Take up the White Man's burden -
Have done with childish days -
The lightly proffered laurel,
The easy, ungrudged praise.
Comes now, to search your manhood
Through all the thankless years,
Cold-edged with dear-bought wisdom,
The judgement of your peers.

Rudyard Kipling

Typeset by Jonathan Downes,
Cover and Layout by SPiderKaT for CFZ Communications
Using Microsoft Word 2000, Microsoft Publisher 2000, Adobe Photoshop CS.

First published in Great Britain by CFZ Press

CFZ Press
Myrtle Cottage
Woolsery
Bideford
North Devon
EX39 5QR

© CFZ MMXX

ISBN: 978-1-909488-63-2

WILD COLONIAL BOY
(A childhood with animals
in Hong Kong)

Jonathan Downes

HONG KONG, KOWLOON AND THE NEW TERRITORIES

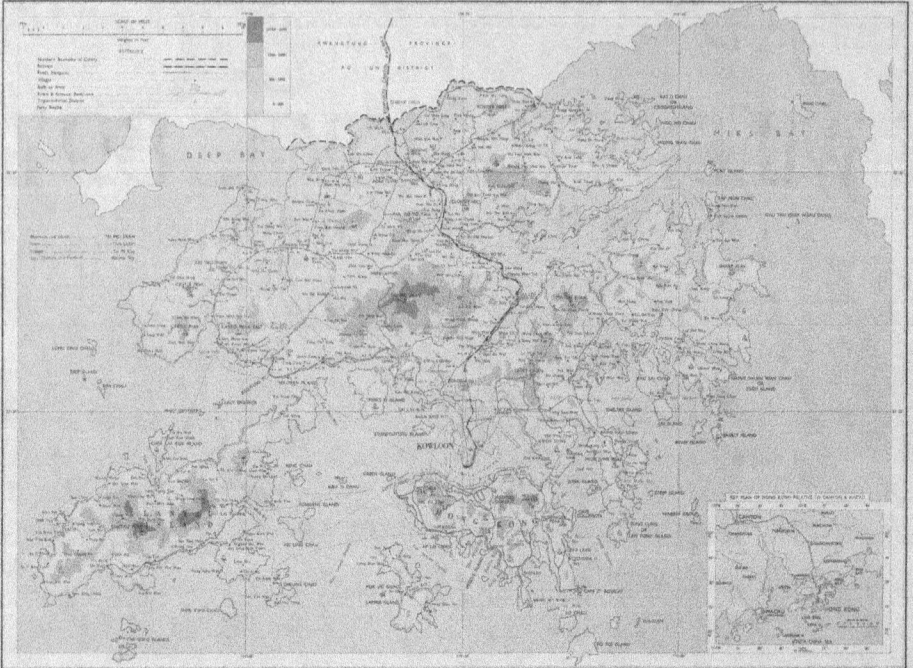

For my wife, who died just as I finished this book,
and who is undoubtedly the bravest woman I have ever known
(1956-2020)

For my Mother (1922-2002)
For my Father (1925-2006)
For 'Mother' (1929-2020)

and

For my little brother Richard (1963-)

and

For my godson Greg who has begun to discover the magic of HK, for Richard
Muirhead but for whom, for Olivia who has facilitated me getting it together to write
the blasted thing, and after ten years of me faffing around bullied me into finishing it,
for Louis who goodnatuedly helped me edit it, and for my Granddaughter Evelyn –
may her childhood be as magickal as, but happier than, mine was

Mount Austin Mansions c.1966

The coyote is beautiful. He moves through the desert delicately, aware of everything, looking around. He hears every sound, smells every smell, sees everything that moves. He's always in a state of total paranoia, and total paranoia is total awareness. You can learn from the coyote just like you can learn from a child.

A baby is born into the world in a state of fear. Total paranoia and awareness. He sees the world with eyes not used yet. As he grows up, his parents lay all this stuff on him. They tell him, when they should be letting him tell them. Let little children lead you.

Charles Manson

Come to the Peak. Ha! Ha!

Some hyperaesthetics scream out to suppress
Cracker-firing; while others direct their rebukes
At aeronaut zoomers. Some try to redress
The false notes of gramophones, saxophones, ukes,
My bête noire is that oiseau de mauvais augure
Who advises in accents impeccably pure,
        "Come to the Peak. Ha! Ha!"

If my Sunday is blank, in my mid-level flat
For an afternoon's nap, I sometimes extend.
I toss and I turn, try this side and that,
But repose is a mood that I can't comprehend.
"Oh is there a breeze in this island!" I cry
And that fiend of a bird makes the scoffing reply,
        "Come to the Peak. Ha! Ha!"

And when I'm invited to tennis up there,
And climb on a tramcar at Kennedy Road,
Should it chance that a dripping wet fog fills the air
And the universe feels like a vault for a toad,
As I take my last mouthful of dry atmosphere
The bird on the hillside lets loose a grim jeer —
        "Come to the Peak. Ha! Ha!"

I play golf at Fanling on a dazzling day,
When the ball is a basilisk's eye in the grass.
If I'd kept my eye on 't, I venture say
'Twould have blasted my eyesight.
        I was out of my class.
I foozled my putts; sclaffed shots off the tee,
And each time I swore, the bird echoed with glee,
        "Come to the Peak. Ha! Ha!"

In a thunderstorm once on Dairy Farm Hill
I sailed with my car, even backed in reverse.
Get out and get soaked? Or wait here until
The tropical storm clouds of summer disperse?
That was the question I asked of the night,
That bird in the coarse grass replied with delight,
        "Come to the Peak. Ha! Ha!"

From Stanley or Shek-O, to Castle Peak Bay,
Cheung Chau to High West or the Taimoshan crags,
Be you outdoors or indoors, you can't get away
From this bird which incessantly, tirelessly brags.
Who first was the wretch with the disarranged brain
That instructed a bird to proclaim the refrain
        "Come to the Peak. Ha! Ha!"

                    Robert Simpson 1933

Foreword

by Richard Muirhead

I have known Jon Downes for most of my life (apart from an interlude of between around 1971 and 1994) and I am happy to thoroughly recommend this book.

In *Wild Colonial Boy* Jon takes us back to the early 1960s to early 1970s and his time growing up as a child in end-of-Empire Hong Kong and also Britain with memories of the wild life and culture he recalls from those days. Jon and I lived on The Peak on Hong Kong island about a mile apart from each other at a time when the British Empire was in gradual decline as, tragically, was the sub-tropical environment in which we hunted butterflies and pretended to be train drivers.

Jon provides no knee-jerk blanket condemnation of Empire which is so "hip" to do as I write this in the Summer of 2020; but a balanced and nuanced qualified assessment of its failings and benefits, such as an appraisal of British naturalists Gerald Durrell, Geoffrey Herklots and indeed Jon himself, though he is far too civilised and modest to indulge in crass self-promotion. What Jon has done is too weave natural history, cryptozoology, Forteana, culture, history and - of course – autobiography, into a beautiful and at times moving tapestry.

What is more remarkable is (despite frequent proclamations to the contrary) Jon`s phenomenal memory for creatures and events from his childhood. I lived studied and played in the same geographical area and era as Jon did yet I can only remember about 10% of what he can. These memories of his shine through a tragic background of Jon`s developing mental illness which is also something I can relate to although my issues began much later in life. Jon`s total honesty throughout the book and his attention to detail shine throughout in refreshing contrast to the boorish self-promotion of much of our contemporary mass media.

This book is unique, similar in some respects to *Gweilo: Memories of a Hong Kong Childhood* by Martin Booth, but different in that Wild Colonial Boy will fulfil the curiosity of naturalist and cryptozoologist alike in a deeper way. Indeed, there is no book about Hong Kong quite like this one. It does a great service in providing a kind of time capsule, not just of a certain period of Jon`s life but of a world, late Colonial Hong Kong and its wildlife, now almost forever gone. Please buy it for a friend, relative or especially a child you know, in the hope that like Jon and myself, that child will also grow up with a love for the planet`s much endangered wild life.

Richard Muirhead
July 2020

Chinese red fox (*Vulpes vulpes hoole*) Hong Kong Botanical Gardens
(*Hong Kong Naturalist*, Vol 5, 1934)

Prologue

You all live by yourselves, no matter how crowded you may think that you are in a room full of people, you are still by yourself, and you have to live with that self forever and ever and ever and ever.

Charles Manson

During the late spring of 1968 I was eight years old and I remember sitting in a geography lesson in Peak School on Hong Kong Island. I was not a good pupil, and my schooldays were far from successful, but for some reason this particular geography lesson remains fresh in my memory half a century years later.

My teacher, a Mrs. Alexander, a lady of whom I can remember almost nothing apart from the fact that she hailed from Northern Ireland and lived in the same block of flats as my family at Mount Austin Mansions, was explaining about the geography of Hong Kong. It was only then, after having lived in Hong Kong for the whole of my conscious life, that I realised quite how small it was, and began to be aware of the peculiar nature of the land in which I lived.

"By the time you are my age," said Mrs. Alexander, "Hong Kong as you know it will not exist any longer." This was an extraordinary concept for an eight-year-old to grasp, and so I missed the next sentence while I grappled with it.

"Hong Kong is not a country in itself," she continued. "It is run by people in England, another island on the other side of the world."

I knew this of course. My father worked in that unfathomable entity of the "grown-up" world called "The Government," but it was only then, as Mrs. Alexander pointed out, that the relative positions of Hong Kong and the United Kingdom on the map of the world (large portions of which, even then were still coloured pink) that I began to grasp the distances involved. As the bell rang for the mid-morning break Mrs. Alexander finished her lesson with words that remain fresh in my mind nearly three decades later.

"Hong Kong is not a country, it is a Crown Colony. When you have boys and girls of your own there won't be any colonies left, and you will be able to tell your children how you lived in a little piece of history," Mrs. Alexander added.

For political reasons, although Hong Kong was still legally a Crown Colony, it began to be known as a "Territory" somewhere in the middle of the decade after Mrs. Alexander's lesson. I was not aware of this politically correct nomenclature and managed to mortally offend one correspondent, in a letter about Sea Serpents, by referring to "The Colony of Hong Kong."

It is of course now a Special Administrative Region [SAR] of the People's Republic of China, but for reasons of etiquette, I use the term "region" except when quoting directly from another source, or referring to Hong Kong's position in Colonial History.

The name doesn't matter because the place will always remain. Despite the encroachments of Communism, Urbanisation and Pollution, the Bamboo Snakes will still live in the thickets and people walking in the hills will still see the scurry of paws as ferret badgers disappear into their holes in the ground. The animals of Hong Kong, who care little for politics, will remain as enigmatic as ever.

From an early age I had been interested in animals. From that point of view, Hong Kong was an ideal place to grow up. Whereas my counterparts in the United Kingdom would have had to make do with foxes, badgers, and hedgehogs, I had the South China Sea as my playground, and the entire Continent of Asia as my hinterland. I could see large swathes of Tropical Forest from my bedroom window, and I was surrounded by exotic and beautiful, wild creatures. My mother always claimed that the first word I spoke was "zoo." As Gerald Durrell's mother claimed exactly the same thing, I do not know whether to take this piece of information *cum grano salis* or not. Four-and-a-bit decades on, it doesn't really matter. What does matter is that I had a remarkable child had - from a zoological point of view at least as far back as I can remember, my mother used to read stories to me, and one of my favourites was the *Jungle Book.*

In those days, Kipling's prose had yet to be perverted and adulterated by the black cloud of Disney, and I revelled in the glorious stories of animals and men in the Indian sub-continent. My mother always encouraged me in my interest in natural history, and when I was five or six years old she acquired a book written by G.A.K. Herklots and titled *The Hong Kong Countryside.* I still have it today, and of all the thousands of books in my collection it is probably the one that I have read most over the years. Much to my joy, many of the animals as described by Kipling also lived in my own backyard. Hooded Cobras and Kraits lurked in the undergrowth surrounding the playground where I went each day after school.

All the way through my schooldays, my mother had a mortal fear that I would be bitten by a poisonous snake - but luckily, for me at least, this never happened (well it did once, but I am still alive so no great harm can have been done). There were mongooses (not the same species as Rikki Tikki Tavy, but close enough), porcupines, wild red dogs or dholes; and every evening, if you went to the right place, you could see the massed hordes of dog-faced fruit bats venturing forth into the gathering dusk. Even Shere Khan and Bagheera had relatives in Hong Kong - the last leopard was shot in the late 1950s, and there were reports of tigers visiting the wilder parts of the New Territories every winter throughout the 1960s. It was truly a magical place for a young naturalist to grow up.

As I got older, my interest in natural history grow, and I filled every inch of my bedroom with jam jars, shoe boxes, and fish tanks that all contained a wide variety of the local fauna. Much to the eternal credit of my mother and our amah Ah Tim, I got away with it, and over the years I learnt much about the husbandry of small creatures - something that has stood me in good stead throughout my adult life.

My mother encouraged my interests in natural history and the written word, and, ironically, on the same day that Mrs. Alexander had so radically overthrown my worldview, my mother figuratively kicked it into touch. Every Thursday she would go into town to play tennis at a venerable institution known as the Ladies' Recreation Club (LRC). After a game of tennis and a leisurely lunch with her friends she would go to the Central Library and get out library books for my young brother and I. One day she found me a book titled *The Amazing Zoo That Dudley Drew,* about a young boy forced to spend the day in bed with a cold. Mind-numbingly bored, he spent the day drawing pictures of fantastic animals. Although the intricacies of the plot escape me, these wonderful creatures came to life and wandered around his house. I became obsessed with this book, and talked about nothing else for weeks until my parents had to threaten me with having the book banned from the house if I didn't shut up. You would have thought that my mother would have learnt her lesson after that, but no. When I came back from school after my fateful geography lesson with Mrs. Alexander, I found that my mother had got me a book that would literally change my life. It was called *Myth or Monster* and introduced me to the concept that there were, indeed, monsters living in the world - and furthermore ones which were even more extraordinary than anything that had been drawn by young Dudley. This book introduced me to the Loch Ness monster, to sea serpents, to the Yeti, to its North American cousin, Bigfoot, to the fearsome Mngwa - the brindled, grey, killer-cat of East Africa, and to the mystery beasts of the South American jungle.

This was heady stuff for an eight-year-old. I read the book in one sitting, had my tea, went to bed early and read it again. The next morning I woke up, my head and heart filled with a new determination.

"I'm going to be a Monster Hunter when I grow up," I announced at breakfast. And I meant it. I'm not going to rewrite history and pretend that my parents were wholeheartedly supportive of my childish outburst, because they weren't. To be quite honest, I can't remember what they said. I can imagine, however. I was at the age when children want to be astronauts, or train drivers, or soldiers, and my parents can easily be forgiven for not taking this momentous and life changing decision seriously. However, the die was cast, and any chance of me leading a normal life had gone completely out of the window.

For weeks after my new discovery, monsters and mystery animals of all types dominated my thoughts; and together with a couple of friends who were equally obsessed with the natural world, I made a map of the immediate area surrounding the block of flats in which we lived. On this map we had plotted the places where birds had nested, where we knew that the local agamas - large, chunky lizards with armoured scales and long tails - lived, and the place in the thick woodland which surrounded the ruins of a hotel that had been bombed out during the Second World War, and where we knew there was a breeding colony of Hodgson's porcupines. To this map was added a fair smidgen of wishful thinking, as we mentally exaggerated a small colony of feral dogs which lived on one of the hillsides into a pack of wolves, and spent our evenings and weekends combing the forested sides of Victoria Peak in search of fearsome tigers and leopards, which we knew from Herklots had once lived there, and which we were convinced still did.

Ironically, it turned out that Hong-Kong was indeed a hotbed of monster-hunting activity. There were, indeed, mystery animals living there, although my investigations into them would not take concrete form for another 25 years. However, even at the age of eight, my monster-hunting research was starting in earnest.

My earliest investigation was into the foxes of Hong-Kong. The local race of the red fox (*Vulpes vulpes hoole*), was - at least, according to accepted disciplines - extinct in the colony. However, one evening some friends of my parents had come around for drinks and I was astounded to hear one of them say that one evening they had actually seen a fox peering over the low stone wall of their garden perimeter. These people were unusual in Hong Kong "Ex-Pat" society in that they had a garden. Most of us - including my family - lived in large, opulent and luxurious blocks of flats. These people - and since my mother's death I have no way of finding out who they actually were - lived in one of the few luxury bungalows which had been reserved for higher echelons of the colonial government.

The Red Fox is an important part of the British zoo-iconography, and it is perhaps because of their "sporting" connotations that they have been persecuted throughout their range. Something notable about the British abroad, is that wherever they go, "the unspeakable" has an unfortunate tendency to pursue "the uneatable" at the slightest possible opportunity, and Hong Kong was no exception. Although their activities have now ceased, the Fanling Hunt was a notable part of life between the wars in the New Territories and has some reasonably important zoological implications. Herklots wrote:

> "The fox of the plains and lower hills of South China is a sub-species of and is very similar to the European red fox; it is paler in colour and lacks the black spot on each side of the nose. There is more gray on the flanks and thighs, the fore feet have less black, and the red tones are less fulvous and more chestnut than the European Red Fox.

Head and body length 26 inches, tail 16.5 inches to the tips of the protecting hairs. Foxes occur both on Hong Kong Island and in the New Territories though they are not often seen. The Chinese name is hung oo lei, (Red Fox)."

It was generally accepted, however, that by the mid-1960s, although there may have been a few isolated specimens in the wilder parts of the New Territories or on Lantau Island, there had been no foxes to speak of in the colony since before the Second World War. However, my mother's friend had seen one - and when you are eight years old grown-ups are infallible. *The Mystery of the Mysterious Fox of Victoria Peak* (as I fondly and slightly-absurdly dubbed it) engrossed me for weeks, and I made a complete pain in the arse of myself, interviewing as many residents - and their servants - as I could, and asking all of them the same question: Had they seen a fox? This early experience of mystery animal investigations taught me some valuable lessons. People are, on the whole, idiots. If something doesn't interest them, they don't understand why it should interest anybody else. They will do their best to poke fun, and generally deride anybody who is doing something that they personally perceive as pointless. Sadly, as I discovered at the early age of eight, most people find monster hunting to be completely boring.

The natural world is of no interest to most of the human race. They can only understand it if it is emasculated rainforest, and if the inhabitants are very safe and controllable, as they are on the television screen in the corner of your sitting room. People, on the whole, are just not interested in going out into the wilds to look for strange things themselves. I found as a child, that whereas the adult world - and that included my teachers - were happy to encourage me to collect butterflies, for example (the natural world is perfectly acceptable when it is killed, pinned to a piece of cork, and left to dry), children were supposed to be seen and not heard. When a child takes it upon himself to wander around asking impertinent questions from his elders and betters he has suddenly crossed over from being a genial eccentric to being a threat. Sadly, this is not a characteristic reserved for children.

As an adult monster hunter, I have found that exactly the same thing tends to happen. If I were to confine my zoological researches to creatures such as birds, butterflies, and small mammals, nobody would have a problem with it. It is only when one ventures away from the well-trodden paths of orthodoxy that one encounters a problem. As an adult even when one is the director of the world's foremost, monster hunting research organization (and, furthermore, one which has as its President a national hero who has been decorated by the monarch), society will hold either deride you, or treat you like a complete lunatic. Truly a monster hunter is without honour in his own land.

The second lesson that I learned was to respect - and did my best to understand - cultural differences. Whereas the Europeans that I spoke to on my quest for the South China fox either made silly remarks or told me in no uncertain terms to go away, the Chinese were much more interested. They told me of their encounters with foxes of many different shapes, sizes and colours. I was too young to understand. I thought that - in some peculiarly inscrutable oriental manner - they were being as annoying as the adults of my own race. It was only when I consulted my bible - Herklots - that I realised how wrong I was being.

Herklots pointed out that in Cantonese, the term "Fox" has a number of different meanings. He noted that several local animals were named foxes by the Chinese. The little spotted civet is known as *t`sat kan lei* (seven striped fox), the Chinese civet, *sam kan lei* (three striped fox), the masked palm civet, ng kan lei (five striped fox), and the ferret badger, *kwoh tse lei* (fruit eating little fox).

It was all beginning to make sense. However, it didn't go anywhere near to explaining what it was that my mother's friend had seen, or the animals that the Chinese people that I had I spoken with had described to me were; and no one apart from my mother's friend had ever seen anything even vaguely resembling a European red fox. Then came my breakthrough. With the innocence of an eight-year-old, I had assumed that Herklots's book was the definitive account of the fauna of Hong Kong. I hadn't realised that the book had been written eight years before I was born, and that a lot had changed over the intervening years.

In 1968, it was 16 years after Herklots had written the book, and, it transpired that Herklots hadn't even been living in Hong Kong when the writing of the book was completed. It was basically compiled from his pre-war nature diaries and from articles that he had written for the prestigious journal *The Hong Kong Naturalist* that had been published between 1929 and 1941. The information on which I had come to rely was therefore - in some instances - nearly 40 years out of date. This was my third great discovery: just because something is written in a book does not necessarily mean that it is accurate.

Armed with these new discoveries and revelations, I pressed on, I like to think, like a junior Sherlock Holmes - albeit perhaps a little precocious one. Each afternoon, in the summer of 1968, as I trudged up and down Mount Austin Road, to and from the ruins of what had once been the Governor's summer palace at the summit of Victoria Peak, I revelled in my new found knowledge. All around me were exciting mysteries just waiting to be solved.

One afternoon I spent over an hour watching a pair of hair-crested drongos - strange crow like birds with peculiar lyre shaped tails - killing and eating a small King Cobra. Another afternoon, I was sidetracked from my quest for the truth about the Victoria Peak Fox when I saw - for the first and only time on the island - a pair of barking deer running, startled, into the thick undergrowth at the bottom of Mount Austin. I stealthily followed them into the woods as my heart pounded in my ear-drums. Sidetracked in their headlong flight to get away from me, the two tiny deer ran into a rotten log with the tiny hooves. It fell apart to reveal an entire universe: peculiar millipedes, like tiny elongated armadillos, came tumbling out. Two local giant centipedes, *Scolopendra* and *Scutigeria* bristled at me, waving their antenna menacingly. Most excitingly were three small toads that glared at me accusingly at with bulbous eyes - not unlike those of an elderly alcoholic sleeping in a shop doorway.

The slopes of Mount Austin were covered with rhododendron trees - some of which stretched to a height of 20 or 30 ft above me in the forest canopy, and the incessant babble of a family of white faced laughing thrushes filled the tropical air. Above us all in the azure blue sky, two or three black kites circled lazily.

Forcing myself into a mode of self-discipline (that I have to admit to I have seldom managed to achieve on a regular basis in the half century that followed), I continued my journey up the winding road towards the house where the sighting taken place. I promised my mother that, under no circumstances, would I be so presumptuous as to bother her distinguished friend in person. Even at the age of eight I could understand the logic in that. After all, he had already told me everything that he knew - and he wasn't particularly interested anyway. All he had seen was a very familiar animal - a red fox (that, with the benefit of hindsight, I can see he probably pursued on horseback over the Home Counties during his youth), peering at him over the low stone wall of his garden. He had no idea that there was anything exciting about the incident, and to him I was merely the slightly annoying small boy who used to get in the way and ask pointless questions about something about which he wasn't particularly interested. However, I hadn't promised my mother that I wouldn't do any detective work in the location where the fox had been seen.

Doing my best to get into character, I reached into my school satchel, took out the slightly battered Red Indian headdress that my mother had given me as a Christmas present, and using one of the lipsticks which I had purloined from her dressing table, I carefully applied my war paint; then, suitably garbed, I made my way through the undergrowth on all fours. Stealthily, I crept around the outside of the perimeter wall. By this time, I was in such a heightened state of excitement that I was sure that I would see a fox lurking behind each and every one of the bushes and trees. Sadly, I saw nothing.

As well as Red Indians, other cultural influences were at work upon me. I was an avid reader of Enid Blyton's *Secret Seven* books in which a small band of precocious, upper-middle-class children, ran rings around the police and solved baffling crimes by dint of crafty detective work. In an attempt to emulate this second set of heroes, I did my best to search for clues. However, the clues were spectacular by their absence. I therefore only had one option open to me. I would have to follow in the footsteps of the Secret Seven and make a map of the crime scene. The fact that there hadn't been a crime was no particular obstacle to me.

My grandfather had given me a compass that was worn on my wrist like a wristwatch. It had never worked, and I had no real idea how to take a compass bearing, but it was

- after all - one of my few items of quasi-scientific equipment, and I was determined to make use of it. I paced the length and breadth of the garden and perimeter wall. Every few yards I consulted my spectacularly useless compass in the vain hope that I would be able to extrapolate some data from it. After about half an hour's work, I had created a crude - and with hindsight a completely useless - map, of which I was very proud, and bore it home in triumph to the corner of my bedroom which I fondly called my laboratory. Here I kept my microscope, my natural history books, my shell and butterfly collections, and various small creatures imprisoned in a variety of makeshift aquaria. Sadly, when I looked back over the events of the day, I had to admit to myself that whilst the adventure had been fun, it had not really brought me any closer to the truth.

The next day in school, I confided to my best friend William about my problem. He suggested that we should go and ask his mother for advice. His mother was a slightly remote figure, but one of whom I was in great awe. She was a real scientist - albeit an anthropologist - and she was one of few grown-ups to actively encourage me in my endeavours. After school I went back to William's flat and diffidently approached his mother. I was always fascinated by his mother's study. There were books everywhere, and various niches around the walls contained a variety of archaeological and anthropological specimens. Most of these seemed to be ancient pottery, but also included a few adze heads and shapeless pieces of metal that William and I fondly believed were instruments of torture, but which were with the benefit of hindsight, compass mountings from eighteenth-century sea-going junks. William's mother was very interested in my quest and she reached up to one of the voluminous bookshelves and brought down a thin blue paperback that I later found out was entitled *Mammals of Hong Kong* by Patricia Marshall. I took the book and sat cross-legged in the corner of the room.

Once again, I found that my hero - Herklots - was ridiculously out of date. Several of the mammal species that he had listed as being common in the colony were now, in fact, extinct. Moreover, the book had only been published the previous year and it was as up-to-date a tome it was be possible to get. Manfully resisting the temptation to become side-tracked in descriptions of some of the more exotic creatures such as pangolins and civet cats, I turned the section dedicated to the South China Red Fox. Suddenly my mystery was solved. Marshall wrote:

> "Now very rare, a few pairs only living in the New Territories. Of the two foxes released on Hong Kong Island in 1965 one was subsequently killed by a car and the other illegally trapped."

So, there *had* been foxes on Hong Kong Island within the last few years, after all. William's mother showed me how to interpret the references at the end of the book and we discovered that the fox that had been hit by a car only a few hundred yards from the place where my mother's friend had seen one. Furthermore, it had been killed only a few weeks after the sighting had taken place. I had solved what I like to think was my first monster hunting mystery.

The next day at school I went rushing in to tell my teacher and classmates all about it. I shouldn't have bothered. My friends were completely uninterested, and my form teacher told me tartly that if I wanted to amount to anything in life I should concentrate on my nine times table rather than searching for animals that were of no possible interest to anybody. I knew then that most adults were not like William's mother. I made a silent vow that when I grew up I would be like her rather than like the boorish and unimaginative people that a benevolent colonial administration had entrusted to nurture the growth of a generation of young minds.

And I hope that I have been (and I still don't know my nine times table)..

Preface

Pain's not bad, it's good. It teaches you things. I understand that

Charles Manson

It was just after Christmas 1977. I was living in Bracknell, Berkshire, renting a room from a couple who seemed dreadfully old to me, but who were probably younger than I am now. I can't actually remember their names but it doesn't really matter. I had no money, and was doing a job that I hated, erecting plasterboard partitioning in offices for a company called Stocker Office Services who only gave me the job in the first place because the bloke who ran it was a friend of some people who owed my father a favour. He was a nice chap, and unlike the couple with whom I lived, who were unremittingly dull, he was actually very kind to me, and - thirty-five years on - I feel mildly embarrassed that I can't remember his name either, although he had a pretty red headed daughter called Adele.

I had spent an uncomfortable Christmas with my family back in Devon. 1977 had seen me being thrown out of school, sacked from my first job, and unsuccessfully trying to claim unemployment benefit. They had bailed-me out (as they saw it) by getting me the aforementioned job in Bracknell. I was desperately unhappy, and - not for the first time - completely confused with the way that my life was going. It was to be another fifteen years before the occupational health department of Exeter Health Authority was to tell me that I was bipolar, and thus provided some the sort of an explanation for the way that my life had run over its first three decades.

During the Christmas holidays my mother suggested that I write a book about my childhood in Hong Kong. I thought it was a terrible idea; my childhood had been a peculiar one, and on the whole it was not a time that I wanted to revisit. I know that she meant kindly - after all, over ten years before she had introduced me to the works of my favourite author Gerald Durrell. In particular, during long lazy afternoons sitting against the trunks of coconut palms in the garden of the Repulse Bay Hotel, she introduced me to a wonderful book which told the story of Durrell's childhood on the Greek island of Corfu. It was a book which was to shape much of my life, but - like so many other things of importance to me during my formative years - it wasn't at all what it seemed.

My impression from the book was that Durrell - unlike me - had been possessed of a remarkable, and idealised family, who had ensured that he had an idyllic childhood. By the time that my mother suggested that I write about my own childhood, I was already aware that my family were far more flawed. Whereas Durrell had written amusingly about the foibles of his family, I didn't think that there was much amusing to say about my own tortured and emotionally inconsistent brood. It wasn't until many years later that I realised that the Durrells and the Downeses had far more in common than I ever thought.

Fast forward from the dying days of 1977 to the dying days of 2002. By this time I was in my early forties, a diagnosed manic depressive trying to put the memory of a nasty divorce, and several other unsuccessful relationships behind him. And oh yes, I was the director of the Centre for Fortean Zoology which was based in my ever-so-slightly squalid two up two down, red brick house in one of the less salubrious suburbs of Exeter. As I have written elsewhere, the cumulative results of my mother's death earlier in the year, and a string of other stuff that I don't want to go into here, resulted in me having the worst nervous breakdown of my life.

The next day I awoke in my uncomfortable hotel room bed feeling absolutely lousy. My head was spinning, and I was hallucinating. We managed to negotiate breakfast and find our way back to Paddington Station, where - by the statue of the little bear made famous by Michael Bond - I collapsed. The worst bout of depression that I have ever suffered hit me like a ton of bricks. How I got back to Exeter I don't know, but when I got home Richard and Graham put me to bed and I stayed there for the next three months.

And for three months I did nothing but sleep and read. Probably the most important book that I read during this enforced rest was Douglas Botting's biography of Gerald Durrell. In my autobiography I comment upon its importance to me:

> "By the beginning of December I was beginning to feel better, and whilst I was still too unwell to leave my bedroom, I could - at last - read again. During the weeks leading up to Christmas I read Douglas Botting's biography of my hero Gerald Durrell. With my brain cells fried to hell it was a long, slow and laborious process but I found that every page was fascinating. I had not realised it, but Durrell's life had paralleled my own in so many ways. However, he was a giant of a man in every way, and without him conservation as we know it today would not exist. Compared to him my achievements - and even those, which I hope that the CFZ will manage in my lifetime - are very minor indeed. The irony is, however, that in the same way that there are definite parallels between his professional life and mine, our private lives, and in particular our strengths and weaknesses are very similar. Like me, he was terminally bad at relationships. Like me, he had probably married the wrong woman (the first time at least), and, like me, his wife had eventually left him because of his increasingly bizarre behaviour. However, in his character flaws - like everything else - he was bigger and better than me. He drank himself into epilepsy and eventually to death, had wild and untreated fits of mood swings and depression and whilst he was capable of great generosity and love, he was also capable of being viciously mean spirited. However, he was aware of his faults and remained remarkably modest about his

achievements."

But it was some years later that I realised quite what an epiphany the book had triggered in me. I had been fascinated to learn the truth behind Durrell's three books about his childhood in Greece. Botting pulled no punches; the idyllic childhood had not been quite so idyllic after all. As the three books progressed, Gerry admitted to his elder brother that they were becoming less and less based in reality. Even at the beginning, Durrell had edited events to suit the demands of the narrative. The five members of his family had not - after all - lived together for five years of bohemian anabasis.

Larry had spent much of the period living with his first wife Nancy in a completely different house elsewhere on the island. Their relationship was a stormy, and somewhat peculiar one, and in 1937 they left the island altogether and visited Paris with Henry Miller and Anais Nin, although they eventually returned. When the rest of the family returned to England at the beginning of World War II, Larry and Nancy remained in Greece, and after escaping to Egypt after the German invasion, the couple separated acrimoniously. Nancy appears nowhere in Gerry's trilogy.

Gerry's gung ho middle brother Leslie was far less wholesome than he is portrayed in the book, having sexual relationships with several of the servants, and making one - at least - pregnant. Gerry's sister Margo was always unhappy with the way she was portrayed, and believed until her dying day that Gerry had used her as a comic foil for the other characters. Even the ever-lovable mother of the family turned out to have been a borderline alcoholic, and it appears that Gerry, like Leslie, also had his fair share of sexual adventures with Greek peasant girls at a surprisingly young age.

When I read this, I felt much happier. I had been a journalist for many years on and off, and was quite aware of the journalistic adage that one must never let the truth get in the way of a good story. The fact that the Durrell family's real exploits have been somewhat more sordid than the ones described in the books (especially the second and third volumes) didn't matter. They were glorious books which had given me years of pleasure, and the fact that it turned out that Gerry had made a lot of it up didn't detract from that.

But it certainly made me feel better about my own family.

Both my parents had been heavy drinkers; I am not sure whether they were *actually* alcoholics, but I am certain that some would define them as such. I am also certain that at times in my life some could have used that definition for me as well, but that is mostly another story. My father was a strict disciplinarian, to the extent that would certainly have seen him in prison, and my brother and me in care, would his parenting techniques have come to light these days. And I, too, had embarked on my sex life at a far younger age than is generally smiled upon these days. I had spent many years bemoaning the fact that my childhood, and my family as a whole had been pretty fucked up, only to find that it was not that different from the un-idylicised childhood of my greatest hero.

But basically it took me another ten years to even start thinking about writing this book. Ten years in which my father died, I remarried, and the CFZ finally became what I had always claimed it was; the most important cryptozoological research organisation in the world.

And so, as we near the end of the winter 2012, a 52 year-old Jonathan Downes embarks on the task of writing the story of his life from the age of one to the age of 11 and a half.

But it's been another eight years since then. The fifty-two-year old Jonathan Downes wrote about 35,000 words, and then got distracted onto other things. The fifty-seven-year old Jonathan Downes wrote another 10-15,000 words, and then, with the invaluable help of his beloved stepdaughter, Olivia, who is also his secretary, he decided that the only way that this blasted book would ever get finished is if took a leaf out of Charles Dickens' playbook and he started to serialise it in one of the magazines that he publishes.

And so, although it might well be considered to be enormously off topic for a magazine which is usually wittering on about politics, drugs and rock and roll, Jonathan and Olivia sat down each week to write that week's instalment of what eventually turned into this book. And, dear reader, that is why you are now sitting there, hopefully in a comfortable armchair with a mug of hot cocoa beside you, reading the longest book that Jonathan (by now a widower of sixty-one) has ever written.

This explains a slightly peculiar facet to the way that I have written this book. I have written things like: "looking back upon these events from the perspective of a sixty year old", or a 55-year-old, or a 58-year-old or whatever, and despite the fact that this is mildly confusing to the reader, who is basically following the story of my childhood in what I hope is reasonable chronological order, I have kept it in, because to do otherwise would – I feel – detract from the honesty of the narrative.

And I am the author, and I can do what I bloody well wilt.

If I'm honest about it, and I always do my best to be honest in my writing (except when it's making jokes at Nick Redfern's expense, whereupon anything goes and I will make up the most disgraceful libels) I'm writing it in order to put my life into some sort of perspective. I'm writing for myself as much as anyone. There is also the added complication that for nearly 20 years my old friend Richard Muirhead and I have been writing a book called *The Mystery Animals of Hong Kong*. In fact, "writing" is probably too strong a term. We have been collecting material for the book which we will probably eventually write, but we have done it in very much a desultory manner, and have taken large breaks to do other things as and when we felt like it. However, for some time, I have realised that I have far too much material for a single volume, and that - again, if I'm honest - the book I had planned would have been such a rambling tome, mixing cryptozoology, natural history, folklore, ghosts, history, and large chunks of both Richard's and my own lives, that it probably would have been unreadable. Therefore in the interests of producing a readable tome when we finally get round to writing it, I decided it was probably best to write my own memoir of my childhood as a budding naturalist as a separate volume.

Some years ago I wrote:

> Everybody lies to their husbands,
> Everybody cheats on their wives,
> Everybody loves their children,
> But everybody fucks up their lives,
> Everybody climbs up the mountain,
> Everybody falls down again,
> And when you scratch the surface everyone's insane.

I spent much of the time between 1996 and 2007 in therapy. It did me no end of good, and I recommend it to anybody who even has the slightest whiff of mental health problems. And as, getting older, I have come to the conclusion that there is no such thing as sanity, I think that therapy - as a sort of secular confession - is a very healthy thing for anyone to do.

Philip Larkin wrote:

> They fuck you up, your mum and dad.
> They may not mean to, but they do.
> They fill you with the faults they had
> And add some extra, just for you.

And I doubt whether a truer word was ever written.

For most of our lives my parents and I didn't like each other very much, but we always loved each other, and although they did some appalling things to me, I did some pretty bad things to them, although none of us meant to. My father and I finally made peace a few months before he died in 2006, but my mother died with us all still semi-estranged. I want to look back upon our shared experiences in the 1960s; a decade during which everyone else was letting it all hang out, but we were still playing the century's old games of Empire upon which the sun was never going to set.

I have just about come to terms with my own dubious sanity. Like all human beings, the seeds of what I have become as an adult were sown during my childhood, and I had some wonderful experiences, but I have always carried a lot of guilt about my childhood and now, I think it is the time to put them all into perspective so that I can get on with the rest of my life.

I hope that whilst I doubt whether the resulting book will be anywhere near as entertaining as Gerald Durrell's books about his childhood, that this book – as it pans out – will be a little more honest than his was. I also think that it is an important book to write, if only because it describes a time that is completely gone, and which will never return. It describes animals and places that no longer exist, at least not in the way that I knew them, and as we face ecological collapse with all the attendant horrors that it will bring, it reminds us that there once was a gentler and kinder time. And it reminds an ageing widowed diabetic who cannot walk unaided, feels nothing beneath his knees, and may not have that many more years to live, that there once was a time when he had a subtropical jungle as his playground.

CHAPTER ONE
Buxey Lodge

"How old am I? I'm as old as my mother told me. How's that?"

Charles Manson

My family, or - to be more exact - my mother, my father and I, arrived in the crown colony of Hong Kong in early 1961 on a P&O boat called the S*S Carthage*. My father told me many years later how he took one look at the bustling metropolis from the deck of the ship as it sailed in through Lei Yue Mun Strait and hated it. My mother, on the other hand, loved the place and so – when I was old enough to make rational judgements – did I.

However, it is quite understandable that my father should take up his new job as Senior Executive Officer in Her Majesty's Overseas Civil Service hating and resenting it, and also – to a lesser extent – why he resented me so much.

My father had spent the latter half of the war as a radio officer in the Merchant Navy. He survived the Battle of the Atlantic, even though he was torpedoed, struck by lightning, and swept overboard – twice – in a gale. After coming ashore in 1947, he married my mother and the two of them moved to North Devon where my mother was a village school teacher, and my father started a career in agriculture, apprenticed to a farmer called Mr Lee-Fowler in Westleigh, between Bideford and Barnstaple.

But my mother had always had a desire to travel. She had been brought up on the Africa stories of Henry Rider-Haggard, and Edgar Wallace, and she had always fancied being married to a latter-day Sanders of the River, so – according to my father – she bullied him into applying for a job as an Agricultural Officer in the British Protectorate of Nigeria. I have always had a sneaking suspicion that this wasn't entirely the case. My father had spent the war as a glamorous young man in a sexy uniform. He had travelled the world and enjoyed a relatively affluent lifestyle. They had money problems during their early married life, and I am sure that the austerity of post war Britain was not much fun to a young man used to the wartime fleshpots of New Orleans (a wicked place, he always said, no place for a young man away from home for the first time), New York, where he drank with the famous boxer Jack Dempsey (on his deathbed, whilst I was working for a tropical fish magazine, he was amused to hear that Dempsey had given his name to a particularly pugnacious cichlid), and post war Singapore, Penang and Australia. Barnstaple and Combe Martin must have seemed very staid in comparison.

According to Wikipedia:

> "Rationing was in some respects more strict after the war than during it—two major foodstuffs that were never rationed during the war, bread and potatoes, went on ration after it (bread from 1946 to 1948, and potatoes for a time from 1947). Tea was still on ration until 1952. In 1953 rationing of sugar and eggs ended, and in 1954, all rationing finally ended when cheese and meats came off ration."

We arrived in Hong Kong sometime in early 1961. I have been somewhat of an amateur historian (amongst other things) for years, and I quite often meander onto historical subjects when I am writing about Fortean Zoology or the more arcane aspects of rock music (which are the two things that I write about most). However, invariably I have had sources of information upon which I can draw, but in the case of my own little history, there are very few of these.

Some of the things that my Father did during his time in Hong Kong impacted in a small way upon the events upon the World Stage, but these are not really relevant to the main crux of this story, which is about my memories of my childhood, how I became who I am today, and the animals and people (mostly the animals) that I met upon the way. Both my parents have died (my Mother in 2002 and my Father four years later) and although once-upon-a-time I would have asked them about the more abstruse details of my early life, there is now no-one left to ask, and I don't suppose that it matters much anyway.

It also must be said that both of them (in their own peculiar way) were fairly unreliable witnesses. I had always been told that my family had arrived in Hong Kong on a luxury liner belonging to the famous Peninsula and Orient (P&O) line. The truth is somewhat more prosaic.

The *RMS Carthage* was one of two ships brought into commission in 1931; known as 'The Far East Sisters' the Carthage and her sister ship the *Corfu* (which is an amusing lexilink, when you consider what I wrote about the parallels between my life, and that of the late Gerald Durrell, in the prologue) spent the next thirty years on the following route: London (Tilbury Docks) to Southampton, Gibraltar, Marseille (UK bound only), Naples, Port Said, Suez Canal, Aden, Bombay, Colombo, Penang, Singapore, Hong Kong, Shanghai, Kobe and Yokohama "India and Far East Mail" service. This is exactly the sort of thing that my parents would have loved, being redolent of the days of the Raj, and a gentler time when Britannia did indeed rule the waves, and all she had to do to prove it was to send in a gunboat of two to quell the uppity natives.

I don't want to appear hypocritical here. If I was faced with the choice of travelling in a leisurely and gentlemanly style by ship, drinking pink gins on the quarterdeck and playing shove ha'penny with the First Mate, or travelling by air (and you must remember that a BOAC Boeing 707, may have been state of the art for the time, but was considerably less comfortable than the long-haul flights of today, and I dislike them badly enough) then there is no question as to which I would have chosen. I, too, would enjoy the ritual of dressing for dinner, and hobnobbing at the Captain's Table, and I too would have enjoyed playing the old Colonial, with my lovely wife Corinna by my side humouring me by pretending to be a *Memsahib,* but unlike my parents I would never have taken it seriously.

During the journey I (not for the first time, and certainly not for the last) managed to screw everything up by becoming ill and nearly dying of pneumonia, and my parents made friends with the Captain, who for the next ten years or so would come to visit us whenever he put ashore in Hong Kong, and became known as Uncle Mike. I always got the impression that whilst my parents liked him a lot, they never really approved of the fact that he had married a Japanese woman, considering that to be almost as bad as 'going native'. However, being friends with the Captain was the sort of social cachet that my parents always enjoyed, and – now I come to think of it – for the rest of their lives, whenever they took a cruise somewhere they always did their best to befriend a senior crew member or two.

Maybe I am being unfair here. My father had always loved the sea, and the only reason that he left the Merchant Navy was to marry my mother, and I know that whilst he never had any regrets about his decision, that the sea is – indeed – a harsh mistress, and she is one who always had a hold over him. But it is an unarguable fact that my parents were gentlefolk of the Empire, and as the Empire inexorably receded into history they never really recovered, nor forgave the people that they held to be responsible.

Both my parents actually came from relatively ordinary backgrounds. There was landed gentry on both sides of my family, but they had gambled or pissed or whored away the land a long time before either of my parents were born. Both my grandfathers had fought with some distinction in the First World War (my maternal grandfather in the Royal Flying Corps, and my paternal one in the Royal Horse Artillery), but both of them were in mildly straightened circumstances after the war, and by the time my parents were born (Mum in 1922, Dad in 1925), they were both working as travelling representatives for the Prudential Insurance company, but my Grandmother never let my father forget, and my Uncle Tim never let my mother forget that their respective families had once been far more important in the scheme of things, and so – as soon as they had the chance to flee the austerity of post-war Britain – my parents decided to reinvent themselves as the county gentry that they would have been if circumstances had turned out differently.

In Nigeria my mother had been through several miscarriages, and when she finally *did* give birth to my sister Arabella, the baby died within hours. My mother nearly died too, so when she was pregnant with me my parents decided to take no chances, and my mother flew back to England; my father joined her for my birth, but very soon the whole family was back in Africa. However, once again, I nearly died, and as my father wrote in his unpublished autobiography:

> "We became quite neurotic about the baby's health. It dominated every conversation and haunted our dreams and after a couple of dreadful months, we decided that we could not continue to live under such tension, so with reluctance we agreed that Mary and the baby should to home to England and that I should either resign or apply for a transfer to another colony. In April 1960, Mary and Jonathan left Nigeria for the last time."

It was only at the age of 53 that I sorted out the timeline for the first time. My parents had always told me that my mother and I had stayed in England for nine months after I had been born, and that I didn't actually know my father until I was nearly a year old. Over the years I have repeated this story to my various therapists and have been told that:

1.   My Father had never had a chance to bond with me
2.   My parents had not been together during that important post birthing period, meaning that my relationship with both of them was somewhat awry
3.   That when my Father did eventually come to reclaim his wife and son from his in-laws, he was a virtual stranger to me

...and various other bits of pop psychology which made perfect sense to me at the time and got me to feel that it wasn't actually my fault that my Father didn't like me very much. Or, if I am to be honest that I didn't like him very much either.

Actually, or so it turns out, none of that was actually true (except for the bits about my Father and me not liking each other overmuch!)

I discovered, one day in 2012, from going through my Father's papers, during a break from doing the index in the latest book by Dr Karl Shuker, that everything that I thought I knew about my early life was wrong. I spent the first eight months of my life with both parents, and then between April and September 1960 my mother and I lived with my maternal grandparents in Grately, Hampshire, before my Father rejoined us and we lived together in England for at least four months before taking a long, leisurely sea voyage to the Orient.

Our first home in Hong Kong was a rococo block of flats called Buxey Lodge.

Hong Kong in the late 19th Century really was the 'wild frontier' of the British Empire, and some of the biggest success stories were from people who certainly didn't fit the current viewpoint of the British Empire as being racist, and Anglocentric. Sir Catchick Paul Chater, for example, was born Khachik Pogose Astwachatoor, to an Armenian family in Calcutta in 1864, and moved to Hong Kong in 1864, where after working in a bank for some time, he became a bullion broker. Four years later he went into partnership with a Parsee businessman called Hormusjee Naorojee Mody. They built a number of houses including two named Buxey Lodge, (presumably named after Mody's uncle, Jehangirjee Buxey) one of which had been converted into flats for mid ranking Hong Kong Government officials in the late 1950s.

However, it had echoes of its pre-war grandeur, and the gardens (which had once been magnificent), but which had been largely destroyed during the Japanese occupation back in the war years, still had vague echoes of their former glory. They were still fringed with rather shabby marble balustrades, and boasted a magnificent summer house which always smelt of stale urine.

I was very young when we first moved there, but it is the place of my earliest memories. The first thing that I remember is of my Father encouraging me to take one of my first faltering steps. He was very thin and had a cigarette in his hand, which means that it would have to be from 1961 because early in 1962 he had a cancer scare and quit smoking for good. My other memories mostly involve the gardens where, either with my Mother, or with Ah Tim the amah who doubled as nursemaid, I would play for hours, and where I took my first faltering steps towards communion with the natural world. I don't remember whether there were swings or roundabouts, but I do remember – vividly – an old dead tree stump that I used to climb, the dusty green palm trees which, with a magnificent flame-of-the-forest tree provided the only natural shade, and the ever present jungle covered hillside which towered high above us.

I was too young to be allowed to play in the jungle by myself like I did only a few years later, but I was certainly aware of it, mostly because I was forbidden to venture into it for fear of snakes and other deadly wildlife which Ah Tim and my Mother were certain would be lurking behind every tree waiting to attack me.

I adored Ah Tim, who was basically a second mother to me, and I loved the occasions when she would take me for afternoon walks when my mother was busy doing something else. I enjoyed walks with my mother as well, but somehow walks with Ah Tim, and occasionally her husband Ah Tam, were far more exotic.

One of my favourite walks was to a Buddhist shrine near the Portuguese Consulate in the old sector of Victoria City in Hong Kong. This has probably long since been pulled down for redevelopment, but when I was a small boy in the early 1960s it was still a poignant reminder of a more gentle and relaxed age. The buildings were set in a small public garden, and it was one of my favourite places when I was about four years old.

There was a huge, ornate, pond with a gothic stone fountain in the middle of it, and although to the best of my recollection the fountain never worked and the pond was always clogged with weed, it was the first time in my life that I ever saw Koi Carp. These magnificent fish swam lazily through the weedy water and entranced me, starting a love affair that has continued on and off ever since. However, the strangest thing about these carp was that no-one knew where they had come from. The pond had been built at the beginning of the century, and the garden was one of the few parts of the city to have come through the Japanese dive-bombing strikes in 1941 relatively unscathed.

After the war, naturalist G.A.K. Herklots was called to look at a pond like this. It hadn't been cleaned out since 1922, but there was no egress from any other body of water. Even then Victoria City was a fairly polluted area, and this tiny pond was a veritable oasis – probably the only piece of fresh, clean water for many miles. The workmen cleaning out the pond were amazed at the amount of wildlife that had taken up residence there. There was a thriving family of Paradise Fish (*Macropodus opercularis*) several large freshwater crabs (which were then known as *Potamon hongkongiensis*) and a large number of different freshwater shrimps. There were similar fauna in my pond and there were also the two large koi carp that I was to write about on occasion twenty years later.

Now, if one is prepared to suspend one's scepticism for a while one can imagine the crustacea arriving in egg form on the legs of visiting water birds. Possibly even the paradise fish. It would seem highly unlikely but it would seem just about possible. But how did the koi carp get there? They were at least twenty years old, and no-one admitted responsibility for having placed them there. Devotees of Charlie Fort will no doubt immediately decide that they had teleported there by some strange biomechanical mechanism unknown to man. However I'm not too sure. I like to think that perhaps, some elderly Chinese fish keeper, realising that war was imminent, decided to place his beloved pets in the fountain hoping that somehow, the fact that it was adjacent to a shrine to the Lord Buddha – protector of all living things – would protect them from harm during the forthcoming conflict.

If this little fantasy of mine is true, then the old fishkeeper's plan certainly worked, because when I last saw the fish, when I went to Hong Kong for the last time in 1980, they were still there. I hope that if, as I fear, the area has long since been modernised, the fish will have been moved to another safe haven, because as well as being magnificent creatures, they are an enduring childhood memory, and as such very dear to me.

I used to sit for hours gazing into the murky waters, fascinated by the fish and the other animals that I saw in this Lilliputian ocean. Ah Tim would sit, and chat away to her friends, all of them smoking pungent cigarettes and putting the world to rights as I would see what I could see in the deep green waters of the fountain. There were the big koi carp of course, moving effortlessly and serenely through the water, but there were the smaller paradise fish that made their bubble nests amongst the dank green reeds. I watched fascinated as the aggressive male guarded the bubble nest, chasing away all potential intruders, even taking on one of the enormous koi that must have been twenty times its body mass, as his tiny larval offspring wriggled away in the bubbles.

The little garden overlooked Hong Kong harbour, and I used to sit by Ah Tim's side watching the great ships come to and fro. There were usually Royal Navy warships in port, and often troopships from Vietnam full of American military personnel (often quite gravely wounded) wanting a few days r+r in the brothels of Wan Chai. Once I remember seeing a big black square rigged schooner, with a small tunnel belching out black smoke alongside the graceful, if slightly sinister, sails. I never did find out who she was or what she was doing in Hong Kong harbour, but several years later when I discovered the books of Arthur Ransome, I decided that she must have been the *Wild Cat* undoubtedly *en route* to the mysterious islands of Missee Lee. The fact that Ransome's book was set some three decades before my birth and that the *Wild Cat* had burned to a crisp and sunk at the beginning of the book, never actually occurred to me.

At the gates of the tumbledown little garden were two enormous stone lion dogs (remember I was only about four at the time, and so the term 'enormous' is a relative one). Ah Tim used to lift me up on them so I could ride them like a make-believe horse, and as she did she would tell me the how these peculiarly grotesque beasts keep devils away and guard children while they sleep.

Many years later, in 2012, my wife and I were in a Garden Centre in Bideford, when I saw a large garden ornament of one of these iconic creatures from my distant childhood, and Corinna bought it for me as a 53rd birthday present. One of my dear adopted 'nephews', Max was staying with it, and took great exception to what he saw as a cheap and nasty garden ornament from a cheap and nasty garden centre. And I tried to explain how for fifty years I have known exactly what they do, and why, and that I wanted one to be a gatekeeper of my house in Devon, and look after me as I sleep (because I have never really grown up), but these days children don't believe in devils or evil spirits, and I fear the tale was lost on him.

Apart from my parents and Ah Tim and Ah Tam, the grown-up world didn't really impinge on me that much, but I do remember one adult clearly. He, too lived in Buxey Lodge, and he was a butterfly collector. I remember being fascinated as I followed him around the garden at Buxey Lodge, cheering happily whenever he caught a butterfly, but secretly hoping that my favourite one – the great orange tip (*Hebomia glaucippe glaucippe*) would get away, which it usually did. He was the first adult to actually teach me anything about the natural world. He took me by the hand

and showed me the different species of caterpillar, and what butterflies they turned into. He explained that each caterpillar turned into a different type of butterfly and showed me which ones were which.

But perhaps most importantly he impressed upon me that it was OK to catch caterpillars and rear them as long as you let go all the butterflies you didn't want for your collection, so they could fly free and live to beget another generation of little flying creatures to bewitch another generation of children and entomologists.

When I was very small, my Mother befriended a huge orange cat that belonged to one of the neighbours, and which she called `Thomas`. Whether this was its *actual* name, or whether it was just a name that my Mother had bestowed upon it, I don't know, but one of my fondest memories of my life before my little brother was born in the summer of 1963, is of sitting on my plastic potty answering a call of nature whilst a huge friendly orange cat rubbed itself adoringly against my bare legs.

In early 1963 my life changed forever. My parents solemnly informed me that I was going to have a little brother or sister. I was quite impressed with the news, and spent several weeks trying to persuade my poor Mother that they should call the child – boy or girl – 'Jonathan' to avoid confusion, but they ignored what seemed to me like an eminently sound idea.

The last six months of my Mother's pregnancy were not easy ones for her, and I know that, with the memory of my sister's death still fresh in their minds, they were seriously considering sending my mother back to Hampshire to have her second child, like they had done when my birth was imminent. But from what I can gather, neither of them liked that idea overmuch, and Hong Kong in 1963 was a far more civilised and sophisticated place than the backwoods of Northern Nigeria had been in 1958, and medical services were incomparably more improved. So the whole of my family stayed put in the Orient; my father getting more and more bad tempered because of stress, overwork, fear for his heavily pregnant wife, annoyance with his irritating son, and the fact that every pore of his body was aching for a cigarette, and my mother alternately nest building and throwing up.

I was put more and more into the care of Ah Tim and Ah Tam, and so I found myself – even at the tender age of three or four going to places that I would otherwise never have seen. And these are experiences which have stuck with me ever since.

Every afternoon, Ah Tim or her husband used to take me out for a walk. Ah Tim would usually take me to the little Buddhist shrine with the fountain where I would reawaken my acquaintance with the two huge koi, and with the pugnacious little paradise fish, but Ah Tam used to take me deep into the secret heart of the city itself. Even at that tender age I was beginning to be fascinated by animals, so – being kindly folk – they usually took me to somewhere where I could see wild animals, but being Cantonese, they took me to places where there were usually being sold for food.

The Cantonese are a race of gourmets; their food is some of the best in the world, and they usually insist in having it as fresh as possible, which means that many of their food animals (and as well as domesticated beasts, they also eat a bewildering range of wildlife) are kept alive under horrible conditions until it is time for them to be slaughtered for the dinner table.

As an adult, I am appalled by the concept of unsustainable bushmeat from anywhere in the world, and I will always do whatever is in my power to campaign against it, but back at the age of three or four I was fascinated by the rows of cages of wild animals that I would see every time that Ah Tam took me for my afternoon walk to the market. I saw various species of civet cat, racoon dogs, ferret badgers and even the shy and beautiful leopard cat. All of those species (except for the *tanuki* or raccoon dog) are native to Hong Kong. Back in the 1960s there were three species of civet cat living in Hong Kong. The largest, the large Indian civet became extinct some time in the 1960s or 70s, but I well remember seeing them waiting like prisoners on Death Row in their bamboo cages. I thought they were dogs, and happily prattled on about the stripey dogs I had seen when I returned home to my doting (but distracted) parents at the end of the afternoon.

On other afternoons we would go to the Bird Market. Cantonese are keen cage bird devotees and lavish enormous amounts of devotion upon their songbird pets. However, at least at the time (and you must remember that this all happened about half a century ago, and things may well have changed over the intervening years) this devotion did not stretch to captive breeding, and very nearly all the birds on sale were wild caught. However, once again as a small child the ethical considerations of what I was looking at didn't bother me overly, and I started a love affair with aviculture that has lasted ever since. I was particularly fond of the softbills like the hwameis, laughing thrushes and bulbuls, and I looked forward dearly to the day when I would own some of my own.

I used to eat some of my meals with Ah Tim and Ah Tam in the servant's quarters, and I soon found myself chatting away in Cantonese to them as much as I did in English. It is an ability that I soon lost, but even now – half a century or so later – I still dream in Cantonese, and those who have shared my bed will attest that sometimes I wake up in the middle of the night jabbering away in an Oriental language that I no longer understand.

Even at the age of three I realised that life if you were a Chinese servant was not the same as life if you were the son of a middle ranking Colonial Service Officer. The servants quarters didn't have air conditioning, and the walls were roughly whitewashed instead of wallpapered, but to my great joy, every evening a host of little geckos would come out of hiding and skitter across the ceiling in search of insects.

When my mother was well enough she would take me to the Botanical Gardens, which was my first experience of a zoo, albeit a small, smelly and rather shabby one. It was a gloriously run-down remnants of the colony's imperial past. Stately, and slightly dishevelled, statues of governors long forgotten, British monarchs, and luminaries of the East India Company were scattered around an expensive park around which had been carefully terraformed, with the minimum of imagination, to resemble one of the less salubrious municipal boating parks in - say - Croydon, Surbiton, or one of the other backwaters of suburban Surrey. But it was a constant source of delight to me as a small child. Even the most rosy of rose-coloured spectacles cannot detract from the fact that the animal exhibits at Hong-Kong Botanical Gardens of the 1960s were a smelly and rather nasty disgrace. They consisted of three or four aviaries, some semi-wild monkeys (more about them later), and five or six rather shabby cages about the size of my living room and that contained a variety of not particularly spectacular zoo exhibits. The exhibits changed fairly rapidly. At the time, my mother intimated that this was because the animals went on holiday. Now, it seems perfectly obvious that this shabby and tawdry little menagerie had a high turnover of exhibits purely because the cages were so unsuitable that the inhabitants died with monotonous regularity.

The ever-shifting population included, at various times, Celebes apes (now known by the less exotic but far more accurate name of Sulawesi crested macaques), an elderly and rather motheaten Asian black bear, some coatis, an extremely large reticulated python, and a large, greenish-brown monitor lizard.

From my earliest years, I have been always been fascinated by reptiles, amphibians and fish. This monitor lizard in Hong Kong, however, was the first one that I had seen. I was familiar with Komodo Dragons from my picture books about animals; but seeing a monitor lizard - albeit only three or four feet in length - in the flesh was a true revelation. I remember squatting on my haunches outside the cage, and gazing at the miserable reptile in awe. It sat there on the bare concrete floor of its cage, motionless for much of the time; though occasionally it would slither unenthusiastically towards the foetid pool of stagnant, green, scummy water that served both as drinking water and its bath.

Having shared a bedroom with a monitor lizard for several years, I am more conversant with their mores. Roger, my late lamented Nile monitor liked nothing more than to defecate in his water, so it had to be changed on a regular basis to avoid it becoming an open sewer. This knowledge may help one realize why this glorious lizard was only resident at the Botanical Gardens for a brief period before - like so many of its predecessors - going on "holiday."

The upper part of Victoria Peak was encircled with a number of footpaths that partly, or wholly, circumnavigated the mountain. It was my family's practice to go into the countryside for walks on Sunday afternoons; and on one Sunday afternoon in 1964 or 1965, we were walking along the footpath which heads from Magazine Gap into the forested interior of the island.

One of the defining characteristics of the mind of a small child is the way that it accepts everything at face value. Despite having a patchy, but in places surprisingly deep, knowledge of the fauna of Hong Kong I was not particularly surprised, therefore, when during our Sunday afternoon walk, my family was confronted by the very same - or, so I thought, at the time - monitor lizard who had so recently "gone on holiday" from the Botanical Gardens crossing the footpath in front of us. It was greenish brown in colour and stared straight at me accusingly, with little beady black eyes, and disappeared into the undergrowth that flanked the tiny footpath.

The Chinese water monitor has occasionally been found in Hong Kong. If I had thought about it - and I am not going to do a Stalinist rewrite of history and imbue my five year old alter ego with insights that I certainly didn't have at that time - I probably would have thought that the monitor lizard that my family and I had seen near Magazine Gap had been of the species. But it wasn't. The water monitor is a distinctive lizard with a rather beautiful pattern of yellow dots that has given it the alternate name of golden water monitor. It is also a much more delicate creature than the slightly chunky lizard that I had seen both in the botanical gardens and - albeit for a few seconds - in the wild. The water monitor is the only member of its family in Hong Kong, or indeed in most of China. If the animal that I had seen was not a water-monitor, what on earth was it?

Much to my joy, nearly 30 years after my original sighting, I discovered supporting evidence for the existence of a hitherto unknown species of large monitor lizard in Hong Kong. Over the years I have been collecting bound copies of *The Hong Kong Naturalist.* Sadly, it has become prohibitively expensive in recent years. A complete set was sold very recently for over £14,000. However, I have been collecting individual volumes as and when I can, and I have photocopies of many of the more interesting articles from the remaining volumes. One of these - amazingly - contains an account of the capture of a lizard that appears to be an unknown species of monitor, from Victoria Peak.

"On the 21st January 1930 a lady walking along Lugard Road was frightened when she saw what she thought was a "miniature crocodile." With the help of a passing policeman, some Chinese coolies, and a "Japanese gentleman who was passing" they cornered the creature. With great presence of mind the unnamed Japanese gentleman took off his coat and threw it over the animal. The lizard later allowed itself to be dumped in a sack and to be taken to a police station and ultimately to the Botanic Gardens where it "was placed in a cage." The creature was examined by Dr Geoffrey Herklots, the most famous naturalist then living in Hong Kong. His description read thus:

Total length - 22 inches, head: 6 inches, tail: 1 foot 6 inches.
Breadth - At neck 2 inches, middle of body 6 inches, in front of hind limbs 2 inches, middle of tail 1 inch.
Depth - Base of tail 2 inches, groove along back and beginning of tail, ridge along rest of tail.

*Colour - Above brown-grey, or deep olive, with yellow spots or hands, below a
dirty yellow, neck no distinctive bands,
Eyes - Open and close independently, lower lids move upwards. Iris a marbled
pale Vandyke brown with a very narrow white or very faintly yellow circle
immediately next to pupil.*

Herklots noted that this was only one of several records of strange lizards seen both
on Hong Kong Island and on the mainland at the time. It was initially identified as
Varanus bengalensis, a species that isn't actually found in China. It was also
tentatively identified as an African species - *Varanus albiguaris*. The surviving
photographs, however, suggest that it was not either of these species. It is also certain
that it was not the indigenous Varanus salvator so what was it?

Today, exotic animals from all over the world are kept as pets, and escapees
undoubtedly can and do become established in the wild; however, the international
trade in exotic reptiles was almost non-existent seventy years ago. Therefore, the
suggestion that the lizard that died soon after capture was an escaped African species
can, I think, be discounted.

Unfortunately, the originals of the photographs were destroyed during the Japanese
occupation of Hong Kong during the Second World War, as was the preserved body
of the unfortunate reptile. Two rather substandard pictures are all that remain. For
what it is worth, however, I am convinced that the animal that I saw, and the creature
photographed by Herklots, were of the same species. Precisely what it was remains a
mystery.

But all this was in the future. I was just happy to be entranced by the rich foetid smell
of a overheated, badly kept zoo, and the two things that impressed me most were the
Celebese 'apes', bad tempered though engaging monkeys with impressively shaped
and brightly coloured hindquarters, and a friendly cock silver pheasant, with whom I
fell in love, and named 'the bird with the red hat'. Indeed for months, even after my
baby brother was born I would say my prayers each evening, entreating my maker:
"God Bless Mummy, Daddy, baby Richard and the bird with the red hat".

I remember also getting righteously indignant for the first time over an animal-related
issue when the local residents complained about the noise made by a male argus
pheasant who lived in one of the aviaries. The *South China Morning Post* carried a
number of complaints, and calls for the poor bird to be silenced. I was most incensed!
The argus pheasant had far more right to live in the mid-levels than did people, I was
convinced, and I held forth vociferously on the subject for several weeks. Sadly, after
all this time I have no idea what happened in the end, but I am sure that it didn't end
happily either for me or the bird.

In June our little family became a foursome when my brother Richard John Downes
joined us. My first memory of him was the evening that he and my Mother came
home from the hospital. I was intrigued by watching my mother breast feed, and even

more intrigued by the contents of Richard's nappies which were very smelly and a pungent bright yellow. I remember it clearly to this very day!

Then one day everything changed again. Mummy and Daddy told me that we were all going 'home'. But we *are home I said and burst into tears, which infuriated my father, who administered strict chastisement as was his habit. We were going 'home',*

to England. And I would never see Buxey Lodge again.
Herklots' mystery monitor

CHAPTER TWO
At Partridge Piece

"I'm not of this generation".

Charles Manson

As I grow older I realise that I was not the only member of my family unhappy with the way that I was treated by the other members. I think that this social description could equally well apply to more than a few other members of my family as well.

My mother, who cut her eye teeth on the tales of derring-do of Rider-Haggard and Edgar Wallace had actually made the transition from Nigerian frontierswoman to demi-Memsahib quite well, but my father hated it. Both of them drank too much, and I know that it was a shock to come back to England, full of tales of Empire, to find that no-one was interested. As my father wrote in his unpublished memoirs:

> "Our home was amongst the ancient sunken lanes, the windswept moors and the green fields of Devon, but for the time being our 'home' was very much where we hung our (bush) hats, and at present this harsh, sunbaked territory was our 'home' - we were with people for whom we had developed an affection, people like big fat, smiling Pius and the wizened old trader with the wise eyes, with people like Sergi, Moses, Ignatius, and with 'Audu-in-the-bush'. These had become our friends and we felt a great more at home with them than with our loving parents, who never could understand why we had to go traipsing off to Africa when we could live in far greater comfort, close to them in England."

Although my mother enjoyed this new world of cocktail parties, tennis and the sort of vicious socialising which takes place amongst women whose husbands are all quite prepared to stab each other in the back in order to get promotion, my father hated it.

Whenever I hear the Roy Harper song *I hate the White Man* I think of my poor beleaguered father; an untreated manic-depressive, self medicating with increasingly large doses of gin, with a happy wife with too much time on her hands and two small children, the elder of whom was already showing the signs of the mental health issues that had blighted his own life.

These days, I like to think that someone in authority would have seen the cracks forming, and might have done something. But they didn't when I went through much the same psychological end game twenty years later, and I very much doubt whether anything would be any different in the new Britain of the 'big society'. Mental illness amongst over achievers is one of the last great taboos. It is perfectly acceptable to be mentally ill if you live in poverty, are ill-educated, or downtrodden by 'the man'. But if you *are* 'the man', then you had damn well better snap out of it and pull yourself together. My father's upper lip was so stiff that I am glad that he never grew a moustache, and with every further day of his torment it got stiffer and stiffer, until it threatened to take over not just his body, but his soul.

In Hong Kong I never really saw my father. In England I had no option.

We spent nine months in a little red brick cottage called 'Partridge Piece', in a hamlet called Ogdens, just outside of Fordingbridge in Hampshire. This was fifty years ago, as I write, and my memories are perforce very fragmented. So I looked it up on the internet and fairly soon found a photograph of a house which rings absolutely no bells in my memory whatsoever. According to one of the property websites, it has an estimated value of over a million. Apparently it is a desirable residence which last sold for £750,000 in 2006. I wonder whether the new owners know about the ghost.

I may not remember much about the building itself, but I *do* remember the ghost. Or rather, I do remember my parents talking about the ghost, because - although I was, apparently, the only person to actually see it, I have absolutely no memory of the fact. But, piecing together things from various memories, I can tell you what happened, both at the time and in the immediate aftermath.

Apparently my family had been plagued by low-level poltergeist activity. Knowing what I know now about things parapsychological, I don't think of such things as having anything to do with the spirits of the dead, and the fact that there was a teenaged girl in the house who was going through some emotional upheavals at the time, tends to explain it all to my satisfaction, at least with the benefit of hindsight. We will come back to the enigmatic figure of the emotionally disturbed teenage girl later in the narrative, because I am doing my best to keep my natural inclinations at bay and keep this narrative in some sort of logical and chronological order.

As I have explained elsewhere, my family - particularly my Father - were very traditionally religious, and my Father became convinced that the windows that slammed for no good reason, the warm pebbles that materialised in mid air, and the sound of footsteps that could be heard padding steadily across the floor of the upstairs rooms, were manifestations of something demonic, or at least cries for help from an unquiet spirit. Once again with hindsight I am very pleased that my father had never read anything by H. P. Lovecraft, or else his imagination would *really* have started working overtime.

He did some digging, by talking to the neighbours and to some of the regulars at the local pub, and came back with the story of a macabre event which, allegedly, happened some thirty years before, in the years immediately leading up to WW2.

The house had then been inhabited by an elderly woman, who lived with her grown-up farm labourer son, who was - what these day's one would probably call - educationally subnormal. Please remember that I am piecing this together from memories of what happened half a century ago, tempered with what happened when I discussed the affair with my father one night many years later when he was on his deathbed and we had both been drinking heavily. Neither of these are the best, or at least the most accepted ways, for a diligent researcher to do his homework.

It appears that this couple had a peculiar, incestuous relationship. For many years the people in the village had ignored them and let them get on with their lives in peace, but for some reason this changed. I have no idea why, how, or what, but as a result of the ensuing scandal, the farm labourer lost his job, killed his mother/lover and hung himself. It would be so easy here to insert a macabrely written Gothic horror story, but despite all my efforts, I have not been able to find out anything more about the affair, and all that I know is the bare bones of what I have told you.

My Father then tried to communicate with the ghost. He named the spectre 'Hob' which is revealing in itself.

A hob is a type of small mythological household spirit found in the north and midlands of England, but especially on the Anglo-Scottish border, according to traditional folklore of those regions. They could live inside the house or outdoors. They are said to work in farmyards and thus could be helpful, however if offended they could become nuisances. The usual way to dispose of a hob was to give them a set of new clothing, the receiving of which would make the creature leave forever. It could however be impossible to get rid of the worst hobs. Hob is the root word from which both Hobgoblin and Hobbit are derived, but it is not the sort of thing that one would expect a middle ranking Civil Servant, part time Naval Officer, and wannabe Churchwarden to know.

Apparently his attempts to communicate with the spirit were vaguely successful. One night as my father was putting me to bed, I apparently asked him what the white thing that was following him around was. This horrified my poor father. He was quite happy to carry his own little bits of psychic research, but he was so full of guilt about my sister's death, and the series of obstetric problems that my mother had suffered that he was appalled at the idea that he could have done anything to harm his eldest son. So he turned to 'Hob', and told him to follow him out into the garden, where he threatened 'Hob' with exorcism if he ever scared me or my brother again. The fact that neither of us were scared didn't enter into the equation, but it has to be said that his threats seemed to have worked, and the psychic disturbances pretty well dried up for the rest of our stay there.

However, there is another explanation which I would like to consider. My parents had engaged a Nanny - a Scottish girl in her late teens or early twenties. She was called Judy and I totally adored her, and in return she spoiled me rotten. However, in my chequered career as an investigator of Fortean phenomena, I have found that more often than not poltergeist and allied phenomena including quite a few ghost sightings are often found in houses where there is an emotionally disturbed girl somewhere a few years on either side of puberty. Now, fifty odd years later, I have no idea when Judy went through the menarche, but I do know that whilst she was living with us, her father - in Scotland - was taken ill suddenly, and died soon after she had returned from visiting him.

This was probably the first time that I recognised that my father could be the most unreasonable old bastard on the planet. Judy was understandably distraught, and terminated her employment with the Downes family so that she could be with her family, and my father hated her for it. He let her go with the worst possible grace and ranted about the poor girl in the most vicious of terms for many years to come. I still remember the shouting, the tears and the rants with terror. For the first time, but by no means the last time in my life I found myself in the position of knowing that my father (whom I loved very much, even though I was terrified of him) hated someone that I also loved very much, and this set up the first of many irresolvable conflicts within my already fragile psyche; conflicts which would eventually threaten to tear me apart again and again and again throughout my life.

I have no way of knowing whether 'Hob' appeared, before, after or during the horrors of Judy's departure, but I would hazard a guess that they were somehow linked. After her's and Hob's departures from our lives my relationship with my parents got progressively worse. My father was a true believer in the Victorian ethos that one spared the rod only if one wished to spoil the child, and I was physically chastised for every transgression real and imaginary. I don't want to spend the whole of this chapter vilifying my poor father for the way he treated me; he was under an enormous amount of pressure at the time. He was doing something arcane on behalf of both the Hong Kong Royal Naval Reserve and the Hong Kong Freemasons (I have never found out exactly what, although I have my suspicions) and his elder sister was dying of cancer. His relationship with his sister Mary had always been a stormy one, and - from things that I heard him say to me and others over the years - I think that he thought that she should have handled her final illness with more of a stiff upper lip, and that she was being selfish and bringing unwarranted stress onto the other members of the family. This is, of course, an absolutely horrific thing to have said, but it was an ongoing *idee fixe* of the man. Judy, my Aunt, and later me at various times in our lives were just letting the side down when we submitted to overwhelming emotions. Somehow, in his twisted worldview, to show emotion was somehow vulgar, and un-British.

But he probably should not be blamed completely for this attitude. As I wrote somewhere else recently, when I was nineteen or twenty I was an unemployed punk rocker, who wrote bad poetry. When he was the age that I was drinking my way around North Devon, smoking marijuana like there was no tomorrow and doing my best to get a succession of local floozies to take their clothes off, he was being torpedoed in the Battle of the Atlantic, and being washed overboard, and eventually having life-saving surgery without the benefit of an anaesthetic. Things like that, I would imagine, tend to have unpleasant knock on effects upon one's psyche.

But Daddy got more taciturn, drank more, and as I reacted to this by behaving more peculiarly, he punished me harder, setting up a vicious cycle that was to last for decades. Apparently, although I have no memory whatsoever of it, I totally screwed up my brother's Christening by shutting my hand in the church door and having to be rushed to A&E (or whatever they called it back then), and my paternal Grandmother was so upset by the way that my father treated me that she refused to come and stay with the family again. Why she didn't actually do something about it I don't know, but - if I am going to be honest about the matter - what on earth *could* she have done?

One day my maternal grandparents took me to Muddiford, a tiny village (as it was then) on the Dorset coast, and taught me to catch minnows with a glass jar and a string. I was totally absorbed in this and when we took the little fish home, put them into a large goldfish bowl which I had been given. I spent hours looking at them and marvelling how the little streaks of silver that one could see darting across the bed of the river, were actually fully formed little creatures; it was the beginning of my lifelong love affair with fishkeeping. However, like so many other of my love affairs throughout my life, it ended messily, with tears, recriminations and anger.

My two cousins, Pené and Patrick were visiting us. I was about four years old so they were about eight or nine, and far more sophisticated and worldly wise than I was. They were also devotees of the surreal humour of people like The Goons, whereas we didn't even have a television set. One day I was babbling on about my fish, and saying that unlike the fish in my colouring books they didn't have huge multicoloured bubbles coming out of their mouths. "Better give them some bubble mixture" quipped my cousins, not realising for a moment that I had no idea of irony (I still haven't, much of the time) and that I would take them at their word. So I poured bubble mixture into the goldfish bowl and killed my beloved fish, and my father shouted and ranted at me for my wanton cruelty, and - once again - beat me severely.

< Author's note: I want to stress here that none of this was my cousins' fault. They were not to know about the complex state of my part of the family, and the mental health issues of those within it.>

My mother acquired a new hobby (or it might have been an old hobby that I was too young to know anything about). Whenever we went on our family walks through the forest that autumn and winter, my mother would collect moss of different colours and shapes, and attractive little pebbles and twigs, which she took home to Partridge Piece. There, she would make intricate little moss gardens in a series of Pyrex glass soup bowls. I was fascinated by this level of intricacy, which reminded me of the magnificent model train layout in the window of the toy shop in Fordingbridge high street. Later, the memory of these miniature little worlds that she so painstakingly created came back to me as I first tried to decorate fish tanks and vivaria for myself; always doing my best to recreate a slice of the habitat natural to the creatures that were to inhabit it. Sometimes I got it completely wrong, with disastrous results, but I always tried.

And right from my earliest days as a wannabe zoo-keeper, I always hated the model shipwrecks and mermaids that less zoologically minded fish keepers insisted on putting into their tanks. I am still of this mindset today, and I am sure that most of this comes from my mother's moss gardens back in the winter of 1963.

I always loved my mother's bedtime stories, and in particular her tales about a small brown rabbit, called 'Brown Rabbit'. This remarkable lagomorph lived in a burrow in the corner of a huge field, in which stood an old oak tree that contained a wise old owl, who always managed to sort out the various problems that Brown Rabbit had with his day-to-day life. Brown Rabbit was remarkably like the four-year-old Jonathan. He kept tadpoles in an old tin bowl and did most of the things that the four-year-old me enjoyed doing.

During our sojourn in the New Forest, we were visited by one of my mother's cousins, who I think was called 'Cousin Betty'. She was older than my mother, and I haven't heard of or about her for years. And as my mother would have been 98 this year, had she lived, I think it is highly unlikely that she is still around.

But, just in case, and in the even more unlikely scenario that she is reading this, I would like to proffer many apologies for my four-year-old gaucheness.

One night, during my cousin's stay with us, she offered to tell me a bedtime story. For some reason, I had severe forebodings about this and politely said that I would rather a 'Brown Rabbit' story from my mother, who glared at me and told me not to be rude to my relative. I apologised contritely and went to bed, dreading what was to come next.

The bedtime story was even worse than I had feared. It was a cautionary tale about some child roasting chestnuts in front of an open fire, and managing, somehow, to burn the house down. I started to shake and then scream. I had bad dreams based upon this for many years to come, well into my adulthood. But, although my mother calmed me down, I was still chastised physically for my rudeness, and – what Roger Waters would no doubt have called "another brick in the wall" – was firmly cemented into place.

My father was a keen member of the Hong Kong Royal Naval Reserve, and on several occasions during our sojourn in the New Forest he went on training courses, most of them only lasting a matter of hours, during which my Mother and one or both of my Grandparents would take me to the little zoo in Southampton. I remember a king penguin and an Andean condor (or possibly a king vulture) hunched miserably on what looked to me like one of those stands old fashioned pet shops use for parrots, but - sadly - I can recall nothing else.

On another occasion my grandparents took me to the museum in Salisbury, and I became fascinated by two of the exhibits; a family of stuffed great bustards, and a pair of spoonbills. Both these are birds that I have studied to a certain extent ever since. I was fascinated, and as usual when I get obsessed with something I talked about nothing else for days, which - once again - brought down my father's wrath upon my head.

The great bustard was formerly native in Great Britain and a bustard forms part of the design of the Wiltshire Coat of Arms and as supporters for the Cambridgeshire arms. It was hunted out of existence in Britain by the 1840s. In the 1960s there were a number of privately funded attempts to reintroduce the species onto Salisbury Plain, and in 1970 the Great Bustard Trust was formed. Their efforts are usually thought to have been a failure, but in the late 1980s, as I have written elsewhere, I had a run in with something that I truly believe to have been a specimen of this species just off the A303 as it traverses the plain.

All is not over for this species in the UK. In 2004 a project overseeing the reintroduction to Salisbury Plain in Wiltshire using eggs taken from Saratov in Russia was undertaken by The Great Bustard Group, a UK Registered Charity that aims to establish a self-sustaining population of great bustards in the UK. They laid eggs and raised chicks in Britain in 2009 and 2010. In March 2015, the group's latest press release stated proudly:

> "The spring is truly with us now with males displaying at two of our release sites. Last year's birds are still apparently making their way back to the place of release with a new group of three being found yesterday. One group of three young males are still located on the south coast in Dorset, and show no signs of moving so far.
>
> Of the 33 birds released last year the GBG can locate a minimum of 12 individuals which gives a survival rate of over 36% which is the best the project has achieved. This figure is also notably higher than the survival rate in a healthy established population. We expect a few more birds to be located during the spring."

The Eurasian spoonbill is another species that was extirpated from the UK in the late Seventeenth Century, but due to hard work by British conservationists, a small breeding colony was formed in Norfolk early in the 21st Century. There were still no more than a dozen British resident birds by the Spring of 2013 when Corinna and I, together with our friend Lars Thomas the Danish naturalist and his sons, were at Fremington Quay in North Devon over the Easter weekend when, nearly fifty years after I saw the dried, and as I found out when I went back to the museum and chatted with the curator in the early 1990s, whilst I was on a few days break from a Steve

Harley and Cockney Rebel UK tour, rather misshapen and moth-eaten Taxidermy specimens for the first time, I finally saw one of these magnificent, if slightly goofy looking birds, alive on home soil. I assure you that it was well worth the wait.

About the only thing from that period in the New Forest that I look back upon with real fondness was the relationship that my parents struck up with an elderly retired RAF officer, who had settled down to a life in a tiny cottage in the middle of the woods and a career as an amateur naturalist. I can't remember his name, and I can't remember anything about him except for a neatly-trimmed head of silver hair, and a shabby tweed jacket which stank of shag tobacco. He took us into the depths of the forest to go and watch the fallow deer, and in particular one albino hind that he had been following for years. Even now, half a century later I remember the sheer primal joy of creeping up upon and then watching something which my father assured me only a handful of other people had ever seen.

I squeezed his hand in sheer joy, as together we stared at the perfectly formed white creature standing like a hornless unicorn only a few yards in front of us. That was a moment that has stayed with me ever since.

That Christmas I first became aware of events on the world stage. My grandfather bought me a stamp album for a Christmas present, and my parents had contacted all their friends from around the world for piles of postage stamps that I could soak off their envelopes and affix into the appropriate portion of the album. I was perfectly aware that the young Queen Elizabeth, then still only in her thirties had her head on all the British, and all the Empire stamps, but who was this fresh faced man whose face was on all the stamps my parents' American friends had sent them?

It was of course President Kennedy, shot down in cold blood only six weeks or so before, and my parents explained this to me, but not in the tones of reverence that so many people were to use when talking about the martyred JFK. They were convinced to the end if their days that he had been an inveterate womaniser who financially supported the IRA, and together with Mahatma Gandhi (he was anti-British despite all we did for him), General de Gaulle (he has never shown any gratitude for what we did for him during the war) and the Duke of Windsor (a filthy, Hun-loving traitor) his name was never spoken in the Downes household except when absolutely necessary!

We flew back to Hong Kong in the late spring of 1964, and I truly felt that I was coming home. Here was a warm, nurturing place that I understood. A place where there were little lizards which crawled up the pastel coloured stucco walls, where the sights, sounds and smells of the tropics were everywhere I walked, and where - since my father went back to work almost as soon as we returned - nobody shouted at me or hit me. It was paradise.

For reasons probably to do with the innate inefficiency of the Urban Services Department we were unable to move int our new apartment up on Victoria Peak, so we spent some weeks living at the old Repulse Bay Hotel on the south side of the island. Looking it up in an idle moment on the internet I see to my sadness that the hotel is now a rather horrid looking 37 story complex called. 'The Repulse Bay' which claims to offer "an oasis of tranquillity and nostalgia" but how it can do it whilst being a monstrosity shaped like a bright blue satellite dish I have no idea.

I am not the only person appalled by the new development. On the excellent Old Hong Kong website Gwulo, 80skid writes:

"A typical Hong Kong tragedy. Hong Kong and Shanghai Hotels demolished the hotel in 1982 to build blocks of flats as property prices rocketed. Protests about knocking down such a elegant piece of Hong Kong's history were ignored. The bubble burst after demolition and the site was left sitting empty. For some reason (books vary on the motivation), the main hotel building was eventually rebuilt a few years later as part of the new development when prices recovered. But it's just a fake. On the development's web site they say:

"The opening of The Repulse Bay Historical Gallery illustrates the Company's continuous efforts to preserve the legacy of The Repulse Bay for the enjoyment of both local and overseas visitors."

Some irony! HSH, who tore down the building and reportedly auctioned off the contents, still own the site."

But I was there when it was still real and was a bastion of what remained of the Empire, and back in 1964 there was still a surprisingly large amount of Empire left. While my baby brother lay in his carry cot making gurgling noises, my mother and I revelled at being back in the country that we loved, far away from a motherland that neither appreciated, understood or wanted us. My best memories of these six or seven weeks are of my Mother teaching me to read from the pages of completely unsuitable books by Gerald Durrell, although I note with hindsight she left out the worst of the alcohol jokes and the account of the bored chimpanzee engaging in autofellatio. But by the time we left the hotel, a few days before my fifth birthday, Jonathan was well on his way to being able to read. I remember sitting on my mother's lap as she read to me tales of exotic animals, exotic people and copious gin drinking, and decided then that when I grew up I would hunt for strange animals and drink a lot of gin.

And guess what readers.

I did.

My worst memory of our stay at the hotel was of an American boy who had a puppet theatre with which he 'entertained' the assembled children every afternoon. I can't remember why, but I was terrified of these puppets, and finally managed to get out of having to sit through another scarifying performance by being copiously sick all over myself, and several other small children. To my great pleasure I was *persona non grata* at the puppet shows ever after, and Mummy and I used to go for long walks on the beach instead. One day, during these walks I found a dead seasnake, something that fascinated me. I was perfectly aware what a snake was - Gerald Durrell had caught, and been bitten by, enough for that not to be a problem for me. But why did this one have such a strange flattened body? I didn't know, and neither did my mother, so she went to the bookshop just round the corner from the hotel and bought two magnificent books, *The Hong Kong Countryside* and *A Pocket Guide to Hong Kong Birds*. I have them both still, and I don't think that I have read any books more in my life.

My mother and I discovered that the mystery snake was *Hydrophis cyanocinctus* the banded sea snake, one of six species of seasnake found in the waters of the former colony. Peculiarly, although I heard about them on a couple of occasions, this was my only encounter with an actual specimen, albeit a dead one, and the only time I was ever in my life to see living ones was four years later at the Royal Perth Show in Western Australia, but we mustn't stray too far ahead.

The same day, I was startled and scared by a noise of earth-shattering proportions that came from one of the scaffolding towers that stood at intervals along the beach. As children do, I had just taken them for granted. Animals, living or dead, were worthy of my investigation, plants could be if they were spectacular enough, but the works of men were just stupid, vulgar and beneath my contempt, so I had never actually done anything to find out the purpose of these tall watchtowers, because I simply wasn't interested. But now I was.

The howl of what I later found out was a WW2 era air raid siren pulsed out across the bay, and all the bathers hurriedly left the water, the teenagers amongst them screaming in terrified delight as they enjoyed the frisson of danger. Mummy pointed her finger and I could see a triangular grey fin break the water. Suddenly two shots rang out, but it seems that the watchman on the shark watchtower was not as good a shot as he had been a watchman and the deadly fish leisurely swam back out to sea.

CHAPTER THREE
Mount Austin Mansions

"I never thought I was normal, never tried to be normal".

Charles Manson

We moved to our new home, Mount Austin Mansions, in the spring of 1964. This was my first *real* home, because although I had lived in at least two places in Nigeria, spent nine months or so at Mole End, and then lived at Buxey Lodge for a couple of years, and then at Partridge Piece, Mount Austin is the first place that I lived about which I had a narrative memory, and although I am sure that the good and bad bits of my life prior to 1964 will have done all sorts of peculiar things to my psyche, and helped keep several highly paid therapists in custard powder and knickers for quite a few years, Mount Austin is the first place that I lived that really matters to me.

Ironically, a far better writer than me also lived there about ten years before me. His name was Martin Booth and I mentioned him in passing earlier in this book. My old friend Richard Muirhead lent me his copy of Booth's seminal book *Gweilo* and it helped me through one of my serious bouts of illness in the winter of 2008/9. Reading it opened a window into my past and I kept on remembering little pieces of my childhood; joyful and sad, innocent and not.

As in so many things in my life, the fact that both my parents are dead may have allowed me to write this book, but it has hindered my research massively. Both of them (my mother in particular) were polymaths who knew a bit about an awful lot of subjects, and I have no doubt that if they were still alive, not only would writing this chapter have been a heck of a lot easier, but various inaccuracies which I am sure have slipped through, would almost certainly not have. But, on the other hand, if either of them had been still alive, I would have been too embarrassed to include large chunks of what I am *actually* writing in this book. So, I guess that it all works out in the end.

As far as I can ascertain, the story goes back to 1868, (just over 20 years after Hong Kong became a British colony) when John Gardiner Austin was appointed as Colonial Secretary in Hong Kong. During his ten-year tenure he built a house on The Peak which his friends nicknamed 'The Austin Arms'. Soon after he left the colony, a hotel with the same name was built on the land which by then had been named 'Mount Austin'. Austin's house, was apparently a bungalow, and the newly formed 'Austin Arms Co. announced their intention to buy the site of the 'Austin Arms', and build and keep a large 'First Class Residential Hotel' on it. Whether they demolished Austin's original bungalow and rebuilt it, added bits on to it, or simply appropriated the name I don't know. It doesn't really matter after all this time, although I have to admit that I am OCD enough to want to find out.

The 'Austin Arms Hotel' lost money almost from the beginning, and the 1892 Extraordinary General Meeting reported income from the hotel (so it's obviously open for business), but also notes a loss of capital and tried to blame the failure of the project on the machinations of Mr. Findlay-Smith who owned the far more successful Peak Hotel (more of that later). Findlay-Smith protested his innocence, and by 1895 the ill-fated hotel became known as 'The Mount Austin Hotel', but this too was presumably not a great financial success, because in 1897, according to the *Hong Kong Telegraph*, 29 May 1897, "... the Military Authorities ... have purchased the Mount Austin Hotel from Messrs. J. D. Humphreys and sons for 100,000 pounds sterling." The Army redeveloped it as 'Mount Austin Barracks', and I have no idea what happened to Messrs. J.D. Humphries and sons.

The Mount Austin Barracks was damaged and fell into disrepair during the Japanese occupation of the colony, between 1941 and 1945, and it was demolished in the mid 1950s, and a cluster of apartment blocks, named 'Mount Austin Mansions' were built on the site. Some of these were allocated for housing senior civil servants and the others were allocated for housing senior Naval officers and their families. Martin Booth lived in one of the latter blocks, I lived in one of the former.

A photograph from *Life* Magazine taken just after the war shows how irreparably damaged the barracks was. And it also shows a deep trough of waste scrubland on the opposite side of Mount Austin Road. This was filled in and levelled and became the Mount Austin playground which still remains there today. I know that this area is artificial from my own experience, because back in about 1969, a couple of years after my family had left Mount Austin, I was visiting friends who lived there, whilst the Urban Services Department were doing something arcane with the drains, and we discovered – much to our delight – that there were huge concrete storm drains, tunnelled beneath the playground. My parents (and, as far as I can remember, my friends' parents – strictly forbade us to explore them, so (of course) as soon as their backs were turned, we did just that.

The Rise and Fall of the Third Reich had just been on television, and it had captured the imagination of all the children in my peer group. World War Two only ended 14 years before I was born, and as I will describe, Hong Kong had been particularly severely affected, and the scars of the conflict were all around us. All the children played war games. Apart from more secretive activities that I shall mention elsewhere it was the most consistent recreational activity amongst the younger generation (my fascination with the natural world marked me out as being 'unusual' amongst the Mount Austin kids), and on this particular occasion, although I was excited at the prospect that there might be all sorts of peculiar animals down there (there weren't), the consensus decision was that we would play 'Hitler in his Bunker'.

I can't remember the details of the game. I am sure that it involved a lot of rushing about with toy guns and shouting *Seig Heil,* but the thing that most impressed me was the idea that I was exploring a world which not only my parents, but – by association – the entire grown-up world had never seen, and because they (to a man) seemed to abhor getting grubby, would never see. The tunnels were so big that the eight-year-old me (who was a bit above average in size, but not massively so) could walk through without stooping. On my belt I had a torch and a sheath knife that had been given to me by my maternal grandfather during our last visit 'Home'. In these unenlightened times it seems extraordinary that a young boy be given a four-inch hunting knife, but I was massively proud of it, and brandished it (as an essential example of an explorer's equipment) whenever I could.

I was not individualistic enough to actively flaunt the game that the majority of children were playing. Indeed, at that age (and for many years to come) I was so neurotic and insecure that I would not have considered doing so. I cannot remember the details, but I imagine that I managed to get to play the part of a guard or something, and so managed to sneak off 'on patrol' whilst the other kids were re-enacting the last days of the Third Reich.

Gingerly I tiptoed through the tunnel. Clutching my torch in my sweaty left hand, and my knife in my right I deliberately aimed the torch beam as far ahead of me as I could. In the gloom I could see movement; was it a snake? A Porcupine? The ghost of a Japanese soldier? But each time I got there I would find that there was nothing at all. The movement had been the result of my over-active imagination. On the sides there were smaller tunnels going off at right angles. I could probably have fitted into them, but it would have been too small for me to have turned around, and this is where my meagre reserves of courage deserted me. I kept to the main tunnel, and carried on until I reached the end, where there was a thick metal grille.

So, I turned around and retraced my steps, and with each step I took it became eerier. My footsteps echoed as if someone had recorded them and played the result back through a plate reverb. I could no longer hear the voices of my playmates at the other end of the tunnel near the entrance, and then – to make it a hundred thousand times worse – the battery in my torch began to run out and the light, feeble already, began to splutter and dim. My over-active imagination started working overtime as I inched my way back.

Although it was the dry season, the tunnel (which presumably would have been full of water in the rainy season) had about an inch of stagnant slimy goo in the bottom, and whilst that had not seemed too much of an issue during my outward journey, on my return trip, by the failing light of my rather ineffectual torch (sorry Grandad, but it was crap) I had to inch myself along to avoid slipping and falling. The silence was deafening. By this time I was convinced that my friends had left, forgotten that I had been with them, and that the workers from the Urban Services Department would have finished whatever arcane thing that they were doing, and resealed the drains leaving me underground to die a lonely and terrifying death alone in the dark.

Of course, nothing like that happened at all. I am assuming that you – the reader – had already worked that one out for yourselves as, over forty years on, I am sitting at my computer writing this story. Through some accident of acoustics, and as acoustics is a subject about which I know less than nothing I am not going to even attempt to explain it, the sound of my companion's voices just didn't carry into the tunnel. I had been too excited to notice this on the way out when I was convinced that I was going to make some enormous cryptozoological discovery or other, but on the way back, when I was less fuelled with adrenaline, and the only discovery I had made was a metal grille of no cryptozoological significance whatsoever, the silence was horrifyingly noticeable.

So, I made my way back to my friends, who by this time had tied the younger sister of one of them to a chair and were preparing to interrogate her. The girl, whose name I forget after nearly half a century, threatened to "tell Mum, if you don't knock it off", and we all climbed up the access vent, through the manhole cover and into the light. What happened next I don't recall.

It is exceedingly difficult trying to piece together events with historical accuracy, when your main source of information is the internet. Wikipedia, for example, was a noble idea, and often works well, but in many cases it is confused, or just simply wrong. For example it confuses the two different hotels, and the apartment blocks which were built on their sites: Mount Austin Mansions and Peak Mansions, and it is only because I lived at both of them that alarm bells began ringing in my head. I think that I have got the chronology right, but again – for the purposes of this narrative – it doesn't really matter. But what *does* matter – again for this particular narrative, which is a subjective history of me, rather than an objective history of the Crown Colony of Hong Kong – is to give some sort of an overview of the place.

It was the first time in my life that I felt like I was part of a community outside my family, because as the flats were specifically designated as quarters for married, middle ranking Civil Servants, nearly each of them was inhabited by a young family. On the whole, the older children were packed off to boarding school back in the UK, and so, when I arrived round about my fifth birthday, there were lots of other children to interact with, and most of them were under the age of about 12, the older children arriving back in time for the long school holidays full of talk about miniskirts,

"Swinging London", and all sorts of other things I didn't understand.

There were three main sets of activities that we of the younger generation found irresistibly fascinating. The first was long and complicated games of soldiers. All the boys took it for granted that when they grew up they would join the armed forces. Whether this was because National Service in the UK had finally only finished the year before, and - like "Swinging London" - the reality of a purely volunteer army had not yet reached Hong Kong, or whether it was because most of our parents had seen action of some sort either in WW2 or during the internecine anti-Communist squabbles that followed as the former jewels in the crown either fell or were forced out, I don't know. However, I suspect that - like so many peculiar facets of our shared childhood - it was because of the unique socio-political situation in which we found ourselves; tended by servants whose relatives (we believed) were massing just across the border to kill us.

The second activity into which we all threw ourselves wholeheartedly was "Cowboys and Indians". It was the first time that I had ever come across TV culture; we never had a television before we moved to Mount Austin, but when we did it opened a whole new world to us. Or in fact it opened our eyes to an idealised America - a land of the free when vicious redskins (who looked suspiciously like the inscrutable yellow skins whom we saw ever day) were shot on sight if they stepped outside their allotted role as servant or sidekick. As I wrote in *Monster Hunter* (2004):

> "I feel so sorry for the youth of today. To them, the Native Americans are people who have fuelled an entire industry of homemade dream-catchers, statuettes of the Great Manitou, and home self-improvement courses in Native American spirituality. To my generation, there was something completely different. We saw them on television at least three nights a week, either killing or being killed by cowboys, or - like my hero Tonto - assisting a slightly inept Lone Ranger to behave like a 19th century analogue of Superman. Fuelled by my in-depth knowledge of Indian which I had gathered from watching episode after episode of the aforementioned Lone Ranger and Bat Masterson - I knew just what to do."

It would be so easy with the benefit of four decades hindsight to throw myself into some sort of psycho-social theory claiming that I usually claimed the role of Red Indian chief because I felt an innate link with their spirituality and notions of one-ness with nature. But that would just be a piece of convenient literary prestidigitation. I usually chose to be a Red Indian for a much more simple reason; my mother had bought me a wigwam and a head-dress for my birthday!

In fact, it wasn't a wigwam at all, but I wasn't to find that out for many years. It was a fairly ordinary tent made out of bright yellow canvas, and with a porch flappy thing that I could sit under pretending to smoke the pipe of peace and complaining that the white men with whom I had been dealing spoke with a forked tongue.

So the die was cast; I could once again, conveniently try to rewrite history and say that this was the beginning of my life as 'an outsider', as I had deliberately allied and identified myself with the underdogs, soon to be exiled to reservations where they could drink their lives away. Goodness me, it would be so easy to do, but it just would not be true. I was always the Red Indian because I had the tent, the hat and a rather nifty set of bow and arrows (each resplendent with real goose feathers and a rubber suction pad on the tip). Sometimes, even when one is barking mad and writing one's own childhood autobiography, a cigar can be nothing more than a cigar).

The third, and in many ways the most engrossing activities of the lives of nearly every youngster there, both boys and girls, involved taking our clothes off. Of course some of this was nothing more than the outpouring of what Brian Aldiss once described as ur-sexuality which many (if not most) children have indulged in for centuries, and which successive generations of adults have done their best to claim doesn't exist. But some of it, I believe, is something far more primal, and far more interesting.

As I will describe later, I lived much of my childhood vicariously through the pages of children's books, and I was always vaguely unsettled by one aspect of the adventures of my heroes. Jennings, William *et al* played most of the games that my friends and I did. They played Cowboys and Indians, they played soldiers, they went catching tadpoles, and they even made camps deep in the woods like we did. However, they never hid in these camps and took their clothes off, luxuriating in the freedom, naughtiness, and forbidden excitement of it all. Of course, I rationalised, it might be too cold in England (the memory of the horrible winter of 1963 was still fresh in my mind). However, when I was in my first year of school in England, seven or eight years after I first came to Mount Austin, that I first read Mark Twain's *The Adventures of Tom Sawyer*, and there in Chapter Sixteen was the validation for which I had searched.

The eponymous hero of the book together with his friends Huckleberry Finn and Joe Harper have run away from home, and are camped out on an island in the middle of the Mississippi river. Whilst there they play at being "Indians" and run around naked and streaked with mud, as an ultimate rebellion against the world from which they are hiding. I think that this was much the same for us in mid 1960s Hong Kong. These acts of rebellion (later in the decade, at least) were probably tinged slightly by the accounts of hippy love-ins, and the public nudity at rock festivals such as Woodstock, but these were acts of rebellion as well, albeit acts of rebellion tinged with hormones that we - at that time - didn't possess.

I find myself in a difficult position here. Received wisdom is that when children play games which involve furtive disrobing, they do so purely out of curiosity. But that is not how I remember them at all. Brian Aldiss' description of such things as ur-sex is – in my opinion – more accurate; it is, indeed, sexual and it is a natural part of child development. But when Aldiss attempted to write about such things he came dangerously close to writing pornography, and this is something that I not only have no interest in doing, but have no intention of doing under any circumstances, so, although these games were a significant part of my childhood, I will not write about them further.

Childhood in Hong Kong was particularly hierarchical. Not only did we (with very few exceptions) not play with the Chinese children, but we didn't play with children outside the confines of our particular age and social grouping. The older kids were off at boarding school in the motherland, or were attending the two institutions of secondary education - Island School, and KG5 (King George Fifth) in Kowloon - and were almost entirely sequestered from us youngsters. The Europeans in the Colony were - in the main - from three different sources: trade, the military, and the government. Each of these three groups of people lived in completely different geographical locations and hardly ever mixed socially. We, of course, were part of the third of these groupings, and so the social contacts of my contemporaries and I were as rigidly controlled as if we had been in purdah. This is probably the reason that we all did roughly the same things, and enjoyed the same pursuits. The fact that we were the same age and didn't play with children older or younger than us is probably the reason that bullying was rare and even the activities that we took great care to keep from our various parents never became properly sexual until we were quite a bit older.

The flat space that Mount Austin Mansions, and its predecessor has been built upon had been hacked out of an area of hillside presumably by coolies with or without the aid of dynamite, three quarters of a century before, but little effort had been taken to landscape the area, as I am sure would have been done these days.

There were a number of blocks, and although I remember exactly which one we lived in (it was the one nearest the road with the huge *feng shui* fig tree behind it) much to my chagrin I cannot remember the name of our particular block, and as it has since been knocked down, I can't even take you there. Around the different blocks of flats and the various utility buildings that serviced them, there was a network of smooth asphalt roadways. Behind it was a sheer red sandstone cliff at the top of which was a small patch of those white lilies one only sees at funerals, and one of the big blocks that I believe was inhabited by families of the Colony's Royal naval contingent.

The red-brown sandstone cliff was very crumbly, and perfect for a small boy to dig entrenchments for his toy soldiers, and over the years it had acquired hundreds of these miniature earthworks which had played host to all sorts of games of make believe for successive generations of Mount Austin children. I decided that the winding asphalt roadways which looped around the different apartment blocks were a great river (modelled vaguely upon the Great River that traversed the land of Narnia in the glorious books by C S Lewis) and that the islands of green grass were just that, different island countries. I called the one that included the red sandstone cliffs 'Magic Land' and anointed myself as its king. There was nothing in the slightest bit magic about it, but the name stuck. Whether I told anyone else about this I don't remember, and after half a century it doesn't matter overly. Probably the most exciting thing about Magic Land was the colony of iron wire snakes that lived at the bottom of the red sandstone cliff.

At the time the only thing that I knew about this species was that they were called *Typhlops braminus* and that they were the only species of iron wire snake in the colony. Both those assertions are completely untrue. Iron wire or flowerpot snakes are found throughout the tropics and subtropics, and there are over three hundred known species. There are actually now three species known from Hong Kong - the common blind snake (*Ramphotyphlops braminus*), the white-headed blind snake (*R. albiceps*) which can be told apart by having 20, rather than 18 scale rows (*R. albiceps* has 20) and having a white snout, chin and throat and a disputed third species, *Typhlops lazelli* which was described by Wallach & Pauwels, as recently as 2004 from two specimens found in 1988 and 1992 on Hong Kong Island, and given the common name of Lazell's blind snake 香港盲蛇 although it is so rare that most people will never see one.

In fact the sad truth is that most people will never see *any* blind snake. Not because they are particularly rare; *R braminus* is distributed across large swathes of Asia and Africa and has even been introduced to parts of North and South America, and Australia, but because of the fact that they are small, vermiform and completely fossorial, which means that most people will, if they are lucky enough to encounter one, think that they are a worm. Indeed, I did the first time that I saw one. I had the small boy's fascination with worms, and had built a wormery which I kept on my bedroom windowsill much to my mother's suspicion. Even by the age of six or seven I knew that the best way to catch worms was to use a watering can to emulate the gently falling spring rain, and I was happily engaged in doing this one day when a peculiar looking worm wriggled to the surface. It distinguished itself from the rest of the earthworm population of the world by not having a clitellum or saddle, and most exciting of all, when I looked closer I could see that it was covered in scales.

I watched it for about ten minutes before returning it to the earth. Although I dearly wanted to keep it as the first really exciting exhibit in my zoo (which at that time consisted of a guinea pig and my wormery) I knew that my mother's hatred of snakes would prevail and that I would never be able to get away with keeping it. Sadly I watched it wriggle away to subterranean freedom, not realising that I would never see a live specimen again. Over the years I was to find a number of dead ones (which like most of my collection of biological ephemera was donated to my school or thrown away by my parents when we finally left Hong Kong in early 1971.

The discovery of this fascinating, perfectly formed little creature was a real eye opener to me. It was just another piece of evidence to add to my burgeoning theory that there was a whole world that grownups knew nothing about, that there was a world full of things that most people ignored or sneered at, and that it was a world that was far more fun to live in than the world of bourgeoise conformity. basically, I have been living there ever since.

My interest in earthworms was fuelled by the widespread belief amongst my peers that giant earthworms could occasionally be found after particularly heavy rain. This was fuelled by an entry in one if the animal books which my Grandfather had given me whilst I was at Partridge Piece which included a picture of one of the giant African worms *Microchaetus rappi* which can allegedly exceed 6m in length. It proclaimed that there were other species of giant earthworms found across the globe, and that there was even one that was found in Europe. So, of course, I reasoned that I had already proved that there were things living right under our noses that no adult would believe, so why not giant worms in Hong Kong? As far as I am aware no specimens have ever been caught in Hong Kong, but they have been reported from Japan and even from elsewhere in China. In September 2012 the *Daily Mail* reported:

> "An earthworm measuring half a metre in length has stunned neighbours after being found in the gutter outside a house. Li Zhiwei, a worker from the Forestry Bureau of Binchuan County, was putting some dates out to dry in his backyard when he spotted the massive invertebrate. 'It looked like a snake. I looked carefully and found it was actually a huge earthworm.' he said."

So it would not overly surprise me if one day something similar is found in Hong Kong.

As I have mentioned widely in my inky fingered scribblings, my whole (totally flawed, and crushingly disappointing) conception of the Motherland was from children's books, which I started to devour avidly at about the age of six and which I have been reading happily ever since. This very week I was very tempted to purchase a boxful of Richmal Crompton's *William* books on eBay, and it was only because I am in the middle of rearranging my bookshelves, and am presently surrounded by teetering piles of books wherever I look, that I didn't succumb to the temptation. What I didn't realise until recently, however, was how much the children's literature of the 1960s and 1970s had affected the landscape in which I found myself once my family moved to Mount Austin.

On the rear, ground floor of each of the apartment blocks were peculiar round, porthole like windows which were known to all and sundry as 'spiggy holes', presumably from a 1940 story by Enid Blyton and on the hillside opposite and above us was a ruin which served as playground for us all. It was known to everyone as 'Grey Walls', presumably from the title of the 1947 adventure story by Malcolm Saville. Although the ruins are still the, the name didn't last. A couple of decades later according to a conversation with Jemma Irvine on a Facebook Group called 'Mount Austin Mansions Alumni' it was known as 'The Japanese Wall' because it bordered onto property owned by The Japanese Consulate, although whether or not it did when I there is another of those questions to which I neither know or need an answer.

We were always told that it had been a hotel which was destroyed during WW2 like so much else of old colonial Hong Kong, but after some discussion on the monumentally excellent *Gwulo* website, but it turns out that they were the ruins a block of flats, designated as Numbers 10 and 11 The Peak. I am indebted to Gwulo member GW who went in search of the ruins for me, and finally identified them.

He wrote that the story of the partial demolition of the building that stood on this site is told in *Resist to the End* by Charles Barman (ISBN 978-962-209-976-0). Barman was a Quartermaster Sergeant in the Royal Artillery during the Battle of Hong Kong. The book is his diary. The book contains two entries for 11th December 1941. There are two entries for the same date as the original diary was subsequently rewritten in an expanded form. One of the entries (Page 19) is from the original diary, whilst the other (Pages 14-16) is the expanded version.

To summarize, on 11th December 1941, Barman was informed that the Number 2 Gun at the Mount Austin Mobile Artillery Battery was unable to fire on targets in Lai Chi Kok as the gun was positioned so close to No.10 (according to the original version) or No.11 (according to the expanded version) The Peak that the building obstructed its line of fire. The solution? Fire at the building to reduce its height. This was achieved in two volleys.

On a humorous note, Sergeant Barman fired on the building in the belief that it had already been evacuated by its tenants, the Royal Army Pay Corps. Apparently not however, as he was berated shortly afterwards by an enraged Captain Thompson who emerged from the ruins complaining that he'd been relieving himself inside when the shelling started!

It was an unofficial but generally accepted children's paradise, and - in common with most of the other children whose families were stationed at Mount Austin Mansions by a beneficent government - we claimed it as our own. I was very happy to read that many years after I had left Jemma and her friends, "played for hours and hours up there on the hillside - scrambled up through the trees or we climbed up the waterfall.".

We explored it over a period of years and found some treasures which would have made our parent's hair curl with horror. For example, decades of disuse and mini landslides converted what had once been the servant's quarters into a long, narrow, snake infested alleyway which led to what had once been a small garden with an orchard attached. It backed onto some tennis courts presumably owned by the Japanese Consulate (which seemed oddly appropriate).

The first day we discovered it, we rudely interrupted a pair of young people, whom I presumed at the time were Chinese, but were probably Japanese, presumably something to do with the Consulate staff who - if they had been lepidoptera - would have been described as being *in cop*, in a small summer house overlooking the aforementioned tennis courts. We were not as stealthy as we would have liked to have believed, and I will always remember the sight of two naked Oriental young people screaming abuse at us until we withdrew.

On subsequent visits we were much more circumspect about our explorations, but - to my memory (and it *has* been about half a century) - we never met human beings again, although we occasionally thought we heard a barking deer, and always encountered the impressive Cantonese garden lizards (*Calotes versicolor*) which were extraordinarily common in the area, coming out in the heat of the midday sun to bask in the tropical heat.

We were particularly impressed by the discovery of the orchard, which still contained apple and pear trees which occasionally bore fruit. Because they had been untended for a quarter of a century, they were rangy and would not have impressed a horticulturist, but the apples and pears were delicious, and all the more exciting for having been gathered by our own fair hands.

I was surprised to find from the photos that GW took of Grey Walls in the spring of 2015, to find that they were completely overgrown and had been absorbed into the jungle. Checking with Jemma I found that they had been the same in her day as well. But when I lived at Mount Austin Mansions in the 1960s, and when I returned to the Colony for a week in 1980, they were open to the sky, as they had been ever since the British shells had felled them as war was just about to start in the Far East. They were a platform of tiled floor, where generations of children could play their own furtive games unfettered by adult intervention.

The way that the ruins have been absorbed into the ever-spreading verdant jungle reminds me of a poem by Rudyard Kipling that appears next to the story *Letting in the Jungle* in *The Second Jungle Book* (1895)

> Veil them, cover them, wall them round —
> Blossom, and creeper, and weed —
> Let us forget the sight and the sound,
> The smell and the touch of the breed!
> Fat black ash by the altar-stone,
> Here is the white-foot rain,
> And the does bring forth in the fields unsown,
> And none shall affright them again;
> And the blind walls crumble, unknown, o'erthrown
> And none shall inhabit again!

We shall return to Kipling again, as I have returned to Kipling again and again in my long and convoluted life. But I am getting ahead of myself.

When we first moved there I was only five years old, and scrambling up and down the hillside was still a couple of years away. Every afternoon in the sunny weather my Mother and I, having left baby Richard up in the flat with the baby Amah, Ah Ling, would cross Mount Austin Road which led from the Peak Tram terminus up to the summit of Victoria Peak, and explore the grassy field that lay opposite Mount Austin Mansions. This was the field which was to become the Mount Austin children's playground; a transformation which first started in 1967 when the Urban Services

Department built a lavatory block, a not very convincing pagoda shaped shelter, and a series of concrete paths. But when we first moved there it was an almost empty oblong shaped field of unwatered grass lawn with a single, and rather shabby, workman's hut in the middle of it. The eastern side was bordered by Mount Austin Road and a simple wire fence. A steep bank with a few large palm trees fell down to the flat expanse of grass, and there was a simple earth track that paralleled the road for the entire length of the park.

Along the western perimeter of the park was the foot of the jungle covered hillside of which more later. Along the southern edge was a long drainage ditch, which led into an underground culvert and the storm drain which I described earlier in this chapter. At the other end of the ditch was a small, red brick basin which collected the water that fell down the waterfall which bisected the hillside, and which for much of the year was a stagnant trickle, but which in the rainy season became a magnificent cascade that poured down the rocks leaving great trails of flume. At this time of year, if you were lucky, you would catch a glimpse of the virulent green cascade frogs, which only ever seemed to come out and be counted at the times when the water thundered down the almost vertical rocky watercourse.

These little frogs, with their comical pointed noses and bright green sides were always one of my favourite Hong Kong amphibians, and later on, when I was in a position to keep and try to breed various of the local small wildlife, I always dearly wanted to try and keep them. But not only could I never manage to work out how to replicate their specialist habitat in captivity, but I never managed to catch more than one specimen at a time, and even at that age I knew that you needed both a mummy frog and a daddy frog in order to breed them.

There was another species of cascade frog in the streams coming off Victoria Peak, and - bizarrely, as this is nowadays considered to be the rarer of the species - in my day it was very much more common. This was the Hong Kong cascade frog, a slightly smaller brown creature which was easier to find and catch. I never managed to breed it, but I reared its tadpoles to froglet status on many occasions. My mother, seeing the suckers on the end of the toes of the little frogs, which even immediately following metamorphosis were quite chunky little fellows bigger than the top joint of my thumb as it was then (and remember that I was quite a chunky little fellow myself), was convinced that they were treefrogs, and - quite reasonably explained to me - that as we couldn't have a tree in the flat, it wouldn't be fair to try and keep them. So I always let them go.

Along the northern border of the field was another concrete culvert which had a slow trickle of water, about an inch deep, running through it. On one occasion, much to my mother's horror, we saw a small black snake making its way downstream with the current. My mother always had a horror of snakes, which had not been helped by an occasion that took place when she and my father had been in Nigeria long before I was born. She had been 'communing with nature' in the makeshift rattan privy, with its dried palmleaf roof, (as she so delicately put it) when she heard a rustling sound, looked down, and there was a green mamba sitting only about eighteen inches from her feet. Pulling up her knickers with one hand, she made a hasty retreat, trying to keep as far away from the deadly reptile as possible, which she managed, although, in doing so, she managed to knock the structure down with the snake still inside.

My parents always had dachshunds when they were in Nigeria, mainly because, although they may have been originally bred to hunt badgers, they were very good at dispatching the snake population of any district where they set up camp. Incidentally, while writing this passage, I found out that the breed is much older than I had originally thought, and despite their Germanic name, do not originate in Europe. Some writers and dachshund experts have theorised that the early roots of the dachshund go back to ancient Egypt, where engravings were made featuring short-legged hunting dogs. Recent discoveries by the American University in Cairo of mummified dachshund-like dogs from ancient Egyptian burial urns may lend credibility to this theory.

On another occasion in Nigeria, my mother had a very close encounter with a spitting cobra, and she only survived because she had been wearing sunglasses, which protected her eyes from the deadly projectiles of venom.

So, my mother's natural antipathy towards the snake tribe had some roots in experience, although she was completely neurotic about it. She was convinced that one day, the whole family would be slaughtered in our beds by a rapacious serpent, and the discovery, several years later of a baby Indian cobra under my bed, where it had been brought in my our cat, did nothing to discourage the phobia.

I went to nursery school every morning; a particularly impressive establishment run by the wife of the legendary Billy Tingle, of which more later. But apart from the fact that I know that I spent a year or so at Mrs Tingle's Nursery School, I cannot remember anything about it. But in the afternoons Mummy and I would explore, if it were not too hot, and if it was, she would take her deck chair and sit in the cool shade of the edge of the rhododendron forest which covered the steep hillside whilst I methodically investigated the various creatures that could be seen within only a few feet of her repose.

For some reason that I cannot remember, her favourite spot to sit was at the far northwest of the field, surprisingly near to where we had seen the small black snake. Perhaps she had believed me when I told her that G.A.K Herklots had assured me that all the poisonous snakes in the colony were more or less striped, and that this particular creature was a uniform black in colour.

There was a dried-up watercourse, which I believe had once been another waterfall, until the stream which fed it had been diverted to keep it away from human habitation. This was part of the European terror of mosquitoes. Even as recently as the mid-1960s I remember being incandescent with rage because some meddling busybody from the USD had poured oil into one of my favourite ditches to kill all the mosquito larvae, killing a whole plethora of other little creatures instead. I remember haranguing the poor workman about it, which made no difference as he couldn't speak English and my faltering Cantonese was sufficient to talk nonsense with my Amah, but completely inadequate for me to try and explain to a poor beleaguered workman who was, after all, only trying to do his job, that the mosquito larvae in that particular ditch were not *Anopheles*, and so were not carriers of malaria.

On one particularly magickal afternoon, which remains clear in my memory even now, a huge swarm of iridescent rainbow coloured flying beetles must have metamorphosed together, because everywhere you looked, there they were. I tried to catch them in my hand, but soon gave up as mostly they were far too fast for me, and on the odd occasion that I managed to catch one it would be so badly injured by the process that my innate humanity took over, and I realised that I would far rather see them flying free. No, that's not true. I would have much rather seen them in an impressive glass vivarium like the ones I had seen in the insect house at London Zoo with Grandad the previous year, but that was not to be. It turned out that these beetles were a species of *Lytta* wrongly called *Cantharides* but known to impotence sufferers across the world as the uncomfortable and - apparently - totally useless aphrodisiac, 'Spanish Fly'.

On other days I would climb the dry watercourse, which consisted of black or dark grey stones completely different to the light grey stones which comprised the waterfall at the other end of the playground, but my Mother would always call me back down before I got too high up, and being a generally obedient child at that age, or at least one who knew which side his bread was buttered, and who didn't want his afternoon explorations with his Mother curtailed, I always came down, so I never did find out what was at the top. A few years ago my friend and colleague, the well-known Australian cryptozoologist and author Tony Healey was passing through Hong Kong, and visited the playground for me taking hundreds of photographs. One of them showed the watercourse, still as inviting and mysterious as ever, and half a century after I first encountered it, I found myself wondering what was at the top.

I think it probably leads what were in my day, tennis courts, attached to one of the big houses on Mount Austin Road, which I as I recounted above, I learned so many years later were owned by the Japanese Consulate.

At the bottom of the watercourse there was (and for all I know, still is) a mound of congealed asphalt left over, presumably, from the manufacture of the culvert. I loved that heap of builder's detritus, and it became all sorts of props in my various activities, whether it was Crusader Castle, Robin Hood's Oak, or Red Indian encampment.

The culvert was not only the northern boundary of the playground field, it also marked the end of civilisation and the beginning of the somewhat disturbing unknown. It was full of fleshy shrubs with giant leaves. We called them 'Elephant's Ears' and I discovered whilst writing this chapter that they are actually something called the elephant's ear taro, (*Colocasia esculenta*) is not only edible, but cultivated in many places across the tropics as a cash crop. This surprised me, because as children we all knew not to pick them because the juice from the stems would bring you out in a painful rash. I also found out this evening that the toxicity of the plant is because of large amounts of Calcium Oxalate, which can also cause kidney stones.

Golly.

For years, even when we were too old to need the constant supervision of doting and watchful mothers, my friends and I used to play on the dried-up water course on the north side of the playground.

I remember on one occasion making a pond in one of the huge rents or crevices between the rocks. This was not as stupid an idea as it sounded. On the waterfall on the other end of the playground, there were many such ponds which had occurred perfectly naturally. And each of them had – as I shall describe later on in this narrative – an individual and highly idiosyncratic biotope within it. So, when one of my friends brought out his pet terrapin – one of the red eared sliders, originally from North America, which have now spread as an invasive species across much of the world – we decided to make a pond for him to play in.

We worked quite hard at this, not only bringing buckets full of water from the culvert on the south end (when I say 'buckets full' I want you to think of a brightly coloured, child's beach toy, rather than anything more substantial). One of my friends and I then climbed up the hillside to the top of the waterfall, and found waterweed and a few small water snails, which we gently removed from their original home and took down the hill, across the width of the playground, and up to our new pond. We put them in, and then introduced Terry the terrapin, who swam around in an unenthusiastic manner.

Then we went in for lunch, bolting our food so we could rush out to see what Terry was doing in his new home.

And guess what?

Terry was nowhere to be seen. For such unassuming creatures, baby red eared sliders are notorious escape artists. We all felt extremely guilty, but fifty plus years later, when *Trachemys scripta elegans* has become an invasive species in Hong Kong, causing no end of environmental degradation, I harbour a fond thought that one of these dangerously invasive reptiles was originally called Terry, and that only now he and his compadres are getting their revenge upon the human race.

Although the turtle species with which I was most familiar with as a child was

Trachemys scripta elegans, there are a number of species which are, or at least were, native. I truly longed to see one or more of them in the wild, but never did.

I have written elsewhere about how *The Hong Kong Countryside* by Geoffrey Herklots was my bible for many years. But many passages in it were either confusing or enigmatic. For example, he wrote that, "The reptiles recorded from or likely to occur in the Colony are two marine turtles, one large headed tortoise, six terrapins, three mud turtles, about fifteen lizards.."

I know that this even confused me as a boy, although I would quote it *ad nauseam* to any adult that would listen. I had a classmate called Jonathan Rigg, who lived in that relative rarity on Hong Kong island - a house that stood alone in its own grounds - and I remember one day when visiting him, telling his mother proudly that we were going to go in search of animals on this list of Herklots's. She smiled indulgently at us, and sent us on our way, but I don't think we ever caught anything more exciting than snails.

As a minor addendum to this story, fifteen years or so later, I was driving from Barnstaple to Exeter when I picked up some hitchhikers. I got chatting to them, and it turned out that one of them was actually at university with Jonathan. I sent him my good wishes, but never heard anything from him again.

Such is life.

But if you're reading this, Jon, please get in touch. It would be lovely to hear from you.

But, once again, I have gotten diverted.

I have spent many years trying to work out what Herklots meant by his uncharacteristically vague list. After all, it bears very little relation to the Testudines currently known or suspected to be living in the Hong Kong Special Administrative Region.

For example, Herklots refers to a "big-headed tortoise".

I assume that Herklots, being an English gentleman of the old school, would be using the word "tortoise" to refer to such chelonia that live mostly on dry land. There are only three species of land tortoise living in the whole of China, and although two of them are allegedly found in parts of South China, I have not been able to find a single record of either species from Hong Kong.

Richard Muirhead, however, found this reference in the *Journal of the Royal Geographical Society of London* vol. 14 (1844) p.115: "The only animals found on the island are a few small deer, a sort of armadillo and a land-tortoise".

This is actually quite interesting, because when it refers to "a few small deer" that does imply there are more than one species of deer living on the island. As we shall see, for years, this was not considered to be the case. The only known species of Hong Kong deer was the Chinese muntjac (*Muntiacus reevesi*). But then, around about the turn of the current century, the creatures were re-classified as being Indian muntjac (*M. muntajk*), a species more commonly believed to exist – as the name implies – in India and Indochina. But this reference which Richard (and you will be hearing a lot more from him later) discovered during one of his trawls through the archives, implies that it was always known that there were two species of "small deer" living on the island.

The "armadillo" is almost certainly the Chinese pangolin (*Manis pentadactyla*), which is not an armadillo by any stretch of the imagination, but is covered in scales and still lives on Hong Kong island today. But the "land-tortoise"? Apart from Herklots's enigmatic reference, this is the only other record we have ever found of a land tortoise in or around Hong Kong.

And why call it "large-headed"? There is a remarkable little creature called the big-headed terrapin (*Platysternon megacephalum*), which is, you will not be surprised to find out, a terrapin with a big head. But this creature is almost completely aquatic, living in the larger hills and mountain streams, particularly in cascade pools. It requires shaded and fast-running water, and is mostly carnivorous, although it will eat some plant matter. But to an Englishman like Herklots, for whom a "tortoise" was purely a terrestrial vertebrate, I cannot imagine that he would have referred to megacephalum by this description.

And what are "mud turtles"? And why are three of them allegedly living in Hong Kong? I have always assumed that he used this term to refer to soft-shelled turtles; delightful creatures which are found across the warmer parts of the world and which have faces reminiscent of The Clangers; a popular children's TV show of the 1970s, and which, according to Olivia, has been revived in recent year.

The term "mud turtles" can refer to about twenty small New World species in the genus *Kinosternon* (ironically, which used to contain *megacephalum* at one time), and a totally unrelated genus of African side-necked turtles containing seventeen known species. But I have never heard of anyone using this term to describe soft-shells.

But, assuming that this was what Herklots was referring to, it is actually a very good description. But three species? There is only one that is known to live in Hong Kong, and like so many other Hong Kong Testudines, the details of its existence in the former British colony are more than slightly confusing.

In a roundup of Hong Kong reptiles and amphibians, written by J. D. Romer, who took over from Herklots as being the doyen of Hong Kong natural history, and whom I met once or twice as a child, there were only a very few records of the Chinese soft-shell (*Pelodiscus sinensis*) in Hong Kong, and he suggested that these were purely lucky reptiles that had escaped the ignominy of a cooking pot. But more recent books on the subject have claimed that this charming reptile, that I have kept in my own collection on a number of occasions over the years, is actually quite common, and can be seen basking on the shores of many of Hong Kong reservoirs, and according to Martin Booth was even in Pokfulam Reservoir ten years or so before the times about which I write.

But this is the only species of soft-shell turtle that is known to occur there. However, there is one record of another species; the wattle-necked soft-shelled turtle, which was found in Kowloon reservoir in 1980. The School of Biological Sciences at The University of Hong Kong suggest that this turtle had most probably been deliberately released form captivity, as the species is commonly imported into Hong Kong from other parts of south-east Asia for food.

And what the third species of soft-shell turtle was, if – indeed – this is what Herklots was referring to when he talked about "mud turtles", I have no idea. If anybody reading this can help us out, I would be immensely grateful. It has been a mystery that has been bugging me for well over half a century.

The exact nature of what Herklots had in mind when he said there were six species of terrapin in Hong Kong is also difficult to ascertain. The Reptiles of Hong Kong website, maintained by the School of Biological Sciences at the University of Hong Kong, mentions eight species known from the region, but two of them – the Malayan box turtle (*Cuora amboinensis*) and the Chinese box terrapin (*Mauremys mutica*) - are Asian species which have been released either by accident or by local Buddhists, who purchased them at food markets and released them as a holy act of contrition, and the eighth is the ubiquitous red-eared slider. Of the other four, one – Beale's terrapin (*Sacalia bealei*) – was not discovered in Hong Kong until 1977, fifty years after Herklot was writing. It is an extremely rare species, and even at the time of writing, in 2020, only six specimens have ever been found. And the Chinese striped terrapin (*Ocadia sinensis*), is only known from one specimen, as reported by Herklots himself, when one was dug up in a dried up pond in Stanley Village during World War II. A large terrapin resembling *O. sinensis* was seen in Lamtsuen river in 1980, but the identity could not be confirmed. The website continues, saying:

> "At present, most suitable habitats in Hong Kong are badly polluted or with too little aquatic vegetation to sustain viable population of this terrapin.
>
> Sometimes sold in local markets. Occasionally seen in fishponds or urban parks."

So, like the mud turtles and the elusive 'big-headed tortoise', the exact nature of this part of Herklots's list remains as elusive to me as it did when I first read it all those years ago.

There were various itinerant and completely unlicensed tinkers who occasionally made their way up Mount Austin Road to sell fruit, nuts and brightly coloured sweets.

My mother, always more protective than most of her peers, completely forbade me to ever have anything to do with these old men, presumably fearing that their wares would be riddled with cholera and other diseases. There was also a salacious rumour (and I have no idea how true it was) that one of these old men was a child molester, and as most of the ex-pat mothers seemed convinced that every catamite in the whole of South China was itching to get their hands upon British colonial children; this was another reason why we (me in particular) were all told to give these itinerant tinkers a wide berth.

Needless to say, none of us paid any attention to these rules; the sweets they sold tasted so much better than their more legitimate counterparts. Forbidden fruit, blah blah blah.

On one occasion, one of these aforementioned tinkers 'set up shop' on the highly trimmed grass sward in front of one of the blocks of Mount Austin Mansions. And on this occasion, he had a wonderfully exciting companion. It was a full-size Reeves' Terrapin, which is still the commonest native species of chelonian in the region. My friends and I admired this beautiful reptile and even attempted to buy it, realising that it was almost certainly destined to be eaten. Either our bargaining powers were not up to scratch that day, or – more likely – we just didn't have enough money, and the remarkably bad-tempered old man shooed us away. From a discreet distance, my friends and I kept him under surveillance. Morally, we were certain, that stealing the unfortunate terrapin in order to save its life would be a completely admirable course of action.

All of his potential customers having buggered off, the old man stood up and, turning away from us, urinated copiously all over the white stucco wall of the apartment block that housed some of his Colonial masters, and – as he did so – the terrapin made a dash for freedom and climbed into the bottom of a drainpipe, never to be seen again. Ever since, I have hoped that - the storm drain systems of that part of Victoria Peak, at that time at least, being more primitive than one would have liked to hope - the unfortunate reptile had a streak of luck that afternoon and finally managed to successfully reach freedom.

More out of form than any belief that we would find it, every time I passed that particular drainpipe over the next three or four years, I would look to see if the terrapin was there.

It wasn't.

A year or so later I discovered the Narnia books of C.S.Lewis. My favourite was, and is, *Prince Caspian* in which the eponymous prince, together with four travellers from our own spacetime continuum, and a bevy of talking beasts and mythological creatures wage a guerrilla war against the usurping Telmarenes - humans descended from a bunch of marooned pirates, whose backstory seemed very similar to that of the Pitcairn mutineers. One of the things that struck me about the Telmarenes in the story was that they all seemed deathly afraid of the forest, and refused to enter it under whatever pretext. This was something to which I could relate massively, because my mother and the other European women, and - indeed - the amahs and other servants who one saw occasionally on the playground field, would never venture into the forest. Even the older children wouldn't. It was if something happened to the British expat with the onset of puberty, and they were no longer drawn to the dark green caves with leaflitter for the floors and leafy rhododendron branches for the walls. We knew every inch of those hillsides, and often made little huts deep in the undergrowth, in which we would carry out our furtive little games, secure in the knowledge that they might be only forty or fifty feet away, but that those in authority over us would never venture into the jungle to see what we we doing. So whilst our mothers sat on the flat grassland below us, chattering, reading or crocheting we would play innocently, and sometimes less innocently, in the undergrowth secure in the knowledge that we would never be caught.

And we never were.

As much fun as could be wrested out of the playground field, I much preferred the days when Mummy would put baby Richard in his pushchair, pack a picnic tea, and the three of us would go off exploring. There were three main places that we would go, but my favourite was the circular walk around The Peak along Harlech and Lugard Roads. Just before he died, my father published a book which showed the links between the two British colonial possessions in which he had served, and that link was largely down to Lord Frederick Lugard. A 19th Century statesman, soldier, and diplomat, he was Governor of Hong Kong from 1907 to 1912, and Governor of Nigeria a few years later, and he was a tireless worker for The League of Nations, and the international fight against slavery. He was a remarkable man, and as I worked on my father's book during the long and slow summer of 2005, I came to admire him more and more.

But forty years before that 'Lugard' was just the name of one of my favourite walks.

From my earliest days, my mother encouraged me in reading, writing, and the pursuit of natural history, and she helped me keep my first nature diary, which I suppose was the progenitor, or at least the distant ancestor, of the blog that now, as a late middle-aged cripple living in North Devon, I still write every day of the year.

She made me a butterfly net out of a broom handle, a wire coat hanger and some patterned muslin that had once been part of one or other of what, until the day she died, she would always refer to as her unmentionables. Crude, and slightly embarrassing it might have been, but it did the job, and armed with it, a cowboy hat and a carrier bag containing various receptacles, mostly jam jars, we would embark on our foray.

The little plateau which contains the upper terminus of the Peak Tram, and in my day also contained a couple of small shops, a flower stall, the Garden Cafe, some ruins, and a white, almost cubical building with two peculiar, copper green domes on top of it, is one of the most iconic sites on Hong Kong Island. Even after many years of Chinese rule (at the time of writing) it is still called Victoria Gap, and whilst it is now site of the Peak Tower, and the Peak Galleria, with only the renamed Peak Cafe being even slightly recognisable from the place of my youth, it is still the junction of a number of important roads. Harlech Road was built some time before 1906. It meets several roads, namely Mount Austin Road, Lugard Road, Peak Road, Old Peak Road, Findlay Road and Hatton Road. We shall return to most of these roads at different places in this present book, but for now a slightly plump middle aged woman pushing an infant in a pushchair, and accompanied by a small boy wearing a cowboy hat and clutching his aforementioned collection of quasi-scientific impedimenta is walking past the Garden Cafe, and taking the left hand fork in the road, which almost immediately takes them into a tunnel of trees which eventually leads out into a straight path which, on the right hand side affords the earnest traveller a glorious view of the southern half of Hong Kong Island, and Lamma and Cheung Chau islands, and a myriad of smaller ones. On the right-hand side there is a sheer cliff which is peppered with exotic looking lichens and small alpine plants.

Presently one reaches a beautiful little waterfall, and as a child I always wanted to climb up it, but my mother told me - sternly - that the rocks were too slippery and sharp, and that I would be sure to tumble to my certain death. She was probably, right, and I never did climb up, although I eventually found out what was at the top of it. But that is another story and you will have to wait a few more chapters for it.

Then - and it always crept up on me, and we were there before I realised it - the path widened significantly, and we reached a small rest area. it was on the left-hand side of the path, and consisted of a couple of wooden park benches and a litter bin, but for some reason my mother, Richard and I had made it our own. Unlike the far bigger rest area about a quarter of a mile further on, there was never anyone there (although I discovered, to my amusement, many years later that a mate of mine's ex-wife had mislaid her virginity on the very same bench about twelve years later).

We would sit there for about half an hour. Richard would gurgle happily in his pushchair, my mother would read the latest novel by Georgette Heyer, and I would chase after butterflies, and occasionally catch one. On the odd occasions that I did, I would bring it back to show Mummy, and ensconce the poor creature in a jam jar so that my mother could draw it, before I let it go. The butterflies were mostly Pierids (the yellows and whites) but over that summer my mother drew four or five different ones, and on one glorious occasion I even caught a swallowtail *Papilio memnon agenor,* and bore him back in triumph to my mother to draw, but he escaped as I was ineptly trying to transfer him to his temporary glass prison.

It was on these walks that I took the first faltering steps towards an understanding of phylogeny. At first I just delighted in the myriad colours and shapes which fluttered around the flowers in the long grass, but soon I began to recognise that some of these butterflies were more closely related than others. On one memorable day I caught one of the various white butterflies are still referred to as 'cabbage white' and I bore it in triumph to my mother to draw. After she had diligently done so, and the tiny creature had been released to get on with its lepidopterous lifestyle, I caught one of the little yellow butterflies which I have never actually been able to identify for certain, but I think it was a grass yellow (*Eurema hecabe*). I asked my mother if she could put the drawing of what I insisted on calling a 'cabbage yellow' on the same pages of a picture of the cabbage white, because they were related.

"How do you know that dear?" She replied. And the seven-year-old me who was nowhere near as articulate as I like to think that I am an adult, ummed and errred and said something about them being roughly the same size. To which she said that a goat and a dog were roughly the same size, and the conversation was over.

What I should've said, and what I've been kicking myself for the last 50 something years for not having said, was that they had the same shaped wings, very similar black markings, and they flew in a remarkably similar manner. But not for the first, and certainly not for the last time in my life my uncharacteristic inarticulateness when dealing with my elders and betters, let me down.

The only other wildlife that we were nearly always guaranteed to see on this walk were earnest black rhinoceros beetles which would always be found in the middle of the path where unpleasant small boys would stamp on them. Anxious for them to avoid such a horrid fate I would always pick them up and gingerly transfer them to one of the bushes on the side of the path.

After a while we would carry on our walk, and soon we would be at the much larger recreation area that I mentioned before. As all small boys were in my day, I was pretty badly obsessed with guns, and the fact that here one could see, what had been (until recently) a shooting range, fascinated the heck out of me.

The 1906 Public Works Department report reads:

> "At the request of the Volunteer Reserve Association (Hong Kong Volunteer Corps), a new rifle range was constructed at the Peak. The butts are situated on the eastern slope of High West and the firing points below the Harlech Road, at ranges 200, 300 400 and 500 yards. The targets which were obtained from England, are of Jeffries' Patent 'Wimbledon' type and a small building has been constructed for them when not in use. The range was finally handed over to the Association in October."

I have one claim to fame at this point, although it is not a very exciting one. Every memoir I have ever read of children who grew up in Hong Kong, whether in book form or on a website, which mention this quondam firing range, describes how as children the authors used to search for bullets and cartridge cases, and amassed a fine collection. A few years later as a schoolboy, some of my friends said exactly the same thing, and because they showed me the evidence, I had no choice but to believe them. However, from the age of about six until we left the colony five years later, I intermittently searched diligently for such things whenever we were at The Butts, but I never found a thing. Eventually, disappointed by such an unfriendly providence, I gave up.

This part of the walk, which is actually the junction between Harlech and Lugard roads, is also the foot of another local mountain; High West. It is actually only 494m high, but is still just about a mountain, although whenever I called it such as a child, my Father would get angry with me, and accuse me of being silly. He never would believe me that according to the American definition, at least, a mountain is a hill over 1,000 feet, and High West was about 400ft higher than that. As quite often happened during my childhood the fifth commandment would be quoted at me, and if my father was in a particularly censorious mood I would be spanked. Like with most things I soon learned to keep my quest for knowledge to myself.

It was many years later that I climbed High West for the first (and only) time, but the place always sticks in my memory for its colony of Chinese francolins. This small partridge-like bird, is almost impossible to see on The Peak, but almost impossible not to hear. Its call has been homophoned into the phrase "Come to the Peak Ha Ha", or if you are one of the people who live nearer the sea level "Come to the Peak No Fear". This story goes back to the days when only the social elite, and the higher echelons of Government were allowed to live on the Peak, and the further up the mountain you lived, the more important you were. the Governor himself lived at Mountain Lodge right at the summit, but more of that in a minute.

Somewhere in my completely out of control files, I have a poem on the subject that was written sometime round about the time of WW1, but, unless a benevolent providence brings it to the surface it is unlikely to end up in this book.

You will remember that my mother had bought Geoffrey Herklots' *Field Guide to Hong Kong Birds* during our delightful sojourn at the Repulse Bay Hotel, but it was during the second half of our regular walks around the mountain, that the little book really came into its own. because this was the part of the journey in which the quest for butterflies was forgotten, the net was packed away and stowed in the back of Richard's pushchair, and Mummy and I became birdwatchers. The first bird that I remember identifying was the black tailed kite, a subspecies of the black kite.

The black kite (*Milvus migrans*) is a medium-sized bird of prey in the family Accipitridae, which also includes many other diurnal raptors. It is thought to be the world's most abundant species of Accipitridae, although some populations have experienced dramatic declines or fluctuations. Current global population estimates run up to 6 million individuals. Unlike others of the group, black kites are opportunistic hunters and are more likely to scavenge. They spend a lot of time soaring and gliding in thermals in search of food. Their angled wing and distinctive forked tail make them easy to identify. This kite is widely distributed through the temperate and tropical parts of Eurasia and parts of Australasia and Oceania, with the temperate region populations tending to be migratory. Several subspecies are recognized and formerly had their own English names. The European populations are small, but the South Asian population is very large.

It is still the bird that I think of first whenever the name of Hong Kong is mentioned. They were, and I hope still are, always to be seen soaring, sometimes in ones and twos, and sometimes in quite remarkably large numbers, on the thermals high above the island and the harbour. this is the bird that generations of British soldiers stationed in India and the Middle East referred to as 'shite hawks' from their habit of frequenting rubbish dumps, open sewers and latrines. It is probable, I would hazard a guess, that they were more likely to feed upon the rats and other vermin, particularly the snakes that fed on the rats, that everyone knows frequent such areas, rather than, as is often believed, eating human excrement itself. They are noble looking birds, and when I was courting my late wife, she was living in Lincolnshire, and every time we travelled to and from her home to mine we would pass through one of the areas in which the red kite (a close relative) were being reintroduced to the UK. Regularly, therefore, we would see the signature forked tail and sweeping wings silhouetted against the sky, and my heart would skip for joy at a brief glimpse of such an old friend.

There were two or three species of bulbul that we would always see on our walk.

The word bulbul derives from the Persian for nightingale, but in English, bulbul refers to a family of about 130 small to medium sized songbirds that are distributed widely across tropical and subtropical Asia and Africa, of which six are found in Hong Kong. My favourite has always been the red whiskered bulbul *Pycnonotus jocosus* - a small bird a bit bigger than a European robin, but with a longer tail and a magnificent triangular crest of feathers. They are gregarious, and cheerful little birds, who rush about the smaller branches of the great trees, alternately foraging and squabbling with each other. They have a distinctive song, make good cage birds and are apparently reasonably easy to breed in captivity, although I only ever kept one pair for a very short time just before my family left Hong Kong, and so I can't actually confirm this from personal experience. The name comes from brilliant red patches on their cheeks, but I have always been impressed by the small black line next to the beak which looks for all the world like the pencilled on moustache sported by John Waters, the auteur and film director responsible for a whole series of appallingly bad taste transgressive cult movies.

As the journey continued, so the microclimate changed, and there was one particular stretch of Lugard Road, about 70% of the way around the mountain which was always particularly humid. here my persona changed again, and Mummy and I would always play an ongoing game in which we were explorers hunting big animals for zoos. My literary diet of Gerald Durrell was, after my sixth birthday seasoned by

Mummy telling me a series of (slightly sanitised) tales from the pen of H Rider Haggard, and so it was as a six-year-old Allan Quartermain, that I gingerly approached three enormous water pipes that crossed over above Lugard Road like a surreal suspension bridge. Why did I approach them so gingerly? It was because these were the elephant traps that we had laid on the previous occasion that we had circuited the mountain, and one always had to be particularly careful when negotiating a trap full of elephants.

There was something vaguely sinister about this stretch of the road, because it was here that the huge, black and yellow *Nephila* spiders would weave their enormous orb webs, several feet across. The silk produced by these webs is so strong that it is not only insects that fall victim to them. On more than one occasion I found dead bats, presumably Japanese pipistrelles, dead, and wrapped in a shroud of spider silk. And once I found a newly fledged red whiskered bulbul, which was still alive, and so carefully using a pointed twig to stave off the spider, my mother and I rescued it and released it to fly away in search of new adventures. It is actually a matter of some contention amongst zoologists whether these spiders are actually capable of eating large warm-blooded prey, but I suspect that they are.

The huge *Nephila pilipes* is one of the most impressive looking creatures that I have ever seen, purely because it looks so unnatural and artificial. Commonly known as the northern golden orb-waver or the giant orb weaver it is found over a huge swathe of southern Asia including Japan, China, Vietnam, Cambodia, Taiwan, Malaysia, Singapore, Myanmar, Indonesia, Thailand, Laos, Philippines, Sri Lanka, India, and Papua New Guinea. It is commonly found in primary and secondary forests and gardens. Females are large and grow to a body size of 30–50 mm (overall size up to 20 cm), with males growing to 5–6 mm. But the thing that has always got to me is that they look like toy robots with machine applied enamel paint. They are totally implacable, ruthless killing machines, and they cannot but deserve one's respect, if only for being just so totally far out.

Half a century later I interviewed the artist Roger Dean who is responsible for some of the most iconic album cover paintings of the progressive era, and I was so tempted to suggest he incorporate *Nephila* and the centipede *Scolopendra* into a future masterpiece. I don't know why I didn't.

Our walk would always end with a quick visit to the Dairy Farm ice cream kiosk, where - if everything had gone according to plan, and I had refrained from being more than averagely irritating - I would be rewarded with a small tub of my favourite mango flavoured ice cream, before we wearily trudged back up the hill to Mount Austin Mansions.

About half-way up Mount Austin Road, there was a footpath that went off to the right, and up to the southern end of the Mount Austin Mansions campus, for want of a better word. I always wanted to take this path, I suspect to my Mother's chagrin, because it was considerably steeper than the main road, and she was the one who had to propel my brother's pushchair up the slope. But at the top there was a large clump of *Mimosa pudica* a South American plant with the peculiar property of closing or folding its leaves if you touched them. How it had ever got there I have no idea, because there were no other cultivated plants here except for a dull flat lawn, but these little leaves always fascinated me, and so I would run ahead to touch as many leaves as I could before my long suffering mama caught up with me. We would usually rest there for about five minutes, and on one occasion, I was grubbing about in the undergrowth by the Mimosa looking for something when I found a small gold ring, which I presented proudly to Mummy as buried treasure. Enquiries with the Police lost property department proved fruitless, and it stayed in my mother's jewellery box for the rest of her life.

The other place that I would go with my mother was in the opposite direction. Instead of walking down the hill to Victoria Gap, we would walk up the hill to Victoria Peak Gardens, right up at the summit of the mountain. The gardens were built around the ruins of Mountain Lodge, which was the summer residence of the governor until it was demolished after WW2. The site covers three different levels, and although, from what I understand it has since been developed, landscaped, and sanitised in a way that I am sure would make me terribly unhappy. The highest level was based around the ruins of the lodge itself, the middle was a gentle slope of scrubby woodland which I used to explore looking for the huge nests of the communal paper wasps, and where the royal blue Chinese bellflowers, peeked their heads above the long grass, and if we were lucky we would see a magnificent blue magpie. However, from what I can gather, it has been replaced by a gaudy and tasteless approximation of a traditional Chinese garden. Like so much of the Hong Kong that I knew as a child it has been modernised out of all recognition.

But when I knew it, it was the lowest of the three levels that was my favourite, because there was a little silver stream that rose from a spring surrounded by an ornate walled enclosure. The stream flowed through the lower level and down into the hillside below where it became the waterfall that I described cascading above the Mount Austin playground field, and then eventually to the waterfall that flows down to, and below Harlech road, and eventually down to Pokfulam reservoir on the south side of the island. About a quarter of the way along the stream was a small pool, like a miniscule salmon pool in a Scottish river. When we first went there, this little pool was the home of a couple of dozen little silver fishes, which I strongly suspect were the same ones that Martin Booth wrote about in *Gweilo* in which he describes his childhood about a decade before mine. In the book he wondered how fish got up to the top of a mountain.

Well, that is one small zoological mystery upon which I *am* able to shed some light. Two species of tiny livebearing fish *Gambusia affinis* and *Gambusia holbrooki* are originally from the southern states of the USA, but their common name of mosquitofish gives a pretty hefty hint as to why the two species have been introduced across large swathes of the tropics. Even today several species of livebearer - a family of fish naturally found completely in the New World - are found naturalised in Hong Kong. These include *G. affinis* and the guppy, *Poecilia reticulata* which is best known as an aquarium pet. However, they have also been introduced across the globe to control mosquitoes, coming to Hong Kong in the years immediately following the first world war. Although it has never been confirmed, I am fairly certain that *G. holbrooki* also exists in the region. One day I intend to go back and find out.

By the beginning of 1966 the little livebearers had gone, but I still visited the pool most springtimes to catch tadpoles. They were the little black tadpoles of the short legged toad *Megophrys* which for some reason appeared to be the commonest species at the top of The Peak. It was Gospel amongst the children of my peer group that the way that you successfully reared tadpoles was by feeding them dried scrambled egg when they first hatched, and scraps of bacon suspended on cotton as they grew older. Surprisingly, for quite a few years I reared successive generations of froglets on this unlikely diet.

June to October is typhoon season in Hong Kong. For those of you not in the know:

> "A typhoon is a mature tropical cyclone that develops in the western part of the North Pacific Ocean between 180 and 100E. This region is referred to as the Northwestern Pacific Basin, and is the most active tropical cyclone basin on Earth, accounting for almost one-third of the world's annual tropical cyclones. For organisational purposes, the northern Pacific Ocean is divided into three regions: the eastern (North America to 140W), central (140 to 180W), and western (180 to 100E). The Regional Specialized Meteorological Center (RSMC) for tropical cyclone forecasts is in Japan, with other tropical cyclone warning centers for the northwest Pacific in Honolulu (the Joint Typhoon Warning Center), the Philippines and Hong Kong. While the RSMC names each system, the main name list itself is coordinated among 18 countries that have territories threatened by typhoons each year. The Philippines use their own naming list for systems approaching the country."

A few years later typhoons were always a source of joy to the younger generation, because they meant several days off school which, for me at least, was a great amenity. But the first typhoon that I remember took place sometime in the autumn of 1964, when we were still very new at Mount Austin Mansions. It had been raining and blowing for days, with a reasonable amount of damage to trees up on The Peak. The whole family was getting stir crazy, and on the first day that my father was back at the Colonial Secretariat, my long suffering mother decided to take my grizzly little brother, and me for a brisk walk up to Victoria Peak Gardens in order, as she put it, to "blow the cobwebs away".

I remember the walk as if it were yesterday. There were fallen branches everywhere, and the banana trees were bent double, their boughs pulverised into a nasty pithy mess. There had been mini landslides everywhere, and parts of what had been a glorious swathe of subtropical woodland more resembled bits of the battlefield of the Somme. just before we reached the old Mountain Lodge gate house, which was and is the only part of that particular piece of Imperial grandeur that is left standing. We walked along the road which led along the edge of the ridge which overlooks the lowest of the three levels and right plonked in the middle of the green sward was an enormous tree uprooted by the storm.

As you may have gathered by now, I had a very overactive imagination as a child, and I immediately saw the felled tree as a pirate ship that I wanted to be the captain of, and so I asked permission and started to clamber down the bank towards the bottom, when - suddenly - I heard my mother scream. I stopped with a jolt, and looked down towards the tree trunk, which was beginning to slither away. It was a Burmese python, one of the largest snake species in the world, and certainly capable of eating a six-year-old boy. I clambered back up the bank, and my mother and I stood, holding hands, and watching in awe as the great reptile, which must have been washed out of its normal hiding place, slithered into the nearest bit of forest and out of our lives forever.

It was the only time I ever saw a wild python, in Hong Kong or anywhere else for that matter, but the memory has remained with me ever since. Up until she died in 2002, my mother would periodically remind me of our shared adventure, and we would reassure each other that we had not imagined it.

CHAPTER FOUR

Peak School

There is no way that you can know the taste of water unless you drink it or unless it has rained on you or unless you jump in the river.

Charles~Manson

I never set out to write a history book here; there are many books on the history of Hong Kong, mostly written by far more accomplished authors than I. This book is basically my own personal history, but bits of the history of the wider world keep on jostling at the door to be allowed in, and being a kind-hearted sort of chap, I am often prepared to acquiesce. In the early 20th Century the prep school on The Peak was housed in the red brick building that us now the Peak fire station. In 1954 the headmistress, Miss Bicheno, entreated the leading architect if the colony to help her get new and improved premises. These were found on the site of what had once been The Peak Club, an establishment which in 1913, using the sort of prose which would, for decades, give fuel to the fire of anti-imperialists, John Stuart Thompson described as:

"The Peak Club I know of no place where music, lanterns, romantic mountain scenery, seascapes far below and delightful society in an alien setting combine more pleasantly than at the Peak Club, Hongkong. Above the passing clouds which now and then whirl around as in Rubens' pictures, over the purple Pacific Ocean which foams around hilly islands, over the high hills as you ascend from the royal colony of Victoria, on a terrace, they have graded a velvet lawn. Here the military and naval bands are brought for a promenade concert in the soft night of the fragrant Orient, beneath Bowring's "wide Cathayan tree". The band of the Royal Welsh Fusiliers, from Mt. Austin barracks, plays the stirring Welsh national march, The Men of Harlech. The men sing the chorus : "See ! the bonfire light before ye. How its fiery tongues do call ye. Come as one to death or glory. Heroes of the fistfight. "Lest by fire they kill and plunder, Harlech ! Harlech ! make them wonder At thy power that none can sunder; Freedom thou wilt live." Flowering plants in large coloured Chinese kongs are set out everywhere. The stars and moon shine. The pictured lanterns gently swing, and the horn lanterns of Ningpo are opal soft. The light flashes from swords, uniforms and jewels. The blue-gowned Oriental servants noiselessly pass refreshments. Not a Chinese house is in view, though half a million Chinese live hidden in the foothills."

In 1954 a modern building was constructed on the ruins of the club, which had been dealt a fatal blow by enemy action during the war, and - according to Google Earth at least - it appears to be one of the only parts of my childhood apart from the house in which I live now, which has remained relatively intact, although according to the Peak School website, the great playing field is now covered in tarmac.

When I first went to Peak School, the younger classes still attended the original building at Gough Hill Path, which was known to one and all as "Little Peak School" but after a year or so my classmates and I went *en masse* to the main school. And on the whole I hated it.

I was totally unprepared for school when I first started going in the spring of 1965. It seemed totally unfair that I had to go to an ugly red brick building every day, that I had to sit politely in a classroom with twenty other children learning stuff that I either already knew, or just completely didn't understand. I had been reading for some years, and was already reading the books of Gerald Durrell and C S Lewis, so why did I have to sit learning about the dull lives of those insufferable little idiots Janet and John and their stupid dog?

I could already write, although my spelling left a bit to be desired on occasion. I was already writing stories massively derivative of the Narnia books, and so didn't understand why my smart new pen and pencil set was taken away from me by these boorish teachers, who expected me to write in the broad capitals as designed by some woman called Marion Richardson, with an enormous thick pencil which was supposed to be better for children's hands to hold.

And then there was homework. One day it was spelling; a list of simple words that I could grasp immediately, and the next day it was sums; something I have never understood. Fifty years later I still count on my fingers, and I never understood any mathematical principles until I learned to programme sequencers and drum machines in the early 1990s. Apart from that, mathematics has always been a closed book to me, and the five-year-old Jonathan was quite happy that it should remain so.

Within a week I was bored and bolshy, and within a fortnight I was beginning to be disruptive. Then, at the end of the first few weeks I went home one day to find that a letter from my headmistress had arrived in the post. I was totally unprepared for anything so unfair. It appeared that the school authorities liked me about as much as I liked them, and used their command of the English language to its full to tell my parents what a difficult child I was. "Jonathan will not conform" they wrote, and my parents were mortified. I had let down the honour of my family they told me, and my father took me into his study, took down my trousers, made me bend over, and caned me, raising up big bloody welts on my buttocks.

He then wrote to the school boasting about what he had done, and giving the teachers written permission to chastise me in any way that they thought fit. I cannot remember whether they took him up on the offer, but I do know that my father caned me regularly throughout my years at Primary School, and by the time I reached puberty I was not only terrified of him, but wanted more than anything to earn his approval; something I never really did until the last few months of his life.

"Jonathan will not conform", repeated my teachers again and again. But what was I supposed to conform to? How could I conform to a world where semi-literate idiots like Janet and John wandered about, vaguely looking up into the sky and saying "see the aeroplane go up, see him fly", and marvelling at the dull antics of their retarded puppy, when there was the glorious prose of Kipling to entrance me and take me to a world that actually made sense to me.

My Mother loved Kipling and introduced me to both his poetry and his prose when I was a very young boy, and I saw so many parallels between the life of the young herdsboys in India of eighty years before, and my life in Mount Austin Mansions during the 1960s. One of my favourite passages was from *The Jungle Book:*

> "Then they sleep and wake and sleep again, and weave little baskets of dried grass and put grasshoppers in them; or catch two praying mantises and make them fight; or string a necklace of red and black jungle nuts; or watch a lizard basking on a rock, or a snake hunting a frog near the wallows. Then they sing long, long songs with odd native quavers at the end of them, and the day seems longer than most people's whole lives, and perhaps they make a mud castle with mud figures of men and horses and buffaloes, and put reeds into the men's hands, and pretend that they are kings and the figures are their armies, or that they are gods to be worshiped. Then evening comes and the children call, and the buffaloes lumber up out of the sticky mud with noises like gunshots going off one after the other, and they all string across the gray plain back to the twinkling village lights."

The life of a village child in 1880s India seemed so much more productive and logical than did the life of a scion of the last days of the empire, being prepared for a life of drudgery, to be prefaced by a number of years in a British public school where sparing the rod, spoiling the child, an obsession with sport, and compulsory homosexuality was the norm. So I daydreamed most of the time, spending only as much effort as I absolutely had to on lessons which I was seeing more and more as a stupid irrelevance. One day a teacher told the class that a pony was a young horse. I politely put my hand up to explain that she was wrong, and was sent to the headmistress for my impudence. On another occasion a teacher humiliated me in front of the whole class, calling me an imbecile, because - when asked why would we want to go to Switzerland - instead of answering that I wanted to experience winter sports, I answered that I wanted to see green lizards (*Lacerta viridis*). I didn't give a damn about ski-ing, but as there was only one species of true lacertid in Hong Kong and I longed to see one of these brilliant verdant living jewels in the flesh.

So, I soon became a problem child, and ended up being put with the other problem children at the back of the class, where I spent my days alternately plotting mischief, daydreaming about Narnia or the adventures of Mowgli, and wondering what Janet would look like if she ditched her stupid brother and their retarded dog and took her clothes off.

A problem was that the other two or three 'problem' children were classed as such because they truly had learning difficulties, and so were given schoolwork that stretched them even less than the normal dull activities of the class. Whereas I was just the over-intelligent child of alcoholic parents who truly believed that the break-up of the British Empire meant the end of civilisation as we knew it, and that anything that had its genesis later than about 1935 was probably either the work of the Devil or communists. So I sat with the underachievers, and became more and more of a burden to the school, and an increasing embarrassment to my parents. And all around me the British Empire continued to crumble.

At the age of six, I was quite understandably considered not old enough to walk the mile or so to and from school like the bigger children, and my Mother had never learned to drive. There is a (quite possibly fallacious) story in the collective mythology of the Downes family, that my Father had tried to teach her to drive whilst they were living in Maidugari in Northern Nigeria. The story goes that my Father had chosen a huge, empty expanse of dried floodplain to act as location for this inaugural driving lesson. The vast plain was completely empty except for the desiccated stump of a baobab tree, and an elderly man leading an equally elderly goat. My mother put her foot on the accelerator instead of the break, and unwittingly hit all three of them.

There were no such things as school buses in Hong Kong in those days, and so I was ferried to and from school by various other 'School Mothers'. Sometime during our first October at Mount Austin Mansions, there was a thick mist enveloping The Peak. But even through the looming grey fogbanks, I could see far more people than was usual. I politely asked the lady who was driving us what was happening. She grinned back at me in a pleasantly conspiratorial manner. "Just wait until tomorrow", she grinned. "You will have the time of your life".

I don't think that I have ever been as excited as I was that night.

The Chung Yeung Festival (重陽節) falls on the ninth day of the ninth lunar month. Similar to the Ching Ming Festival in spring, the Chung Yeung Festival is when entire families congregate at cemeteries to engage in age-old practices of ancestor worship. My Father always told me that it was part of a worldwide tradition of Great Flood legends (he had always been very much into the work of the - now, generally discredited - Immanuel Velikovsky). I believed this for many years, but apparently the festival is actually rooted in a Han dynasty (202 BC to 220 AD) legend in which a soothsayer advised a man to take his family to high ground for the ninth day of the ninth moon. The man complied and the next day discovered that all the inhabitants of his village had been slaughtered, while he and his family had been spared by leaving for the hills. In Hong Kong, people go to the great outdoors for a picnic on this day, with many people eating special cakes called 'ko'. The name sounds similar to 'high' or 'top' in Chinese and people eat them in the hope of being promoted to high positions.

The next day dawned bright and fair. I am intentionally using Enid Blytonese here because I this was the beginning of one of the most precious subset of childhood memories within my mental folder of such things.

There were stalls all along Mount Austin Road, from the flat bit alongside the playground opposite the apartment block in which we lived, all the way down the hill to the flat bit between the Peak Tram terminus and Peak Mansions (all now demolished and apparently replaced by something called the Peak Galleria, which I am rather pleased to say that I have never seen in the flesh, as it were.

Over the years this festival became known to my family as 'Up the Hill Day', and it became one of the things that I looked forward to more than anything each year. It was the only time in my childhood I had ever seen helium balloons, and - especially after reading Joan Aitken's *Black Hearts in Battersea* - I bought as many as I could afford each year in a vain attempt to be able to try and make a working model of the balloon in which Simon and his fellow protagonists flew over wolf-ridden England.

There were also stalls selling plywood and *papier mache* childsize reproductions of the sorts of vintage Chinese weapons - swords, battle axes and halberds - that are now only seen in period kung fu movies. My friends and I bought loads of them, and - squealing with delight - had pitched battles with other kids up and down Mount Austin Road. With hindsight I can see that this was the only time that we children actively socialised with our Chinese counterparts. Oriental and occidental children frolicked together as our indulgent parents looked on smiling. It was as if we had stopped being *Gwei Lo* and they had stopped being servants and employees, and for one day a year, we were all just people. And furthermore, people who were allowing ourselves to enjoy each other's company.

No wonder 'Up the Hill Day' is one of the happiest memories of my childhood.

For reasons I have never been able to understand, amongst the stalls selling toy weapons and gaudily coloured pictures of scenes from Chinese mythology, was a stall which sold small dried dead fish. There was a row of these unfortunate creatures, and I found out later from a friend of my parents who was a keen fisherman that these were often found in the same area where fisherman hunted shrimps and prawns, and had the colloquial English name of sand darters. I bought one of them and it stayed in my collection for decades, and it may even still be in the loft of my house in Exeter together with a porcupine skull, a horseshoe crab shell and other treasures.

I liked it because its armour plating make it look prehistoric, at least to my eyes, and it took pride of place front and centre in my ever-growing museum. Bizarrely, however, this fish came back to haunt me. During the second half of 2004, when I was living in a tumbledown farmhouse outside Crediton, with a girl who shall remain a fairly minor footnote in my lifestory, I received an email from an old nemesis. Back in the late 1990s Scandinavian cryptozoologist Jan Ove Sundberg took exception to something I had said as a joke, and accused me of being an alcoholic, and furthermore of being a disgrace to my country and to Cryptozoology. I quite possibly *was* an alcoholic at the time, but it was none of his damn business, and the two of us had a rather unpleasant exchange of vitriol in one of the more well-known forums for cryptozoological discussion.

But, six years later, I was all loved up, and more prepared than usual to accept extended olive branches when they were waved in my direction. He sent me a photograph of what was unquestionably a sand darter and said that it had been found in a bag of frozen shrimps from somewhere in Asia. I wrote back telling him the story of "Up the Hill Day", and I don't think I ever heard from him again.

Each Christmas (like every other English-speaking school at that time, and probably to this present day) there was an end if term play. The first of these that I could remember was a dramatic masterpiece called *The Magic Postbox.* It was set in a small English village where they had such things as postmen and red post boxes and the villagers would greed the aforementioned functionaries of the Royal Mail with a cheery "Good Morning Postie", and the village children were friendly and kind and respectful and didn't try to nick the hubcaps off the postvan whenever it was stationary for more than a few minutes.

I assume that this *magnum opus* was written by the class teacher (whose name has vanished in the mists of time) because I truly doubt whether it could have been the work of a professional writer. The only line of dialogue that I can remember took place at the end after the pseudonymous postbox which had appeared in the middle of the village around the time of the Winter Solstice, had disappeared as mysteriously as it had appeared. "It must have been a magic post box belonging to Father Christmas", said someone or other. And therein you have the whole of the plot. All fine and good as far as it goes. But things were soon about to get complicated.

There were about seventeen children in my class. Some of them, like me, were quite prepared to sit back and be part of the audience, or - at best - be villagers who didn't actually have any lines but had to gasp with astonishment, every time the bloody postbox ended up in a new location. But there were about a dozen wannabe thespians, and only four speaking roles. Therefore, Miss Whateverhernamewas re-wrote the script meaning that there were now three magic postboxes, three village policemen (who all said much the same) and the starring brace of cute kids - a boy and girl called Fred and Barbara who kept on following the peripatetic postbox on its travels round the village, were replicated three times. Even to the six-year-old me, the story didn't make much sense. I politely said as much, and was sent to see the Headmistress for my pains. I could see that the Headmistress agreed with me, as did my Mother later on, but I was sternly told not to be cheeky, and to go and stand in the corner, which I did for the rest of the morning.

I was also told that I was not going to be allowed to play the ever-so-important part of a villager in *The Magic Postbox*, and together with another pupil - a slightly rebellious girl called Katie who had also been excluded from the production for some heinous crime or other, were not even allowed to watch the play, and instead had to stay in our classroom behaving ourselves. I was actually quite disappointed at not seeing the play, but on the plus side, we had an interesting session of show and tell, and I did find out what girls looked like beneath their clothes which was an enormous item ticked off my bucket list.

That Christmas was the first time that I discovered that there were such things as school reports. And, guess what, mine was terrible. At the age of five the syndrome that was to well and truly define my school career until I was expelled from a crappy public school in North Devon thirteen years later, was established. And my Father physically chastised me for having dragged the family honour through the mire. I didn't know what it meant, but I was consumed with guilt for having done so. This pattern of physical punishment and guilt tripping would continue for the next decade and a bit.

But something nice *did* happen that Christmas. One day just after my school report had come and gone, my Father bundled us all into the family's Triumph Herald, and we drove to somewhere in the Repulse Bay area, from whence we returned with a small Siamese kitten called Augustus (soon shortened to Gus or Gustus). He was the first animal with whom I had a real relationship, and we spent many happy days playing complex games. As my toddler brother was still far too young to be a playmate in any meaningful sense of the word, Gustus became an essential part of my games, being Algy to my Biggles, and - later - Ginger to my William. It was probably from Gustus that I acquired my lifetime suspicion that dogs and cats are not carnivorans at all, but little people wearing fur coats, and ever since all of my cats and dogs have talked in their own voices, had their own complex personalities and mythologies, and been my day to day companions.

A few weeks into the brave new world of 1965 the outside world impacted upon mine again. Someone called 'Churchill' died, and for a whole week, there was what I would now call a thumbnail inset picture in the top right hand of all of the television programmes. It showed a fat old man with a strange domed building (that looked a little like a bit of the Tiger Balm Gardens) behind him. It must have been some feast day or other because they were shrouded in what looked like firecrackers. And all the adults that we met were terribly upset. Some of them even cried openly, which was completely unheard of in front of children or servants.

There was a widespread belief amongst the children in my class that Churchill's ghost had been seen crossing the playground above the school, and on the hillside opposite Mount Austin Mansions, and as a result there was a spate of ghost stories doing the arounds of the younger generation. Despite the fact that I had been the epicentre of what appears to have been a very real bout of paranormal activity in the New Forest during the summer of 1963, this was the very first time that I had ever been aware of the concept that - as Shakespeare is said to have said - there were more things in heaven and earth. Until then, I believed that my parents knew everything, and that they were the last word in all knowledge. From then on, I realised that this wasn't necessarily so, and that there were things that other people believed, and even *saw*, that were not necessarily described in my family's received philosophy.

My Auntie Mary had died sometime in the previous year also, and this added to my newly found sense of the mystic. I went through the first episode of another syndrome which has come to me at various times of my life, and became very religious. The fact that I had a member of my very young family sitting up in heaven with the Almighty certainly made the afterlife seem more interesting, and I mused quite intently on the meaning of death, and what would happen when I died. Basically all the stuff which George Harrison wrote about in *The Art of Dying.*

As an aside here, round about the turn of the Millennium I was head over heels in love with a devout Roman Catholic girl called Linda. My parents liked her quite a lot until Linda told them that the most holy thing that one could do was to meditate upon the hour of one's own death. For some reason which I don't really understand, my parents were terribly angry that she said this, and took against her entirely. I never told them, or her, that I had been doing this terribly holy thing way back in my childhood, and still did it more than I liked to admit.

Maybe I was a saint, but I have to say that I think it is massively unlikely.

But I started meditating, although I'd never heard the term, and didn't know that this was what I was doing, and whenever I could get away with it I would lie on the floor of the great school hall, and gaze up at the whitewashed ceiling. I could see nothing else but smooth white paint, and when doing this it was easier to turn off my mind, relax and drift downstream. It was 1966 after all, although I wasn't to hear *Tomorrow never Knows* for another 10 years.

And I would meditate upon my own death, and I decided that when I died I wanted it to be in the Peak School hall staring up at the white ceiling.

At Christmas my Grandad had sent me an exciting book about animals which I still have to this day. I devoured it eagerly, and as - a week or so after Churchill's death - there had been a bout of severe weather meaning that we couldn't leave to go to school (whether it was a typhoon or not I cannot remember, and it doesn't really matter) so I stayed indoors reading Grandad's book and playing with my toy soldiers. My Mother whom - it will be remembered - had been a schoolteacher back in

England, devised a clever game involving times tables and toy soldiers, which she used to teach the rudiments of school sums to the assembled youngsters who were stuck inside the flats, but it was Grandad's book that fascinated me most. I was particularly interested in the description of bamboo bats; The lesser bamboo bat or lesser flat-headed bat (*Tylonycteris pachypus*) is one of the smallest species of mammal, not much bigger than a large bumble bee, and is native to Southeast Asia. Grandad's book described how they were so small that they could live inside a bamboo stalk. This totally enthused me, and - especially as there were thick groves of bamboo along parts of the forest verge of Mount Austin road, I managed to convince myself that I would find one.

The day that the rain finally left, Mummy stuffed my brother into his pushchair, and the three of us went on a brisk walk down the hill to the Peak Tram terminus where there was a sweetshop and a stall selling cut flowers. For some reason, that day the flower stall had several different types of gladioli for sale. Gladioli were always one of my Mother's favourites, so she decided to buy some. As the wizened old Chinese man who ran the stall reached for a bundle of flowers for her there was a tiny little flapping of wings and something the size of a large bumble bee flew out of the bucketful of flowers, and towards the open entrance to the terminus. "Tylonecteris!!!" I shouted excitedly and inaccurately, and - ignoring my Mother's oft repeated strictures that I should stay with her at all times - I ran after it, brandishing my cowboy hat as a makeshift net. My Mother bellowed at me angrily (for such a ladylike woman she could yell like an angry water buffalo if she wanted to) but I ignored her as I leapt into the air, flourished my hat and caught the tiny creature.

A few minutes later, after having been severely reprimanded by my Mama, I looked at my capture, and found that it was not a bat after all, but what I now know to be a fairly nondescript moth; probably some sort of Notonid. However, nearly half a century later, while I was starting work on this book I was pleased to discover that two species of bamboo bat have now been discovered in the region, and that - if the stars had actually been in my favour - I *could* have caught one of them back in that day after the rain.

On the south side of Hong Kong Island, there is a huge natural harbour called Tai Tam Bay. It is here that I spent some of the best, and some of the worst times of my childhood. The bay is so large that it probably should be called an inlet, or something, because the word 'bay' conjures up visions of British seaside holidays, complete with donkey rides, and overpriced ice-creams, instead of what it actually is; an expanse of deep, sheltered, and relatively calm water between two long capes which jut out into the South China Sea. To the East is Cape D'Aguilar, which according to my very bad Portuguese means 'Cape of the Eagle'. As a child I always assumed that it was so named because it was one of the very few places on Hong Kong Island where the white headed sea eagles still nested (or, at least they did half-a-century ago - I have no idea whether they still do, and sadly suspect that they don't). It was only a few years ago but I discovered that I was completely wrong; despite the inviting lexilink, the naming had absolutely nothing to do with avian fauna of the area. D'Aguilar was a relatively obscure 19th century civil servant of Jewish and Austrian extraction, about whom I know absolutely nothing, although I suspect that he must have been reasonably important, to have had such an important geographical feature named after him. Here I should point out that dear Richard Muirhead pointed out to me that this man of whom I knew nothing was actually the first Lieutenant Governor of Hong Kong for five years from 1843. It is a very good job that I gave him the manuscript to have a shufti at before I went to print.

And to the West is Stanley Peninsula; from a historical point of view, as well as from a Fortean one, one of the most important geographical features of the island. About halfway down the peninsular is the village (now, apparently the town) of Stanley, and between Stanley and the sea is a large, grey, forbidding, high security prison. It was opened for business, if the incarceration of malefactors can be described as 'business' in 1937, but within four years its whole *raison d'etre* would change entirely. It was still a prison, but instead of housing the aforementioned malefactors, it was housing civilian prisoners of war. Because, in December 1941, the British Crown Colony of Hong Kong was invaded, successfully and overwhelmingly, by the Imperial Japanese army.

After the war it returned to being a civilian prison, and - until they were phased out in the mid Sixties - it was where condemned prisoners were kept, and indeed executed, the final such execution being in 1966. However, in stark contrast to this grim reality, there was (and presumably still is) a private beach attached to the prison. It is called Tweed Bay, and was reserved for the use of prison officers, police officers and their families, and also for the use of any other middle to high ranking civil servants within the Hong Kong government, who were prepared to pay what I remember my father used to complain was quite a hefty subscription fee.

From about 1965 for two or three years, my family - my mother (who used to tut disapprovingly at the young women in dashing two-piece bathing costumes), my father (who, I have a sneaking suspicion, was more impressed at the sight than my mother was), my little brother (who just toddled around happily, having to be restrained from eating the occasional dead seagull, or lump of rotting seaweed) and me - went there at least once every weekend during the spring and summer months. I spent my time investigating the local fauna, and staring shyly at the girls paddling by the shore. I paid no attention to them when we were at school together in our prim, old-fashioned uniforms, but at the beach, in bathing costumes, shrieking with delight as they ran in and out of the surf, they were oddly alluring, and the six or seven year old Jonathan was both tongue-tied and confused.

But ignoring the female of the species for the moment, for my years in thrall to them have not yet quite begun, this little cove was another place where I discovered the incredible diversity of life which was laid out like a smorgasbord before me. One of the first things that I discovered were the elongate black sea cucumbers, which lolled on the sandy floor of the bay like leathery legless hippos. If you picked them up, like Gerald Durrell had described in *My Family and Other Animals* they did, indeed, squirt out water, but I was more intrigued by the description in *The Hong Kong Countryside* where Herklots told how they, under duress, would also disgorge their very entrails in a revolting method of self-defence. As Herklots explains, the respiratory system of these extraordinary echinoderms, the commonest Hong Kong species of which grows to between eight and ten inches in length, instead of being situated near the head as in most higher animals, including our own species, is placed right at the other end of the elongate, oval-shaped body, near the anus.

This mechanism consists of a pair of 'respiratory trees' which extract the oxygen from sea water that the sea-cucumber 'breathes' in. These respiratory trees are covered with a mucous substance which becomes very sticky when exposed to sea water. If seized by a crab or other predator, the bold *Holothurian*, by an effort of will, ruptures its anus and disgorges the respiratory trees onto the marauding predator, which then becomes immobilised as if it was dropped into liquid latex whilst the sea cucumber slides off, surprisingly gracefully, and one imagines with somewhat of a smirk on its face, to fight another day (presumably once the respiratory trees have grown back).

Herklots tells the story of how, at a "bathing picnic" at some time before the war, he had been using these hapless invertebrates to bombard his fellow picnickers, when one lady took a sea cucumber, and dropped it inside the bathing costume of one specific eminent professor "who like Esau was a hairy man". The irritated echinoderm did what it does best, and disgorged its sticky payload all over the poor professor, with the result that the poor man was forced to shave parts of his body which never usually saw a razor. History does not relate what happened to the sea cucumber.

I knew enough about human physiology and anatomy, to be aware that adults had pubic hair, and so I found this story not only desperately amusing, but with a *frisson* of sexual naughtiness that made it appeal even more. I tested Durrell's reports that these peculiar creatures could squirt water, and that they made an excellent water pistol on a number of occasions, but I always thought that subjecting the poor animal to enough stress to force it to rupture its own anus was both cruel and distasteful, and the idea of putting one in a rock pool with a crab in order to test the hypothesis under laboratory conditions was just nasty. So I never did see for myself the remarkable defence mechanism that these relatives of the starfish had evolved to a fine art over aeons.

Another relative of the starfish was also common in the shallow rock pools which fringed each side of the beach. These were great, black sea urchins of the Genus *Diadema*. I always found them totally fascinating as they moved around the rock pools surprisingly quickly like some sort of roving robot in a tacky 1950s science fiction movie. For my sixth birthday in 1965, my father gave me a face mask and snorkel, and this allowed me to drift, face down, in the warm shallow water, and see several other sorts of sea urchin which never seemed to come inshore so that they could be imprisoned for a while in the rock pools for my delight.

One of the things that fascinated me most on my excursions around Tweed Bay were the blue buttons (*Porpita porpita*) which came into coastal waters in large numbers each September. They are superficially similar to jellyfish, but are actually colonial hydroids; a colony of hydrozoan polyps. They are about the size of a British 5p piece, bright glue and fringed with tentacles. The blue button is a *Chondrophore*, which is a group of cnidarians that also includes *Velella* and *Porpema*, and are passive drifters that live on the surface of the Indian, Pacific and Atlantic oceans in both tropical and subtropical regions, sometimes in large numbers. Their sting is not strong enough to pierce human skin and so as a child I picked them up and examined them with impunity, marvelling at their rather predatory blue beauty.

The *Chondrophores* are similar to the better-known *Siphonophores*, which includes the Portuguese Man o' War. These latter creatures were rare in the colony during my time there, and indeed during the time that Herklots spent in Hong Kong, but I saw them drifting along like a deadly sky blue flotilla on a few occasions, and once even managed to get up close and personal with a single specimen which I found in one of the larger rock pools off the beach.

The only jellyfish with which I ever had a traditional encounters were the tiny, colourless 'jelly bug' which I was always told, and Herklots intimated, were a tiny species of jellyfish, but which are now apparently known as 'sea lice' and are now recognised to be the juvenile form of various species of *Cnidarian*, in which the nematocysts are fully functional despite the near microscopic size of the creatures. When I came to write about this, sitting in my favourite armchair, with my iPad balanced precariously on my unfortunately large tummy, and my badly behaved and overly neurotic Jack Russell asleep on my knee, I decided that I had better check mine and Herklots' memory, and so I belatedly discovered the true identity of these annoying little beasts. I also unearthed another piece of information about them which, jogged my memory about another episode from my childhood which for about half a century has been buried deep within the soggy gooey bits of my hypothalamus. I don't remember which beach it was, or any other details of the day, but I was swimming with a bunch of other children, under the care of an older boy of - say - fourteen. We must have swum into the middle of a bloom of these tiny terrors because I remember feeling as if a dozen red hot needles had been pushed into my right arm, and I burst into tears and swam for shore.

Another of the party was much more badly stung than I was, and had to be helped back to shore by our teenage protector. Luckily said protector was a Boy Scout, and even *more* luckily the Boy Scouts in the further flung reaches of Her Majesty's realms were taught far more esoteric things than merely how to prepare for Bob a Job Week, and helping old ladies across the road. Our companion, whom I vaguely remember was called Donald, but about whom I remember absolutely nothing else, was screaming in agony, and great angry red welts had erupted all over his trunk.

What happened next astonished all of us, and I am amazed that it has remained hidden in my subconscious for all these years. The Boy Scout, picked Donald up, stripped off his swimming trunks, pulled down the front of his own trunks, and urinated all over him, to the accompaniment if the massed giggles and gasps of the assembled children.

Immediately, as if by magic, Donald stopped crying, and within seconds his skin returned to its normal colour. The Boy Scout counted to a minute ("one Missisippi - two Missisippi" etc) and when he reached sixty, took little Donald down to the shore, washed him off, and put his swimming trunks back onto him, and the event was over. I had forgotten entirely about it, until, whilst researching Jelly Bugs, I found a reference to urine being used commonly to treat jellyfish stings, and that - half a century on - it is still believed widely in Hong Kong. In fact, it seems that the jury is still out on the subject; depending on which phase one is in, human urine can be either alkali or acid, and so may alleviate the pain or even make it worse.

With my scientific reasoning hat on, I am suppositioning that as:

1. Donald was young, and possibly delicate
2. So were the jellyfish
3. The Boy Scout was also healthy

That his urine was probably in the right phase, and that it managed to work a certain degree of micturation magick, but that the sheer shock value of what the Boy Scout did shocked Donald back into some degree of equilibrium, and that all was well that ends well. This stuck in minds of all the revolting little boys who witnessed it because for some months my friends and I would boast that we knew how to treat jellyfish stings, but unless my memory is hiding any more deep dark secrets, as far as I remember, I was never in the position of being able to out this knowledge into action. And I think that I would probably have remembered.

Another jellyfish that I first read about in Herklots' all-encompassing tome, and which I have wanted to see ever since is *Craspedacusta sowerbii*, one of the world's few species of freshwater jellyfish. Actually, if we are going to be pedantic about it, this species isn't a jellyfish at all, but a colonial hydroid like the blue buttons I described above. At the time Herklots was writing, and indeed for many years after, although they had been reported from many parts of the world, but it was unknown from whence they had originated. The first ones recorded in Britain had been in a huge tank containing enormous waterlilies from South America, and so for a while it was supposed that the species had originated in the slow waters of the Amazon. However, the current thinking is that they originated in the Yangtze Basin, and so the ones noted by Herklots from the University of Hong Kong in 1940, where they were found in a tub containing waterlilies imported from East Africa, and locally sourced water chestnuts, and the ones reported post war in Kam Tin, had probably not travelled a spectacularly long way to get there.

Every few years there are reports of them from slow moving canals, and flooded gravel pits in the north of England, and one of these days I will get it together to go and see them. It is on, what I believe in the current vernacular, is known as my 'bucket list' of things to do before I die.

I don't remember there being a particularly diverse variety of seashells on this particular beach, at least not compared to some of the beaches that I would visit a few years later, and they mostly seemed to be limpets and winkles. However it was at this little beach that I first started my lifelong love affair with chitons. There are about 940 species of chiton in the world, sometimes known as sea cradles or "coat-of-mail shells", or more formally as *Loricates*, *Polyplacophorans*, and occasionally as *Polyplacophores*. Chitons have a dorsal shell, which is composed of eight separate shell plates or valves. These plates overlap somewhat at the front and back edges, and yet articulate well with one another. Because of this, although the plates provide good protection for impacts from above, they nonetheless permit the chiton to flex upward when needed for locomotion over uneven surfaces, and also allow the animal to slowly curl up into a ball when it is dislodged from the underlying surface.

I have always found something completely irresistible about these peculiar, woodlouse-like molluscs. The fact that unlike most molluscs they can roll themselves up into a ball is one aspect that has always endeared them to me, and the fact that they have remained almost unchanged for something in excess of 400 million years, is another.

I started a collection of sea shells, which I kept for many years, giving them to my ex-father-in-law in the late 1980s, which - as he ceased to be my father-in-law in 1996 - is something that I have been mentally kicking myself for ever since. The jewel in the crown of my early seashell collection was a specimen of *Conus textile*, a rare and incredibly beautiful shell with (as the binomial specific name implies) a textile like pattern in orange, brown and white. They were very rare in Hong Kong, which was probably a good thing, because - as I took great pleasure in telling everyone to whom I exhibited my collection - they were deadly poisonous. Like all species within the genus Conus, these snails are predatory and venomous. They are capable of "stinging" humans, therefore live ones should be handled carefully or not at all. The conotoxin of this species is extremely dangerous to humans.

From what I can gather, the species is considerably more common now in Hong Kong waters than it was back in the 1960s when I was there. My original supposition was that this is as a result of climate change, as I suspected that Hong Kong was actually at the most northerly part of the species range, and warmer waters might well encourage the species to venture north but a quick shufti at the Aquabase distribution map for the species, shows that it is found as far north of the coast of Japan, and so this cannot be the case. Over the past 20 years I have come to realise that biotopes are not permanent, and neither are the ranges of the species which live within them.

It is part of the accepted narrative within current western society that Nature lived in harmony with each other until the white man came along and fucked it all up. Whilst this is true up to a point, there are a myriad of reasons why species change their range and even go extinct. And they are not all anthropocentric. Whilst I have no idea why my favourite Hong Kong seashelled creature has changed its range over the past 50 years, and in the grand scheme of this book it doesn't really matter, the further I go along the path laid out for me by my Uber-mistress of Crypyozoology, the more I realise that the fluctuations and changes in animals' ranges are something incredibly important within the whole field of Cryptozoology and should be given far more attention.

I think that my favourite seashells were, and are, cowries of which there are 248 known species worldwide. How many of them actually occur, or occurred, in Hong Kong waters I have no idea, but I would hazard a guess at several dozen. Peculiarly I have only ever seen two living cowries in my life, despite the Hong Kong beaches, particularly in Tai Tam bay, being full of them. One was in Hong Kong when I was about eight, and the other four decades later at the Shirley Aquatic Centre in the West Midlands.

The children who played on the beach invariably tried to scare each other with the ever-present spectre of shark attacks. But there was no shark observation tower, and to the best of my knowledge nobody ever got attacked by a shark there, or indeed anywhere else in Tai Tam Bay during the time I lived in Hong Kong. However, there is a reference to a shark sighting in 2012, and - ironically - it seems that the first known fatal shark attack in Hong Kong history (which means, realistically, the first attack on a European in the years since the British arrived) could well have taken place in that very bay.

In the waters of the bay was an island called Lo Chau or Tweed Island, from which the bay got its name. It was strongly believed by the local children who had heard about the mysterious prisoner encountered by The Count of Monte Cristo on his island fortress that a very dangerous prisoner (believed to be either Chairman Mao or the wartime Japanese Governor) was isolated there. This was, by the way, despite all the evidence to the contrary ie. that Mao was very much alive, and Takashi Sakai and his replacement had both been executed back in 1946. There was also the small matter that there were no buildings on the island, and no supply of water, although, of course, we all believed that there was an underground labyrinth where the nameless prisoners were imprisoned in the darkness. What horrid little beasts children are.

Reg Harris special (war) correspondent for several journals in Australia who was based in Hong Kong, filed the following report on September 25, 1945 for *The Argus (Melbourne, 1846-1957):*

"Man Killed by Shark at Hong Kong

Police-sergeant H.W. Jackson was the victim yesterday of the first known shark attack at Hong Kong while he was bathing at Tweed Beach shortly before dusk. He was frightfully mauled and died within a minute of being rescued by Captain A.M. [sic] Braude, Hong Kong Volunteer Defense of the Hong Kong Telephone Company.

Tweed Beach is a popular swimming area near Stanley internment camp. Sergeant Jackson, who was interned for nearly four years, was awaiting repatriation to London. Large sharks have never been seen in Hong Kong bathing waters. It is believed that this one must have followed a ship in."

The excellent *Gwulo* website gives more details:

"On August 17, 1945, news was received that the Japanese had surrendered on August 14 and the guards were withdrawn. However, it was not until August 29 that Admiral Harcourt's fleet was seen off Stanley. The fleet anchored in Hong Kong harbour and at 5pm Admiral Harcourt drove to Stanley Internment Camp. The National Anthem was sung and the flags of all nations represented in the camp were raised. A bugler sounded the Last Post in memory of those who had died. The hymn, "0 God Our Help in Ages Past" was sung.

With Liberation those police officers that were fit were allocated duties pending repatriation. Jackson was still quartered at Stanley during this period and took the opportunity to take a daily swim in the fine weather. In early September he was booked on an RAF flight out but, being a bachelor and enjoying the weather, he gave up his place to another officer who was anxious to get home to his wife and family. On September 22 the Royal Navy put on a film show at the Queen's Theatre where Lance Sergeant Norman Gunning met Jackson who told him that he was again booked on an RAF flight out the next evening, September 23.

The next day Jackson returned to Stanley to pack his kit and to have a last swim at Tweed Bay, near the internment camp. As he was taking his last swim Jackson was attacked by what was assumed to have been a shark. Captain Braude, HKVDC, and Inspector Nolloth heard Jackson's shout and went into the water to assist: him. When they pulled him out he was still breathing but he died seconds later on the beach. A subsequent inquest heard that Jackson's injuries were "consisting of two-thirds of a circle torn from the right buttock. In the upper part wounds extended to abdominal cavity and Intestines were hanging out the back." The official cause of death was "shock and haemorrhage.""

The children of my time, were convinced that Sgt Jackson had been killed by officials determined that he should not get to the island and reveal its secrets. I wonder how many of those children grew up to become conspiracy theorists. Something else believed in implicitly by all the kids who visited the beach was that "someone" had once killed a huge great white shark in the bay, and that if you knew the right spot to dive, you would be able to see its body; something that several kids claimed to have done, despite the fact that the cadaver of even the hugest shark would have disappeared as a result of predation from invertebrates and smaller fish in a matter of hours, especially in sub-tropical waters like these. However, such stories added a *frisson* of danger to our escapades on the beach, and - with the benefit of hindsight - I think that successive generations of grown-ups encouraged these stories to deflect children from discovering the real history of the beach.

It wasn't until I read *Prisoner of the Turnip Heads* by George Wright-Nooth that I realised something quite appalling. This little beach, where - apart from the occasional nanny or other servant - everybody was white and upper-middle-class (at least), had - during the darkest days of the Japanese occupation - been the execution ground. The sand where my brother and I built sandcastles, and where - religiously, each time we visited - I put together the battered old paddling pool that I used as a makeshift aquarium in which to observe the myriad small (and not so small) creatures of the deep that I had caught, was soaked with the blood of incarcerated prisoners who had been caught trying to escape, Chinese coolies convicted of any of an enormous range of perceived crimes against the imperium of His Imperial Majesty, and American air force personnel unlucky enough to have been shot down and captured. Some of them had been cruelly tortured or otherwise ill-treated before the sadistic Japanese soldiers, or their lackeys - Formosan mercenaries, and renegade Indian troops rebelling against the Raj - had tired of their sport.

When my family returned to the United Kingdom in 1971, one of the strangest things that the 11-year-old Jonathan had to get used to, was dealing with old people. I had hardly ever met any. Although there was a burgeoning Chinese middle class, I never met them. Practically my entire social circle, except for the servants, was English and from the Home Counties. I knew one Dutch boy, one American family, and one very pretty Indian girl who was in the same class as me at school. However, her father had been a Maharajah until such things ceased to exist when the British left India in 1947, and being *ci devant* royalty, meant that everybody treated her as if she was white.

As described in the previous chapter there were three almost entirely distinct social groupings within the European population of Hong Kong. My father went to Hong Kong as a senior executive officer, and left as the acting Assistant Colonial Secretary, so we were fairly high up in the pecking order of the government families. But one thing that the government, the navy, the army, the police and all other Europeans employed by or in the administration had in common was retirement age. All but the very senior had gone back to the leafy lanes of Surrey to retire by the time they reached their early Sixties. So there were no old people in my family's social circle. Neither were there the disabled, the handicapped, or the infirm. The social Darwinism of Her Majesty's Overseas Civil Service made sure that such people were quietly shipped back to Blighty. So, I think I can be forgiven, when - at the age of seven - on Stanley beach, I was taken aback when I met a wrinkled old Englishman with white hair and no legs. He was also drunk, and very very angry!

I had no idea what I had done wrong. Apparently the old man thought that I had been staring at him in an impertinent manner, and for this I was publicly humiliated, when my Father gave me a bare bottom spanking in front of all the people on the beach, which included various school chums of mine, and Sunila, the pretty young Indian girl who would have been a Maharanee in an alternative universe. Then I was made to publicly apologise to the old man, who - or so it turned out - had been a senior Army officer in the First World War, who was interned and tortured by the Japanese in the Second, and had, as a result of that, had both his legs amputated above the knee.

I think that the old man was shocked at the severity of my punishment, and he soon calmed down, called me to him, and even did his best, in a clumsy drunken way, to comfort me. And somehow, through some peculiar machinations of the grown-up social world, the next weekend my entire family was invited to have Sunday lunch with the old man and his household in a large house in the New Territories.

Until then I had only visited a handful of actual houses in Hong Kong. The Downes family had always lived in apartments in huge Edwardian blocks of flats, designated as a lodge or a mansion. And so the opportunity of having a REAL garden in which to play was a very strange and unusually welcome one for me. I know now that there were far more places in Hong Kong that my family and I could have explored, but that - for whatever reason - we didn't, and that despite it being a small colony, I never did visit most of it.

By the way, for those of you not in the know, the New Territories (新界) is a peninsula that constitutes one of the three main regions of Hong Kong, alongside Hong Kong Island and the Kowloon Peninsula. It makes up 86.2% of Hong Kong's territory. Historically, it is the region described in The Convention for the Extension of Hong Kong Territory in 1898. According to that the territories comprise the mainland area north of the Boundary Street of Kowloon Peninsula and south of the Sham Chun River which is the border between Hong Kong and Mainland China, as well as over 200 outlying Islands including Lantau Island, Lamma Island, Cheung Chau, and Peng Chau in the territory of Hong Kong.

The New Territories were leased from Qing China to the United Kingdom in 1898 for 99 years in the Second Convention of Peking (The Convention for the Extension of Hong Kong Territory). Upon the expiration of the lease, sovereignty was transferred to the People's Republic of China in 1997, together with the Qing ceded territories of Hong Kong Island and Kowloon Peninsula.

The New Territories contained practically all of Hong Kong's farmland, and back in the sixties was still remarkably rural. The wildest area, then and now, was the Sai Kung Peninsula on the eastern side of the colony. This is truly the area that gives the lie to the idea that Hong Kong is nothing but a concreted urban wasteland. By Hong Kong standards, and remember that the entire colony has an area of only just over 1,100 square kilometres, it is a vast area of relatively unspoiled wilderness. Consisting of volcanic rocks covered with thick forest, which acts as home to many of Hong Kong's larger species of wildlife, the region was even more remote when the Downes family lived in Hong Kong half a century ago. This all changed in about

1970 when an ambitious waterworks scheme, the second such scheme in Hong Kong's history got underway.

The roots of the scheme were in the Communist inspired riots of 1967 which I will deal with elsewhere in this book. As a direct result of these, mainland China ceased sending fresh water to the British Colony and as a result there were serious water shortages. Luckily, and as far as I am able to ascertain, totally coincidentally, the Colonial Hong Kong Government had already started work on one ambitious reservoir scheme some years before. Plover Cove Reservoir (船灣淡水湖), located within Plover Cove Country Park, in the north-eastern New Territories, is the largest reservoir in Hong Kong in terms of area, and the second-largest in terms of volume. It was the first in the world to construct a lake from an arm of the ocean. Its main dam was one of the largest in the world at the time of its construction, disconnecting Plover Cove from the sea. Synchronitically it was finished a year after the Communist riots, but it soon became apparent that another, similar project was needed.

The High Island Reservoir scheme was, in many ways, even more ambitious.

High Island or Leung Shuen Wan (糧船灣洲) lay in the sea off the southeast coast of Sai Kung Peninsula, Hong Kong. The reservoir was created by constructing two main dams. One was built at the west of High Island connecting it with the Sai Kung Peninsula at Yuen Ng Fan (元五墳). The other was built in the southeast of High Island, connecting it with the Sai Kung Peninsula near Po Pin Chau, a stack island. Three smaller dams were also constructed in valleys around the reservoir. Aqueducts totalling 5 miles in length were also constructed to transfer water from streams around Sai Kung Peninsula to the reservoir. Construction spanned 10 years from 1969 to 1979. Two roads were created as part of the scheme, crossing over the dams, and it was these roads that opened up the area to more regular visitors from the city. However, half a century ago, when the reservoir system wasn't even a gleam in a planning officer's eye, the area was very difficult to access, and so had not changed much in several hundred years.

Pak Sha O was (and according to Google Earth still is) a small Hakka fishing village near the coast where the Pak Sha O river (白沙澳河) flows into the South China Sea. The village probably dated from about 1600 when the first Hakka settlers arrived in the area, having migrated from Central China, and probably from Northern China five hundred years before that. Although they are only a subgrouping of Han Chinese, the Hakka people have a very distinct cultural identity, with their own language and cuisine, although their religion and folklore appears to be similar to most other people in the region. Historically they have always been an agricultural people, but as most of the prime agricultural land in the region had already been taken, they settled in less ideal areas and grew crops in smallholdings and kitchen gardens. I had visited the village from the sea one weekend, when a family friend took us out in his boat, but I had no idea, that deep in the forest there were still some big houses that dated back to the days of the Chinese Empire, and even less idea that the old man that I had unwittingly upset at Stanley Prison Beach lived in one of them.

Now, remember now, that my little brother was about three when these events took place, and that both my parents are long dead. Also remember that I was a behaviourally disturbed five or six-year-old at the time, and that all this took place over half a century ago, and that an awful lot of water has flowed under an awful lot of bridges, and an awful lot of brandy has flowed down my arterial system since then. So, although I am writing this, utilising my failing memory as best as I can, I am not going to claim 100% accuracy, nor would that be a particularly wise thing for me to do if I were going to. I remember the name Pak Sha O, and it looks roughly the right place on the map. However, all the accounts I can find say that all the area beyond Tai Mon Tsai was inaccessible from land except by foot until the roads were built in about 1970.

But as Pak Sha O is way beyond Tai Min Tsai, and I have a distinct memory of my father driving the family Sunbeam Herald deep into the forest to visit the elderly gentleman whose acquaintance I had made in such an inauspicious manner, then one of three things has happened. The two most likely scenarios are that either Wikipedia is inaccurate (fancy that) or my memory is completely awry. However, there is a third, and much more exciting scenario. From all the available evidence, the elderly gentleman, who I only ever knew as 'Uncle Simeon', and whose real name - if I ever knew it - I have long forgotten, was an important enough figure in the infrastructure of the colony, both then, and over the previous three decades, to have been granted privileges that normal citizens of the colony, European or Chinese, could only dream at.

I saw one such privilege with my own eyes; the man whom I assumed was his houseboy, although even I realised that he was somewhat old for such a junior post, had a holstered pistol prominently displayed on his belt, and the guard on the gate had an assault rifle. Private gun ownership was strictly forbidden in Hong Kong during the sixties, and whilst I had seen firearms, they had only been carried by uniformed policemen or soldiers. But here were people in civilian clothes who were openly, not to say ostentatiously armed. With the benefit of half a century's hindsight it does not seem impossible that Uncle Simeon could have built himself a private road, or even that His Excellency the Governor, had diverted public funds to pay for one.

Our first visit set the scene for the ones which were to follow. In those days before the tunnel and mass transit railway that now go underneath the ancient harbour, the only way to cross to the mainland was by ferry, and as I remember it, the various car ferries were nowhere near as exciting or romantic as the much lauded Star Ferry which has been plying its trade across Hong Kong harbour since the early 20th Century. We then drove through the city which in recent decades had spread like a fungus over the barren rocks and scrubland of this particular spur of southern China and into what was then mostly farmland. Flat paddy fields, with the occasional water buffalo, and the Hakka women with their peculiar fringed hats and their black pyjamas.

But it wasn't long until we reached the forest, and although I was used to playing in the thick rhododendron forest on the sides of Victoria Peak, somehow this forest seemed much wilder and much more exciting. I would like to embroider history here and say that the forest was full of wildlife, but it wasn't; not that we saw, at least. But there was something disturbing and intractable about it, something unforgiving and unwelcoming.

At the time I didn't recognise the significance. There was a small side road off the main highway, and about a hundred yards in, a huge gate that barred further access along the road either on foot or by car. There was a small hut by the side of the road, and as we approached, two men in uniform - both European - came out to meet us. My father switched the engine off, and got out of the car to meet them, and they spoke in hushed voices, which I - a nosey little fellow - strained to try and hear, but to no avail. I was, however, impressed to see that they both carried what looked suspiciously like machine guns. It didn't strike me for many years that it was unusual to see two Europeans carrying out such a relatively menial task as being guards to an obscure stretch of road. This was the sort of job that was always entrusted to Chinese policemen or Gurkha soldiers, and to see two white faces there, would seem to suggest that the thing they were guarding - whatever, or whoever it was - was of above average importance.

We drove through the thick forest, and although I let my imagination run riot, and supposed that all the larger fauna described by Herklots would be there; all three civets, the dhole, so familiar from Kipling, and even tigers and leopards, although there hadn't been a conclusive tiger sighting since 1947, and the last leopard had been shot during the year of my birth, six or seven years before.

Then the forest died away and the little dirt road opened out into a clearing where half a dozen neat little houses with the peculiar tiled roofs of Cantonese architecture, and looming over them all, what seemed in comparison to be a huge old house in the Imperial Chinese style. As my Father was pulling into the parking space, 'Uncle Simeon' came hobbling out to meet me, accompanied by two extraordinarily beautiful young Chinese women, whom I know now were probably in their late teens.. They were wearing the sort of silk pyjama-like tunics that, with the benefit of fifty years experience of such matters I know that one would see on a period television drama being worn by the concubines of a Chinese warlord, or - more prosaically - by the staff at a high class Oriental knocking shop (although I shall admit here and now that my experience of both is purely theoretical). My Mother had a look of horror on her face which I totally misinterpreted. "I'm not staring at him, I'm not!" I assured her in a secretive whisper which was probably audible half a mile away. She shushed me quiet, but it was true. I wasn't staring at the old man who was coming over to greet us, or his female companions. I was far too busy staring at the two huge, cast iron barred cages, that were over to the right. One of them contained a pair of fierce looking and unimpeachably impressive wild boar, and the other something that I had always wanted to meet; a masked palm civet.

"You like my animals, Boy?" Uncle Simeon grunted at me as soon as he was close enough. Terrified that if I replied wrongly I would find myself being beaten again, I nodded. "What's the matter, Boy? Cat got your tongue?" He grunted cholerically at me. I looked back at him mutely, scared to speak unless I said the wrong thing, and scared to look anywhere in the direction of what I knew were his prosthetic legs. I had seen the film of *Reach for the Sky*, and of course *Treasure Island* had prepared me for the concept of wooden legs, and so knew, in theory at least that things were possible. Part of me was fascinated by the idea and wanted to see how they fitted on and how he could walk with them. I knew that all that was left of either leg were battered looking stumps several inches above where his knees had presumably once been, but for the life of me I couldn't work out how he would be able to walk. But walk he could, after a fashion, but as he hobbled closer I could see by the look on his face that he was in extraordinary discomfort, and that each step was causing him some considerable pain. There was also a strange creaking noise, which sounded just like the bellows of wood and leather that my Grandmother Rawlins used on her log fire back in Hampshire.

"Come with me" he ordered, reaching his hand out to me. Speechless, and terrified, I put my hand in his and walked slowly with him over to the cages. The masked palm civet or gem-faced civet (*Paguma larvata*) is a civet species native to the Indian Subcontinent and Southeast Asia. It is classified by IUCN in 2008 as Least Concern as it occurs in many protected areas, is tolerant to some degree of habitat modification. It was one of three species of civet to be found in Hong Kong at the time, although the largest, the large Indian civet has since been almost certainly extirpated.

It was fifty years ago from the time that I am sitting in my favourite armchair in my tumbledown cottage in North Devon, with my wife's pet crow in the kitchen making strange barking noises that it has learned off the smaller of our dogs, but I remember the sights, sounds and smells of that lunchtime in the tiny village like it was yesterday. Uncle Simeon and I spent what seemed like two or three happy hours watching the pair of civets (for the creature I had seen had a slightly shyer mate hiding in the darker interstices of the cage) playing happily in the branches of some long-dead tree that had been placed in the cage by one of Uncle Simeon's bevy of staff. The civets chased each other through the branches with what seemed like boundless energy, engaged in a glorious game of catch-as-catch-can. They even came and took juicy morsels of fruit from our hands. It was a magickal afternoon and I cherish it still.

Uncle Simeon was not the only expat who had a private zoo. An elderly army officer living just around the corner from Peak School had two large cages in his garden which was overlooked by one of the small roads that crisscrossed that part of The Peak. One contained a rather motheaten Asiatic black bear, and the other a pair of coatis. But even at age seven, I knew that these animals were not *bona fide* Hong Kong species, and so - although I enjoyed it when either my Mother, Ah Ling, or Ah Tim took me past them on our afternoon walks - they did not give me the frisson of excitement that I got every time I was able to tick off one of the species from the checklist contained in *The Hong Kong Countryside.*

Although I had been terrified of him from the first time that I met Uncle Simeon, the barriers soon dropped and I found myself increasingly at ease in the company of the irascible old man, and his ladyfriends. However, our acquaintanceship was to be a disappointingly short one. My Father had six weeks annual leave owing to him in the early summer of 1966, and when we returned to Hong Kong in the July, he told me that Uncle Simeon had died. I have never found out exactly who he was, although all the evidence that I can remember would suggest that he was a very important man indeed, but he remains in the more obscure byways of my brain as one of the people who was unwittingly responsible for making me who I am today.

I had grown up quite a lot in three years, and so - this time - I was excited about our imminent trip back to the Motherland. We were to visit my Maternal Grandparents in Hampshire, spend a few days in London, and then to Guernsey in the Channel Islands for about a month. My Paternal Grandmother living then in Chester, it was deemed that a cross country trip from Hampshire to the north of England would be too complicated to arrange, and so she came to visit us in the Channel Islands.

I was particularly pleased that we were going to the Channel Islands, because - by then - I had read most of Gerald Durrell's books and was inordinately excited at the prospect of visiting his zoo in Jersey, that was - apparently - the shape of zoos to come, and completely unlike the other zoos that I had visited in my short but eventful life.

Both then and now, most children of the age that I was in May 1966 did not (and do not) read for pleasure, and the books aimed at kids had more pictures than words, and what plotlines there were, were simple and facile. But I have already told you what I thought about Janet and John and their stupid dog, and how I had been given my first C S Lewis book the Christmas before, and adored it. I have also explained how my Mother taught me to read, and instilled a love of books into me which has stayed in my psyche to the present day. I have also described how she was the first to introduce me to the glorious prose and expansive vistas of Gerald Durrell, and it will - I suspect - not come as a surprise to anyone to learn that I soon became a firm fan.

One of the things that my Father *did* insist on, and something for which I shall be eternally grateful, was that all the bookshelves in the apartment were open to me, and that I was encouraged to read what was therein. Okay, this meant that I was introduced to the *Kama Sutra*, to *The Koran* (as it was spelt in the translation I read a few years later) and even *The Thoughts of Chairman Mao* some years, or even decades before most of my peers, but it did mean that even as I came to realise that the grownup world was unfair and unappealing, I was introduced to ideas and practises that would shape my burgeoning emotional life. Some of them (like one of the particularly umm interesting chapters of Vātsyāyana's prose) taught me things that I was determined to implement as soon as I could, and others, like the prose of Gerald Durrell gave me concepts that have stayed with me long after my obsessive desire for sexual experimentation became a diabetes-quashed memory.

It is ironic that neither of my parents were particular fans of Gerald Durrell. In fact, after his 1975 divorce, he became yet another of the people (like Oscar Wilde, and the aforementioned Gandhi and the Duke of Windsor) about whom my Father would snort derisively, and my Mother would always change the subject as quickly as possible if he was ever mentioned at the dinner table.

It was my Godmother who was the Gerald Durrell fan. Phyllis Greenfield had been a friend of my mother when she was doing her teacher training during the earliest days of the Second World War, and upon my arrival into the world in August 1959, she became my Auntie Phyll. She was someone else that my Father didn't like, but she was always very kind to me, and fed my burgeoning library every Christmas and Birthday. Somehow she had been a friend, or an associate at least, of Enid Blyton, and so I received several of her books before they had actually been released.

For reasons which I didn't understand at the time, but probably had more to do with class consciousness and snobbery than literary merit, Peak School had a blanket ban on 'comics'. I was to discover the glorious anarchy of *The Beano, The Dandy* and *The Beezer* some years later, but for the moment the only such periodical that I read was a weekly 'magazine for children' called *Treasure,* which did indeed contain comic strips, but they were ones of an educational or morally uplifting tone.

There was the ongoing saga of adventures in 'Princess Marigold Land' where - each week - the eponymous protagonist (a youngish girl, probably the spiritual forerunner of the current crop of Disney Princess movies which so delight my granddaughter) each week managed to thwart the evil plans of the Wizard Weezle (as I think his name was) in a wholesome manner. There were the adventures of 'Cuddles the Jam Rabbit', a rabbit who liked jam and always made a mess whilst eating it, and of course 'Beep Beep the Bubble Car', who carried out his activities selling bent MOTs from some lock up in Lambeth. (I made up the last bit).

I have a vague idea that it was published by the same people who published *Look and Learn* (a publication for older children which I read until I discovered *The New Musical Express* when I was about fourteen) and so, there were regular educational features, and - by happenstance (although I tend to believe my old friend and mentor Tony 'Doc' Shiels when he growls that "there's no such focking thing as a focking coincidence yer Saxon bollix", in a Hibernian accent rich as figgy pudding) - a week or so before we left Hong Kong for the UK, there was a feature in which 'Beep Beep the Bubble Car' travelled around London with a stupid crow whose name I don't remember (although I do remember that he always heeded help with his schoolwork in the shape of solving a riddle or a maze or suchlike).

As a result of this, I drew up an amazingly detailed (for a six-year-old) list of places that I wanted to see. These included Trafalgar Square, (I wanted to feed the pigeons, and I also owned the Ladybird biography of Lord Nelson), St Paul's Cathedral (I was an avid stamp collector, and the commemorative stamps that had been issued the year before to mark the passing of Sir Winston Churchill featured the iconic image of the dome of St Paul's during the Blitz) and Leicester Square tube station (I have no idea). But the most important things on the list were the Natural History Museum and London Zoo. I had visited both with my Grandfather three years before, but I had only been four years old and my memory of the visits was very patchy.

Only two things really stick in my mind from those first visits. One was visiting the famous Guy the Gorilla, now stuffed in the Natural History Museum, but then very much alive in Regent's Park. The other memory, however, is far more important in terms of my own family history.

On one of the landings of the Natural History Museum was a stuffed greyhound. His name was 'Mick the Miller' and he was the most famous racing greyhound of all time. He was also - allegedly - a canid directly responsible for my presence here on the planet. According to my Grandad, it had been a bet of a tanner (sixpence) on this sagacious and fleet-footed hound that had allowed him to take my Gran out in their first date. He had been a gallant (if slightly inept) fighter pilot in the Royal Flying Corps, and she had been a beautiful young land girl, dashing enough to wear trousers and drive a motorbike, but still aristocratic and charming enough to catch the attention of Flight Lieutenant Rawlins who was a scion of the family responsible for circus and funfair rides across the South of England. She also had lovely legs (according to my Grandad).

My Gran's family who were shabby gentry fallen on hard times, had not actually sunk so low as to accept someone they believed was a Gypsy and a Jew into their family (my Father believed that he was both, I don't mind either way even though it means that I am officially unemployable under the Nuremberg Laws) and so the young couple eloped after a shockingly short time, although whether this was still courtesy of Mick the Miller, history doesn't relate.

However, there is one thing wrong with my grandfather's story. It is complete nonsense. Mick the Miller was indeed a male brindle Greyhound. He is still celebrated as the first great racing greyhound to compete in England (although he was born in Ireland). Despite a short three-year racing career, his achievements were highly publicised around the world and by the end of his career he had become an icon in the sport.

Even now, he is one of the most famous racing greyhounds of all time. His achievements include winning nineteen races in a row, including the English Greyhound Derby on two successive occasions. He suffered an injury at Wimbledon Stadium whilst racing which broke the streak, and once recovered was beaten in the attempt to win a third Derby title. He went on to appear in films, and is still considered by many to be one of the greatest sporting heroes in the UK.

But it wasn't born until four years after my mother in 1926, and for my grandfather's story to be true, this doughty greyhound would have had to have been whelped sometimes during the First World War. By the time my grandfather told me the story he was 78, which six decades before I write this was a much older age than it appears to be now. So, whether he just got his greyhounds mixed up, which seems unlikely as Mick the Miller was allegedly the first British racing greyhound, or whether he was suffering from the beginnings of the senile dementia which was eventually to kill him, or whether he was just making up an amusing story for his grandson, I have no idea. But I'm slightly disappointed to have found out the truth.

However, in the intervening years, my knowledge of the natural world had expanded massively, and I had another list (which I portentously named my 'animal itinerary') of things that I wanted to see in both locations.

We flew from the old Kai Tak airport on Kowloonside, Hong Kong on four different occasions during the 1960s, always on old BOAC Boeing 707s, and - to be quite honest I cannot really differentiate between the different times. What I do remember is that we would always stop off at Karachi airport to refuel, and that it was always so unutterably hot there that both Richard and I would be copiously and messily sick. We would always stop off at New Delhi airport, where I was impressed to see that you could buy tableaux featuring stuffed mongooses (yes, they are mongooses not mongeese) facing up to equally stuffed Indian cobras. Rudyard Kipling had already led me to expect this sort of thing from the subcontinent, although I was not sure whether it still went on post 1947 when the British had left. My parents had been so scathing about Gandhi and Nehru, (although it has to be said that they were also surprisingly scathing about Lord Mountbatten, the final Viceroy) and the six-year-old me could well imagine these newly independent iconoclasts, being so anti-British that they banned mongoose/cobra interaction purely so they could thumb a nose at my beloved Kipling (the poet of Empire said my Mother).

We also stopped off somewhere in the Middle East, either in Lebanon (then known as the 'Riviera of the Eastern Mediterranean' and a must go-to spot for the jetset) or somewhere in what was still called 'The Persian Gulf'. On one massively disappointing occasion it was Athens.

About the only thing that I enjoyed learning back at Peak School were the Greek Myths. The teacher had a thick coffee-table type book with exquisite water colours and line drawings and a whole multitude of amazing stories about the adventures of Perseus, Theseus and other heroes. The book started with Gaia and ended with the beginning if the Trojan War, and I devoured it whenever I had the chance, and always looked forward to the lessons. Ever since the Internet gave me access to Amazon and eBay, I have been trying to find a copy of it (and the other books that shaped my childhood such as an equally enormous tome on Red Indian lore, which told you how to make feather head-dresses, impressive fake eagle claws, and a whole slew of vicious looking weapons) but have never managed to find either, if any of you reading this can help me out, please contact me through the CFZ website.

So when I heard that we were going to stop off at Athens, my young mind went into overdrive, and somehow I imagined that we would be visiting sacred groves where centaurs grazed. When we - instead - found ourselves in a dull modern airport, I was massively disappointed. My father bought me a postcard of a slutty looking Aphrodite with a fag (cigarette not American homosexual) sticking out of the corner of her mouth. He thought it massively funny, but I didn't understand it at all.

We arrived in London, which was much greyer, duller and dirtier than I had been led to believe from my reading of *Treasure* and the adventures of Paddington Bear. It was May 1966, and - when I met and made friends with Mick Farren a lifetime later - he told me that 'Swinging London' was in full swing, and its nightclubs were full of the grooviest people on earth. However, we were in a shabby hotel somewhere in the heart of the teeming Metropolis, and all I can remember was that my brother (aged three) screamed incessantly, I had an infected hangnail on my thumb upon which my Father had to perform a crude operation with a big darning needle and a bottle of Dettol, and it was my first experience of hard shiny lavatory paper.

My Mother went out to - as she called it - 'forage for dinner' doing her hunter/gatherer thing around the local cornershops and delis. I can't remember what we ate, but I do remember having to drink some rather nasty sour apple juice that made me feel sick. What I *do* know is that we managed to pack an enormous lot into the next few days, and that I saw all the places on my list (even the tube station that I have no idea why I wanted to visit, I fed the birds (tuppence a bag) in Trafalgar Square, and we saw London Zoo twice; the second time getting to Regent's Park by boat through the canals of Little Venice!

My memories of the zoo are fairly fragmented. I remember seeing the back of a sleeping aardvark and hearing its stentorian snore. I remember going for a ride on the back of an elephant, and - during a ride on a tame pony - causing a minor furore by trying to dismount when the animal was still moving just like one of the characters in *The High Chaparral*. I remember the Snowdon aviary, and not being impressed by the name of the architect because I didn't know who Princess Margaret was, but thinking the thing to be spectacularly ugly, although I was impressed both by the Mappin Terraces and the nocturnal house.

But it is the Natural History museum that sticks in my mind most. I remember the huge preserved *Rafflesia* - the largest flower in the world, and the huge blue whale, which - at the time - I still believed was a stuffed specimen rather than a model. I remember the dinosaurs and the enormous butterfly collection, but the thing that impressed me most, and indeed still did the last time that I saw it, was the Rowland Ward pavilion which included huge stuffed animals portrayed on what I fondly believed was a realistic diorama of the African veldt.

This, added to my memories of my Mother's moss gardens a few years earlier, was the beginning of a lifelong fascination with dioramas, which led me to attempt them with model railway sets, toy soldiers, and - eventually - with tropical and sub-tropical fishtanks, the apogee of which is a fishtank in my sitting room at home in Devon which is an attempt by me to recreate a vista of a place where I spent some of my happiest childhood hours. But more of that in a later chapter.

After a few days in London we travelled to Hampshire where my Gran and Grandad lived, and then we flew to Guernsey where we spent the next four weeks.

Although I had started my investigations into seashore wildlife back in Hong Kong, it was my time in the Channel Islands at the age of six during which I first got my head around littoral biology. For about forty years I was convinced that I had imagined it all, but when in 2006, Corinna and I visited Jersey I found that the enormous expanses of clear shallow water, and the vast shore zones were just as I had remembered them. The shorelines of Guernsey are very shallow and go out a long way, and there are a fascinating selection of different types of habitat. As a child, well -meaning relatives gave me a lot of books, mostly published by Ladybird, or in the excellent Observer's Guides, which detailed different aspects of the British countryside and shoreline. And I studied them avidly. So avidly, in fact, that I knew much of them by heart.

There was one problem. Although I could recite much of the Ladybird book of rockpools by rote, I didn't live in Britain. I tried very hard to extrapolate the animals that I saw around me in Hong Kong from the animals described in the books but to no avail.

It was all very well having a book which told you about the winkles, cockles and dog whelks of the British Isles, but such a reference work was completely useless when you were trying to identify cowries, cone shells and giant clams, let alone horseshoe crabs and mantis shrimps. But for the first time I was in a place where I could wander untrammelled (something I hadn't realised about the vast expanses of beach at low tide was that my parents could sit down on deckchairs and keep a watchful eye on us whilst we wandered for what seemed like miles) and where I could actually identify the creatures I caught.

And so I wandered for hours with a small net and a couple of jam jars with string handles, catching, watching and generally grokking the magnificently diverse fauna of the Guernsey shoreline. Of course my first forays into the world of marine aquaria ended in tragedy. I had spent a very productive day hunting and took two large jars of shrimps, crabs and tiny dabs (flatfish no bigger than the top joint of my thumb) back to the guesthouse where the landlady had told me indulgently that I could keep what I was already privately thinking of as my marine zoo. The morning after I ran downstairs excitedly to find that most of them were dead or dying, except for the crabs which were merrily feasting upon the corpses of their unlucky fellows.

With tears gushing down my face I grabbed the jars and ran out of the house down to the jetty which was only a few hundred yards away. Luckily the tide was in and I poured what remained of my marine zoo back into the sea from whence they had came, and vowed that I would never again try and keep marine creatures as pets until I knew better how to keep them happy. It was a promise that I didn't completely keep, but it was a policy that I have pretty much followed ever since. Over the years I have tried to keep rockpool tanks on several different occasions with more or less unsuccessful results, but I suspect that sooner or later I shall try again, because each time I do I am convinced that I shall succeed.

I still remember the excitement of the day that I first found beadlet sea anemones. They were in a tiny pool left by the tide on the leeside of a rocky outcrop. Like the young protagonists of L P Hartley's *Eustace and Hilda* I watched, fascinated as they caught and devoured a small shrimp, but unlike the titular Eustace and his big sister I knew enough about the subject not to try and rescue the hapless crustacean. Overjoyed by this discovery I ran back up the beach to where my parents were sitting, and dragged them back down the beach to see. But the beach was, as I have already described, a very large one, and there were lots of rocky outcrops, and I never found the rockpool or its inhabitants again.

Above the tideline there were sand dunes peppered with marram grass, and most days we would set up camp just where the dunes met the splash zone of the beach, and I became fascinated with the sand hoppers that lived in this peculiar liminal nomansland. They seemed to be neither one thing nor another; together with little insects that my Father called sand fleas, they were neither land animals nor marine ones, and I was fascinated by the way they eked out an existence amongst the rotting seaweed at the utter high tide mark.

Some days we would go for long walks along the clifftops and, again, my lifetime fondness for sea pinks and the peculiar succulent plants that live, buffeted by the salt wind, on the utter edges of the land, come from those family excursions in the May of the year that The Beatles released *Revolver.* I remember my Father bought me my first kite, which I flew on the thermals high above the springy turf of the cliffs. I named her Queen Katie, and was inconsolable when - following my Father's suggestion that I try to fly her all the way 'home' - she got stuck in a tree and I lost her forever. I remember crying my six-year-old heart out, and I remember being severely chastised by my Father for some transgression or other that I cannot remember, and I remember that a few days later I was gifted a copy of *The Voyage of the Dawn Treader* and a new kite which I immediately Christened Queen Katie II. I have no idea whatsoever what happened to 'her'.

Thus the pattern of my childhood: animals/books/physical punishment/fear continued in the remnants of the Duchy of Normandy as it had in and around the Fragrant Harbour. So it did. So it would do. And so for ever and ever, so mote it be.

Then, for a week, my Paternal Grandmother arrived for a visit and everything changed. From what I understand, my Father had an uncomfortable relationship with most of his family caused partly because of his treatment of me, partly because of his drinking, and partly because of the Colonial *pukka sahib* persona which he had adopted since going overseas. My Grandfather had died sometime in the decade before I was born, as a result of injuries sustained whilst in the Royal Horse Artillery during the First World War. I was terrified, because my Father told me that she was a witch (and so, according to my cousins, she was) but at that stage I identified witches with the evil ones from the pages of the Narnia books. And so another slice of terror entered my life. This is totally unfair on my Father's Mother who was a kind, if somewhat straight-laced old lady. But she had a shock of white hair, was nearly blind (from the glaucoma for which I am tested every year, and because of which the remnants of the National Health Service still give me free eye tests.

There was no love lost between My Father and my Grandmother. My Father once told me later in my childhood that he didn't love his Mother, but that he respected her greatly. This came as an enormous culture shock to me, as the idea of someone *not* loving either of their parents was something that I truly didn't understand. I found out many years that she actually had been a witch, and that she had initiated at least one of my young cousins into the craft. I grew up to be a Pagan fellow traveller (if I can steal terminology from the Fifth International) and reasonably successfully graft together the precepts of the Goddess with those of the man Jesus, whom I believe was a very real historical character and laid down a succinct and admirable list of rules to live by. At the same time I try to leave the lore of the Church of England behind, finding it judgemental and often vulgar, and do my best to give the teachings of both St Paul and Gerald Gardner as wide a berth as possible, as I believe they were both self-serving oiks, who - intentionally or not - perverted rich and beautiful ideas for their own ends.

But I digress.

As I have already intimated, the main reason that I had been excited about going in holiday to the Channel Islands was that I was a Gerald Durrell fanboy *par excellence.* And for months I had been telling anyone who would listen that visiting Jersey Zoo would be a unique experience, because Gerald Durrell had invented a new kind of zoo and that it was going to be something completely different to anything that we had experienced before.

Well it wasn't. It was crap.

And for many years it remained one of the biggest disappointments in my young life. My first impressions of it were that it looked home-made, and that some of the cages looked less impressive than the big hen coops where Gran and Grandad kept their chickens. I had been particularly looking forward to seeing the tuataras, but all there was to see was a ramshackle arrangement that looked like a badly made lean-to garage, and the pair of unique reptiles, which - whilst they looked a little like lizards were nothing of the sort - were nowhere to be seen.

I am sure that there must have been something worthwhile there, but to a downtrodden six-year-old for whom Gerald Durrell had assumed an almost Godlike status, it was a horrid shock. Six years later I read Durrell's book *Catch me a Colobus* which explained a little about what had happened. Durrell and his then wife Jacquie had been on a series of extended trips, either making films or catching animals, but were shocked when they came back from the extended visit to Malaya and the Antipodes which is described in *Two in the Bush* to find that - in Durrell's words – "my precious zoo was looking shabby and unkempt and that it was almost bankrupt". Durrell took over direct day to day management of the zoo, and the project was eventually saved.

I found out more when I read Douglas Botting's biography of Gerald Durrell many years afterwards. Apparently he had started the zoo with a bloke called Ken Smith with whom he had worked at Whipsnade, and been on several of his more high profile expeditions. It appears that Smith was Durrell's business partner, and had been manager of the zoo for its first four years of existence. Apparently there was a massive falling out between the two men, which resulted in Smith leaving the island and moving to Devon where he started a number of zoos, most notably Exmouth, which I remember with no great fondness and which was (according to Getty Images) closed on humanitarian grounds in 1980.

On first reading Botting's book over the Christmas of 2002, I had a quick shufti online to see if I could find any corroborating evidence, and found plenty. I wrote Smith off as a bad, or at least a misguided, egg and thought very little about him for the next fifteen years. However, about an hour before writing these words I went back online and found that in the intervening decade and a half Smith's reputation has been through some sort of sea change, mainly due to a book by Russell Tofts, which I finally got around to reading as I finished preparing this manuscript for publication.

And boy was it an eye opener.

I already knew from Douglas Botting's biography of Durrell that he was a prodigious drinker, and an out of control alcoholic for much of his life, and that he could also be a bit of a dick. It appears from what Russell writes that there were faults on both sides. Gerald Durrell was indeed a bit of a dick to Ken, but – then again – they were totally different people with different mindsets and different views of what a zoo should be. To Gerry, Ken was dull and money oriented. To Ken, Gerry was an annoying hedonist with very little grasp of the realities of day to day existence.

But it also looks as if Ken left voluntarily rather than being pushed. And then that – for the rest of his life – Gerry tried to expunge him from his personal history.

But that is not the weirdest thing. It turns out that in the years leading up to the Second World War, Ken Smith worked as an insurance agent for the very same company that both my grandfathers worked for, and in the same area of the Cotswolds. They must've known each other. And then, even more peculiarly, I found myself quoted in the pages of the book, in the very same passage that I had been hoping to expand. The universe truly is a very strange place.

And the book also tells us quite a lot about the way that reputations are made and lost both before, and in these days when the information superhighway has blazed its inimitable way through all of our lives, and also underlines the fact that who are the good guys and who are the bad guys is very much a matter of historical perspective.

But back in 1966, visiting the zoo was the first big cultural disappointment of my young life, and I remember being very tearful as a result of this; something which - once again - provoked my father's ire, and probably (although I can't actually remember whether it did or not) resulted in another of my Father's stern Victorian beatings. These not only hurt like hell, but were both humiliating and upsetting. My poor Father seemed to truly believe that sparing the rod did, indeed, spoil the child, and often preceded the chastisement with a lecture of the "this is going to hurt me more than it will hurt you" variety. And afterwards, secure in the knowledge that he had carried out his holy duty, he would tell everyone about it. I still have a horrible memory of one Christmas in Hong Kong when - the day after I had been caned for having had the worst school report I had ever been given (and that is saying quite a lot) the family were out for a brisk constitutional, and we met a family whose children were in the same class as me, and whom I disliked massively.

My Father proceeded to tell them all how he had caned my bottom on the previous day, and then asked me in front of them whether I had deserved it, and whether I was pleased that I had been beaten for the good of my character. There was only one acceptable answer to that, and as I gave it I could see the unctuous grins of my schoolfellows, and could foretell the barrage of teasing and vitriol that would be awaiting me when I returned to Peak School after the holidays. I was not wrong.

The whole experience of visiting Les Augres Manor was such an unpleasant and traumatic one, that I didn't go back for over forty years. However, on my return at the age of 47, I knew far more about life, the universe and Durrell than I had done back in

1966, and Corinna and I had a lovely time and were very much impressed with what we saw. Indeed, I think that Jersey Zoo is one of the best zoos I have ever visited, certainly the best British (yeah, I know that the Channel Islands are Crown Dependencies rather than *de facto* parts of the United Kingdom, but you know what I mean) zoos that I have ever visited, and certainly the best small zoo that I have seen anywhere in the world.

We still had several more weeks left of our stay on Guernsey, and I looked forward to many more hours of Marine Zoological studies. Once I had got my head around the fact that I was not going to be able to keep my makeshift jam jar aquaria going for more than an hour or so, my relationship with my studies was a much more comfortable one.

One day at very low tide, I found an ormer; one of the creatures for which the Channel Islands are best known. Ormers are the British term for various members of the abalone tribe; large ear-shaped gastropods which are apparently very good to eat, and which also reveal great stocks of Mother of Pearl nacre on the insides of their shells.

Ormers are considered a great delicacy in the British Channel Islands. Overfishing has led to a dramatic depletion in numbers since the latter half of the 19th century.

"Ormering" is now strictly regulated in order to preserve stocks. The gathering of ormers is now restricted to a number of "ormering tides", from January 1 to April 30, which occur on the full or new moon and two days following that. No ormers may be taken from the beach that are under 80 mm in shell length. Gatherers are not allowed to wear wetsuits or even put their heads underwater. Any breach of these laws is a criminal offence which can lead to a fine of up to 5,000 or six months in prison. The demand for ormers is such that they led to the world's first underwater arrest, when a Mr. Kempthorne-Leigh of Guernsey was illegally diving for ormers, and was arrested by a police officer in full diving gear.

I sat back on my haunches and watched this elaphantine sea snail amble slowly but determinedly across a seaweed covered rock, leaving a wide wake of bare stone behind it. A few days later, high above the tideline I found the empty shell of an even larger specimen, which I kept in pride of place in my seashell collection, and it is presumably still in the possession of my ex-Father in law, unless of course he got bored with the shells and threw them away.

During the period when my Grandmother had been staying with us, my Father had rented a hire car, and - as a family we went off to explore the island. Sadly, I remember little of this except for several visits to a tiny chapel in the St Andrew district that was covered in seashells, and mosaic pottery.

It was created in 1914, by Brother Dodat, who planned to create a miniature version of the grotto and basilica at Lourdes, the Rosary Basilica. Some articles in the *Daily Mail* said that it "is the smallest functioning chapel in Europe, if not the world". The chapel is non-denominational. The chapel was originally built by Brother Dodat in March 1914 (measuring 9 feet long by 4.5 feet wide). After taking criticism from other brothers, Dodat demolished the chapel. He finished a second chapel in July 1914 (measuring 9 feet by 6 feet). However, when the Bishop of Portsmouth visited in 1923, he could not fit through the door, so Dodat again demolished it. The third and current version of the chapel started soon after the last demolition, and measures 16 feet by 9 feet. Dodat went to France in 1939 and died there, never having seen his chapel finished.

We also paid various visits to the island of Sark and the even smaller island of Herm. My memories of these two islands are all mixed up with each other half a century later, but I do remember my parents being very impressed to learn that Sark was the last feudal society in Europe, a state of affairs that persisted until 2008, and - from what I can gather - is still in existence in a kind of bastardised form with the Seigneur being a semi-hereditary ruler. My best memory of these visits was (I think) on Herm, when - whilst stalking through the long grass, picking wildflowers, and generally trying to get on with my life, I came face to face with a wild rabbit. We were only about a foot apart, and my immediate thought was that it was a cat of some description, but then it pricked up its long ears and bobbled away through the undergrowth, leaving me rather pleased with a wildlife encounter which was nothing to do with anyone else and completely my own.

About a week before our leaving the Channel Islands, my Grandfather was taken ill, and my Mother had to fly back to the mainland to care for him. I have no memory of what his ailments were, but apparently they were serious enough for my Mother to have to stay in England for a month or so, whilst my Father flew back to Hong Kong with me and my brother. The last few days in Guernsey were not happy ones. It was bucketing down with rain, and so, Richard and I were forced to stay in the guest house sitting room playing with the two resident cats, whilst my Father had long interminable telephone calls with my Mother in Hampshire. Even at the age of six I realised that my Father was convinced that my Grandparents were just being manipulative, that they had never forgiven my Father for having taken their daughter to foreign lands from which she only occasionally returned, and were not above pulling a fair degree of chicanery in order to ensure some quality daughter-time. The fact that I am pretty sure that it was my Mother who dragged my long suffering Father into the Colonial Service, so she could experience for herself the things she had only ever read about in *Sanders of the River*, never occurred to them.

My only memory of the trip back to England, was that the flight was continually delayed because of bad weather, and that we were stuck in a German airport for two days because of fog, whilst my little brother cried incessantly for Mummy.

Apart from that, Dad bought be my first Biggles book, and a War Comic about someone called 'Battler Britain' who flew a Hawker Hurricane catapulted off the deck of some sort of merchant ship. I had books, I had chocolate, and my Father was too busy dealing with my fractious younger sibling to pay me much attention.

And best of all, I would soon be back in my beloved Hong Kong. I felt an unfamiliar emotion.

I   was   happy.

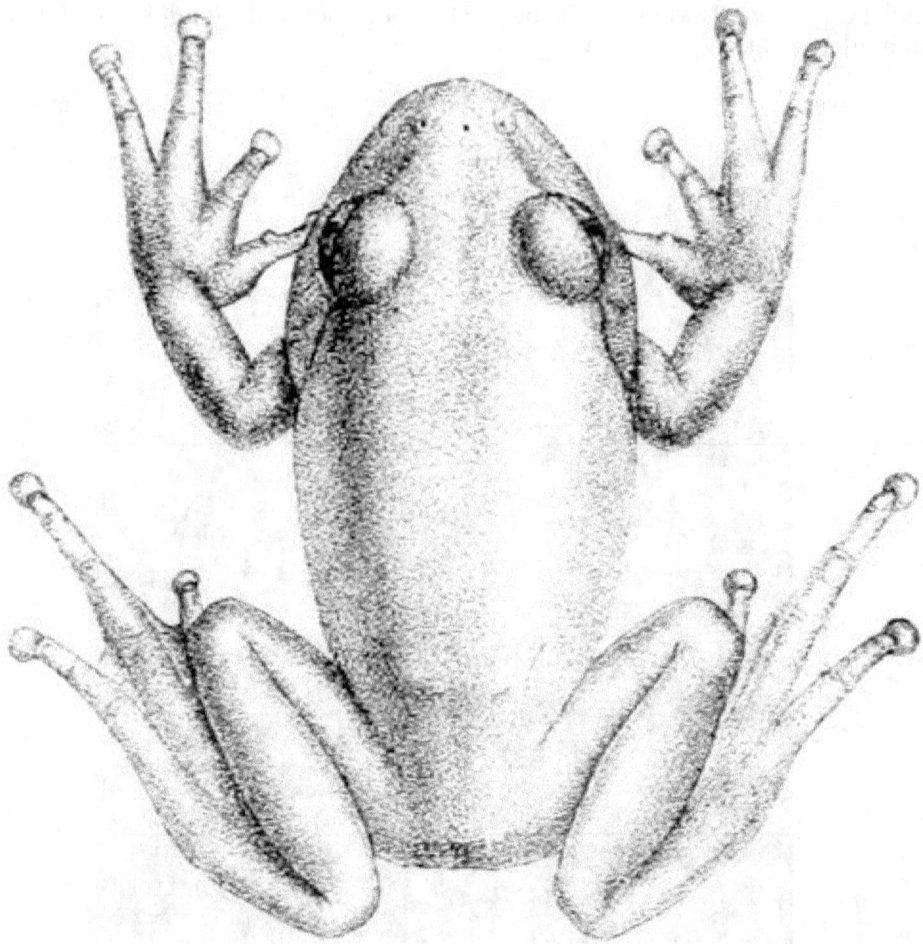

CHAPTER FIVE
The Bathroom Nature Table

Getting up every day and going through this again and again is hard.

Charles Manson

So, for the first (and not the last) time in my life, I tried to start a museum. That September, when I started my new year at school, my classroom had, for the first time, a Nature Table. And it was pretty bollocks, to my way of thinking. On each of my visits to London, as you have read, I had been taken to the Natural History Museum in South Kensington.

It was, and still is, one of my favourite places in the world. On my more recent visits there it has gone down quite considerably in my opinion, because it has decided that it is its role in the world to be an educational resource for Britons of all ages, and from all social backgrounds, rather than a meeting place for the cognoscenti from across the Empire. When I first went there I found myself feeling that I was part of a continuum that went back via Darwin to Pliny the Elder, and I felt myself having a truly religious experience. Alongside my fellow seekers after truth I gazed in silence and awe at case after case of preserved animals, and felt that I truly was worshipping at the great altar of a cathedral dedicated to the glory of Mother Nature.

I do not want to be a grumpy old git, although I am rapidly approaching the age when that is a perfectly valid ideology to adopt, but I truly feel that - just like the Church of England - in re-evaluating their approach to appeal to a wider demographic, many British museums will end up appealing to no-one. Certainly, although I understand why the museum does not anymore sponsor the killing of animals for exhibits, and - as a vegetarian, and fellow traveller of the more radical animal rights activist community – it is a decision with which I have to agree on moral grounds. And I understand the motivation behind clever, imaginative and well-designed interactive exhibits, aimed at stimulating inquisitive young minds. But I seriously doubt whether any of the hundreds of noisy school children who bustled along the long stone corridors came away feeling like they had become part of a continuum that led back to anyone except possibly one of the more crass Children's TV presenters.

But my first visits to the Natural History Museum had left me with a very high bar to aim for, and, as the classroom nature table didn't even begin to emulate that bar, and so I decided to do something of my own. The apartment in which we lived in Mount Austin Mansions had two bathrooms; one which was an *en suite* appended to my parents' bedroom at the end of a corridor, and the other was the one used by my brother and me, and those visitors who paid us a visit. But there was a third lavatory, in a remarkably large room in the opposite corner of the flat to Richard's and my bedroom, and it was very seldom used. But it had a very wide windowsill, and several small tables that weren't actually used for much, and I knew exactly what I wanted to use it for. And - showing a level of liberal understanding which I never understood then, and don't really understand now - my Father (my Mother still being in Hampshire with his in-laws) gave me permission to use the windowsill and a small table opposite the lavatory pan, as my own Nature Table (although I always privately called it the Downes Museum). And I diligently set to work.

To start off with I had my shell collection from various Hong Kong beaches, augmented vastly by my collection from Guernsey, and - in a valiant attempt to replicate the glorious dioramas that had so impressed me in South Kensington - I exhibited them in what I thought was a massively imaginative matter - by displaying them in the lid of our old twin tub washing machine which had blown up when my Father realised that he didn't know how to use it - on a bed of playsand and filled with water. I had even gone to the effort of dissolving a pack of kitchen salt in it, so the seashells would be exhibited in their natural state.

At the age of seven this made perfect sense to me, and I proudly explained my methodology to all the people who I ushered into the bathroom to gaze with wonder upon my Nature Table. But it wasn't just a polymorphous collection of seashells. I also had a large and impressive swallowtail caterpillar which sat, cheerfully, munching its way through the leaves of a small citrus plant that had been given to the family as a 春節 present the previous Chinese New Year. Sadly, before the impressive six inch larva had been able to pupate, it fell off the plant, and wandered into my shell exhibit where it drowned in salt water. I was distraught.

However, my proudest exhibit was a small, wrinkled and very dead foam nesting frog, probably *Polypedates megacephalus*. It was actually completely desiccated, and - these days, with the benefit of half a century's experience - I would have kept it as it was. But I remembered how many of the soft bodied creatures which were on display in the British Museum (Natural History) had been bottled in some sort of preservative. So I determined to find out what this liquid was.

I always did my best not to interact with my father more than I needed to, and so, I asked the only other adult authority figure available to me; Ah Tim. She, bless her, gave me the benefit of her vast experience in cooking both Oriental and Occidental cuisine. Apparently one of her previous employers at some point between arriving penniless in Hong Kong in 1949 during the second bloody Civil War between the Kuomintang and the Chinese Communist Party, and starting to work for the Downes family fourteen years later, had yearned for the pickled onions that were such a part of his life in rural England, and which were unavailable in Hong Kong. And so Ah Tim learned to make pickled onions, and when I asked how to preserve something in fluid, she gave me a bottle of clear vinegar, which I carefully used to preserve my frog.

As anyone with even the slightest knowledge of biochemistry will doubtless know, it did nothing of the sort, and - instead - started to dissolve the wretched creature. And, even the seven-year-old Jonathan realised that a semi dissolved batrachian in a foul smelling soup was unlikely to impress anyone, so - with great regret - I consigned it to the lavatory, where it left an unfortunate stain on the porcelain which no amount of scrubbing was ever able to remove.

I have been working with my childhood friend Richard Muirhead on a book about the mystery animals of Hong Kong in a desultory sort of way for many years now, and as part of my ongoing research for this project, which will eventually reach fruition (honest) I subscribe to an internet newsgroup called Old Hong Kong, which occasionally does what it says on the tin and sends me photographs of Hong Kong in the years between the wars, and the post-war years before it became the unbridled mouthpiece of *lassaiz faire* (and non-*lassaiz faire*) capitalism, and was still a bastion of colonial architecture, and – possibly even more important – colonial values.

Sadly, most of the time the old Hong Kong newsgroup just sends out up to forty invitations to invest in the foreign exchange market, buy Viagra, or look at amusingly illiterate but semi-graphic pornography which is mildly embarrassing when someone is looking over my shoulder as I do my emails. However, I continued to subscribe to the newsgroup and despite the unkind slurs from my friends and co-workers, not to mention my nearest and dearest, it is not because of emails from people like XxX Dubai Aunties XxX with titles such as **[old_hongkong] 18+ Compilation of Girls with Niplslipz** and **[old_hongkong] ..:: $ex with Asian women in Australia ::..**, but because occasionally I get a gem.

Like this one.

In amongst all the unwanted, though mildly amusing rubbish, was one called **[old_hongkong] When Insect Attack what Happen**, which included a picture which to many people probably looks like a badly photoshopped excerpt from a third-rate horror movie, but brought back vivid memories of some encounters from my childhood that I had completely forgotten.

Between the years of 1966 and 1970 on several occasions (my brain is trying to say that this happened every summer but this is, to be honest, just wishful thinking) there were enormous swarms of dragonflies, which terrorised children at the school. When I say swarms, I am talking of an obscene mass of insects, tens or even hundreds of thousands strong, which appeared to have forgotten the typical good-mannered hunting strategies common to the *Odonata* and flew willy-nilly into each other, into walls, and into the faces of the terrified children.

From memory, they were an orange/brown colour, which corresponds well with *Pantala flavescens,* which is, according to none other than James Tutt – one of the founding fathers of modern entomology (cited by Wikipedia) – the most widespread dragonfly on the planet. It is also (again, according to Wikipedia) known in Hong Kong as the 'typhoon dragonfly' as it arrives with, or shortly before the seasonal rain.

A brief look at Google indicates that these swarms still take place. According to one couple writing on their religious-themed blog **http://everydayadventuresinfaith.blogspot.com/2009/07/dance-of-dragonflies.html**

…they do indeed swarm just before the typhoon:

> "The most fascinating signal of the approaching storm was the dance of the dragonflies. As the barometric pressure changed yesterday, the dragonflies came out in swarms. As a creature of the wind and water, in the Chinese culture the dragonfly symbolizes change. Its iridescent wings are incredibly sensitive to the slightest breeze, and so we are reminded by their "dance" to heed where the proverbial winds blow lest we run into stormy weather".

They then decided to quote from Psalm 107:28-30:

> When they cried out to the LORD in their trouble,
> and he brought them out of their distress.
> He stilled the storm to a whisper; the waves of the sea were hushed.
> They were glad when it grew calm, and he guided them to their desired haven.

Which is all very well, but I have to say that I don't see the relevance.

If indeed the insects that I encountered as a child were *Pantala flavescens* then the fact that they migrate to the former British colony does solve one of the conundra that have been mildly bugging me for the last five decades.

You see, the dragonflies weren't the only species of tropical insect who – at least in the days when I lived in Hong Kong – were wont to swarm. Flying ants, termites, small beetles, aphids (which on one occasion turned up in their thousands on the ceiling in my museum bathroom and various types of Lepidoptera swarmed fairly regularly. It was only the latter that were quite as spectacular as the dragonflies. I remember in 1970 when there was a magnificent glut of silkmoths – probably Cynthia moths *Samia cynthia*. Herklots, in his seminal work *The Hong Kong Countryside* (1951), notes on page 69 that three different species of the *Danainae* or monarch butterflies were also known to swarm in the winter months in Hong Kong. I recall also seeing a swarm several-thousand-strong of a yellow and black day flying moth that forty-five years later I am completely unable to identify. However, the swarms of these other insects were all caused by mass emergences from the larval state. One used to see the adults in the process of emerging from their chrysalides, or – in the case of termites or flying ants – emerging in the tens of thousands from their communal homes.

Even as child I was aware that dragonflies emerged into adulthood after a protracted adolescence as aquatic nymphs. Indeed, I kept the nymphs of several species in my various makeshift aquaria on my bedroom windowsill and once or twice even managed to rear them to adulthood. I had always imagined that these obscene and completely daunting swarms of dragonflies terrorising the neighbourhood for more than a day had all emerged from their nymphal state at the same time. But how could they? There were very few ponds and streams on that part of Hong Kong island, and I was very familiar with the inhabitants of most of them. Sure, there were usually one or two dragonfly larvae to be seen but nothing even approaching the amount of biomass it would have taken to produce these immense swarms, which were like something from the imagination of Clark Ashton Smith.

I decided once the subject had come back into my head after a gap of (terrifyingly over half a century, to look up the causes of dragonfly swarms. Google prodded me towards a blog called **http://dragonflywoman.wordpress.com/.**

She informed me that there are two known types of swarming behaviour:

The first are – as alluded to above – migratory swarms which she describes as effectively rivers of hundreds of thousands of dragonflies all flying in a different direction and covering large distances. She says that these swarms are like bird migrations or the migrations of monarch butterflies, ie a large number of individuals travelling together between habitats and usually made up of a single species. As far as I can remember, all these insects were of the same species, however Christine L. Goforth, who is the dragonfly woman, says that one of the diagnostic characteristics of this type of swarm is that they move very quickly and may appear and disappear in a matter of minutes. She also says that the dragonflies in this type of swarm typically follow significant waterways and fly high above the ground.

The second type of swarm identified by Ms. Goforth is the static swarm. These swarms contain far fewer individuals than migratory swarms (twenty to one thousand instead of tens of hundreds of thousands) and are highly localised. Individuals in the swarm will remain restricted to a very small area (like one field, or yard, or hill) and fly in a circular or figure of eight pattern about one to twenty feet off the ground, usually over a grassy area. She goes on to say that these are feeding swarms and may contain one or several species of dragonflies in equal proportions.

Neither of these descriptions actually tick all the boxes. Although the characteristics of the swarms I encountered as a child were far more likely 'static swarms', and indeed they were usually congregated with their epicentre around a grassy area (either the playing field at Peak School or the grassy playground that apparently still exists at Mount Austin). These were in enormous numbers, and despite the fact that I (alone amongst my terrified compadres) found these swarms fascinating and did my best to observe and interact with the wallages of insects, I have no memory ever of seeing any of them hunting or eating their prey. I remember this with a fair degree of certainty because on other occasions I used to watch *Anaciaeschna jaspidea,* the common evening hawker, or the glorious *Anax immaculifrons* hunting and eating its prey and I was very aware of the hunting strategies of the *Odonata.*

I am only too aware of the fact that dragonfly woman is writing nearly half a century after my experiences, and that times have changed for invertebrates (as they have changed for all of us) in the intervening years. For example, I remember in 1971 catching, marking and releasing nearly 400 specimens of the two cabbage whites *Pieris brassicae* and *P. rapae* simply in one day within the confines of my garden here in North Devon and the garden of Well Cottage next door. These days one is lucky to see three or four in a day. So with the photograph sent to me in a parcel of soft pornography proving that my memory is not defective, what actually were these dragonfly swarms on Victoria Peak, Hong Kong Island, during the years when my contemporaries back in Blighty were experiencing the Swinging Sixties?

In Canada in 1979 I witnessed the beginning of the migration of monarch butterflies *Danaus plexippus* and the sheer biomass of hundreds of thousands of insects was an awesome sight that has stayed with me ever since. However, I wondered then as I wonder now, exactly where this huge number of butterflies had come from. I had been in my little suburb of Toronto all summer, and had seen the unmistakable caterpillars on milkweed plants quite commonly. But the caterpillars weren't there in their millions. I wondered then whether certain areas, and indeed certain trees, were for some reason obvious to the orange and black patterned insects, but obscure to the amateur naturalist intent on grokking this entomological experience in its fullness – designated muster points from whence the horde of butterflies could, once whatever biological trigger was necessary, fly thousands of miles down to Mexico.

I wonder whether, rather than a large swarm of migrating insects having arrived in Hong Kong just before a typhoon, the opposite could have taken place. Perhaps individual specimens *of Pantala flavescens* from all over the former British colony, the former Portuguese colony of Macau and quite probably large chunks of Guangdong Province of mainland China, had gathered together on Victoria Peak, using it as a sort of departure lounge before – with the typhoon as its impetus – beginning an enormous migration which could take them half way across Asia.

If anyone reading this can add to my knowledge of the subject, please get in touch.

During the Colonial twilight of the mid 1960s, my mother was a member of a venerable institution called The Ladies' Recreation Club (LRC).

It was there she played tennis and had morning coffee with her friends, and where - amongst other things - I learned to swim. It was exactly what the name implied; a social and sports club for the wives of Colonial Service Officers. I had assumed that, like so many other relics of Hong Kong's Imperial past, the LRC would have been swept away on the surging tides of progress. However, as I sat at my computer writing on a balmy Sunday afternoon in 2002, I entered the name into my Internet Search Engine, and there it was.

If you look at the picture on the front page of their website, you will see a patio just above the swimming pool. Back in the 1960s it boasted two large tanks containing koi carp. During the summer term, the weather in Hong Kong was so hot that primary school children used to start school an hour or so earlier in the mornings, and have the afternoons off. Invariably at least three afternoons a week, my mother would take my little brother and me down to the LRC to swim, whilst she would spend the afternoon chatting to her friends.

One of these friends was a terribly fierce-looking American lady called Mrs Ingersoll whose husband had been something to do with the Kennedy Administration. I was always terrified of her, because she was tall and thin, with blue rinsed hair, a hooked nose, pince nez glasses and a distinct aroma of gin. However, being a well brought up lad I was always polite, and when we met up at the LRC, she would take me by the hand over to the enormous tanks which held the lugubrious looking koi carp and tell me, in a miasma of gin fumes how Mr. Kennedy/Mr. President/ Her darling John (depending on how drunk she was) had adored koi, and how they could have saved him. I was only four years old when President Kennedy was shot, and was far too young to know what the fuss was about, but I know now that for many people it was the defining moment of the 1960s.

I had only the vaguest idea who President Kennedy was, and at the time my only motivation was to get away from this horrible alcoholic woman, and back into the swimming pool, so I didn't really pay much attention to the story. At the time I vaguely assumed she was trying to say that if the President had kept fish instead of being President, he wouldn't have been killed, but even for a seven-year-old this didn't make much sense. I have since vaguely wondered whether Kennedy ever had fish-ponds, either at his private residence or at the White House. Flushed by my success in locating the website for the LRC, I chased around the Internet trying to get information about whether there was, indeed, a pond full of koi carp at the

Presidential Official Residence - but to no avail. I therefore did what I always do when my avenues of research come to a sudden halt - I telephoned Nick Redfern.

Nick is an old mate of mine who is the author of several bestselling books on UFOs and conspiracy theories. He lived an uneventful life in the west Midlands where dressed in black with a shaven head, he listened to punk music and investigated UFOs, until much to everyone's surprise he met a beautiful Texan lady, upped roots and disappeared off to live near Houston. We still keep in touch on a regular basis, and help each other out with our researches. He wasn't at all surprised to have me telephone in the small hours to talk about koi carp. Much to my surprise he burst out laughing. "I've got something that you can use", he chuckled down the phone, "God knows if it's got anything to do with your story, but it's a connection between JFK and koi carp".

Ten minutes later I got the following e-mail:

"Jonny, here is the info on Agent Koi. This story is very little known even in JFK assassination circles. I don't know why he/she uses that name, maybe the story is 'fishy' or, like a koi, keeps getting bigger. But anyway this is the story.~

Agent Koi worked in US Army Intelligence from 1973-1978 and was involved with a declassification team. Koi says that in 1974 he/she read a file from 1965 that started out as a criminal investigation of five army employees. Koi did not want to specify the nature of the investigation, but it was found that three of the five had links to certain people allegedly involved in the JFK assassination at Dealey Plaza, Dallas on 22 November 1963. So the story goes, based on the 1965 investigation, the three people were in Dallas on five occasions in the ten days leading up to the assassination, and each time were filming Dealey Plaza (this info supposedly came from another army informant), the grassy knoll, and the book depositary where Oswald supposedly was etc. what became of the films is unknown, but Koi claims suspicions were raised that they were made to give the real assassins a good layout of Dealey Plaza etc. Koi says nothing conclusive was ever proved, but all five men retired within 12 months from the army on various grounds. Koi says the file he/she read was shredded. That's it."

This was a new twist. Was Mrs Ingersoll something to do with the elusive Agent Koi? Maybe her husband - a US Government Foreign Office Attache (often, according to my Cold War spy thrillers, a euphemism for high ranking CIA operative) - WAS the elusive Agent Koi. Maybe she was Agent Koi herself? Unless this is all a coincidence, it seems certain that Agent Koi was involved far earlier than the Conspiracy Theorists now believe.

So there you have it. That is the entire story as far as I know it, and as far as Nick Redfern knows it. If Mrs Ingersoll is still alive (which is doubtful as she was considerably older than my late Mother), I have no idea how to contact her. So the matter has to rest. However, if any readers are ever in Hong Kong, please do go along to the LRC in Central District and see if the koi carp tanks are still there for me...

It is mildly interesting that my introduction to the Fortean aspect of the JFK assassination took place so early in my life. After all, it was only three or four years after the dark deed had taken place.

Over the years, many of my friends from college (not the least being Nick Redfern) have become interested in various aspects of this undeniably mystifying historical event.

It has been linked with a whole string of other unfortunate deaths, most often Marilyn Monroe, and it has been suggested that there is some sort of link to a shadowy cabal set up in the wake of the Roswell crash of 1947. If you believe this set of theories, JFK was just about to reveal the truth behind this alleged UFO incident, and was shot by order of Majestic 12 to stop him revealing it.

However I once spent an evening with the editors of the British, and American, leading conspiracy theory journals, and by the end of it I didn't give a toss who had killed Kennedy.

But something that does interest me is the link between Lee Harvey Oswald, the Kennedy murder investigation, and a peculiar belief system known as Discordianism. I would not go so far as to say I am a follower, but I am certainly what the Fourth International would have called a 'Fellow Traveller', and I find the subject inalienably fascinating. Discordianism is either a parody masquerading as a religion, or a religion masquerading as a parody; it doesn't really matter which side of the coin you come down on. One of the people responsible for starting Discordianism was Omar Khayyam Ravenhurst, better known as Kerry Thornley, who together with a childhood friend called Greg Hill, who had adopted the *nom de guerre* of Malaclypse the Younger, authored the religion's text *Principia Discordia, Or, How I Found Goddess, And What I Did To Her When I Found Her.* Thornley was also known for his 1962 manuscript, *The Idle Warriors,* which was based on the activities of his acquaintance, Lee Harvey Oswald, prior to the 1963 assassination of John F. Kennedy.

There are other links with the investigation into the Kennedy assassination, but this is neither the time nor the place to look into such things. But I would strongly suggest that you do so.

Hail Eris.

I have already explained how my family had employed a family of Chinese immigrants; refugees from the mainland, in the wake of the second half of the Chinese civil war, which had seen Generalissimo Chiang-Kai-Chek and his cronies exiled to the island of Formosa. At some time after 1964, Ah-Tim and Ah-Tam had been joined by Ah-Tam's teenaged niece; another refugee, Ah-Ling; a strikingly good looking young woman with gorgeous red hair, indicating that one of her recent progenitors had come from the Philippines. My parents, not only allowed her to move in to the servant quarters at the back of our apartment, but - realising that the career path for such an attractive, though penniless, member of the human race was likely to be a sordid one - paid for her education, rather than see her end up as a prostitute in Wanchai like something out of a novel by Richard Mason. This was, as far as I am aware, a piece of pure altruism on their part, and I always think of it whenever I hear, or read, people ranting about the evils of the British Empire.

They also gave her a job; the birth of my little brother had been a painful, life threatening and difficult one for my mother, and for many years afterwards, she was in poor health. Therefore, the advent of a charming and vivacious young woman who could be a 'Baby Amah' and look after Richard (who she immediately nicknamed 'Little Pig'), and - to a certain extent, at least - babysit me, must have been a veritable godsend.

I don't want to bang on about this, because the main purpose of this narrative is to tell the story of my childhood in a land that no longer exists, rather than bellyache on about my mental health problems, but my sanity was continuing to deteriorate, and I will be the first to admit that I was not an easy child, and must have been quite hard work to deal with.

Richard and I both adored Ah-Ling, and never considered her (or indeed, any other members of her family) to be 'inferior' because they were 'servants'. They were adults, which meant they were to be treated with politeness and respect, and like her aunt and uncle, were basically considered by my brother and me to be part of our family.

For some reason, during the early months of 1967, Mummy was again absent from the Downes' household. I vaguely remember her having to go into hospital, but as both of my parents are now dead, and my brother was only three years old at the time, there is nobody I can ask, and it doesn't really matter now anyway. But, as my father was - as usual - working exceedingly long hours, and Ah-Ling took over the various maternal roles for a week or so. These included sitting out in the shade of the great banyan tree at the south-westerly corner of Mount Austin Playground, while my brother played in the dirt, and I (plastic WWII helmet jammed onto my seven year old head) searched for wildlife in the long grass. When we had tired of these activities, she would tell us stories.

Chinese folk tales tell of fox spirits called hli jīng that may have up to nine tails (Kyūbi or Kitsune in Japanese). Many of the earliest surviving stories are recorded in the *Konjaku Monogatarishū*, an 11th-century collection of Chinese, Indian, and Japanese narratives.

Many of the stories of Kitsune are reasonably well known in the west these days, mainly because of the popularity of manga, anime, and associated Japanese culture. But, try as I have, I have found non-scholarly collections of Chinese folk tales to be few and far between. What makes things worse is that, as Ah-Ling was from a partial Filipino family, and I have vague recollections that other parts of her family were from various locations in China, which is one of the largest countries on Earth, it is impossible to say now whether the origin of the folk tales that she recounted to us was Cantonese or not. Indeed, as she later went on to work with her husband in one of the more highly regarded parts of the burgeoning Hong Kong film industry (and no, this is not an euphemism), I would not have been surprised if she had utilised her talent for storytelling and made these stories up. But she told us many stories, about the adventures of fox fairies, and the human beings that they befriended, and the pantheon of characters from her stories joined the characters from the Narnia books, and other scions of juvenile English literature in the ever growing occupation of entities who lived in my head.

I particularly liked the story about how a fox fairy (whose name I have completely forgotten) made friends with two little boys called Jonathan and Richard (coincidental? I doubt it), and how the three of them went searching through the deep forest on a hillside which seemed to be very much like that of Mount Austin, in search of a ruined temple.

Ah-Ling was very protective of us, and didn't allow us the leeway that was permitted by my mother. We had to play close by her, and not wander away into the forest. I quite understood this, when it came to 'baby Richard' as I still referred to him, and - I have to admit - sometimes still think of him now (despite the fact that he is a high-ranking Army Officer) but highly resented that I, at the grand of age of seven, was not allowed to venture into the forest by myself.

As I have always noted, one of the reasons why *Prince Caspian* was always my favourite of the Narnia books, is that I could understand the social situation described whereupon the invader Telmarines were frightened of the forest, because all the adults I knew - both European and Chinese - seemed to share a similar antipathy towards the forest that surrounded us. Even back in the mid-1960s, I could not rationalise that it was because of the magical talking creatures, dwarves and satyrs, that lived there, because - sadly - I realised these creatures didn't live on this side of the wardrobe. But, hardly any of them seemed prepared to venture into the demesne of the trees, and whilst my mother (bizarrely, considering her phobia of snakes) seemed quite happy to allow me to scramble up and down the heavily wooded hillside to my heart's content, untrammelled by adult supervision, Ah-Ling, probably because she was *in loco parentis* to my father, wouldn't allow such thing! But I took careful note of these stories of hers, and made myself a silent promise that, as soon as I was able, I would venture off into the forest and up the mountain, to look for the deserted temple.

My mother returned a week later, and I think that it is probably a mark of the way that children just accept the *status quo* rather than questioning it, that I still don't know where she had been. If this was one of the modern brand of children's books that do not gloss over the gritty realism of the human existence, somewhere along the line the protagonist (me) would discover that I had missed some awful family secret. But, I sincerely doubt that this was the case. Because my mother had suffered strings of gynaecological problems following her miscarriages in Africa before I was born, which meant that her two surviving children had to be born by caesarean, I suspect that, if she did go to hospital, it was something to do with one of these sad afflictions. Sadly, for those of you expecting a dramatic piece of gothic romance here, I doubt whether there are any family secrets to be unearthed, in relation to this at least.

As soon as she was able to take my brother and me out to the playground again (and for those of you who don't remember my earlier description, it was only a hundred yards or so and across the road from the front door of our apartment block), I resumed my explorations of the hillside, but instead of looking for small wildlife in the trees, bushes, and leaf litter of the well-trodden parts of the small forest, I started to investigate areas to which I had never been before.

The forest was bisected by a tall, grey stone waterfall, which led to a small nullah and consequently to a culvert, which defined the southern edge of the playground. The watercourse was a stagnant trickle in the dry season, and a torrent in the wet. It was fed by the little stream which went through the Victoria Peak Gardens at the top of the mountain, and I was always mildly intrigued to find out why such a relatively strong stream of water could - by the time it reached the playground at the bottom - have almost completely dried up. It was only some years later, when I had mastered some of the laws of physics, that I realised that as the sun beat down on the naked rocks of the waterfall, it made them surprisingly hot - too hot to comfortably sit on at any rate - and that this heat also caused the vast majority of the water, which had entered the little nullah above the waterfall with such high hopes, to evaporate before it could reach the bottom. I knew the area between the waterfall and the steep ravine which marked the northern edge of the playground quite well. But now it was time to cross the self-imposed barrier of the waterfall and explore the woods on the southern part of the forest.

I can still remember the sights, sounds, and smells of the Hong Kong jungle, even though it has been very nearly half a century since I lived in the former British Crown colony. The trees, which covered the hillside above Mount Austin were covered in thick groves of rhododendron. Peculiarly, although I can remember them clearly, and I even remember stealing flower buds, I don't remember ever seeing them in bloom. Whether this is because the wild rhododendron do not erupt into the riot of colours displayed by their domesticated cultivars, or whether the memory of a man in his early sixties trying to recall events that took place half a century before is flawed, I don't know.

But I remember the dark greeny-grey leaves of these evergreen bushes and trees, each highly polished as if by a veritable army of faerie housemaids, like it was yesterday. Rhododendrons are quite a successful invasive species in other parts of the world, most notably in the United Kingdom, and I have been in small rhododendron forests in the UK. But they all lack the vitality and polish of their Hong Kong equivalent, and they lack the diagnostic herbal aroma of a natural rhododendron forest at the northern edge of the tropics. For rhododendron forests, when in the place that The Almighty had naturally decreed, have a peculiar aroma, almost like oregano, cooking on a freshly baked pizza. And they are home to a dazzling diversity of tiny creatures. From my earliest years I have been a devotee of butterflies, but whereas some of the butterfly families that I saw as a family have analogues within the families of butterflies found here in the UK, others don't. And it is one of the latter; a beautiful and delicate group of butterflies called *Euploea,* which are always synonymous in my mind with the Hong Kong rhododendron forest. They are closely related to milkweed butterflies like the iconic monarch, which is familiar to everyone living in north American for its mammoth yearly migrations between Canada and Mexico. For some reason *Euploea* have got the English name of `crows`, which has always seemed - to me, at least - to be a completely inappropriate appellation.

Crows are noisy, gregarious, and cheekily outgoing. They are scavengers, scroungers, and chancers, and although they are birds of which I am very fond, they have nothing in common with these beautiful, delicate, and shy forest butterflies. There are several species of these lovely butterflies in Hong Kong, but the ones that I remember best are a dark, chestnut coloured insect, which was only ever found in the thickest part of the rhododendron forest. The chestnut wings, sprinkled with a smattering of little white spots, looking - for all the world - as if some mischievous child had flicked tippex all over them, glided effortlessly between the branches, and the tiny flowering plants on the forest floor from whence they got the nectar, upon which they subsisted. They flew in a peculiarly mechanical fashion, as if they were Lilliputian ornithopters from the pages of a steampunk novel or a progressive rock album cover painted by Roger Dean. I believe that the species was *Euploea mulciber,* but, all the pictures and descriptions that I have been able to find of this species describe it as having blue patches on the forewings, and so it might have been *Euploea core.* However, after all these years, it doesn't really matter. There are four species of *Euploea,* recorded from the former British colony, but it is the fact that then - and now, when I allow myself to indulge in flights of fancy - I thought (and think) of them as the embodiment of strange guardian spirits of the jungle.

Although there were quite a few species of mammal living in Hong Kong, the larger ones had enough sense to keep out the way when they realised that a human being was blundering across their demesne. So, although I knew that three species of civet cat, the little barking deer, porcupines, and quite possibly much rarer creatures like pangolins and leopard cats, were to be found in these forests, I never saw them.

It was some years later, when on a crepuscular ramble through the forests of the Pokfulam hills together with my classmates and a wildlife officer from the Hong Kong government, that we were lucky enough to see a pangolin alive and in its own habitat. For those of you who do not know, pangolins are primitive and highly specialised mammals marked by large, hardened, overlapping platelike scales made of keratin; the same material of which our human fingernails are made. They eat insects, mostly ants and termites, and are critically threatened throughout their range.

Although, when I was a boy, they were lumped together with the anteaters and sloths in an order called the Edentates, it is now believed that their closest relatives are actually the carnivores, such as cats, dogs, bears, and seals.

I vividly remember seeing this beautiful throwback to an archaic past peering indignantly at my classmates and me, before resuming its hunt for tiny insects in the undergrowth as if nothing had happened. In the daylight, however, which is - unsurprisingly, as I was only seven years old - the only time that I wandered through the jungle untrammelled by adult supervision, the only mammals that I ever saw were the tiny, grey, musk shrews, which were named *chuchundra* in Kipling's *Jungle Book.* They are commonly known as the Asian house shrew, and it is as a nocturnal dweller in human houses that it turns up in Kipling's glorious prose. But I only saw them scuttling through the leaf letter of the forest floor as I was going about my furtive explorations.

For some reason, the forest on the far side of the great, grey stone escarpment upon which the great waterfall crashed to the ground during the rainy season, was much wilder and more impenetrable than the well explored jungle on 'my' end of the hillside. It was darker, and the lianas and other creepers hung down far more densely. One could hear the chattering of parakeets high in the forest canopy above, but I don't remember ever seeing any. Strange communal nests of various types of moth caterpillar hung down like grotesque fruit from the forest branches, and - I have to admit - that although I know perfectly well what it was written about - whenever I hear Billie Holiday singing about 'strange fruit', it is these weird bundles of microlife that come to mind. I never found out what it was that these caterpillars actually ate. I never saw them, except as part of a huge colony. Once I opened one of these nests up and tried to count the number of inhabitants, but I gave up as I was approaching a thousand, and carefully closed up my investigation hole and went on about my business. Occasionally, I would see epiphytic pitcher plants hanging off the branches, but the microclimate was not really humid enough for them here. They were much more likely to be found in the more conventional rainforest of the lower lying areas on Lantau Island, for example.

As I have written elsewhere, although the Second World War was over fourteen years before I was born, in many ways - both in Hong Kong and in the UK - the war years were the defining historical points of my young life. Hong Kong, in particular, had suffered particularly badly at the hands of the invading Japanese, and the scars were still everywhere to be seen. During the four years in which Hong Kong was under Japanese administration, the vast majority of what remained of the natural forest had been cut down for firewood, and it was one of the major goals of the colonial British government during the post war years, and of the semi-autonomous Chinese government since 1997, to replace the indigenous forests as exactly as can be managed.

I never did find out whether the forest on the side of Victoria Peak which overlooked my little kingdom of the Mount Austin playground, was indigenous or had been replaced. The fact that in the forty years since I last went there, the ruins of Grey Walls of which I have written elsewhere, have become overgrown by the jungle, whereas they were open to the sky in my day, suggests the latter. But as far as this narrative is concerned, it doesn't really matter.

Because, no matter what the history of these forests was, they still concealed some mysteries to which I - as one of the few children to go poking about away from the well-trodden paths - found myself privy.

Martin Booth, in his remarkable memoir of his childhood in Hong Kong about ten years before I went there, describes how he found the mortal remains of a Japanese soldier half-buried on the hillside. Martin's exploits lived on after him, and - 40 years before I read his book, and 30-something years before his untimely death from cancer - the longer term residents of Mount Austin Mansions remembered him and his family and told stories of how Martin had discovered some of the mysteries of the mountain. I never found any dead Japanese soldiers, nor did I find the remains of an American dive-bomber, which had allegedly been shot down by the Japanese garrison at the top of Victoria Peak and crashed into the jungle.

But I did find a tomb.

The further away I got from the waterfall, the thicker the vegetation became. The rhododendrons had been replaced by what I think are some kind of fig tree, with looping roots that pushed above the ground like fanciful drawings of sea serpents that push above the water. Each of these little loops of wooden root contained a tiny ecosystem of its own. Miniscule moss gardens covering all the colours in the spectrum between verdant green and corpse grey were the home for numerous little insects and other tiny arthropods. Normally, I would have stopped to examine them, but I had different metaphorical fish to fry.

Each of the huge tree trunks was covered in complex knotwork, made up of invasive creepers with small, heart-shaped leaves. I don't think that they were parasitic in any other way, but - like everything else in the forest - they were engaged in a bitter phototropic battle to get as much of the limited supply of sunlight as possible.

This side of the forest was darker, and wilder, than the rhododendron forest that I knew so well, only a couple of hundred yards away. I would love to say that I saw one of the elusive mammalian inhabitants of these dank, tropical woods. But I didn't. I was on a mission, and I was determined that nothing was going to get in my way. And luckily, nothing did.

Hong Kong's hillsides are dotted with the graves of its indigenous inhabitants. One would quite regularly come across these little, semi-circular, stone and concrete structures, which contained an earthenware urn full of mouldering bones. Sadly, some of the other European children of my age thought it was funny to vandalise them, smashing the urns and throwing the bones around in a horrid act of desecration. But, I always treated such finds with reverence, and on the occasions that I found one that had been ransacked by one of my peers, I would try to put the bones back as neatly as possible.

These graves were always found on open land, and so I was mystified to find one of these little mausoleums, deep inside the forest on the south side of Victoria Peak. I couldn't read the Chinese characters, and - even now - I don't know whether the writing on these solitary tombs customarily includes the date of the death and interment of its occupant. But, I figured, the tomb had to be either pretty recent, or very old.

It is one of the matters of historical record that reflects badly on my own people that between 1904 and 1947 Chinese people were not allowed to live on Victoria Peak. This, of course, did not affect residential servants, or the very rich - such as Sir Robert Ho Tung - who would have had no problems whatsoever in persuading the Governor to relax the law as far as they were concerned.

The ordinance was allegedly put in place to prevent the spread of Bubonic Plague, which, by the early years of the 20th Century, had allegedly caused some 100,000 deaths in the region. However, it is hard not to see this piece of legislation as a piece of anti-Oriental 'apartheid', together with other pieces of legislation forbidding Chinese style architecture in parts of Victoria city, and the fact that Chinese people were also banned from entering some of the more opulent hotels and clubs.

During the Japanese occupation of the British colony, over 95% of the forest that remained was cut down for firewood, and this - of course - included much of the forest on Victoria Peak. The fact that the area to the south of the waterfall that I was now exploring was accessible to a small boy expending only a certain degree of effort, would suggest that it would have been no obstacle to Japanese soldiers or their slave workers in search of fuel. So, I reasoned, that the tomb must have pre-dated 1905 because in the years after it became legal for Chinese people to live on The Peak again, for the mountainside would have been naked of trees. Although, I didn't know, and still don't, whether there were actual legal safeguards put in place to stop tombs being built on the hillside opposite a series of blocks of flats inhabited by middle-ranking British colonial servants, I was certain that it would have been frowned upon. From talking to some of the older inhabitants of Mount Austin Mansions, I discovered that the forests had only really taken root within the previous decade, and the tomb certainly looked like it was older than that.

It had been built carefully, nestling in a miniature crevice between two huge, grey, boulders, and great care had been taken to make sure that it was sheltered both from the rain and wind, and from the ever present threat of landslides. When I looked closely, I could see that a little watercourse had been dug so that in the wet season, any run off from the huge grey stone waterfall would avoid flowing over the little grave.

I assumed that it had been built no later than the end of the 19th Century, and I felt both honoured and touched to realise that I was probably the only person left alive in the entire world who knew of its existence. So I took it upon myself to keep the little sepulchre clean and tidy. I carefully brushed the fallen leaves (which were not many in number, as the forest was mainly consisting of evergreen rhododendrons) and even donated one of my precious jam jars (usually intended for keeping caterpillars) and - when I remembered - would pick wildflowers and put them at the graveside.

Some months later, I had an enormous shock.

Being, as you might gathered by now, somewhat of a secretive child, I never told anybody else about the existence of the little grave, and, whenever I was unhappy (which was a lot of the time) I would visit it, secure in the knowledge that I was the only person that knew of its existence. But one day, a year or so after we had left Mount Austin, I climbed the mountain to visit the grave, and found that I was not alone. There was a small bunch of burnt joss sticks in the ground in front of the grave. I never found who it was who had placed them there. Bizarrely, in all my years exploring the hillside, I found that the Chinese inhabitants of Hong Kong were even less willing to venture up there than were their European counterparts, although I never found out why. Fancifully, I assumed that they would be scared of the ghosts, spirits and fox fairies that lived there, and I suppose this is as good an explanation as any other.

A few years ago, one of my friends, the Australian cryptozoologist and explorer, Tony Healy, came to visit Corinna and me at our home in North Devon. We had a lovely few days together, and when he told me that he was visiting Hong Kong on his way back to Australia, I asked him to do me a favour. A few weeks later, he emailed me a large batch of photographs of the Mount Austin playground, and Victoria Peak gardens. Now, I am perfectly aware that it would be quite easy to read all sorts of implications into this, but the photographs all show that, whereas in my day there was no barrier separating the thickly forested hillside from the civilised demeanour of the playground, but now there were little picket fences, statues, and pots of ornamental shrubs all along the bottom of the forest line. These were certainly not enough to stop even the most casual visitor stepping over them and climbing up into the forest above. Indeed, when an internet acquaintance of mine from the Gwulo website went to investigate the ruins that we had once called 'Grey Walls' (as described elsewhere), he did just that. And nowhere did anyone suggest that he had broken even the most minor of bylaws in so doing. But, I like to think that this new delineation between the park and the forest was so that the physical people that lived in the park and the spirits that lived in the forest would each know how to keep to the demesne where each one belonged.

These days, I am sure that I would have played it differently. My natural curiosity would not have allowed me to leave such a mystery unsolved, and I would now keep as close a watch as I was able upon the little tomb in order to try to find out who it was who had visited it. After all, it could not have been a random hiker. Such people, even should they feel drawn to exploring the deep forest, would not take a bundle of unlit joss sticks with them. No, whoever it was must have gone there on purpose with the express intention of visiting the graveside. Even had they originally been the aforementioned conceptual hiker, they would have to have returned at least once in order to light the joss sticks.

I don't think I ever returned after that. It wasn't that I resented the fact that somebody else had started going to the grave, but the fact that they had brought joss sticks somehow implied that they had a more innate connection with whoever it was that was interned there. And, although I had been visiting the grave for a year or so, the fact that it was now being visited by somebody who had shared a greater spiritual connection with whoever it was whose bones were mouldering in the earthenware urn high on the hillside meant that I began to feel like I was no longer the custodian of the grave, but an intruder. Somehow, I felt that the grave could only have one visitor at a time, a bit like a hospital bed in a busy general ward. I'm not sure exactly why, but it still makes perfectly emotional sense to me now over half a century later.

I don't think I ever explored on the south side of the waterfall again either. There were so many exciting things on the northern side, and then as now, I was fascinated by the little creatures that live in fresh water, so there was nothing really to lure me there again, when there were so many little rivulets and tiny ponds to explore on and around the waterfall.

In May 1966, Chairman Mao Zedong announced, 'the cultural revolution', ushering in 3 years of bloodshed and violence across China. As Hong Kong is nothing but a tiny enclave on the shores of the South China Sea, those in power there at the time, were terrified that the violence and mayhem was going to spread across the border to the British Crown Colony. By this time my father was relatively high up in the Hong Kong government, and I realise now that he was far more aware of the threat to all of us 'foreign devils' than anyone else (and I suspect, even my mother) realised.

The Communist party was, of course, banned in Hong Kong but the mid-60s saw a rise in the radicalisation of young people across the world, and would even produce years later a *bona fide* martyr in the shape of 21yr old Jan Palach, who burnt himself to death in Wenceslas Square, Prague, and eventually inspired one of my songs many years later.

According to Jaroslava Moserov, a burns specialist who was the first to provide care to Palach at the Charles University Faculty Hospital, Palach did *not* set himself on fire to protest against the Soviet occupation, but did so to protest against the "demoralization" of Czechoslovak citizens caused by the occupation.

"It was not so much in opposition to the Soviet occupation, but the demoralization which was setting in, that people were not only giving up, but giving in. And he wanted to stop that demoralization. I think the people in the street, the multitude of people in the street, silent, with sad eyes, serious faces, which when you looked at those people you understood that everyone understands, that all the decent people were on the verge of making compromises."

Two other Czech students did likewise later in the year, and in doing so became spiritual standard bearers for the wave of revolution, which was enthusing young people across the globe. Over the years I have met, and become friends with, several of the luminaries of these events; Daevid Allen gave me first-hand accounts of student uprising in Paris, 1968, and Mick Farren regaled me with many accounts of the counter-cultural riots here in the UK.

Not surprisingly, Chairman Mao had enthused young people in his country, many of whom who had formed groups of paramilitary 'Red Guards'; an armed revolutionary youth organisation. It was only days after my mother had returned to the colony that she and my father took me aside to warn me that there was quite likely to be a band of young people dressed in blue tunics, marching along the road at some point in the next few months. I actually think that it is testament to my parents' child-rearing skills, that they did not keep me imprisoned in the flat for my own safety. But rather, they instructed me to avoid such bands of youths, and return home as quickly, and as unobtrusively, as possible, if such people did cross my path. With hindsight, I can see that they were quite right to do as they did. Revolution is a mostly urban preoccupation, and I was highly unlikely to come across such people, whilst about my daily business scrambling up and down the hillside. A few days or weeks later, I was playing cowboys and Indians with my friends on the green sward in front of Mount Austin Mansions, when our war-hoops were rudely interrupted by a chant of "Mao, Mao, Mao Tse Tung" and the sound of what the Rolling Stones would have described as "marching, charging, feet, boy". I suspect that all my other friends had received similar warnings from their parents, because we all stopped playing, and ran for the shelter of the big, concrete, porch which enshrouded the main entrance to our apartment block.

They were, indeed, Red Guards. About 20 of them, and even then I realised how young they looked. I was coming up to my 7th birthday, and most of the kids marching up Mount Austin Road didn't look more than ten years older than me. Unlike their counterparts on the mainland, they did not carry assault rifles, but bore hefty bamboo poles over their shoulders in a similar manner to the way that more conventional soldiers would bear their weapons. We stared at them in awe, until they disappeared up the hill and out of sight.

I am sure that both our collected parents and the Red Guards themselves had expected that children would have been terrified by the experience, but no. Nothing of the sort. It was only a matter of days before the assembled youngsters of Mount Austin

Mansions decided that they, too, wanted to be Red Guards, and had started marching up and down the hill and around the playground opposite, with chunks of bamboo over our shoulders, chanting praise to the author of his little red book. This came to the notice of the mother of one of us, who was absolutely shocked and appalled, and physical chastisement followed for the vast majority of our number. However, much to my surprise - both then and now – my parents appeared to think it was funny, and nothing more was ever said to me about the matter.

Some days or weeks later (it has been over half a century, and my memories are fading, which is one of the reasons I have decided not to wait any further to finish writing this narrative, before 'time's ever rolling stream' bears all my memories away), a suspicious package was found in the vicinity of one of the garages around the back of our apartment block. I would love to say that I had been climbing up the old *feng shui* fig tree at the north east corner of the compound, from whence I would have been able to have a grandstand view of events. However, that would have been a lie. But one of my friends was up there, and stayed totally still so as to avoid being seen by the police, and bomb disposal squad, who rushed to the scene.

The bomb, which is what it *did* turn out to be, had been made inside a jerry can, and was detonated in a controlled explosion by those most competent to do so. My friend described a large bang, a puff of grey smoke, and the cheers of the younger members of the military troop. I heard the bang from all the way up in our flat, but thought nothing of it and was mortified when I found out - later that day – that there had actually been some real excitement in my environs for once! And, although there were riots, and other outbursts of communist backed civil disobedience, for three more tumultuous years, that was it as far as my own experience of the communist Cultural Revolution in Hong Kong was concerned.

But there were other knock-on effects.

That November, for example, some of the parents of Mount Austin Mansions, who were determined to make sure that their offspring stayed culturally in touch with the customs of the Motherland, organised a fireworks display. For some reason, my parents were scornful of the whole idea. I have no idea why, as they were always fiercely patriotic, but I have a suspicion that their allegiance was to the Empire that was rapidly crumbling around our ears, rather than to the homeland in which they had not lived for any length of time for over a decade and a half. I only had the vaguest idea what it was all about (and I have to admit that I was more than slightly scared of the bangs, although I didn't like to admit it) but when I found out that the whole event was tied in with a plot to blow up the Houses of Parliament, I found myself highly enthused.

I knew what the Houses of Parliament were. I had seen the Palace of Westminster during a few days in London earlier in the year, and the fact that somebody could have gotten so close as to nearly having blown the whole thing up, totally fascinated me. I was still desperately miserable at school. Neither the teachers, or most of the other pupils, had any empathy with the stray little fantasy world that existed in my own head, in which stories from Kipling and Enid Blyton were mixed with my ongoing investigations into the wildlife of Victoria Peak, and the strange Cantonese lore that was being taught to me by my Amahs.

So, I hatched an amazing plan. If I were to blow the school up, I would never have to go there again, and instead of being educated, I could stay at home with my mother, read books, and explore the hillside to my heart's content. My half-formed plan was to get hold of enormous amounts of fireworks, and stash them in the cellar of the school. I actually have no idea whether the school had a cellar, and I doubt whether I knew back then either, but I have never allowed reality to get in the way of a good fantasy. I also ignored the fact that the fireworks display at Mount Austin Mansions was significant, because it was the last legal private one to be carried out in Hong Kong for some years. This was precisely because the powers that be were worried about fireworks being cannibalised into incendiary devices; fireworks displays from then on were only to be carried out under the auspices of the Colonial Hong Kong government.

The Chinese custom of letting firecrackers off during social and religious occasions continued illegally. It was frowned upon by the authorities, but somebody in the Colonial Secretariat had obviously decided that – in the interests of race relations – banning them outright, and cracking down on their illegal sale and use, would cause more harm than good.

So my plans to become a second Guy Fawkes were thwarted at birth, and by the end of November, my incendiary arsenal consisted of a box of matches, a bottle of white spirit, and two packets of sparklers.

But even the most rabid revolutionary anarchist has to begin somewhere!

Not unsurprisingly, my conflagratory plans came to nothing, although they nestled in the back of my mind for many years, and gave me a great deal of pleasure each time that I contemplated them. With hindsight, however, this was probably the first of my 'fantasy' plans that I allowed to achieve some sort of objective reality inside my increasingly addled brain. This is a pattern which has happened to me regularly ever since, and - as I get older, and less constrained by the bourgeois constructs that 'most people' like to think of as 'reality' - I tend to try to put my idiotic flights of fancy into action as often as possible. It is surprising quite how often these things are successful, although I am awfully glad to say that my juvenile plans for blowing up my primary school with an amassed hoard of fireworks never got beyond the fantasy stage.

However, there is one other memory of the fallout from Chairman Mao's cultural revolution, which does continue to haunt me. Probably because of my uneasy relationship with both my parents, I had become a furtive child, who made little 'camps' and bivouacs around the sprawling apartment. It had been built a generation before, to a clientele that all had numerous servants, and so appended upon the areas where my family and I lived, there were extensive servant's quarters on the back of the building. And because we only had a relatively small family of servants, several rooms were left unused.

As I was playing in one of them one day in 1967, when I had an experience that I shall never truly forget.

I overheard my father talking to my mother about the likely outcomes of a wave of Red Guards swarming across the border from mainland China, joining forces with the colony's home-grown communist agitators, and sweeping a swathe of terror through the European community. The Japanese invasion and its horrific aftermath, after all, had only taken place just over 25 years previously, and the scars of the four years of rape, torture, violence and - what we would now call - 'ethnic cleansing' were very plain for all to see. And I still remember, totally vividly, how my father gave a service revolver to my mother together with three bullets, one for my brother, one for me, and one for her. Things like that are something that one doesn't forget in a hurry.

Right in the middle of the initial scares of a communist uprising, came an enormous bout of bad weather, with two separate typhoons laying waste to much of the colony. Up on Victoria Peak, we were completely isolated, and my father and his friends and colleagues had a wonderful time playing at soldiers, and civil defence workers: shoring up road verges damaged by landslides, and distributing food and medical supplies brought in on helicopters by the resident British Forces. With hindsight, I can see that this whole episode did an awful lot of good. The young and early middle aged European men of the colony had become so enervated by the imminent prospect of war with the 'Yellow Peril' that they truly needed this spate of natural disasters in order to let off steam. I think that, had they not had this opportunity to protect hearth and home, that relationships between the British and the indigenous Chinese would have suffered a great deal more than they actually did.

There were lots of riots and bomb threats that summer, despite it being the much touted 'Summer of Love' for the cognoscenti both in the United States and the United Kingdom. John Lennon was broadcasting his slightly simplistic message of love around the world at roughly the time that my father made arrangement with my mother to shoot me and my brother, rather than have us fall into the hands of what Bret Harte called 'The Heathen Chinee'. But it was at that point that my father's annual leave became due and we left the tiny British colony, which seemed to be about to be overwhelmed in fire and fury, and fly back to the Motherland.

Somehow, my father had wangled a totally non-standard form of annual leave. What usually happened was that every three years the diligent colonial servants would go back to the United Kingdom for something between three and five months at the end of what was popularly called a 'Tour of Duty'. In theory, at least, the members of Her

Majesty's Overseas Civil Service were liable to be posted to a totally different colony when a new Tour of Duty started. However, by 1967, the sun was already setting on vast swathes of the British Empire, as a doctrine of forced de-colonisation was underway across the globe. So, in practice, especially when you were as high up the colonial service as my late father was, you knew that you would be posted back to whichever colony you had left nearly half a year before.

My father, however, for some reason, between 1966 and 1969, always managed to get 6 weeks annual leave in a single block. How and why this happened, I have no idea, but it does need to be noted upon to explain the locations of some of the various adventures and misadventures described in this book. My family have, I am afraid, a tendency towards self-aggrandisement, although - peculiarly - the truth is usually far more impressive than whatever flights of fancy have been concocted. My paternal grandmother was very proud of her Scottish aristocratic roots, and always claimed that we were somehow descended from the leaders of Clan MacGregor, and drummed into my brother and me that the MacGregors themselves were descended from an ancient Celtic royal family. The name MacGregor actually means 'son of Griogar', which is itself the Gaelicised form of the Christian name, Gregory. I actually have no idea whether I have the blood of Scottish Kings mixed with the red wine and gin which is coursing around my veins, and - truthfully - I don't really care. If you believe the doctrine of 'five degrees of separation' we are all fairly closely related to each other anyway, and although I am vaguely interested to find out what my family has done for - say - the last couple of centuries, what a bunch of people who may or may not have been my forebears did a millennium ago is fairly irrelevant. But it amuses me to find out that the surname MacGregor was banned in Scotland on a number of occasions prior to the 18th century, because the members of that clan were a bunch of unruly and badly behaved yobbos. Perhaps there is something to be said for this genetic stuff after all.

1967 was the year that my grandmother turned 70. In these days of mass communication across the globe where one can talk to anybody that one wants with just a few clicks of a mouse button, it seems incredible to think how - just half a century ago - arranging an intercontinental telephone call so that my father could fulfil his filial duty by wishing his mother a happy birthday, took weeks of arranging (I believe, at the highest governmental level). I know that we all stayed up tremendously late so that the entire family in Hong Kong could deliver our birthday greetings, and when the phone call finally came (something to do with the governmental hotline to and from the United Kingdom) it was a terrible anti-climax. We had a couple of minutes of very crackly and very stilted conversation, which was one of my first slices of evidence that my family are not terribly good at talking to each other.

Soon after, however, my father informed us that when we went to Britain in a few weeks time, we would be holidaying in Scotland. Moreoever, we were going to be camping in a Dormobile, and taking Grandmother with us. Thus, grandmother would be able to take us all to the historical locations of the clan from which we may or may not have sprung.

Oh joy!

Even at the age of seven, I realised that six weeks in a tiny camper van with both my parents and an irascible old lady, was not going to be a barrel of laughs. And guess what, readers?

It wasn't!

And so, once again, the Downes family - two adults and two small children - left Kai Tak airport and flew back to the United Kingdom. I remember none of the details of the flight, but I expect that they were pretty much the same as happened the year before. My brother and I were probably sick at Calcutta airport, as a result of the excessive heat, and my father probably lost his temper with us. But this is all just supposition. I truly can't remember after a gap of over 50 years, and it truly doesn't matter.

It is strange, however, to realise that I am now over ten years older than my parents were at the time of this journey, and I am - perhaps - a bit more understanding of their feelings now than I was back then.

On one of our trips back to England, the aeroplane developed engine difficulties and we had to stop off for an unscheduled stay in Tehran. When I say that to people these days, their view of the Iranian capital is clouded by stories of Islamic fundamentalism, public executions, and a generally repressive regime. However, back in the late 1960s, it was the height of the Shah's power and influence, and Tehran was a mixture of east and west. It was where the emperor's western leanings and espousal of western philosophies such as rights for women – which were so unpopular amongst much of the Iranian ruling classes that they were one of the biggest causes of his downfall in 1979 – met a beautiful, ancient city of low, terracotta buildings, studded with sky blue tiles, with the domes of Mosques glinting beautifully in the sunlight; a vista which my mother told me had not changed since the days of Sinbad the Sailor.

On the one morning I spent in Iran, I awoke at dawn to the sounds of the muezzin calling the faithful to prayer in the way they had done for centuries. I tiptoed out of bed and made my way to the veranda, where I stood in my pyjamas, my eyes wide open in wonderment at the beautifully exotic cityscape laid out below me.

On another occasion, for some reason that I can't remember, we ended up staying overnight in Beirut. Again, when I say this to people who are my contemporaries here, in 21ˢᵗ century Britain, they wince because, to them, Beirut has ever been anything but a hotbed of terrorism, violence, and religious intolerance. But when I was there, in 1966 or 1967, as I wrote earlier, the Lebanon was known as 'the riviera of the eastern Mediterranean', and Beirut was the sort of place where one would have been able to see the Duke and Duchess of Windsor, complete with their collection of overfed lapdogs parading up and down the main streets in the vain hope that somebody would recognise that he had once been a King and Emperor.

We landed in London, and immediately upon leaving the airport, travelled down to Hampshire to visit my maternal grandparents, and after a few days went up to Chester to liaise with my widowed paternal grandmother. I have no memory of the journey, which is probably just as well, and the only memories I have of our sojourn in Chester was visiting Chester Zoo, which even then was one of the best in the country. Here, I saw my first okapi and my first pigmy hippo; two animals that I had dearly wanted to see.

Somewhere along the line, my father took collection of a Bedford Dormobile; a camper van popular in the mid-1960s. The four of us, together with my grandmother, got inside and drove northwards.

It was enough of a shock to realise, while reading this, that at the time of writing (several years before this book was finally published) I am presently twelve years older than my father was, and fifteen years older than my mother was at the time. But it truly shocking to realise that my wife when I wrote this passage a year or two before her untimely death was far less than a decade younger than my grandmother was at the time, and that I am only a few years behind that. *Tempus* certainly does *fugit.*

My memories of our trip to Scotland are far more fragmented than are my memories of our stay in the Channel Islands a year before. This is probably because nothing much of note happened, or at least nothing much of interest to my young mind, whereas, as I've written elsewhere, our stay in the Channel Islands was remarkable for a number of reasons.

I remember being remarkably impressed by the sight of a fully kilted bagpiper, with a remarkable hat, skirling away for all he was worth, by the side of the road as we entered Scotland. Even then, I was aware that this was a stunt put on for the tourists, but I was impressed nonetheless.

Peculiarly, and this is something I don't think I've ever told anybody, when we left Scotland three or four weeks later, I had been looking forward to seeing the same piper who had welcomed us there, bidding us farewell. But I fell asleep in the van, and the next thing I knew, we were back in England. I was beginning to discover the world of the metaphysical, even at the age of eight and so I managed to come up with some fanciful notion that because I hadn't seen the piper saying goodbye, somehow, part of me was still in Scotland. I know this is nonsense, but on the occasions that I have visited Scotland since, I have always kept my eye out for a piper welcoming me or bidding me farewell, and have always been somewhat disappointed that this never happened.

My cousin Pené has been researching our family history for many years, and - sadly - it turned out that much of what my grandmother believed about my family is basically made up, and that even my father cherry-picked what he wanted to believe, and what he wanted to discard, in order to make our family appear that it was further up the social scale than it actually was.

It does appear that, somewhere along the line, some of my ancestors were Scottish gentry of some description, but - I am embarrassed to say - that I cannot remember the details, and that unless I get to speak to Pené at some length before I get to finishing writing this book, I am unlikely to ever tell them to you. But from the moment we crossed the border from England, my grandmother started to instil into my young brother and me that we were dispossessed Scottish nobility, and may even have had royal roots. I already knew about Robert the Bruce from the Ladybird book about him, and I was most impressed that he appeared to have taken career advice from a spider. But that was pretty much all I knew about the history of Scotland.

To confuse matters further, my mother and godmother had provided me with a pile of new reading material for the journey, several of which books I still have today. One of these books was my introduction to the worlds of Joan Aitken. *Black Hearts in Battersea* is set in a fictional early 18th century reign of King James III. In this world, James II had never been deposed in the Glorious Revolution, and supporters of the House of Hanover continue to plot against the Stuart monarchy.

Prince George, over in Germany, held much the same position in this timeline as did 'Bonnie Prince Charlie' in our timeline.

There was even a remarkably clever ballad, which went:

> "My bonnie lies over the ocean,
>   My bonnie lies over in Hanover,
>   My bonnie lies over the ocean,
>   Why won't they bring that young man over?"

It was my introduction to the concept of alternate history, which has been something that has intrigued and fascinated me ever since. But what with this rich and vibrant portrayal of a non-existent Scottish monarchy in Britain, and my grandmother's eager re-inventing of my family's Caledonian heritage, it is not particularly surprising that I ended this holiday with a particularly skewed view of my Scottish background.

My father used to tell stories of how his mother had dragged us round a plethora of tartan shops, trying to buy me a tie in my ancestral MacGregor tartan. The final straw came when, in yet another of these establishments, my grandmother had demanded to know whether the tie that she wanted to buy me was "the *hunting* tartan, or not?" Apparently, she thrust the tiny scrap of plaid at the shop assistant while asking this, in the sort of haughty tone one imagines Queen Victoria using when she told whoever it was that one was not amused.

"This woman is nothing to do with me!" said my father, in mock embarrassment. "I have never seen her before in my life!" and he stomped off to look at the whiskey shop next door.

Earlier that day, I do remember my grandmother wanting to buy me a kilt, but my newly found Scottishness only went so far, and a kilt was still far too much like a skirt for me, and I have never been comfortable with the idea of crossdressing.

Whether or not this was because they wished to encourage their elder son's interest in freshwater biology, or whether it was purely to get Richard and me out of the Dormobile for an hour or so, during the long journey north we stopped off several times at roadside park-ups which were conveniently by the side of slow moving rivers where Richard could go paddling and I could go in search of wildlife.

I soon realised that there was a big existential difference between these slow-moving waterways and the hill streams that I knew and loved so well back in Hong Kong. For one thing, there was a much greater diversity in fish morphology than I had seen back in the orient. As well as fast-moving fish like minnows and dace, which were roughly comparable to the mosquito fish of Hong Kong, and the stone loach were reasonably reminiscent of the weather loach that one saw on occasion, one would get the occasional sighting of a majestic salmon or trout which were far more impressive than the fish of my adopted homeland. There were occasional sightings of tiny, squat-shaped fish that I discovered later were called miller's thumbs, or bullheads (not to be confused with the North American bullhead catfish) but I never caught one, and will not be discussing these fish in any great length until a later chapter. During one of the stops by the riverside, I found a peculiar stone about the size of my two clenched fists, and the thing that made it most peculiar is that if you held it up to the light, it was pale green in colour.

I had an annoying habit of collecting what I called interesting stones from all sorts of places, and whenever I could, burdening my family's baggage weight allowance, and taking them back to Hong Kong with me. My father was usually fairly scathing about my finds, which, with hindsight I can see was not altogether undeserved. But this stone was completely different. Both he and I were really excited about it, and he posited that it could be a lump of arsenic, and continued to say this off and on for the next few weeks.

My parents were surprisingly judgemental people and saw everything in a sort of liverish black and white. I know, especially as I get older and have more insight into my own psyche, that I have similar tendencies, which is why I can identify them in my progenitors with the benefit of half a century's hindsight. They would get surprisingly angry at things that were completely beyond their control; the decision by Canada to change its flag from one which openly celebrated its ties to the mother country to a bicolour design featuring the silhouette of a maple leaf, for example. Both my parents ranted about that for years, and would still bring the subject up occasionally, until their dying days.

If someone or something offended them, they would hardly ever forgive or forget, and – as I had the typical child's belief that my parents were always right – I picked up some of their stupid prejudices, which took me some years to discard. I think that it's an important part of one's growing up when one realises that one's parents are fallible, and I'm afraid that this didn't happen for me until I was in my teens.

Take mortgages, for example. Because my parents had ranted about how the rapidly rising house prices had introduced a whole generation of young people to the joys of only achieving home ownership by getting into sizeable debt, I had no real idea what a mortgage was, and was quite prepared to agree with my parents that they were the work of the Devil. It was only when I had a frank exchange of views in 1982 with the father of my then girlfriend, that I realised that my parents were, once again, talking bigoted twaddle.

For some reason, at the time, my Aunty Anne and Uncle Arthur had done something to annoy my parents. I think it might have been because they suspected them of the heinous crime of voting for the Labour Party in the 1966 general election. Whether they did I have no idea, don't care, and it is none of my business, although in the interests of full disclosure, I voted for Labour under Jeremy Corbyn in the 2019 General Election.

My parents considered that Harold Wilson was somewhere south of Beelzebub in their catalogue of people of whom they approved, and the fact that my father's younger sister could actually espouse such dangerous concepts as Socialism was something up with which they could not put.

So, for the previous twelve months or so I had heard a whole string of disparaging remarks about my uncle in particular. My aunt, as a woman, and as a blood relative of my father, had of course been led away from the path of righteousness by her husband.

None of this really affected me; I only had the vaguest memories of who Aunty Anne and Uncle Arthur actually were, and although I had met them three or four years before during my family's sojourn in Hampshire, they had not impacted significantly upon my memory. However, now was going to be different! My personal ambitions had always been to be some sort of a scientist, and Uncle Arthur may have been (in my father's eyes) very nearly akin to the Bolsheviks, who had battered the Russian Royal family to death fifty years before, but he *was* a scientist. And as such, he loomed high in the list of people with whom I was impressed. And now, with this extraordinary new geological find of mine, which my father continued to insist was going to be arsenic, I was going to establish my scientific credentials in the eyes of my uncle.

Just as an aside, whilst I was engaged in writing this memory of mine down for posterity, I realised that I actually had no idea what arsenic even looked like. So, I went over to those jolly nice fellows at Wikipedia and discovered that it is something called a metalloid; a chemical element that has properties in between those of metals and non-metals. It is found in a number of different forms, and it is found in quite a few different parts of the world, where it is not uncommon. And ummm, none of them appear to be green.

For the next two weeks, my father kept on bringing the subject of my discovery at every possible opportunity and continued to tell me how proud my uncle Arthur would be. So, it could be imagined, that I had fairly unrealistic expectations. Then again, my expectations in all sorts of things in life have turned out to be unrealistic, although by the application of sheer stubbornness and not a little ingenuity, I have sometimes managed to make these expectations come true.

When we eventually got to my aunt's house in a little Welsh town with an unpronounceable name, I couldn't wait to show my discovery to my learned uncle. Proudly, I unwrapped it from various layers of newspaper and proffered it to him, expecting to bask in the praise of a real scientist. He took a brief look at it and told me it was just an ordinary stone, and that it was only coloured green because it was covered in algae. No, I spluttered. It couldn't be. But my uncle was adamant, and – sadly – this whole episode has gone down in Downes family history as the arrogant seven-year-old Jonathan trying to tell his scientist uncle that he had 'misidentified' a compound.

In reality, although I can quite easily have appeared thus, there were mitigating circumstances. I was quite a respectful child and would not have dared argue with an adult, if my father had not spent the previous twelve months belittling him and if my father had not spent the previous two weeks drumming into me the 'fact' that I had made an astounding geological discovery. It is only now, when I am sixteen years older than my father was at the time, and suffering from many of the same character flaws, that I realise the true state of affairs. But, both my Aunty Anne and Uncle Arthur have since died, and - if my parents' view of the afterlife is true - they are now sitting on a cloud somewhere, arguing the toss with my father, and it is nothing to do with me anymore.

I have leapt ahead a bit. But when one is telling a story like this, it is sometimes necessary to play fast and loose with one's narrative. However, I remember how annoyed I was when I discovered how many liberties Gerald Durrell had taken with the timeline in his immortal books about his childhood, and so – although I have to do the same here – I am doing my best always to confess to my literary sins, whenever I am forced to indulge in them.

Back in Scotland, a couple of weeks earlier, we continued to trudge up and down glens where my distant ancestors were supposed to have slaughtered each other with 'rifle and grenade' (as the song goes), and my grandmother's claims of royal blood for the Downes family reached remarkable levels. But, on the whole, nothing much of any significance happened.

It was about a year before I discovered the concept of cryptozoology, but I had - of course – heard about the Loch Ness Monster, and dearly wanted to visit Loch Ness. But, for some reason, my parents wouldn't go any further north than Fort William, and we trundled back down through the Scottish Lowlands again. At one point, in the southern part of the Cairngorms, we went to see the place where reindeer had been reintroduced to the country for the first time in eight thousand years when, due to climate change, they were extirpated. They were reintroduced in 1952 by a Swedish guy called Mikel Utsi, who introduced twenty-nine of them. I was pleased to see that they had prospered. There were about 130 of them ten years ago and are an integral part of the long-term plans for re-wilding the Scottish Highlands. And because of the cuddly cultural connotations (Rudolph *et. al*), there is far less opposition to the burgeoning reindeer population than there has been to reintroduction of wolves, lynx or white-tailed sea eagles. I was impressed by the small herd of chunky looking cervids, which were, of course, familiar to me from the images on hundreds of Christmas cards, but the thing that sticks in my mind is that – high on a mountain above us – were a couple of sizeable patches of snow. And you must remember that this was in July! Snow in the summer? The very concept of it excited my impressionable young mind.

But apart from these, almost fragmentary, memories, I truly don't remember much about the holiday at all. What I do remember, however, is how pleased I was when – at the end of it all – we stepped off the Boeing 707 at Kai Tak Airport and I was on the earth of my beloved Hong Kong once again. My head was full of the soaring bullshit I had been fed about my links to royalty, and – when I returned to school a few weeks later – I irritated the hell out of everybody by repeating my grandmother's nonsense. But already, Scotland seemed an awfully long way away, and - despite the coals of opprobrium that were heaped upon me by teachers whom I had told that, if only history had worked out slightly differently, I would be a prince of royal blood - I was back in the place that I considered to be my *real home!*

Opposite the top gates of Peak School on Plunkett's Road was a row of large, lock-up garages. And in one of them, a Chinese cobbler called Ping Kee had set up shop. He was actually a friendly acquaintance of many of the school children, including myself, and – each Christmas – he would have a makeshift stall selling Christmas trees, and – although my parents bought a large and imposing tree from him each year - he would always let me have a small and commercially overlooked tree for myself, for free. I say that his name was Ping Kee, but – a few years ago – when I was pootling about on Google Earth, I saw an annotation which appeared to imply that the whole building block, of which the lock-ups were only the ground floor, was called

Ping Kee. A fairly thorough trawl through Google has done nothing to clarify the situation, and so I am none the wiser. However, that Christmas, Ping Kee was immortalised in another of the bloody awful dramatic presentations by the Peak School drama mistress.

Ping Kee and the Magic Dragon was a particularly egregious slice of children's drama. It told the story about how a young, Chinese boy, the eponymous Ping Kee, made friends with yes, you've guessed it, a magic dragon. Ping Kee was played by a European child wearing makeup, a Hakka woman's hat and a stupid accent and use of Pidgin English, which I strongly suspect would be banned today because of its innate racism. Johnny Foreigner may still be a rum cove, but one's not allowed to take the piss out of him anymore. And this is probably a good thing.

My role in this dramatic masterpiece was as part of the dragon. The uniform at Peak School included some bright green overalls to be worn during art classes or during any other activity, which might end up with the pupil becoming messy or wet as a side effect of the activity. The 'dragon' consisted of a dozen or so children, wearing these aforementioned green overalls, and crouching down with their hands about the waist of the child in front of them. The child at the very front brandished a magnificent Chinese dragon head, of the sort that one would, and still does, see at the front of a 'dragon' in a Dragon Dance.

Apart from all this, I have no memory whatsoever of what the rest of the plot of this *magnum opus* of this might have been, but what I do remember is that it was one of the things that made my father unreasonably angry. As I have said elsewhere in this narrative, both of my parents had the ability to be remarkably judgemental, and somewhere along the line my father had read something that suggested that the word 'puff' in the children's song *Puff the Magic Dragon*, which was sung with gusto at the end of the performance of this little dramatic interlude, was a reference to both drugs (puffing away on a spliff, one assumed) and homosexuality (the word 'puff'; need we say more) and for weeks he ranted about this at every possibly opportunity, even implying – to my damaged and illogical little psyche – that somehow it was my fault that the teacher was promulgating such pernicious propaganda aimed at destroying the British Empire and all that it stood for. There were, if I remember rightly, two performances, and the whole episode was over. But it did underline for me, if any underlining was needed, that the world of adults was a strange and illogical place.

Many years later I had an acquaintance for used to sing a song called *Puff the Magic Junkie* to the same tune. The lyrics went:

> "Puff the Magic Junkie, he used to sniff cocaine,
> And when he came down from a trip, he'd shoot right up again"

But that is both irrelevant and in dubious taste, so we shall move swiftly on.

Dragons, apart from being the catalyst for a long-forgotten school play, were quite an important cultural motif in Hong Kong. Pokfulam Road is a footpath, just about driveable by emergency vehicles like police cars, ambulances or the Saracen armoured cars used by the army, which I only ever saw in action when troops were brought in to help the civilian population shore up vast areas of hillside that had collapsed in landslides as a result of a particularly nasty typhoon, and the road led from Victoria Gap at the top right down to the Pokfulam reservoir at the bottom. About a quarter of a mile down it was a long stretch of hillside that had presumably collapsed in one of the aforementioned landslides, and as a result it was covered in concrete to a height of seven or eight feet. While the concrete was still wet, somebody – with no little artistic talent – had drawn a beautiful renditioning of a stylised Chinese dragon into the wet concrete with their finger. It was accompanied by several Chinese ideograms, which Ah Ling told me had been made by very bad men, which meant – or so it transpired – that they had been followers of the Chinese nationalist movement, led by Generalissimo Chiang Kai-shek, then hiding out on the island of Formosa. The Chinese nationalist movement was, of course, the same political group who – led by Dr. Sun Yat-Sen – in 1911 had led the revolution that overthrew China's last imperial dynasty (the Qing dynasty). Although there was much more prominence given to the fight against homegrown Chinese communists, those who had been placed into power in Hong Kong were equally worried about the possibility of a popular uprising in Hong Kong, led by the nationalists. After all, they had already established a secure political outpost in Taiwan, and it would make good political and military sense for them to attempt to do the same in Hong Kong and Macau.

But as we know, this never happened, and the only memory I have of a grassroots Chinese nationalist revolutionary campaign was the beautifully executed dragon on the hillside above Pokfulam reservoir.

Another dragon, which was of pivotal importance to Hong Kong, and which I had learned about at a young age, was the one who – depending on who you believed – either had nine humps, or was nine separate dragons (personified in landscape by eight mountains and the Chinese emperor). These made up the geography of what is now the urban area of Kowloon. This was ceded to the British in 1860 by the Imperial Chinese government, but the British did very little to develop it and used the area mostly for tiger hunting. However, during the time I lived in Hong Kong, the international airport of Kai Tak was extended, and the work that had to be done in order to build the new runway, would cause irreparable damage to the spine of one of the nine dragons, and there were many protests about this. Even in the 1960s, the old ideas of *feng shui*, and associated with it the rules of appropriate propitiation to both a pantheon of Gods, other lesser deities, and supernatural creatures like the nine dragons, were still very much in evidence.

I, however, was convinced that there were going to be real flesh and blood dragons lurking somewhere in the wilder parts of the colony. After all, the dragon motif was everywhere; as well as the two examples I cited above, there were dragon boats, dragon dances, and even a popular vein of cheap, locally produced snacks which were surreptitiously enjoyed by most of the local school children, despite the fact that – to a man – our parents disapproved of them, saying that they were unhealthy and probably produced under disgustingly unsanitary conditions. This whole range of snacks – potato crisps, prawn crackers, and weird salted dried seeds – were all emblazoned (or at least the packets were emblazoned) with the image of a stylised Chinese dragon.

Surely there had to be some zoological rationale to explain all these uses of the dragon motif, hypothesised the seven-year-old me. After all, I had already seen a large monitor lizard on one of the less trodden paths near Magazine Gap (described earlier) and I had heard that the colony even had occasional visits from the most fearsome of living reptiles: the Indopacific Crocodile. There were even fearsomely poisonous sea snakes, which one of the books my grandfather had given me claimed could grow up to six feet in length. This was nearly as tall as my father and – again, to the seven-year-old me – my father was massive. So, any of these could, to my mind – both then and now – prove to be a pretty convincing dragon.

I did not know it then, because I hadn't even heard of the term, but this was one of my first forays into rational cryptozoology.

I was surrounded by a rich, and often contradictory, melange of cultural archetypes, religious beliefs and superstitions. And even at such a comparatively young age, I felt compelled to see if I could work out what they all meant. It is something I started young, and which I still do today.

But then, as now, I've found – to my dismay – that these socio-cultural explanations, which take place in a dazzling mix of hard science, real life, and the noosphere may fascinate me, but they are of very little interest (and, sadly, mostly of no interest whatsoever) to my peers. This is a cross that I have had to bear for well over half a century.

Sometime in the second part of the 1960s, my parents decided that they should expose me to the more cultured things in life, and so they took me to a whole series of concerts and recitals by both Hong Kong grown and internationally famous classical musicians. I remember seeing the Amadeus Quartet, for example, but whilst the music was pleasant enough to my ears, it didn't really enthuse me. To be honest, here, no music really enthused me until the beginning of the following decade, when all sorts of stuff that my parents hated because it was played by "long haired twits who probably took drugs" burrowed its way into my synapses and has stayed there ever since.

They also took me to a whole series of performances of various operettas, mostly by Gilbert and Sullivan, but occasionally by other composers of the same ilk. They were performed by a local amateur dramatics society which was also responsible for pantomimes which we looked forward to each Christmas. One of these was *La belle Hélène* by Jacques Offenbach. For those of you not in the know, it is a light-hearted retelling of the Trojan War mythos, with the 'Hélène' of the title being none other than Helen of Troy. And I was totally blown away.

This became one of my periodic obsessions, which anyone who knows me can tell you, still happen relatively regularly throughout my life. And, I was filled with the desire to write a play about the Trojan War and have it performed by the other children who lived first in Mount Austin Mansions, then in Peak Mansions, to where we moved some years later.

My friend Michael and I even spent several weeks trying to construct a large model of a Grecian trireme out of cardboard boxes and chipboard. When we had finished, we thought that it was a remarkable piece of handiwork, but to anybody else it would have just looked like four or five cardboard boxes with badly cut out pieces of chipboard in the bow and the rear.

This obsession flared up a couple of times but basically fizzled out by the end of the decade. My liking for Gilbert and Sullivan, however, didn't, as anybody who will remember me, Richard Freeman and Mark North drunkenly singing *Poor Little Buttercup* at one of the *Fortean Times* 'Unconventions' in the early part of this century, will no doubt attest.

My Uncle Tim was a strangely imposing man. A gentleman farmer in Sussex, he also became the owner of one of the major car dealerships in the county, and was - I believe - the only male member of my mother's family whom my father truly respected. He was very much head of the family, with the sort of air that I pretend to put on when I have to, but which I suspect nobody (even I) actually believes when I do.

Uncle Tim lived with my Aunty Cath in a large house just outside Pulborough in Sussex, and - I found out many years later, after his death - that he also owned the (nearly as imposing) house next door, in which resided his long term mistress. He also had a gun cabinet full of impressive looking shotguns, including my father's gun that he looked after while my parents were in Hong Kong (where private firearm ownership was understandably banned), and a large and boisterous Golden Retriever called 'Timber'. When our torturous trek around the Scottish lowland was finally over, and we had returned to England, plonking my grandmother back in her home in Chester, and - as I have already recounted with a shudder - visited my aunt and uncle in South Wales, just in time for me to unwittingly make a twat of myself, we moved to the south of England to visit my mother's side of the family. Whilst visiting Uncle Tim and Aunty Cath, I had received an early birthday present from him. It was two of the Observer's Books; one on 'Grasses, Sedges and Rushes' and one on 'Larger British Moths'. I still have them today, and - whilst both of them were to be of little use to a budding naturalist who was carrying out his investigations on the other side of the

148

world in a little geographic pinprick, upon which the sun was doomed to set by the time I reached middle age - these two books did do something very important for me. Previous to receiving them, the only books on nature that I had read were aimed at children, and were both picture-led and generalised, but, most importantly, things like *The Ladybird Book of the Seashore* and *What to look for in Summer* took a grossly holistic view of the natural world. They did, of course, include dozens of beautiful watercolours, more or less accurately portraying the animals and plants that could be seen on (for example) the seashore, or in summer, but they made no attempt at classification.

It was not until I held these two Observer's Books in my sticky little seven year old hands, that I realised - with an earth shattering epiphany - that just like the human race, the natural world was divided into families. And in the same way that my own little subset of humanity included my mother's family (the Cosens' and Rawlins' family) and my father's family (the Downes and Smiths and - if you were to believe my grandmother - the Royal MacGregors), the natural world had similar subdivisions of my own.

Of the two books, the one on moths was by far my favourite, and - of the moths - it was the imposing hawkmoths that impressed me most. Interestingly, of the twenty-odd species of hawkmoths which can be found, on occasion, in the British aisles, quite a few of the rarest ones, while being uncommon visitors to Britain, are found over great swathes of the warmer parts of the planet, and - therefore - were the first animals that I could read about in the books that Uncle Tim had given me, which I could see for myself, wild, back in Hong Kong. In the intervening years, the lumpers and splitters of taxonomy have been at work, and some of the species of hawkmoth that I immediately recognised, as I eagerly devoured the little book before me, have now been - on the basis of genetic differences - delineated as separate species, but that is by the by. The silver striped hawk moth, for example, is a rare visitor to the United Kingdom, but I saw it quite often in Hong Kong, and was fascinated to realise that - together with several other bulky moths that I knew quite well - it formed a recognisable family, all the members of which had a diagnostic spike or hook sticking out of the tail of their caterpillars. Richard Ford was, with this book, responsible for introducing me to one of my first important realisation about the natural world.

As recounted earlier, I had always assumed that certain butterfly species were related. The butterfly which my friends and I called the 'cabbage white' which was in fact a subspecies of the small white (*Pieris rapae*) known to generations of English schoolboys by the same name, and was very similar to several yellow butterflies in the genus Eurema. These were quite commonly found in open areas and scrubland in Hong Kong, and which I used to see quite regularly on our family walks around Harlech Road, especially near the old World War II shooting range. But now, I realise for the first time, that such relationships were "official".

These new vistas of the imagination that had been opened to me grew and solidified inside my conscience, and when we got back to Hong Kong, I began diligently trying to work out these complex family relationships between the different animals that I encountered. This was truly important to me, because even my guru Herklots, who had provided a certain number of Latin names of the animals about which he wrote, had still stuck to a pleasantly informal mode of presentation; he called invertebrates 'creepy crawlies' for example, and made no real attempt to classify them.

But, back in Hong Kong, I soon discovered that there were things that I came across on a regular basis, which would never, and probably had never, crossed the path of my naturalist brethren back in England.

One day, for example, just as I was leaving school for the afternoon and preparing to walk down the long, wooded road which lead down to Victoria Gap, an extraordinary insect about six inches long and a beautiful pale green in colour, flew straight towards me and landed on my shoulder. It was a huge, and very beautiful, praying mantis, which - years later - I identified as *Hierodula patellifera,* otherwise known as the great Asian mantis.

I had never seen one before, although I was very familiar with the idea of them from reading one of the most evocative passages in *The Jungle Book* (as referenced earlier) and the chapter in *My Family and Other Animals* when Gerald Durrell describes the pet mantis he had kept as a boy. I determined to do likewise, and, as I had an empty jam jar in my school satchel, ready exactly for opportunities like this, I put the mantis into the jar, together with a small twig which she (I knew she was female because of her size) could sit on until I could transfer her to something more fitting for such a remarkable creature.

I took her home and transferred her to a large, one gallon jar, which had originally contained pickles, and I went out to the servants quarters to ask Ah Tam to make some holes in the lid for me. I then - having placed the mantid in her jar in pride of place in my bathroom windowsill museum - went down to the small stand of elephant grass that grew by the old *Feng Shui* fig tree at the back of the compound, and spent the next ten minutes in search of small insects which my new pet could eat. I kept her for about a week, and she kept me on my toes having to provide for her, and she got fatter and fatter. It was my mother who suggested that this was because she was ready to lay eggs, and told me that I should probably let her go now, so that she could find a "husband" with whom she could carry out this delicate task. My mother was almost certainly completely right, because I have kept various mantides species in more recent years, and noted that when they are ready to produce an ootheca, they develop a very bulbous abdomen, and eat far more than usual.

What I didn't know then,, and only discovered relatively recently from my friend Graham Smith, is that if there is no male mantis present, an ootheca will still be laid, albeit a smaller one, but it will sometimes produce live offspring through a type of parthenogenesis. It is probably a good thing that I didn't know this at the time, because the task of providing for a huge number of baby mantides would have been beyond me, and the eight year old me would have been exceedingly upset when the mother mantid died, as she would undoubtedly have done soon after egg laying.

So, I took her to school, showed her to my classmates, who were mostly completely unimpressed, and at playtime I opened the jar and released her out into the great, wide world. She flew off towards the walled garden of the house on the opposite side of Plunkett's Road. I don't know who owned the garden, but it contained a number of densely leaved flowering bushes, where I felt sure that there would be ample food for her and her young family, and that she would be very happy.

Right in the middle of Queen's Road South in Victoria City, was (and may well still be) a restaurant called *The Parisian Grill*, which - together with *Jimmy's Kitchen* - was probably the most famous of Hong Kong's homegrown eateries.

I don't think I ever went there, but it is undeniable that this little restaurant fulfilled a great cultural purpose for me as I was growing up. Because, presumably as a way of protecting their clientele from the rigours of badly stored foodstuffs in a pre-deepfreeze society, the owners of *The Parisian Grill* had bought a small farm on the southside of Hong Kong island, from where fresh food could be guaranteed for the clients of this upmarket restaurant. This farm was known to all and sundry as 'the PG Farm' and it was probably my favourite place to visit when I was a boy, possibly even eclipsing the Hong Kong Botanical Gardens.

One of the things that I love about the British is their complete lack of imagination. For example a Victorian explorer would spend months trekking across trackless wastes in the middle of Africa, losing the vast majority of his bearers and companions to crocodiles and hostile natives, and eventually find a particularly nasty swamp in the middle of nowhere, which they would promptly call 'Piccadilly'. And I'm not really exaggerating. Indeed, in an amusing twist on this socio-cultural paradigm, a copy of *Whizzer and Chips* in about 1971, had the story of a little African boy and his mother, who were quite understandably pissed off at this paradigm. So, in a graphically illustrated adventure, which I'm certain would never pass the all-seeing eye of the censorious powers that be in these decadent days, the little boy (whose name was Chester) and his mother, clad only in loincloths, paddled their canoe down the great river upon which their village was situated, and eventually reached the sea. They kept on paddling. And they paddled until they reached the coast of the United Kingdom, and paddled up the River Irwell until they found a little village, which they promptly named "Ma'n'Chester".

Although the comic strip would be seen as being impossibly racist by today's standards, it did make a fairly serious point. And it's a point, which - even today - can be illustrated by even a brief look at a Hong Kong atlas. There are, for example, ranges of hills in the New Territories, which an unimaginative bunch of Royal Engineer surveyors named 'The Mendips' and 'The Cotswolds'. And on the south side of Hong Kong Island, there is - what was, when it was named, a small fishing village, but is now the sizable conurbation of - Aberdeen.

Back in the 1960s, Aberdeen was quite a picturesque place. It was the location for a floating village, containing approximately 600 junks, and - according to those jolly nice fellows at Wikipedia - today houses an estimated 6000 people. The people living on the boats in Aberdeen are mainly Tanka, a primitive group of native South Chinese, who arrived in Hong Kong in the 7th to 9th century, and who pre-date the far better known Han people by a considerable period. For reasons which I don't understand, and which are probably not relevant here, the term 'Tanka' is now considered to be derogatory, a bit like 'Gypsy', and is not in common use. The people are generally referred to these days as 'boat people', something that is linguistically most confusing. The term is also used for large numbers of Vietnamese refugees, who turned up in Hong Kong - by sea - fleeing from Vietcong ethnic cleansing following the north Vietnamese victory in the Vietnam War. Between 1975 and 1999, 143,700 Vietnamese refugees were resettled in other countries, and more than 67,000 were repatriated, and it appears that many still live in Hong Kong. Aberdeen floating village, has been in existence for several hundred years, and the temple to Tin Hau, the goddess of the sea, was built in about 1855, although Aberdeen had been an important port for the sandalwood trade, as far as back as the 14th century. Amongst the most famous tourist attractions of Aberdeen are the floating restaurants; enormous seaborne noodle-palaces, which my parents would never visit (not with us, anyway) because they were convinced that anyone who ate there was likely to drop down dead of cholera. Every summer, around about the time of the summer solstice, Aberdeen was venue for the Duanwu Festival, which is far better known, especially to those of us in the western world, as the 'Dragon Boat Festival'.

According to the most popular legend, it is said that the festival commemorates the death of a poet and politician called Ku Yuan, who committed suicide by jumping into Miluo river about 300 years before the birth of Christ. The common people rushed to the water and tried to recover his body, and each year - in commemoration - they hold complex dragon boat races. Dragon boats are long, thin, rowing boats with a crew of twenty two, comprising ten pairs of paddlers, someone steering, standing in the stern of the boat, and a drummer, who keeps time rhythmically. Some of the more traditional boats can have crews of up to fifty, and the boats are rigged with decorative Chinese dragon heads, and tails, as well as lanterns and other pieces of symbolic regalia.

I used to love Dragon Boat Day, and on the occasions that we weren't able to go down to Aberdeen to see it live, I would watch it avidly on television and - indeed - I still do. But my favourite place in Aberdeen was, as I said, the PG farm.

These days, it is the site of the internationally famous Ocean Park, but in my day it was a small, fairly grubby, and very smelly, show farm. In 1953, it was leased from the government by a Chinese businessman called Mr Tse, who kept all sorts of animals there, including geese, turkeys, monkeys, and some black bears, one of which caused somewhat of a scandal when an unaccompanied English child was injured by it.

Mr Tse's son wrote, many years later, that his father kept all sorts of animals here as a hobby. It wasn't a business as such; there were no entrance fees and anyone could simply walk in and spend the day.

It had a large fish pond, and swings and a see-saw for children, but the thing that impressed me most was a large, and quite well stocked, tropical fish shop, which also included such exotics as the local endemic Hong Kong newt, and other paddle tailed and fire bellied newts. There was only ever one species at a time, which would suggest that whoever it was who was responsible for buying in stock, did so from whatever the wholesaler had in stock.

Even at such an early age, I was always far more interested in the 'non-standard' fish like kuhli loaches (*Pangio kuhlii*) and their relatives, and the Oriental weather loach (*Misgurnus anguillicaudhus*), a species which I had been lucky to find living wild on the island. Both of these little fish had become firm favourites of mine to this very day, and, as I sit dictating this to my beloved step-amanuensis Olivia, I can see two specimens of the latter fish swimming around furtively in the tank in the corner of my sitting room.

Oriental weather loaches are so widely bred, both for the pet trade and for food, that they have been introduced to all sorts of places in Europe, Australia and North America, where they have become invasive species. Because of this, it is impossible to tell whether they were originally native to Hong Kong, and I don't suppose it really matters. Because, even if they are an invasive species, unlike other such animals which were also sold widely and willynilly at PG farm, for example the red eared slider (*Trachemys scripta elegans*), which - as in so many other places across the world, including the UK - have become established in most suitable habitats in Hong Kong, where they wreak havoc upon the local wildlife, and out-compete the local turtles, they appear to be completely harmless.

They also sold tortoises of an unknown species. I always wanted one, but for various reasons, my parents would never let me have one, even when - in early 1968 - we moved to somewhere with a back yard. Another memorable fish for sale at PG farm was the common clown fish (*Amphiprion ocellaris*), best known to more recent generations of children as the fish from *Finding Nemo*. I was fascinated to see how they lived in a symbiotic relationship with a large and magnificent species of sea anemone, in the *Stichodactylidae* family, and would spend ages staring myopically into the tank, watching how the sea anenome, who was so highly venomous that its sting could have caused anaphylactic shock in humans, lived completely amicably alongside these pretty little fish that would - under other circumstances - have been a most welcome lunch.

It must have been about this time, that I had burbled enthusiastically to Ah Tam about the different fish that I had seen at PG farm, because one evening, he brought me a large, and slightly cracked, Famille Rose bowl, the sort that even now one is likely to find in one of the more authentic Chinese restaurants. Just type in 'Famille Rose' into eBay, and you will see the sort of thing I mean.

This bowl, however, was two thirds filled with water, and contained a stone, some water weed, and three extremely long loaches. I don't think they were Oriental weather loach, and Ah Tam had no idea what they were, but I kept them for several years until - unfortunately - whilst we were away from the colony on holiday, they fell victim to Augustus the cat.

CHAPTER SIX
Peak Mansions

Look down at me and you see a fool; look up at me and you see a god; look straight at me and you see yourself.

Charles Manson

Right at the beginning of 1968, we moved house. We had been at Mount Austin Mansions since the spring of 1964, and although I had fragmentary memories of both Buxey Lodge and Partridge Piece, Mount Austin Mansions was the only real home I had ever known, and I was understandably upset at the idea of leaving it. However, my mother sweetened the bitter pill for me by telling me that my brother and I would have a much bigger bedroom, a little area that she described as a 'stage', and - most excitingly of all - because it was a ground floor apartment, we would even have a conservatory and an outside backyard.

I believe that our relocation was caused by my father's promotion to the higher echelons of the Colonial Civil Service, because Peak Mansions was home to a motley collection of upper echelon Colonial Servants, including a High Court Judge.

Peak Mansions was built in about 1928, and adverts for flats in the apartment block appeared in local papers towards the end of the year. It was built as private accommodation, but like everything else in Hong Kong, it changed during the war. It was used as a base for the Hong Kong Volunteer Defence Corps during the battle for Hong Kong in December 1941. It was badly damaged in the fighting, and was subsequently used as a base by the Japanese.

As I have alluded to above, despite the fact that I was born fifteen years after it all ended, the Second World War was one of the most important defining influences in my young life. Whilst my peers back in England may well have been enjoying the swinging sixties (although I have a sneaking suspicion that unless you actually lived in the Kings Road with a nice little trust fund to finance you, that the sixties didn't really swing for anyone) I was living in what was then Crown Colony of Hong Kong;

---

the finest jewel of in the crown of a rapidly diminishing empire. And unlike all of the United Kingdom (with exception of the Channel Islands) Hong Kong had been occupied (rather brutally) by enemy forces, in this case the army of the God-Emperor Hirohito of Japan.

Hong Kong was - and is - a very strange place; whilst the rest of China was undergoing The Cultural Revolution of Chairman Mao, Hong Kong was basking in the imperial twilight of an economic boom fuelled by cheap labour and hardworking illegal immigrants. The ever present fear of a communist invasion was fuelled — amongst both the European and Chinese population — by the memories of what had happened in December 1941 when the invading Japanese army spilled across the boarder on the 8th December less then eight after the attack of Pearl Harbour. There were only fourteen thousand allied soldiers as opposed to fifty one thousand of the invading Japanese. Less than a fortnight later, on Christmas Day it was clear that future resistance would be futile and the Governor surrendered.

The next four years were grim ones. The occupying under Rensuke Isogai submitted the colony to a rain of terror. Captured soldiers were tortured and killed, and it is alleged that over ten thousand women were raped by Japanese soldiers.

Twenty plus years later my friends and I played soldiers on the same hillsides which had seen pitched battles between British and Japanese soldiers and we took over a concrete pill box that has been built for the use of Japanese soldiers as our gang hut. In about 1968 one of my friends said that he had seen the shadowy figure of a man in khaki uniform slinking through the tall elephant grass on the hillside. My friends and I poo pooed this whilst allowing a delicious frisson of fear to trickle up our spines. A few days later my Father came back from work with a very stern face. We were never to play in the abandoned pill boxes and gun emplacements on Lugard Road again; the body of a small Chinese boy, horribly mutilated, and his genitals crushed to a pulp had been found there. My Father and all the others of the adult population decided that there was a psychotic killer (presumably with an arcane sexual motive) on the loose. My friends and I knew better — the murderer had been the ghost of a Japanese Soldier still with the rapine motives he had possessed when he had been alive.

After the war, Peak Mansions became used by the Royal Navy, and was subsequently acquired by the Hong Kong Government in 1956 as family quarters for upper ranking civil servants.

Peak Mansions was a fantastic place to grow up, with secret tunnels, gruesome history and several resident ghosts. Probably the most famous was the ghost of a little girl who ended — many years later — as the central character in a novel by Anne Berry the novel goes into an elaborate back story about how a young girl called Lyn Shui was raped, brutalized and eventually murdered during the years of occupation. From my memories of the case, the figure of a young oriental girl, apparently in distress, was seen on a number of occasions running along the corridors of one of the flats. These incidents took place over a number of years but as far as I'm aware nobody ever tried to communicate with her. This is completely at odds with the plot of the novel, during which an ex-pat English girl call Alice builds up a complicated relationship with the spectre .

However on at least one occasion someone did try communicating with one of the ghosts on Peak Mansions. The man in question was the one-time police commissioner Roy Henry, and if you can't believe the word of a police commissioner who can you trust? According to Mr Henry the ghost he met on a number of occasions was a nuisance with woke him regularly in the middle of the night and left him feeling bitterly cold. He did indeed try communicating with it but to no avail.

Many years later, in middle age, I was collecting as many books on Hong Kong as I could find, and someone recommended to me a book called *Prisoner of the Turnip-Heads* by George Wright-Nooth, which told the story of his life as a member of the Hong Kong police (the prefix of 'Royal' had not been added at this stage) in the years leading up to the Second World War, and – most interestingly for me – his life as an internee and prisoner of the Japanese, in Stanley Prison.

It contained an episode of major cryptozoological importance (major to me, anyway), but I learned quite a lot more from it.

Since I was a boy, I had enjoyed reading Prisoner-of-War Camp books. Without exception, they are full of tales of derring-do, where the social norms of Britain's public schools translated seamlessly to a life in captivity.

Well, I went to a British public school, and – believe me – it was much less wholesome than one would imagine from the books of Enid Blyton and Anthony Buckeridge. And, having been confronted with the web of intrigue, bullying, minor theft, corruption and insipient homosexuality, that is found in the real thing, I have often wondered whether life in the POW camps was as wholesome as has always been portrayed.

Stanley was – of course – something slightly different; it was mostly a Prisoner of War camp for civilian internees, and so whatever military discipline might have been found in the establishments set up to contain soldiers, sailors and airmen, was entirely absent. Wright-Nooth describes a complex social situation where bargaining, corruption and theft amongst the internees did indeed take place, and where the hockey sticks were not jolly, and old Etonians were few and far between.

It even goes into some detail about the semi-legendary outbreaks of ritual cannibalism, when certain of the occupying Japanese predated upon their captives. This is something which has often been alluded to, but I have never read about in detail before, and it makes highly uncomfortable reading. This is not a book that I would ever recommend if people read for fun, but it does make it easier to understand why, a year or so after I returned to the United Kingdom in the early 1970s, so many

British people who had lived through the war were bitter about a state visit to Britain from the Japanese emperor.

Despite the fact that adults always like to pretend that children are completely innocent, and know nothing of the nastier side of life, this is just not true. My parents would have been horrified that my friends and I were perfectly aware of the horrible events at Nam Koo Terrace where (or so it has been alleged for the last seven decades) the Japanese had made themselves an impromptu military brothel. We used to tell stories of the ghost of terrified comfort women who were seen running screaming down the street in a state of undress, in an eternal attempt to evade their invisible tormentors. Certainly there have been a string of quite well attested murders, rapes and suicides there ever since as recently as 2003, when a group of middle school students attempted to stay overnight at the building hoping to catch a glimpse of the ghosts. According to the report, three of the female students (who were later sent to hospital to receive psychiatric treatment) claimed to have been assaulted by a invisible attacker.

Interestingly there was a similar, though less *News of the World*esque series of events at the back of Peak Mansions. On the roof of Peak Mansions (where all the children were strictly forbidden to go), there were two huge green domes, which I believe held the mechanism that operated the elevators. However, to me and my friends, they were space stations, igloos, machinegun turrets, or whatever other item of hardware was necessary for the game that we were playing at the time.

One day, in either 1969 or 1970 my friends and I (totally without permission) were flying toy airplanes from the roof, when we looked down to the tarmac path six stories below us and saw a body lying in a slowly expanding pool of blood. We ran down the stairs as quickly as we could and found an unconscious Chinese workman who had presumably fallen out of the window of one of the flats in which he had been working. I ran to find my mother, and even at that age was shocked to find that with no emotion whatsoever she told me to find a Chinese person to deal with it, and being a dutiful son I did just that.

The workman died on the way to the hospital, and I was left with confused memories of seeing my first seriously injured human being, and even worse, my first conscious encounter with my mother's very singular brand of racism.

It was only later that I found out that this particular spot had been the sight of nearly a dozen accidents, murders and suicide attempts. As far back as 1913 a burglar had leapt to his death in this very spot and there had been a steady stream of similar incidents since. I have always been reminded of Andrew Green's famous accounts of events at a house in Ealing where a series of fatal accidents had taken place. Even the teenage Andrew had been rescued by his father just as he was about to jump from the roof, after receiving a compelling mental urge to jump over the parapet in order to have a look in the garden.

Sixteen Montpelier Road, Ealing still appears to exist — at least it was for sale last time I looked on the internet. Peak Mansions was pulled down in around 1990 in order to build a shopping mall, and - believe it or not - the Ripleys Odditorium. It would be interesting to find out if there have been any strange ghostly events there since my time.

In one way, the Hong Kong in which I grew up is a ghost. It was handed back to China in 1997 and the last rays of the setting sun of the British Empire were extinguished forever. Whether this turns out to be a good thing, or bad thing, or just a thing, remains to be seen.

On the hillside immediately behind Peak Mansions were three tiers of ruins. They had originally been an opulent, Victorian hotel, and - as children - we were told that it had been destroyed during the fighting with the Japanese two decades earlier, but this is completely untrue.

The history of the hotel is quite an interesting one. In 1875, someone called N.J. Ede had built a house called Dunheved there, but only six years later it was taken over by Alexander Findlay Smith, a Scottish railway man responsible for the original Peak Tram; a funicular railway familiar to anybody who has visited Hong Kong in the past century and a half. Findlay Smith decided that - with some prescience - a hotel to cater for people travelling up The Peak on his new railway would be a massive commercial success, and he was right. The hotel - which Findlay Smith sold in 1888 - was a popular success. Over the years, other storeys were added, and a two-storey annex was built. However, in 1922, it was bought by rival hotel owners, and because it had been constructed incredibly badly, closed in 1936, and was destroyed by fire two years later.

I don't know when it was finally demolished, but by the time we arrived thirty years after the fire, there was nothing left but ruins! But what fantastic ruins they were! And these, like the ruined Grey Walls, further up the mountain by Mount Austin Mansions, had been turned over to the youngsters of Peak Mansions as a wonderful adventure playground.

On the highest of the three levels, there was even a small cave; or at least we *called* it a cave, although it was really just a concave vertical space in the hillside, about four foot deep. But, the imagination of children is one of the fundamental wonders of the universe, and it became a smuggler's cave, a pirate cave, and base for Robin Hood and his Merry Men during the three years that I lived there.

About thirty feet above the ruins, there was another plateau on the hillside, which when I first discovered it, was home to some derelict but still pretty well serviceable pre-fabricated buildings, which again had been left uninhabited and were used by the local youngsters. However, when it was discovered that various human vagrants and - equally alarmingly, as far as the Colonial Administration were concerned - a small colony of Chinese cobras (which are, of course, deadly poisonous), the buildings were demolished, adding a fourth plateau of wasteland to our alfresco playground.

Immediately to the west of Peak Mansions, there was a 'proper' playground, with a roundabout, swings, and a slide, but I don't think any of the children living at Peak Mansions (and there were about twenty five of us) used it with anything approaching as much pleasure as we did the old ruins on the hillside.

My burgeoning career as an enthusiastic young naturalist was stepped up several notches by our move to Peak Mansions. There were several reasons for this, the most obvious being that – for the first time – we had an outside area that we could call our own. It was only a large, concreted back yard about thirty-foot square, but it allowed my imagination, and my collection of wildlife, to expand enormously.

At one end of the big bedroom, that I shared with my younger brother, was a large double window that looked out upon the yard. The section of the room which contained this window had two little walls about three-foot-tall, across with a gap of several feet in the middle to allow access. This is what my mother had originally described to me as a 'stage', and upon seeing it, I knew exactly what she meant, although it didn't look theatrical at all. My mother told me, that because I was the eldest, I could have this little enclave as an office, from where I could do my homework and carry out the other things which an enthusiastic eight year old could, and would, do. There was a long, broad windowsill, which stretched the whole width of the double window, and – thus – almost the width of my new office. And, much to my surprise, as my parents had always discouraged such things previously, I was allowed to put a motley collection of fish tanks, goldfish bowls, and jam jars upon this shelf, into which I placed a variety of aquatic beasties. In those days, the fish tanks that I owned were all no more than twelve inches in length. They had cast iron frames, that for some reason were always painted a bright enamel blue. I have no memory of how or where I obtained them, but I had two or three of them, spaced out at artistic intervals along the windowsill. Right in the middle, was a tank containing a pair of gold barbs (*Barbodes semifasciolatus var. Schuberti*). I had no idea at the time, but – although this colour strain was developed by Thomas Schubert of New Jersey in the early 1960s – the parent species was actually found quite commonly in the ponds and streams of Hong Kong. Indeed, I had actually managed to catch them on several occasions myself, and had noted – in my mind – that they were morphologically similar to the pair of golden fish which took pride of place in my windowsill aquarium, but had not made the connection that they were in fact the very same species.

At various times I had also had different types of tadpole, dragonfly nymphs, and water beetles, although the two things that I dearly wanted to catch – caddis fly larvae, and the impressively carnivorous giant water bug *Lethocerus* – always eluded me.

Although I didn't know it at the time, I was beginning to embark on the career as a cryptozoologist, which has taken over much of my life ever since. Although I had never seen one, I had received persistent reports that the streams of Victoria Peak contained a bright red crab. Both my parents poo-pooed the idea, saying that crabs were only found in the sea, and that any crab that's seen inland would have been carried there by birds who had caught them at the seaside and then dropped them before they could eat them.

On the face of it, this isn't that stupid an idea. Hong Kong island is, of course, only just over thirty square miles in area, and so one is not ever very far from the sea. But I had read a brief mention in Herklots' *The Hong Kong Countryside* of a freshwater crab species from the New Territories. This one, however, was green, but it did establish that – at least as far as freshwater crustacea were concerned – my parents didn't always know what they were talking about.

However, my instinct for self-preservation, which has not always been as infallible as one would have liked, did kick in at this point, and I decided that it would be an unwise decision to challenge my parents' position on this matter.

I kept on getting these stories for years, and twice – once on the flatbed of the stream which flowed through Victoria Peak Gardens, and once in the same watercourse, but along the manmade channel that took the water that had flowed from Victoria Peak Gardens down the waterfall to Mount Austin Playground – I found the discarded, bright red, exoskeletons of what were irrefutably crab claws. I showed them to my mother, but was told – in no uncertain terms – that they would have been dropped by marauding birds in the way described above.

I was convinced that she was wrong, and from the early months of 1968, I spent a lot of my energies trying to find living specimens of these red freshwater crabs, and even had a fish tank ready primed with fresh water, gravel and plants, ready to receive them.

As alluded to earlier, fresh water has always been a problem in Hong Kong, and, as the relations between the British Empire and Communist China worsened, and it became obvious that the British administration would soon not be able to import fresh water from the mainland, in 1960, an audacious plan was put into action, and work began on what was then the world's first fresh water lake constructed from an arm of the ocean.

The government hired an engineering consultancy to undertake a preliminary investigation, and when they had reported that the plan for damming off an entire arm of the sea was feasible, they authorised the HK$348mil project. The creation of the reservoir necessitated the displacement of a number of Hakka villages, the inhabitants of which were rehoused in purpose build accommodation in Tai Po. The Hakka had migrated southwards from their homeland in northern China about two hundred years before the birth of Christ, and they are an interestingly distinct Chinese race. Sadly their traditional villages are now few and far between and so whilst acknowledging the necessity for the Plover Cove reservoir to be built, I had a horrible idea that much of ethnographical interest was probably lost.

The first phase of the dam was completed in 1968, and for a year or so the drinking water that came out of our taps tasted most peculiar. Although I quite often drank water straight from the tap, it was in complete contravention of my mother's house rules. Because she and my father had spent so many years in Nigeria, where the sanitation facilities were considerably more primitive than they were in Hong Kong, she always insisted on boiling our drinking water. Therefore, the kitchen always contained a small row of green gin bottles, into which my mother would carefully pour tap water that had been boiled, to get rid of her – largely imaginary – bacteria.

Although I blithely drank the water straight from the tap, I was convinced that water from Plover Cove would contain large amounts of sea salt and other coastal chemicals that would not be at all good for my ever growing family of aquatic animals. So, I hatched a plan, and the next time that rain was due (and we were still in the rainy season at this time), I purloined as many buckets, washing up bowls, and other receptacles as I could get away with, and put them out in the backyard to catch the falling rain. Thus, I had a supply of freshwater that had not come from an area that, until recently, had been part of the South China Sea, and would therefore not be harmful to my fish and aquatic invertebrates.

One day, in early 1968, I went with some family friends to a fair that was held somewhere in the Mid Levels. And whist I was there, amongst other things, I won a goldfish in a bowl, which I took back proudly to my collection. The bowl was too wide to fit on the windowsill, and so I hatched a plan that I would build a makeshift table, stretching the entire width of the windowsill, to give myself a completely new area which I could fill with jam jars and fish tanks. I spent ages planning how I would do this, and eventually hatched a plan, which involved planks and bricks, which I had managed to persuade Ah Tam to get for me. But in the meantime, I placed the bowl carefully on top of the wardrobe in the main part of Richard's and my bedroom. However, but with the benefit of hindsight, not unexpectedly, 'Goldy' as I had unimaginatively called him, died after only a few days. Not only does this usually happen with goldfish that have become incredibly stressed out after having been exhibited in a fairground full of noise, bustle and excited small children, but the fact that the fish food that I had been giving it, and which consisted of a weird stale bread like substance to be crumbled into the water twice a day, was totally unsuitable for feeding anything, and Goldy was, sadly, doomed from well before the moment that I won him.

I'm not sure why, but the move to Peak Mansions had one particularly significant knock on effect for me. Within only a week or so after we arrived, I started to receive orphaned or injured birds; mostly fledglings. This had never happened to me up the

162

hill at Mount Austin, and I don't know why things changed so radically. But this established a pattern, which was to continue during the three years that we lived there, and which has continued - to a greater or lesser extent - ever since.

The first of these birds was a young *Zosterops* or white eye, which had been found sheltering inside one of the open garage bays around the back of the apartment block by my friend, William. For those of you not in the know, *Zosterops* are tiny little birds, a little smaller than a sparrow. They have a dull, light green plumage and the eponymous tiny, white feathers around the eye like the most delicate eye makeup put on by the most beautiful of women. Like most of the other birds that I have kept over the years, it was what is broadly known as a soft bill, which means it is an omnivore, who needs both animal and vegetable foodstuffs to thrive.

Even now, over fifty years after the event, I can remember the intense emotion that flashed through my mind as I carried the terrified little creature through the house to the conservatory, where I put it in an impromptu hospital cage made from a cardboard box with one of my mother's kitchen towels in the bottom.

Although my parents didn't encourage me overly in the pursuit of the local fauna, for some reason they were more forgiving and accepting of the various rescued birds that arrived, and allowed me to keep them in the huge Edwardian conservatory through the French doors that led off the sitting room. Sadly, although I perfectly remember my feelings of awe at being the custodian of something so small and helpless, not to say beautiful, my memory doesn't tell me what happened to the little bird. I expect that it died; most of them did, but in this case, I truly can't remember.

I have written critically, here and elsewhere, of the way that my hero Gerald Durrell retroactively edited the events of his young life to make a more cohesive narrative when he wrote them down in middle age. I am truly trying not to do this, and to avoid the temptation of making things any better - or worse - than I remember them. But the important word in that sentence is 'remember'. It comes as a shock, when writing about things that I did and said when I was eight years old, to realise that in less than ten years, I shall be seventy; an age which no amount of dressing up will change from being undeniably elderly. I will freely admit, also, that in the intervening half century, much water has flowed under many bridges, and far more alcohol and - indeed - other substances have polluted my blood stream; therefore, I am more than usually affected by the vagaries of human memory; and let's face it, human memory is not the most reliable of things at the best of times. It also doesn't help that nearly everybody that I knew back then is dead, and that the only two that are not - my brother and my old friend Richard Muirhead - are considerably younger than me, which means that I can check with them on the broader brushstrokes of what happened, but not on the minutiae of everyday life in the Downes household.

I cannot remember what order they came in, but over the next three years there was a fairly steady stream of orphaned and injured young birds, most of which died, some of which were released back into the wild, and others of which became much loved family pets.

There was a Hwamei that, for reasons of alliteration, I called Harold. Hwameis are amongst the most beautiful of the laughing thrushes; three genera of passerine birds primarily occurring in tropical Asia. Most of them are jungle birds, often very attractive and with loud vocalisations. Some of these vocalisations are loud and raucous; the Chinese name of one species means 'Seven Sisters' - an undeniably sexist name which compares the row which the make to the loud cackling and gossiping of a group of elderly Chinese spinsters, gathered at the village well. But others, like Harold the Hwamei, have a beautiful and melodious call, which has lead to them being much prized as cage birds by the Chinese.

The name 'Hwamei' comes from the Cantonese for 'painted eyebrow' and refers to the distinctive markings around the bird's eye, which - coincidentally - is similar to that described above for the tiny Zosterops, but if anything, looks more like the eye makeup of a high class courtesan in a traditional Chinese opera. The bird has a bright yellow beak, and the rest of the plumage is made up of various shades of lush chestnut, and the bird is a little larger than a British blackbird.

But the undoubted king of my avian collection was William.

My parents were close friends with a couple who lived at one of the other apartment blocks on the Peak: Mount Kellett. Mr Wakeford was - from memory - a policeman and - I believe - a fairly senior one, and he, his wife, and son owned (or at least, had shares in) a plush motor launch called *The Pukaki,* who was apparently an 18th century Maori chief in New Zealand. I have spent the last fifty years believing that it was the name of an antipodean bird, but apparently not. It is also - in the current vernacular - something rather revolting that I would rather not describe in these pages, and - I have no idea why anyone would name a boat after an obscure tribal leader, I assume that whoever it was who named the boat had intended to name it after the pukako, one of the most instantly recognisable of New Zealand birds, and just got the spelling wrong. But they could have been referring to a lake named after the aforementioned chieftain or - I suppose - even the revolting social practice described in the Urban Dictionary.

The Downes family used to go out with the Wakefords quite often at weekends, and together we would explore the various small islets, creeks, inlets, and bays that make up the territory of Hong Kong. Although most people think of Hong Kong as being a densely populated concrete nightmare, it consists of over 200 - often uninhabited - islands, most of which are incredibly beautiful.

We would explore this delightful and picturesque archipelago, and - with my naturalist hat on - I delighted in the vast array of tiny biotopes that we would explore most weekends, and - with my eight year old boy hat on - I would revel in the normal childhood pursuits of swimming, diving, and building sandcastles.

One day, early in 1968, probably around Easter time (because only the most foolhardy would go swimming in the sea during the winter, because the cold currents came straight down the Asian coast from Siberia) we were out - with the Wakefords - sailing around one of the islands near Cheung Chau. We had dropped anchor, and were enjoying a picnic lunch (which normally meant potato crisps and sandwiches for me and my brother, and varying amounts of alcohol for the adults) when suddenly the peaceful lunchtime was shattered as Mr Wakeford - sunhat still on his head - gave a gasp of astonishment and dove straight into the water. It appeared, I remember, as if none of the adults knew what was happening either, as the tall and wirey policeman swam steadily towards the jagged rocks just off the shore. A few minutes later, he swam back. I remember that he was doing the backstroke, because his sunhat was no longer on his head. It was - instead - on his chest, and had been co-opted for use as an impromptu bird's nest for an indignant ball of black and white fluff that was squawking vociferously at him.

William had entered our lives!

William (except he wasn't actually called William yet) was a crested mynah (the contemporary spelling seems to be mina, but I am stuck in my ways, and much prefer the old spelling). It is a species of starling which is native to southeastern China and Indochina. Interestingly, in the last decade of the 19th century, the species was introduced to the Canadian city of Vancouver, from where it spread across quite a large swathe of the continent, although it has now become extirpated. They are inquisitive, and intelligent, birds who naturally live in open country rather than forest, and can be seen quite widely in semi-urbanised park land, as well as grass and scrubland.

Jim Wakeford presented him to me, still residing inside his sunhat, and with a gruff voice he told me that here was another exhibit for my zoo. I don't think that he had cleared this beforehand with either of my parents, both of whom looked less than impressed with the idea.

Jim Wakeford was a very tall man; from memory, a few centimetres short of seven foot in height, and I believe - from what my mother told me subsequently - that he had spent the years of the Second World War as a naval officer on board various submarines. I always wondered how he had managed to get in and out of such cramped quarters, and had a delightful mental picture (which stays with me still) of them having to use the same sort of weird tin opener contraption that - to this day - is used on most cans of corned beef. I am sure that this was not the case, but the concept amuses me still.

I don't think that Mr Wakeford's height had any bearing on the matter, but, my parents came from a social background, where one did not criticise another adult in front of children (who were mostly required to be 'seen but not heard') and so they were faced with a *fait accompli*, and William was to live with us for the next three years.

Luckily for him, our picnic lunch, which had been so rudely interrupted, included tomatoes, bananas and hardboiled eggs, and I had enough knowledge of such things to be aware that from these humble ingredients, I would be able to make a delicious repast for the young Sturnid. I cut one of the hardboiled eggs in two, and mashed it up with the banana, before adding a few pieces of finely cut tomato. Then, using a technique which I had honed over the previous few months, and which I still practice occasionally today, I sat cross-legged on the deck (something that I have not been able to do for nearly half a century), plonked Jim Wakeford's hat on my knee, firmly but gently held the bad tempered little bird, and gently squeezed the base of its bill between thumb and forefinger. The little mynah was forced to open its beak, and - using the index finger of my right hand - I pushed a mouthful of the unappetising looking splodge into its beak. It swallowed it with every sign of pleasure, and after doing another couple of times, the small bird got the idea that I was its new 'mother' and gaped for me obediently. Giving it water was more problematical. These days, I would use a syringe, but - although I had such a thing back at Peak Mansions - I didn't have one on the boat. But, I did have a teaspoon, and William drank several spoonfuls of fresh water, before having an enormous bowel evacuation and going to sleep. Looking at William's droppings, I was pleased to see that there was no visible blood and that he seemed healthy. And, although I knew even then that as a 'rule of thumb', most baby birds do not survive, I had decided that as an axiom, if one of my feathered charges survived the first night, then it was likely to have a much better chance of surviving in the long term.

We took William home at the end of the day (still in Jim Wakeford's hat) and installed him in a sizeable bamboo bird cage that I had kicking around. Because the apartment was demesne of Augustus the Siamese cat, the only place that was safe to put William was the conservatory, which was already home to several other rescued birds, a pair of blue budgerigars, and a fat, unattractive white mouse. That night, as I said my prayers, I included William in them, and the Great God Pan must have been listening, because the next day, when I awoke and went rushing to the conservatory, he was sitting up (still in Jim Wakeford's hat) demanding his breakfast. From various books by Gerald Durrell, I had gleaned the information that cod liver oil and Abidec multivitamin drops were very useful in bolstering up the constitution of orphaned young fledglings, and, I always had them in my store cupboard. Bolstered with such useful supplements, the bird became larger, stronger, and more vociferous, and before long, was a family favourite. Even my bad-tempered father, who normally did his best to ignore my burgeoning menagerie, used to come and talk to William, and was even seen surreptitiously feeding him on occasion.

The origin of his name is lost in the mists of time. Indeed, it was lost only a week or so after he was named, because I thought that I had named him William after my friend William Topley (not the country and western singer) who lived with his family in an apartment elsewhere in Peak Mansions. It had been William who had brought me the tiny Zosterops, which had kickstarted my collection of rescued wild birds, and I was sure that I had named the mynah after him in appreciation of this. My father insisted that he had (sarcastically) named him William, or more exactly "Sweet William", because his cage was so odoriferous. For those of you not aware, the original "Sweet William", was Prince William Augustus, Duke of Cumberland, who is best remembered for his role of putting down the Jacobite rebellion at the battle of Culloden in 1746, after which he became a popular hero across much of Britain. However, he was not so revered by everyone; his opponents referring to him as 'Butcher' Cumberland. As I was writing this part of the book, one of the Queen's grandsons got married. As a result, it was a matter of Royal precedent that he would be granted the title of one of the Royal Dukedoms. However, there are only a certain number of these, and, for those of us aware of such things, there were very good reasons why many of these could not have been granted to Prince Harry. One of the most contentious of these would have been 'Duke of Cumberland', because - in a United Kingdom struggling to remain United - the idea of naming a high profile member of the Royal family after the bloke who was most famous for having massacred thousands of Scottish peasants in a most brutal fashion would have been undiplomatic to say the least. The possibility amused me in a malicious sort of way, but - luckily, although slightly disappointingly - somebody involved with the decision making process had both some knowledge of the lessons of history, and common sense; two things which are sadly absent from the CVs of many of the ruling classes and politicians of contemporary Britain.

But I digress, as I so often do. William soon became the tamest of any bird that I have kept before, or since. As soon as one opened his cage, he would hop out onto your finger and sit with his head pointing skywards demanding to be scratched under his chin. Even as an adult, he would occasionally come up to you and gape like a fledgling, which presumably was the bird equivalent of the way that adult cats will come up to their owners, turn around, stick their tails in the air and display their bottoms as if they were kittens allowing the mother cat to check for the presence of tapeworms; a mildly revolting but also touching display of familial submission.

One sunny day, however, disaster struck. I had put his bamboo cage on the broad windowsill of the conservatory so he could bask in the sun; something which he had always enjoyed. The window was open, and an inopportune gust of wind blew the cage over, the clips which secured the top to the base broke, and the cage fell apart. William, who by this time was pretty well fully fledged, flew into the blue yonder. We were all devastated, because the little bird had become a much-loved member of the family. I never expected that I would see him again, but the next morning when I went into the conservatory to feed the other birds, he was there at the window, pecking at the glass to be allowed in. Seldom have I been so happy, and - even now, half a century later - the memory of my relief is palpable.

A week or so after William had returned to us, the family went on a day trip to one of the grassland scrub areas above Kowloon Reservoir. What we were doing there, why we went, and who we took with us, I have no idea, but I do know that it was as a result of this trip that my ever growing menagerie got another new inhabitant.

I'm sure that we had someone, or maybe more than one, with us, because - as was so often the case - my parents were engrossed in conversation whilst my little brother played in the dirt and I went off to explore. The picnic place was surrounded by tall strands of elephant grass, which were nearly as high as I was. I always found these tall grasslands to be absolutely fascinating; they provided shelter for a whole range of different animals, and if one walked through them, one could dislodge a wide variety of different wildlife.

On that day, I was particularly interested in the tiny Chinese button-quail, which flew up from only a few feet in front of me as I walked. The males of this species are particularly impressive, with brilliant blue plumage and a fierce challenging call, all the more impressive for the birds being about the size of my eight-year-old clenched fist.

But all too soon, I reached the end of the stand of elephant grass and found myself in completely unfamiliar territory. I was in an area of scrub and grass land; the grass being identical to the elephant grass which I had just waded through, but being only a couple of inches tall. This khaki coloured meadow was punctuated with jagged granite rocks and the occasional thorn bush, and as my parents and their friends were way back on the opposite side of the elephant grass, it was delightfully isolated, and I felt very intrepid.

I marched on boldly, my butterfly net clutched in my right hand, and a jam jar on a piece of string dangling from my belt.

Suddenly, a pair of bright scarlet wings launched itself into the air before me. Shimmering, whatever it was flew strongly, about a foot above the foliage, before coming to rest on another of the little thickets. When I reached the animal's hiding place, it flew up again. I had never seen anything like it. It appeared to have much less rigid wings than a butterfly or dragonfly, and a wingspan of about four inches. But I couldn't get close enough to it to see what it was.

This happened on four or five occasions before - eventually - my quarry ran out of luck, and flew into a relatively bare area of stone and sun-baked earth. I could see something chunky and brown ahead of me, and - with my butterfly net stretched out in front of me - I did an intrepid and rather painful swan dive upon it. Although ultimately successful from a scientific point of view, it was still one of the sillier things I had done in my young life, because it was far more painful than I had imagined; I was oozing blood from nasty grazes on both knees. However, my bravery, not to say foolhardiness was not in vain, because there, wriggling around indignantly in the depths of my homemade butterfly net, was the largest grasshopper that I had ever seen.

Like my literary hero, William Brown, I never remembered to carry a pocket handkerchief, so I limped back through the elephant grass to where my family was still engaged in their post-picnic socialising, blissfully unaware of the drama that had been enacted only a few short yards away. I oozed more blood with every step, and by the time I got back to my nearest and dearest, I looked like a bit part actor in one of the less salubrious splatter movies. Being, inherently, a truthful child, I told my parents what had happened, but was not at all expecting the coals of opprobrium which were - as a result - heaped upon my forehead. Okay, I had torn my shorts and got them and my shirt covered in blood, but I *had* discovered a very interesting animal which was completely new to me. Surely, even my parents should see that this had been a sacrifice worth making. But, no, they didn't. And, I was punished in some way or other; the details of which have disappeared over the horizon on time's ever rolling stream.

However, much to my surprise, and - I have to admit - even to my surprise when looking back at these events with the benefit of half a century's hindsight, no objection was raised when I decided that I was taking my new animal find home with me. I put a twig and some leaves in the jar with it, and noted - with pleasure - that the grasshopper almost immediately started eating, and it appeared that it had an immense appetite.

It's strange how memory is selective. Whilst I remember the above encounter with this spectacularly hungry orthopterid, and I remember studying it under what I fondly thought of as 'laboratory conditions' (which actually meant putting it in Goldy's old, now empty goldfish bowl, on my desk and peering at it as he ate large amounts of foliage and defecated copiously), but I cannot remember what - if anything - I called it. And I cannot remember what happened to it in the end. However, I *do* remember taking the large goldfish bowl out into the back yard and releasing the huge insect temporarily in an attempt to see it fly once more; the allure of those great scarlet wings being too much for me.

Whereas, in its natural habitat, the great grasshopper (which I knew now was a locust) flew only a foot or so above the plants that covered its homeland, and I had confidently expected it to do the same within the concrete prison of my back yard. However, it wasn't to be, and the huge insect, once given a taste of freedom, flew almost vertically towards what Oscar Wilde would have called the "little tent of blue" high above us, and soon was out of sight. I was heartbroken; this was too soon after William's temporary escape for me to be phlegmatic about the situation.

But the story about me and the grasshopper wasn't over yet!

That evening, my parents had one of their regular cocktail parties at which the apartment would be filled with an assortment of grownups from the high echelons of the Colonial Government. As usually happened, my brother and I were dressed up in posh shirts and bow ties and given the task of handing out drinks. I have recounted these stories to friends of mine over the years, and some of them have been absolutely appalled at the idea of a five year old and an eight year old dispensing hard liquor to their parents' friends, but I have to say that Richard and I enjoyed these occasions. We not only got to dress up in special clothes, but always ended up with a pocketful of tips, usually totalling anything up to ten dollars, which was a huge amount of largesse for us at the time.

However, on our particular evening, my heart was heavy and my mind was full of my recently accidentally liberated pet locust, and I could think of, and talk about, little else. And I gave complex lectures, not only about my lost pet, but about the biology of locusts, to anyone who would listen.

This was my first experience of the phenomenon known as 'Chinese Whispers', although ever since I have thought of it as 'Hong Kong Whispers' in memory of that first manifestation of it. Before long, the story had gone round the assembled throng of slightly pissed expatriates, that I had released a plague of locusts into the backyard, and that they had flown to every corner of the Peak Mansions complex, and that nobody's house plants, fruit or vegetables would be safe.

Now, before we go any further, I think I should explain that whilst the apartment block was six storeys high, and there were only four sets of apartments, each with a back yard attached to the lower most one, above each back yard, each of the apartments had a small veranda upon which - British expatriates being the sort of people they are - the inhabitants took pride in growing miniature flower gardens and even vegetable patches, and the horticultural community was just as obsessed about their cultivations in Hong Kong as they would have been back in the leafy lanes of the Home Counties, which is where most of them came from. So the idea of my wilfully releasing a swarm of thousands of voracious insects was a potential disaster. It wasn't long before my father, with vengeance in his eyes, strode across the apartment to speak to me on the subject.

He took me by the ear and led me out into the back yard, and - with the unpleasant mixture of fear and resignation, which was so much a part of my relationship with my father all the way through my childhood - I waited for the inevitable physical retribution to take place. However, for once, my father seemed prepared to listen to me, and - I realise now - that whereas my mother rather enjoyed swilling down gin with the local colonial 'meat packing' glitterati, he found these occasions to be complete purgatory, and privately thought that most of his guests were a bunch of tedious nonentities. I was just beginning to explain to him what had actually happened, when my eye was caught by something moving on one of the potted geraniums that were the only things that my mother could grow with any consistent success. Hoping for the best, I ran over to it, and retrieved my errant locust. The huge goldfish bowl was still where I had left it, and I returned the great insect to its accommodation. My father burst out laughing, as I explained that this was the only locust that I had ever seen, and that far from having deliberately released a swarm of the insect, I had accidentally released one, and my informative lecture on how some species of the insect do indeed travel in huge swarms had been misconstrued by a bunch of half tipsy adults, who couldn't be bothered to listen to what I was saying, believe that nothing that a member of the younger generation could say would be of the slightest possible interest.

So, hand in hand with Daddy, with my free hand clutching my precious goldfish bowl and locust, my father and I went indoors to tell the assembled throng what *had actually happened.*

The score for the evening was Downeses: 1, the rest of the world: nil.

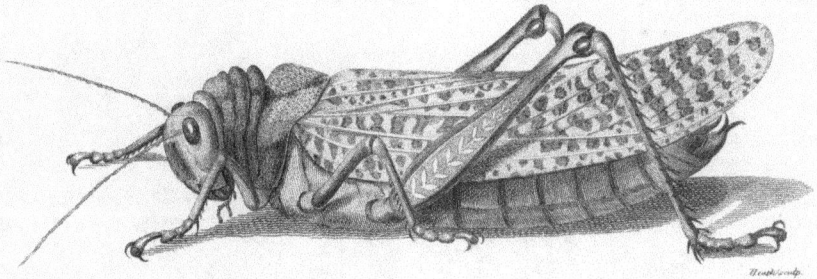

G. cristatus

1803 Oct.¹ London. Published by G. Kearsley. Fleet Street.

CHAPTER SEVEN
Down Under

You know, a long time ago being crazy meant something. Nowadays everybody's crazy.

Charles Manson

I don't know, and I doubt whether I shall ever know, the exact reason why – for the first time all decade – our annual holiday did not take us back to the Motherland. There were, and to a certain extent, still are, fault lines within my family, of which I knew nothing at the time. I *do* know that my father had a difficult relationship with his mother, and I also know – because he told me, many years later – that he had suspected that when – at the end of our 1966 trip to the Channel Islands – my maternal grandparents had manipulated events so that my mother stayed with them for some weeks rather than flying back to Hong Kong with the rest of us, they had done it for purely selfish reasons. And he resented that immensely. Whether that was the reason that we didn't go back to the UK during the summer of 1968, or whether – as he said at the time – he just wanted to show my mother the places in Australia that he had visited immediately after the war, I don't know. And I don't suppose that it matters, really. What *does* matter, is that I was able to visit a number of places that I would never otherwise have seen, and undergo experiences – some good and some bad – that have stayed with me ever since.

We sailed from Hong Kong in a cargo ship that had berths for a dozen or so passengers. The voyage from Hong Kong to Borneo, and from Borneo down the Australia took several weeks, and as I celebrated my birthday about halfway through the voyage – and as we spent at least three weeks (maybe more) in Australia - we must have missed the beginning of the new school term as a result. But, as I hated school and began to resent it more and more, this is no great pity. At least as far as I was concerned.

For some reason, which totally eludes me, we boarded the ship at night, although we didn't actually leave Hong Kong Harbour and sail out through the Lei Yue Mun Straits until the next morning. I remember sitting up in my bunk, in the cabin I shared with my brother, reading the well-thumbed copy of *Swallows and Amazons* that I still have today, whilst Richard, who was only about five years old, took great pleasure in mimicking the sounds of the huge quayside cranes that were loading bales of whatever into the open hatches on the foredeck of our ship.

This was the first of our annual holidays that I was old enough to really experience and learn from, and as we pulled slowly away into Hong Kong Harbour, the foetid smell of which – rich, fruity and disgusting – remains with me still, I knew that we were at the beginning of a great adventure. It was not entirely coincidental that I had decided to bring my Arthur Ransome books with me; they were the best literary reference points that I had for a long sea voyage – even I knew that the pirates of *Treasure Island* lay several centuries in the past – and I wanted a more contemporary set of reference points. The adventures of the Walker and Blackett children may have taken place thirty years before, but Hong Kong in the 1960s – at least, if you were from a family of one of the higher echelon Colonial Servants – had more in common with the England of the 1930s than it did with 'Swinging London', or the summer of revolutions across Europe and America.

Before long, we were out into the South China Sea, the bustle and smell of the 'fragrant harbour' a long way behind us. To my great joy, my parents allowed me to wander relatively freely across the decks, and, thus, I felt more like an explorer and less like the emotionally challenged child of irrational, alcoholic parents.

There was a line of chairs and benches at the front of the foredeck, and these became my own little eyrie from which I could sit and watch the ever-changing seascape, which was laid out before me like a glorious vista as if it had been created for my own personal entertainment.

I was convinced that the oceans before me were going to be full of a whole range of exotic and fascinating wildlife. Probably they were, but I didn't see as much as I'd hoped, although the ever-changing patination on the water and the great white barrel wave of the ship was an endless source of satisfaction to me.

Hong Kong was still a small dot on the horizon behind me when I saw my first dolphin. It rose up from the depths, its vinyl, shiny, mottled grey skin glistening in the tropical sun as it rode the barrel wave. I watched it for a good ten minutes before it disappeared. I hoped that it would be the first of many, but it wasn't. We didn't see another one until we were anchored off the coast of Borneo.

The further away we got from land, the wilder the seabirds became. I was surprised to see how far from land the great white-bellied sea eagles would fish. The common scavenging birds of prey of Hong Kong waters – ospreys and kites – had fallen astern before we had left Hong Kong territorial waters, but the huge eagles stayed with us for the rest of the day, before – too – being replaced by the birds of the open sea.

Towards the end of the first day, I saw my first deep ocean bird; the frigatebird, something with which I was only familiar from books.

William Dampier in 1697 wrote:

> "The Man-of-War (as it is called by the English) is about the bigness of a Kite, and in shape like it, but black; and the neck is red. It lives on Fish yet never lights on the water, but soars aloft like a Kite, and when it sees its prey, it flys down head foremost to the Waters edge, very swiftly takes its prey out of the Sea with his Bill, and immediately mounts again as swiftly; never touching the Water with his Bill. His Wings are very long; his feet are like other Land-fowl, and he builds on Trees, where he finds any; but where they are wanting on the ground."

We never saw more than one a time, but these magnificent denizens of the open ocean were with us pretty well constantly until we reached the Australian coastal waters approaching the Great Barrier Reef.

Somewhere nearer to Australia than Borneo or Hong Kong, there was a small storm, and a tired and battered member of this genus was found on the afterdeck. Knowing that I was interested in animals, one of the crew brought it to me, and I gave it water, and a tin of sardines, before launching it back out above the open ocean. Whenever there was a storm, and we had two or three during the voyage, I would be eager to see what wildlife would have been blown aboard. There was usually something – several birds and on one occasion, a huge silk moth – all of which I gazed at in awe.

One thing that I was hoping to see, (in the sea I mean, not blown on deck by a storm) but never did, was one of the great whales. I never saw a single one and – indeed – have only ever seen one (a tiny portion of hump and the remnants of the spume of what I believe was a humpback whale, near the Pillars of Hercules some years later). But, day after day, I sat in my lonely vantage point, various reference books (mostly totally useless because they were of Hong Kong birds, or the rock pools of the British Isles) spread out around me, as I gazed out into the blue ocean before me, like the lookout boy on an 18th century galleon.

For the first leg of the voyage, at least, my brother and I were the only children on board. This was really quite an enviable position to be in, because – as the only children – we were spoilt rotten by the vast majority of the adults on board. Both the crew, and the passengers, were particularly kind to us, and even my father was happier and less harassed incrementally, each day that we spent at sea.

It was the first time in my life that I was truly in the middle of the ocean. No matter which one direction one looked, and on which deck one stood, there was no land to be seen. I have described this to people I know, and a surprisingly large number of them seemed quite disorientated by the idea. But, I loved it. Each morning, my father and I would complete a little ritual of along the decks, all around the ship, completing a full circumnavigation of the vessel. I don't know what my father did then, but I would invariably go and sit in my little vantage point at the very front of the promenade deck, and stare out to sea, waiting for the inevitable adventures.

Sadly, whales, dolphins and sharks were completely absent on this leg of the voyage, but what we *did* see – every day now – were flying fish. These are delightful silver creatures, that – from my juvenile vantage point at least – looked like tiny piscine versions of the Boeing 707s that had taken us to and from England on so many occasions. I never tired of watching them launch themselves on their perilous journey, as they rode the powerful spume of the bow wake into an unfamiliar (for them) environment.

I wondered then, and continue to wonder now, how common these little creatures must be, because we saw them continuously from our second day out of Hong Kong all the way until we were in Australia coastal waters. They seemed to be a constant: making their perilous leaps above the surface of the water, every minute or so throughout our voyage. Most of these little fish, are around 10" in length, although the Californian flying fish (*Cypselurus californicus*) can reach a length of just over one and a half feet. There are – apparently – about sixty-four known species, grouped in somewhere between seven and nine genera, depending on which taxonomist you believe. They don't fly, of course, but they make powerful self-propelled leaps out of the water and into the air, where their long wing-type fins enable them to undertake a gliding "flight" for some considerable distance above the surface of the ocean. Flying fish live in all the world's oceans but are found particularly in tropical and warm sub-tropical waters, where they live in the epipelagic zone; the top layer of the ocean to a depth of about 200m. This is also often known as the "sunlight zone", because it is the section of the ocean where most of the visible light exists. Something that intrigued me, as I sat happily at the front of the observation deck, alone with the ocean and my thoughts, was how long these "flights" could actually be. I tried to time them, using the second watch on my watch, but with no pre-warning as to when the little silver aviators were going to propel themselves above the surface, my experimentation wasn't all that successful. When I finally gave up several days later, I decided that I hadn't seen any of these flights last any more than about half a minute.

However, in May 2008, a Japanese TV crew filmed a flying fish off the coast of Japan. This particular fish spent forty-five seconds in flight. These flights are typically over a distance of about fifty metres, although under optimum conditions, they can glide as far as four hundred metres. They travel at speeds of more then 43mph, and at a maximum altitude of six metres above the surface of the sea. Something that I was never to test out on this voyage, or indeed subsequent voyages, was the story that I got from one of the massively entertaining, though often zoologically unreliable books by Willard Price was the idea that, like moths, these little fish are phototropic and can be caught by fisherman in small boats, who erect lights on their decks, and hold huge butterfly net type arrangements behind them, waiting for these little fish to be lured to their doom.

I used to love the books of Willard Price. Unusually, for the books of exploration that I read as a child, the two protagonists - Hal and Roger Hunt – are neither English nor *Pukka Sahibs.* By the time of our epic voyage, there were nine books in the series, with another five to be published before the Canadian born author stopped writing them in 1980. Hal and Roger Hunt, sons of world-renowned animal collector, John Hunt, have grown up alongside exotic and dangerous wildlife. In *Amazon Adventure*, the boys' literary debut, Hal is nineteen-years-old, and Roger six years younger. For reasons that I cannot remember, they took a year off school to help capture animals for their father's collection on Long Island. These adventures took them to the four corners of the globe, and as well as encountering some of the most dangerous animals, and natural hazards, in the world, they also had to deal with their literary antagonist, the villainous Merlin Kaggs, who was eventually eaten by a Great White shark. The natives that they boys encounter during their adventures are – with hindsight – rather two dimensional; either villainous or loyal, and whilst I have not read these books in many a year, I still have them somewhere, and, just writing about them here makes me feel like reading them again, so I probably shall. Pootling about on Wikipedia to find out the publication dates, for example, I am interested to see that there is a mini-series of four books, by Anthony McGowan, published annually from 2012. These relaunched the 'Adventure' franchise, with the adventures of Roger's daughter Amazon (aged twelve) and her cousin Fraser (son of Hal, who is a year older). From the synopses I have found online, these seem to be more in line with current politically correct thinking as far as the environment is concerned, with the two children and their colleagues saving wildlife from environmental disasters, rather than capturing them for Americans to gawk at in unnamed 60's zoos. I soon gave into temptation, and bought the new books, and found them – much to my surprise – great fun, and I hope that the series continues.

I have no idea whether what Willard Price wrote about flying fish being attracted to light is true or not. I have seen the assertion repeated at various places online, but I am not convinced. However, back then, I saw no reason why Price's eminently believable statement should not be fact. After all, I was completely aware of the idea that some fish are phototropic.

Back when we were living at Mount Austin Mansions, and were on the fifth floor with a much high south facing vantage point than we had when we moved down the hill to Peak Mansions, every evening just after dusk, one could see the flotilla of tiny fishing boats, mostly sampans or smaller, sailing out into the waters that lay between Cheung Chau and Lamma islands. There, they would rest, and each little boat would sprout a bamboo antenna, on which dangled an oil lamp. Why they used oil lamps rather than electric lights, I have no idea. Indeed, the fact that they used oil lamps was embedded securely in the knowledge base of the youngsters on Victoria Peak, and I have no idea from whence it came. However, this tiny fleet of fishing boats would spend the first half of the night hours out on this relatively calm stretch of inland ocean, light fishing. Whilst they were not as demonstrative as the fishing techniques described by Willard Price, and used both lines and nets to catch the fish which were lured to the surface of the water by their pools of light, this was certainly something which was not only true, but something I had witnessed with my own eyes, when, one evening when an early evening cruise with the Wakeford family overran for some reason, and we sailed back to Aberdeen Harbour close enough to the fleet of tiny fishing boats to see their techniques for ourselves.

So, some fish were certainly attracted to light. Why not flying fish? Why not, indeed?

With hindsight, I can see that much of my childhood natural history explorations were fuelled by information which I got from my reading, which even at the age of eight, was far wider and more veracious than that of most of my peers. Fifty years later, I still live in a house full of books, and read more in volume and a wider range of subject matter than anyone else that I know. However, as at the age of eight, my comprehension of some subjects was limited, so my world view was skewed dramatically towards the results of my forays into children's literature (in particular) which – sadly, for me – was not always the most successful thing that I could do.

It is actually quite a difficult task trying to write a convincing narrative about things which happened half a century ago, to which I am probably the only remaining living witness, as my brother was only just five years old, and his testimony is probably not going to add much to the overall fluency of my account.

So, I cannot actually tell you – for sure – how long it took the ship (which for some reason I remember as being Swedish) to get as far as Borneo. But, I remember our arrival at the port of Sandakan as if it happened yesterday. Sandakan is one of the major towns of the Malaysian state of Sabah, but only five years before we arrived as our first stopping off point on our voyage to Australia, Sabah had been the British Crown Colony of North Borneo. And, as the transition to independence had been generally peaceful, and endorsed by the government of the Motherland, Britain was generally quite popular, and there were still quite a few expatriate Britons living there, still working the same plantations that their families had owned for generations. But only two years before, British soldiers had joined the Malaysian armed forces in a bitter and vicious undeclared confrontation, with the Indonesian army. But being only eight years old, I didn't know any of this, and as the green, leafy island – the third largest in the world - appeared on the horizon, all I could do was dream of orangutans, head-hunters, and spectral tarsiers.

After a week or so at sea (and this is where I truly would like to have been able to say exactly *how* long that leg of the voyage had taken), just being in sight of land was strange enough. But, the smells and sounds of this bustling tropical town wafted out to us long before we entered the little harbour.

We had sailed around the northernmost tip of Borneo some time over the previous twenty four hours, and it is only now, when I look at a map of the area on my iPad, that I realised what an impressive journey we had made. According to Google Maps, the captain must have carefully negotiated the disputed territorial waters surrounding the Paracel Islands, and the equally disputed Spratly Islands, the ownership of which is argued between communist China and four or five other countries in the area. We must have carefully navigated the strait which lies between the bottom of the Philippines and the top of Borneo overnight, because I remember finishing my breakfast and running out onto the deck to see the great, grey-green island get slowly bigger on the horizon. Coming into port seemed – to a child of eight, at least – to take many hours, and I remember that after the various formalities had been concluded, it was dinnertime that evening before some of the passengers were allowed to go ashore. For whatever reason, the Downes family were not amongst them.

However, I was happy enough to sit on deck in my favourite vantage point, and instead of watching the ever-changing seascape before me, sitting enthralled as I watched the pleasingly exotic hustle and bustle of the events unfolding before my eyes.

There had only been a few passengers at the start of the voyage, back in Hong Kong, and I'm afraid that the only one that I remember was an elderly, white-haired, Australian man, who used to join my parents for drinks on the quarterdeck every evening when the sun was over the yardarm. But, sitting at the front of the ship, watching what was happening around me with fascination, I was interested to see that our number had suddenly been swelled. Amongst the gaggle of passengers who joined the ship at Sandakan, were a middle-aged couple who still carried out the traditional British practice of running a rubber plantation, deep in the hinterland. I cannot remember their names (nor that of the elderly Australian), but all three – for different reasons – remain firmly lodged within my psyche to this day.

An hour or so after the new passengers had joined the ship's community, I dragged myself away from the three-dimensional soap opera on the quayside, and joined my family in the bar for pre-dinner drinks.

Not entirely to my surprise, the rubber farming couple to whom I eluded earlier, had joined my parents and the elderly Australian at their table, and a lively conversation, mostly about how – since the British had left – everything had gone to shit, was ensuing.

My mother looked worried. My little brother was coughing and spluttering like a small, pink walrus and was getting noticeably worse. I sat at the edge of the table, nursing a glass of lemon squash, and doing my best to perform my seen-and-not-heard act, but when my mother took my brother back to the cabin that we shared, and put him to bed before making a call to the ship's physician, my father brusquely introduced me to his new friends.

I actually feel mildly sad that I can't remember their names, because they never treated me with anything but kindness and consideration. He looked a bit like Lord

Lucan, with the prominent and rounded moustache that was so fashionable amongst the more conventional members of the British upper classes during the sixties and seventies. She, however, had a taste for big, flowery dresses and even bigger flowery sunhats, which made her look as if every time she appeared on deck or in the mess room, that she had been attending a durbar three quarters of a century before. Together, they gave me one of my only pictures of life as a true British colonial ex-pat rather than a civil servant whose sojourn in a British Crown Colony would last half a dozen 'tours' of a couple of years or so, before returning to the leafy lanes of Surrey, but people who had not only made their homes in the tropics, but whose families had done so for centuries. They were the real victims of the de-colonialisation process, and as the young state of Malaysia found its feet amongst the nations of the world, and grew further apart from Britain, I often wonder what became of this kindly couple, and whether (and if they did, how) they managed to adapt to this brave new world in which they found themselves living.

As well as my enduring interest in the natural world, I was – like most small boys – fascinated by things appertaining to the military, and took it for granted that if I couldn't be a zookeeper when I grew up, that would probably be a member of one of Her Majesty's armed forces. This was, after all, something that every adult male, and many of the adult females, I knew had done. Nowadays, as an aging hippy with a bad attitude and a firm anti-capitalist and anti-militarist agenda, I find it peculiar to look back and think that there was a time that I blindly prepared myself to go out and kill people in the name of God, Queen and Empire, but back then, it never entered my mind that there would be any other options for me. With the benefit of hindsight (good old hindsight), I now know that the ubiquity of military service on the path of every English adult male that I knew, was because National Service had only come to an end a few years before, and before that there had, of course, been the small matter of World War II, which – perforce – sent everybody into (at least, preparing for) conflict and in many cases, threw them headfirst into the war.

So, I was fascinated by my new friend's accounts of his life in the local militias, fighting the communist backed Indonesian insurgency around about the time that I was born.

But he also told me wondrous stories about the animals, and the less tangible "things", which the people living in the jungle – whether of European or local descent – took for granted, and which thrilled me to my very bone.

My mother came back to re-join the party, but she had a serious look on her face. Apparently, my little brother, Richard, had developed some sort of tropical fever of unknown origin, and – to be on the safe side – the ship's medical officer had decided to admit him into the sick bay, in order to monitor his condition. These days, it would be unthinkable for a five year old child to be admitted to hospital (floating or otherwise), without there being a provision for his mother to stay in attendance, at least part of the time. But this was fifty years ago, and furthermore, it was the 1960s, deep in the heartland of colonial and post-colonial Asia; a culture that was vaguely akin to Britain forty years before that. And so, as the two ships nursing orderlies tended to my brother's pyrexia, my mother sat with me and my father, hearing stories about tiger hunting, shooting Indonesian guerrillas, and occasionally glimpsing the mysterious little forest goblins, as she sipped her gin and tonic and waited for the sun to be well and truly over the yardarm.

The next day, the elderly Australian man offered to take me ashore for the day. My brother was still ill, my mother was beginning to take his illness seriously, and I have no memory whatsoever of what my dad was doing. But, we were scheduled to spend two days in Sandakan, while the ship loaded and unloaded cargo, refuelled, and did whatever else a Scandinavian merchant ship does when it spends two days in a Malaysian port.

These days, I can hardly imagine respectful people being stupid enough to let their little boy out of their sight for seven or eight hours, in a potentially dangerous foreign country, and under the charge of someone that they hardly knew. But these were different times, and this is precisely what my parents did.

Together, the Australian and I explored various bits of the outskirts of the little port. Sadly, I remember very little about it. The only things I do remember were him buying me an expensive hand-carved boat (the hull of which I still have and which I pass every day as I stagger downstairs to find out what horrors the new day has in store for me) and that once we were back in his cabin aboard the ship, he made a half-hearted attempt to seduce me. As far as I remember, this was the only time this ever happened in my childhood, and I gently rebuffed his advances, and they were not repeated. And to this day, I have never told anyone about it.

Things like this are supposed to be highly traumatic for a child, but I don't think it did me any great harm, although I am very pleased – with hindsight – to have encountered such an ineffectual molester.

That evening saw me sitting on deck with my parents and their friends, listening agog to the rubber plantation owner talking about some of the more arcane inhabitants of the jungle.

If the eight year old me had the insight of the sixty year old me, he/I would have taken notes, but I didn't, and so – all these years later – I found myself reliant on the half century old memories of a conversation that took place when I was a little boy.

Apparently, or so he said, as well as the jungle tribes of the Murut people, who were – I was thrilled to hear – the last ethnic group in the region to renounce headhunting, there was a nomadic tribe of what he called pygmys, who lived in the wildest parts of the forest and who were very seldom seen.

They were, he said, completely different to the tribes with whom he was familiar, being much smaller and darker skinned. Although, I have been able to find out little about these people, it appears that before the modern humans arrived in southeast Asia, the region was occupied by a race known as the Negrito, which is the Spanish diminutive noun of negro, and simply means "little black person". These people still live in the Andaman Islands, parts of what was then Malaya, parts of southern Thailand, and the Philippines. It is accepted that they once lived far more widely, and that there are ethno-cryptozoological reports of such people in several parts of Indonesia. I have found historical camps of them in Borneo, although in 1912, Charles Holmes wrote:

> "...the wide distribution of remnants of the Negrito race in the island round about Borneo, and in the adjacent parts of the mainland of Asia, renders it highly probable that at a remote period, Negritos lived in Borneo; but in the present time there exist no Negrito community..."

The most exciting survivors of the Negrito race live on North Sentinel Island in the Indian Andaman Islands, two thirds of the way across the Bay of Bengal, towards what was still then called Burma. The precise population of this island is not known. Estimates range from 40 up to 500, however no one has ever landed on these islands and survived.

Any ship, aeroplane or helicopter that approaches the islands is greeted by a hailstorm of arrows. As recently as 2006, Sentinelese archers killed two fishermen who within range of the island, and the Indian government discourages any approach to the island.

I had read about these island warriors in an issue of *National Geographic*, which someone had given to my parents, and – being a bloodthirsty little boy – I was eager to find out whether this semi-uncontacted tribe in the middle of northern Borneo was as aggressive as their Sentinelese cousin. But it appears, not. The rubber planter told me how these tribes came and went, leaving no evidence of their existence, and how he would occasionally leave gifts of tobacco out in the jungle for them.

But these were not the only mystery dwellers in the jungle.

In folklore, the *Batutut* or *Ujit* or *Người rừng*, sometimes also known as "forest people", is an entity said to inhabit the Vũ Quang nature reserve and other wilderness areas of Vietnam, Laos and northern Borneo. A 1947 sighting by a French colonist refers to the animal as a *L'Homme Sauvage* (wild man).

Two *Người Rừngs* were reportedly captured by tribesmen near Đắk Lắk Province in 1971. In 1974 a North Vietnamese general, Hoang Minh Thao, requested an expedition to find evidence of the creatures, but it was unsuccessful.

A professor Tran Hong Viet of Pedagogic University of Hanoi, a researcher of Người

Rừng, reported in 1982 finding footprints in 1970, measuring 28x16 cm., of which he made casts. He had been making an extensive post-war inventory of natural resources, and while collecting specimens near Chu Mo Ray in Sa Thầy District, he came across the prints. A photo of the cast of the print was later published by *Fortean News of the World (Japan Fortean Information Society)*.

Most recently, in 2014, an "ape man" was reported to have been shot in the Bornean jungle and the creature was described as being an "orang pendek"

In 1974, John MacKinnon, best known to cryptozoologists for his involvement in the discovery of the Vu Quang Ox, described his encounter with a huge, upright-walking orangutan:

> "I was nearly home when I saw a terrifying spectacle. For a moment I thought it was a trick of my vision. A huge, black orang-utan was walking along the path towards me. I had never seen such a large animal even in a zoo. He must have weighed every bit of three hundred pounds. Hoping that he had not noticed me, I dived behind a large tree. I was in no state to defend myself, or run from him should he come for me, and I could recall clearly the natives' terrible stories about old, ground-living orangs. I held my breath as the monster passed within a few feet of me and let him get about forty yards ahead before I followed in pursuit. He was enormous, as black as a gorilla but with his back almost bare of hair; Ivan the Terrible was the only name I could think of."

The *orang pendek* has been reported from Sumatra for centuries. In recent years, the Centre for Fortean Zoology has sent a number of expeditions to the island in search of the fabled beast, and we have had a certain degree of success. The Bornean ape man, known as *Batatut*, is far more obscure; although the CFZ's Carl Marshall went to the forest of North Borneo in search of it, some years ago. He was not successful, and all the native stories that he encountered were from Sumatra.

I didn't know any of this, and sat totally enthralled, as the rubber planter told me about the shy, bipedal ape that lived out in the wildest parts of the jungle. He had only seen it the once, although various of the workers on his plantation were more familiar with the animal. If I had known then that I was listening to one of the only European reports of an unknown hominin from the world's third largest island, I like to think I would have taken notes. But I was eight years old, and as the dusk fell - and the fragrant smell of various night flowering plants that I have never been able to identify, but which rolls out over the sea at dusk to greet any sailor lucky enough to be anchored off these shores - I drank my lemon squash and listened, enthralled, to these stories of a world which, even then – had pretty much vanished.

Because my parents' shipboard friends were amongst the last generation of colonial rubber planters, indeed amongst the last generation of colonial anythings, anywhere in Malaysia or Indonesia, stories like this will probably never be heard again. At least not under these circumstances. I don't know what happened to them when we said our farewells some weeks later, when the ship pulled into Sydney harbour, but I have nothing but warm memories of them, and hope that the rest of their lives were happy ones.

The next morning, we were back at sea. We had left Sandakan overnight, or at least after my bedtime, but this time we were not in the open ocean. For the next thirty-six hours or so, we hugged the north east coast of Borneo as we made our way southwards to our next port of call. We reached the little port of Tungku late on the second day after leaving Sandakan. And even from my vantage point on deck, it was obvious that this was a far less sophisticated place than Sandakan. There was none of the hustle and bustle that we had seen at our previous berth; along the quayside were a row of dilapidated wooden shacks, and there was nobody to be seen except a couple of drunken Malay men arguing off to the left hand side, whilst a mangy and emaciated stray dog wandered up and down the quayside indolently.

There didn't even seem to be facilities for us to dock at the quayside, and so we were anchored a quarter of a mile or so offshore. The greasy, grey-green jungle stood over the little town oppressively; it was my first proper view of properly tropical rainforest, and I was disappointed that it wasn't a riot of colour, with parrots, monkeys, and gibbons clambering about the trees making the sort of noises that I had only ever heard on National Geographic nature documentaries. The trees were silent, still and implacable, and watched over the tiny port in a vaguely sinister manner.

Here, in the interests of what our transatlantic chums call 'full disclosure', I'm not actually 100% sure that the second port we visited was in fact Tungku. I know that it was in Sabah and I know that it was a small down-at-heel harbour, but – as of the time of writing this – half a century has passed, and I was never a very attentive child at the best of times. I was convinced that as the jungles on shore and the waters upon which we bobbed contentedly, were full of enormous amounts of fascinating wildlife, that the following day would see me (the naturalist of the ship; some sort of eight year old Darwin, as I self-identified) coming face to face with it all, and making a myriad of ground-breaking zoological discoveries.

So, I went to sleep that night, my dreams populated by dugongs, crocodiles, and spectral tarsiers.

The next day would have dawned bright and fair if we had been characters in the edenic children's books that I read so avidly, and which had done so much to formulate my world view. But, being the real world, it didn't. And I soon discovered why 'rainforests' were called 'rainforests'. It drizzled all day, and the air was so humid that it was actually hard to see where the humidity stopped, and the drizzle began. The island was shrouded in a grey, diaphanous mist, which made the whole place look grubby and slightly sinister.

Following breakfast, ablutions, and everything else, all the passengers went ashore for our long-promised foray into the jungle. Quite a few of the older passengers, who'd obviously been to this insalubrious little port before, had decided to stay on the ship, and so the entire excursion was hacked into two large, open-topped trucks, the beds of which had been modified by the addition of a motley collection of chairs – none of which matched – making them into two makeshift charabancs. I was massively impressed at this new and exciting mode of transport, but most of the adults complained in that very reserved, British way, usually saved for indignant letters about cricket sent to the relevant editor of the *Daily Telegraph.* My hopes of seeing a wide cross-section of the local wildlife started off well; there was a large, dead and semi-decomposed black snake by the side of the road as we boarded the 'tour busses'. Its flesh was turning into a greasy, odoriferous jelly, and about a third of its backbone was already visible. It was, sadly, to be the only item of Bornean wildlife that I would see that day, despite my binoculars and high hopes.

We headed out into the hinterland of the island, but we didn't go into the jungle. This was because there was no jungle. The mighty grey-green trees that we had seen from the ship the previous evening were merely a tiny remnant of what must have been there only a few years previously. Because the whole area had been chopped down, and the jungle replaced by palm nut plantations. Palm nuts originally came from Africa, but because they grow quickly and the oil, which is extracted from the seeds, contains more saturated fats than the oils made from corn, sunflowers, and a host of other plants, this cash crop has become widely cultivated across south east Asia, particularly in Malaysia and Indonesia. These days, the plantations are under increasing amounts of scrutiny, because it is now widely accepted that they cause a great deal of social and environmental harm. Greenhouse gas output has increased, people are displaced by unscrupulous palm-oil enterprises, traditional livelihoods are negatively impacted, and – above all – rainforests with high levels of biodiversity are destroyed in order to produce environmental 'deserts', where practically nothing apart from palm nuts are able to live. It is a similar situation to what has happened with forestry reserves in the United Kingdom; our natural deciduous woodland, where a mixture of broad-leafed trees, various shrubs, and a large number of different ground plants which played host to a dazzling biodiversity, being replaced by serried ranks of non-native conifers, which are great for timber production, but which produce an environment where practically nothing else can live.

For hours, we drove along long, straight, laterite roads; the drizzle permeating our clothes until we were soaked through, and although I jabbered on excitedly about the orangutan that we were "bound" to see "any minute now", we saw nothing apart from laterite and palm trees. At some point, we stopped for whatever reason, and as the party stretched their legs, I snaffled a palm nut from one of the trees and put it in my pocket to take back to Hong Kong with me, at the end of our long adventure. I kept it for years, until it started to sprout a rich carpet of mildew, and my mother – as always, fearing that her offspring would succumb to some nasty, tropical disease – made me throw it away.

Several hours later, when we returned to the dock, we were all thoroughly disillusioned. Even the dead snake had vanished, which was disappointing to me because I had been trying to work out how I could extract the skeleton and take it back onboard the ship.

At the quayside, we got into a couple of small boats with outward motors, and made our way back to the ship. Even now, I was convinced that the brief, quarter mile journey would see us come face to face with dugongs, dolphins, and sharks. Despite this, I sat near the stern, my hand trailing in the water, oblivious to the fact that if there *were* any denizens of the deep in the vicinity, the hand of a little English boy might well be seen by them as a tasty snack. That singularly failed to happen, although the kindly rubber planter told me that he'd had a brief sighting of the curved back, and triangular dorsal fin, of a shark or dolphin breaking the surface for a brief instance. Even then, I suspected, that he was just being nice; trying to make up for my disappointment in finding that the rainforest I had so longed to see just wasn't there anymore.

It is good to note, however, that in recent years, the Indonesian and Malaysian governments have become far more aware of the environmental impact of logging and palm nut cultivation, and that now there are now large nature reserves, the provisions of which are – to a certain extent, at least – respected by the human inhabitants of the region, and the businessmen who own them.

Again, for reasons which remain obscure, we set sail overnight, and by the time the assorted passengers arose to greet another day, we were far out to sea; the coast of Borneo disappearing rapidly on the horizon. It may have been the third largest island in the world, and a dazzling hotspot for biodiversity, but our sojourns on the island had – I'm sad to say – been somewhat of a disappointment. But never mind, I thought, as I resumed my vantage point at the bow of the ship, scanning the horizon before me with my little binoculars and steely gaze. The next stop was Australia, and before we would make landfall, we would be travelling directly above parts of the Great Barrier Reef, which in those days - allegedly - had water so clear that one could look down from the deck of a passing ship and see the riot of colourful animal interactions a few fathoms below.

Time is a very strange thing, and often a remarkably objective one. It is a well known phenomenon that as one grows older, time appears to go past far more quickly. I remember that when I was at school, at the beginning of the summer holidays, the six weeks stretched ahead like a glorious vista of opportunity. Whereas, now, just over a year past my sixtieth birthday, six weeks goes past in the flash of an eye, and even the temporal distance between one year's end and another, seems to go by stupidly fast. So it is that as I look back fifty something years to the Downes family's voyage from Borneo to Australia, I truly can't tell you how long it took. The days on board ship seemed to take place in a temporal universe all of its own, which – both at the time and in my memory – seemed to stretch on forever. But, looking at it from a logical point of view, we were probably only on board for about a week during this stretch of the voyage.

It had its high spots. Earnestly, I had explained the Coriolis Effect to any of the adults – both passengers and crew - that would listen. The practical application of this, and the one that I particularly wanted to see for myself, was the phenomenon by which – allegedly – water swirls down the plughole the opposite way in the southern hemisphere, to the way it does in the northern hemisphere. I have read that when one was actually *on* the equator, the water would go straight down the plughole without swirling either clockwise or anti-clockwise. This was something I was intent on seeing for myself.

On the night on which we were scheduled to actually 'cross the line', I was determined to stay up and see what happened. My enthusings on the matter had apparently effected a large proportion of the crew, and I remember my parents – laughingly – tell all and sundry upon our return to Hong Kong, how members of the ship's crew had stayed up to see the phenomenon for themselves. I, sadly, possibly as a result of my intense excitement on the matter, was ill that night, and so missed seeing what actually happened. I have, for some reason, managed to miss the chance of finding out whether the Coriolis Effect actually *does* work on the times that I have crossed the equator on subsequent equations. Sad, but true.

The next day, there were fun and games on deck. In a light-hearted ceremony which is always carried out on ships containing passengers who have not previously crossed 'the line'. One of the ship's crew is always designated as King Neptune, the ancient Greek sea god and – to this day – widely regarded as Monarch of the Seas. Other sailors are dressed up as highly unconvincing mermaids, who are His Majesty's Attendants, and an awful lot of splashing, and some dunking in the on-deck swimming pool, is the order of the day. The 'Crossing the Line Ceremony' is all good fun, and my brother Richard and I enjoyed it immensely. I would hate to think that this pleasantly bawdy nonsense would be disallowed in these puritan times, because the sight of sailors wearing unconvincing, false breasts and mermaid fish tails, might offend either the LBGTQ or other akin communities. I truly hope not. Another momentous happening, which took place that week, as we sailed across the Coral Sea was the occasion of my ninth birthday. The captain and crew were very kind to me, and not only provided a birthday cake (which I don't think anybody in my family was expecting) but made a big fuss of me, and the captain himself took me up into the wheelhouse and let me 'steer' the ship for a few minutes.

This momentous day, which also included me being given a copy of Geoffrey Herklots' exhaustive full length tome on the birds of Hong Kong (which I still have, to this day), ended with me happily sat on deck in my favourite vantage point, seeing the most exciting piece of marine wildlife on the voyage. To my great delight, a hundred yards or so off the starboard bow, I saw a huge manta ray leap out of the water, high into the air above, before re-entering the ocean in such a streamlined manner that, whereas there had been a significant splash when it left the ocean, there were only a few discernible ripples as it went back in.

In all the years that I have been fascinated by sea life, I still think that this is one of my favourite experiences.

As we sailed by the coast of New Guinea, there was a mild tropical storm, and the next morning I found a huge silk moth sunning itself on one of the ship's bulkheads. It was considerably larger than my nine year old hand, with dark chocolate velvet wings, with a delicate pattern overlaid in fawn.

Then, the next day came. The moment I had been looking forward to for so long; we were to sail over the Great Barrier Reef. I had been enthused once more by my sighting of the manta ray, and I was certain that we were going to see all sorts of glorious marine wonders. But the storm had done its damage, and the sea was a murky, greyish green and everything that I had been told about how those sailors on ships passing over the Great Barrier Reef would be able to see thousands of fish, crocodiles, and whales in crystal clear water, singularly failed to come to pass. I did see two large sunfish, however, and for the first time in my life, I wondered how a creature that seemed to spend its whole time swimming on its side could be even slightly happy with its lot. This was a big disappointment, but it was soon wiped out when we reached our last port of call: Brisbane.

Sadly, I cannot remember anything about Brisbane itself, or about anything that we did whilst we were there, because everything paled into insignificance besides one of the things that we did when we were ashore. We went to a place called the Lone Pine Sanctuary, where I saw koalas and – most excitingly – platypus for the first time. Somewhere, there is a photograph of my brother and me grinning like imbeciles as we held a koala; something which these days is understandably discouraged. But the thing that has stuck in my memory ever since, and the thing that – I think- still counts as the most impressive zoo exhibit I have ever seen in a lifetime of visiting zoos across the world, took place when we entered a small, subterranean viewing passage, which was considerably smaller than my own sitting room, here in North Devon. It was dark, and there were several wooden park benches positioned so one could look at a long, glass window, maybe ten foot high and three times that in length. The window looked out on an impressively adapted little creek, the water of which came about two thirds up the glass, so one could see the water to the depth of about seven foot. There were small fish, and yabbies – peculiar Australian crayfish that I have always admired – but most exciting of all were two small furry creatures, about twice the size of a European mole, and superficially similar in physiology, except for the fact that they had bills like that of a duck. The platypuses (I'm not sure if they're supposed to be platypi or not) swam around visibly, their every move being greeted by a chorus of ooh's and aah's by the awestruck members of the public who sat there, watching them. I was too excited to join in. To see such a glorious primitive creature; one of the few mammals left alive who lay eggs rather than giving birth to live young, was such an awesome experience that I could never find any way of externalising it.

It remains one of my most treasured zoological memories, and – like my sighting of the manta ray a few days earlier – has remained with me ever since, and will continue to remain with me for the rest of my life.

Under any other circumstances, the other animals which were on display at this lovely little sanctuary on the outskirts of Brisbane, would have been an extraordinary treat! There were echidnas (of what species, I cannot remember), for example, but after my interaction with the little platypus family, to see the only other species of extant egg laying mammal was a bizarre anti-climax.

I could have spent a month there, but we were only able to be there a few hours. We went to visit some friends of my parents on the way back, and apart from the fact that they had two dried and lacquered sea horses that I dearly coveted on their mantelpiece, I can remember absolutely nothing about them. But the memory of the oddly elegant little aquatic monotremes remain with me still.

A few days later, after a relatively short trip down the eastern coast of Australia, we arrived in Sydney. We saw the Sydney Harbour Bridge, and my father ranted incessantly about the – then nearly completed – Sydney Opera House. "It looks like a fucking artichoke" he grunted, angrily. I have, I will shamefacedly admit, inherited some of my father's less socially acceptable vices, including his infinite capacity to get angry about things. But my parents were angry about the Sydney Opera House, the Canadian flag, and traditional hymns put to modern tunes, for over four decades; something which knocks my pitiful efforts at directing streams of bile at things I cannot possibly change, into a cocked hat.

I remember very little else about Sydney. It was hot, and grubby, but we went on into the suburbs and visited a wildlife sanctuary. It was, by no means, as exciting as had been the Lone Pine Refuge a few days earlier, and my abiding memory is how callous - and yes, downright cruel – some of the staff were, especially the ones who were charged with taking our particular little party around the zoo.

We visited a paddock containing a bunch of bored looking, grey kangaroos, and the equally bored tour guide explained how kangaroos were marsupials and therefore gave birth to semi-developed youngsters which they nurtured in an external pouch. "Well, duh, any twat knows that", I didn't say, but I asked an innocuous question about how big the 'joeys' are. The bored looking tour guide vaulted over the perimeter fence, wrestled the nearest of the bored looking grey kangaroos to the ground, reached into its pouch and pulled out an indignant and somewhat frightened looking young kangaroo, which he brandished in my general direction.

"Does this answer yer question, cobber?"

I reached into the depths of my antipodean knowledge for a suitable repost.

"Fair dinkum," I muttered, and the tour guide glared at me, obviously considering me - a bloody Pom, no less - guilty of cultural misappropriation (if the term had been invented back then).

And he got his revenge a few minutes later, by suggesting – in complete contravention of the gulag-like signage, forbidding all and sundry from feeding the wildlife – that I give some 'monkey nuts' to an impressive looking galah cockatoo. I still have the scars today, and the memory of the loathsome tour guide sniggering as my mother applied impromptu first aid to my cut finger.

There was also a display of sheep shearing, which seemed, to my nine year old eyes, to be far more wantonly brutal than was necessary.

But the one thing that I do remember about this less-than-happy visit to an Australian zoological establishment, is my first encounter with the magnificent brolga – or Native Crane.

These magnificent birds, which were originally known as 'the native companion', were originally thought to be a member of the heron family, but by 1865, the legendary ornithological artist, John Gould, placed it correctly within the order of Gruiformes. On this summers day in 1968, I was lucky enough to see them indulging in the behaviour for which – perhaps – they are best known; their intricate, ritualised, mating dance. I don't think I have ever seen such oddly beautiful, and apparently choreographed, behaviour in a bird. The performance began with one of the birds picking up some grass, and tossing it into the air before catching it in its bill. The bird then jumped a yard into the air, with its wings outstretched, and continued by stretching out its neck, bowing, strutting haughtily around as if it owned the place, calling and bobbing its head up and down.

There were about half a dozen of these magnificent birds in the slightly shabby paddock, and no sooner had one of the birds started to dance, than several of its companions joined in. I have read, I think in *Two in the Bush* by Gerald Durrell, that – on some occasions – up to a dozen of these ridiculous, but oddly graceful birds, will line up opposite each other and perform a mass dance, like elderly women at a keep fit session, trying out line dancing with more enthusiasm than skill in execution.

Twice during the long coach journey back to Sydney Harbour, where we re-joined our ship, we saw flashes of reddish brown, as something large and long careered across the road, like the proverbial bats out of hell. The bus driver, who was doubling as a tour guide (a far nicer one than the bloke that we had happily left behind at the sanctuary) explained that they were 'goannas'. It was some years later that I discovered that goannas (an inaccurate contraction of the word 'iguana') were actually lace monitors – the second largest lizard known to exist in Australia. They can grow to nearly seven feet in length, including a long, slender tail, which is about one and a half times the length of the head and body. They are common all across eastern Australia, and were once a favourite traditional food of the Australian aborigines.

The largest Australian lizard is, of course, the perentie, which can grow up to a length of just over eight feet, and is found in a broad swathe across the centre of the continent. But once upon a time, there was something far bigger.

Megalania is a supposedly extinct giant monitor lizard, which evolved to pray on the Australian megafauna. And it was the largest terrestrial lizard ever known to have existed. The largest specimens reaching a length of over twenty-three feet, with a maximum weight of approximately 620kg. The most recent fossil remains date to around fifty thousand years ago, and it is quite possible that the first human settlers of Australia might have encountered them, and been a factor in their extinction.

However, there are people within the cryptozoological community who believe that, not only has this enormous lizard survived to the present day, but that it has a far more socio-cultural importance. There is quite a lot of evidence that mariners from China, or at least from countries which lay within the Chinese sphere of influence, reached the continent of Australia centuries before the Europeans did. Extrapolated from this, it has been suggested that some of these mariners may have encountered specimens of Megalania, and taken the traveller's tale back home with them, and that this is where the original concept of the Chinese Dragon came from. Artefacts of apparently Chinese origin have been found in several archaeological sites in eastern Australia, and this hypothesis is not without its appeal. There have certainly been a number of well-attested sightings of giant lizards in modern day eastern Australia, particularly in the Watagan Mountains of New South Wales. Some of these sightings have been made by qualified zoologists, and it seems likely that there is some substance behind them. However, it may not be evidence for the continued existence of the monstrous Megalania. Lengths of animals in the wild are notoriously difficult to guess, and if these unknown lizards move as fast as the goannas that I saw that afternoon in 1968, it would be even more difficult to estimate their true length and mass.

I have always thought that it is more than likely that some species of monitor lizard can grow to a greater length than is currently accepted. Colonel John Blashford-Snell told me of his experiences in Papua New Guinea during the 1970s. He equated some of the 'dragon' and 'dinosaur' sightings which had come out of that mysterious island over the years, with encounters that his team had logged with absolutely massive lizards, with heads the size of a horse's, that he identified as absolutely massive specimens of *Varanus salvadorii*. I see no reason not to believe him, indeed I wouldn't dream of doing so. I have long thought that an aquatic monitor lizard, probably extra-large specimens of the Nile monitor (*Varanus miloticus*), might be responsible for the sightings of 'aquatic monsters' across parts of West Africa. And, carrying on a logical progression from these hypotheses, it is, I suspect, quite possible for the giant monitor lizards of eastern Australia to be explained by outsized specimens of known species rather than something completely new.

But I am feeling in a remarkably pessimistic mood today, as I write this.

We only had one more port of call, before our voyage – the seafaring part of it, at least – was over. And a day or two later, we arrived in Melbourne. My memories of it are of a stately, colonial city, which actually felt more like one of the regional seats of power in the United Kingdom than anywhere on what is arguably the most exciting continent of them all, at least from the zoological point of view. I remember visiting a staid Victorian park – both literally and figuratively – where formal grey footpaths and prim box hedges were the order of the day. I looked with disinterest at a small flotilla of ducks on a small, ornamental pond, and silently willed the lords of time and space to bleeding well get on with it and take us to the next stage of our adventure.

A day or so later, we travelled to Adelaide, the capital of South Australia. To my mild embarrassment, I don't actually remember the details of the journey, or anything much about the city. What I *do* remember, was going into the Natural History Museum and seeing a stuffed platypus. Whilst the animals I had seen, back at the Lone Pine Reserve at the outskirts of Brisbane, had been tiny (the size of a large European mole), this one was considerably larger; the size of a large, domestic, cat. I know now that this discrepancy was almost certainly purely because the animals in the sanctuary had been juveniles, whereas the animal in the museum had – in life – been a large adult. But it intrigued the nine-year-old Jonathan immensely.

Whilst we were in South Australia, I vaguely remember going to another display of farmers shearing Merino Sheep. Again, I was disgusted and quite distressed by the thoughtless, and wanton, cruelty of it all; on this occasion, the shearsmen were so rough that they even drew blood from the poor, unfortunate creatures. Why the Australian farming community were so proud of this baffled – and to a certain extent, still baffles – me.

We made our way to the big railway station in Adelaide, and the next stage of our epic voyage was just about to begin. We were just about to embark on one of the great railway journeys of the world. The Nullarbor Plain (which in Latin, quite literally means 'no trees') is a flat and semi-arid area of southern Australia, and is the world's largest single exposure of limestone bedrock, occupying an area of about 77,000 square miles. For the next three days, we travelled across it by train. Construction of the Trans-Australian Railway began in 1917, and is the longest straight section of railway in the world. Sadly, for nine year old children everywhere, the original line was deemed to be suffering from severe problems with track flexing, and the line was entirely re-built the year after we used it, and as far as I can ascertain, the journey is now far faster and efficient, which is – from my point of view – a sadder thing indeed. Because the three-day journey remains in my mind's eye one of the highlights of my young life.

The plain was a riot of slightly muted, but gloriously contrasting, wildflowers. And I sat for hours, in the plushly furnished and decorated carriage, which I believe was known as the 'Observation Car', looking happily out of the window at the ever-changing vista. I always hoped that this would be my biggest chance of seeing a wild kangaroo, but – in fact – I can't remember seeing any wildlife; just the mosaic carpet of wildflowers that stretched on for mile, after mile, after mile.

Being a little boy with the revolting proclivities that little boys have, I was fascinated and indeed, delighted, to find out that when went to the lavatory, one's bodily waste flushed away directly onto the railway track below; something I'd never seen before and have never seen since. And which, I am sure, would not be allowed by the authorities these days, although I can't honestly see that the produce of the bowels of a few dozen travellers once or twice a week, would have any serious environmental impact upon this enormous area of wilderness.

Many years later, when I discovered the writings of Bernard Heuvelmans, I read about the explorations of Ludwig Leichhardt (1813 – 1848 approx.) who was a German explorer and naturalist, most famous for this explorations in the wilder parts of central Australia.

In a section of his most famous book, *On The Track of Unknown Animals*, which deals with the mystery fauna of the antipodes, Heuvelmans speculates that various claims of sightings of what appeared to be giant rabbits, actually referred to surviving *Diprotodons*. These were the largest marsupials ever known to have lived, and – along with many other members of a group of species collectively known as 'the Australian Megafauna' - they existed from approximately 1.6million years ago until they finally became extinct about 46,000 years ago, probably as a result of human predation, and the destruction of the ecosystem on which they depended by early Aboriginal land management. The largest specimen was approximately the size of a hippopotamus, and superficially resembled a rhinoceros without a horn. There were at least three species, although some authorities that there were as many as twenty. The closest surviving relatives of *Diprotodon* are the koala and the three species of wombat, but – much as I personally would love the enormous marsupials to have survived – I truly cannot see how and why Heuvelmans said that these animals could look like a giant rabbit. Even as a child, I wrongly suspected that this was an exercise in wishful thinking, rather than systematic taxonomy.

Heuvelmans goes on to claim that Leichhardt became completely obsessed with the possibility that these enormous creatures could have survived. He wrote that Leichhardt:

> "...tirelessly carried out several other explorations, and his researches gradually led him to the belief that the *Diprotodon* was not extinct. In 1847, he organised an expedition with the secret hope of bringing one back alive. He set off enthusiastically into the dry heart of the continent and it is known that he reached the River Cogun on the third of April 1848. Nothing more was ever

heard of him, or his companions. The trail of unknown animals sometimes leads to Hell."

It is an emotive piece of writing, but many years later, I was visiting the British Museum (Natural History) in South Kensington, when I met an expert on the life of Leichhardt. She told me that basically, there was no evidence whatsoever that Leichhardt was even slightly interested in *Diprotodons*, and that he had probably been killed by indigenous Australian natives, as had more than a few other European explorers at the time.

But I didn't know anything of that at the time. I was still intently scanning the patchwork horizon for any signs of kangaroos. One of the waiters in the dining car made friendly overtures to me and I told him of my secret desire to see a kangaroo. He told me that there were stories amongst the farming folk that lived on the edge of the Nullarbor Plain, that as well as the familiar kangaroo species – the red and the grey kangaroos – and the smaller wallaby species, there were occasional sightings of truly enormous kangaroos, by those people foolhardy enough to venture into the wilder parts of the plain. There was a truly enormous giant kangaroo (over six and a half feet tall, and weighing over 500lbs), which lived in Australia during the age of the Megafauna, although it too appears to have gone extinct, possibly as recently as 18,000 years ago. Whenever I see people on cryptozoological forums discussing possible survival of Australian species Megafauna, I remember the middle-aged and weather-beaten waiter on that long-ago dining car, and wonder idly whether there was any truth in his assertions, or whether he was just trying to amuse a little English boy during a long, otherwise boring, afternoon.

For some reason, one particular social *faux pas* that I committed on this journey, involved a fairly busty middle-aged Australian woman, who played piano rather well. Every afternoon and evening, she would sit at the grand piano in the Observation Car, and play a mixture of light classical melodies and show tunes. I was overly impressed. Surprisingly, as music has been such an important part of my subsequent life, the nine-year-old Jonathan had not really encountered live music before – outside music lessons at school, that is. There was an acquaintance of my parents, who had lived a few floors away from us in Mount Austin Mansions, who played the piano (mostly songs from *The Sound of Music*, I recall, with a wince) but who did it really rather badly. This woman was – in my eyes, at least – extraordinarily talented, and I told her so. "You play like a professional," I said.

"She is a professional", hissed my father as he led me away by my ear, leaving my mother to apologise profusely to the woman who was employed by the railway company, to entertain their travelling guests. I was chastised soundly though I didn't really understand why, but – it seemed – that once again, I had broken one of the unwritten rules of social behaviour, which even nine-year-old boys of my class and background were apparently meant to know instinctively.

I don't actually remember our arrival at Perth, the capital of Western Australia. But we spent two or three weeks there, which – from the point of view of a nine-year-old stranger in a strange land – was a glorious eternity. We stayed at a small guest house on the outskirts of the city, and whilst we went into the city itself on many occasions, we spent most of our time exploring the countryside and the huge swathe of golden sandy beach, and its adjacent sand dunes.

I had discovered the wonders of sand dunes two years before in the Channel Islands, but these were far larger and seemed to go on forever. They were their own singular biotope and were home to all sorts of fascinating wildlife. One morning, after it had rained lightly the night before, I was enthralled to see the wide range of tiny footprints that could be found everywhere one looked, on the temporarily rain-hardened sand. Even then, I knew that the vast majority of Australia's mammals were marsupials, and I daydreamed happily about potoroos, antechinus, and other small pouched mammals, as well as the few indigenous rodents, which somehow had bucked the prevailing trend and survived upon the island continent when all over placental mammals had failed.

But it was the seashells that really fascinated me. Although some of them were similar in shape and form to the ones with which I was familiar from the beaches of Hong Kong – cowries and conus, for example – others were completely unfamiliar to me, and I soon amassed a sizable collection. My father gave me a pocket guidebook to Australian shells, and I have it still, somewhere, in the depths of my library. With the book in my pocket, I spent much of my time marching intently along the foreshore and much of my evenings identifying, classifying, and sorting the specimens that I had found. When we eventually returned to Hong Kong, they took pride of place in my shell collection but, alas, along with the rest of my seashells, they were given to my ex-father-in-law, thirty years ago. And thus, are lost to me for good.

On one day, we visited the Royal West Australia Show. I have never been particularly interested in agricultural animals, but I well remember my father getting all misty eyed and sentimental when he saw a display of bullocks from the breed which originated in his native North Devon, and – to the day he died – he credited this serendipitous encounter with provoking our next family holiday being to Devonshire, and eventually to our family's return back here to live. I wasn't the slightest bit interested in the endless parades of livestock, but some of the 'sideshows' have stuck in my mind ever since. Mostly the ones involving wild animals. The most exciting of these was a fairly unassuming makeshift aquarium tent, which would never have stuck in my mind at all if it hadn't been for the fact that one of the tanks contained a display of living sea snakes of various species. They were animals that I had always wanted to see alive, and which I never had before, and never have since. There were several different species in a six foot tank, similar to the one that I used to keep my alligator snapping turtle in up until a few years ago, in the CFZ museum. They didn't look particularly happy or healthy, and I wondered then (and continue to wonder now) whether these notorious pugnacious animals had actually bitten each other whilst in captivity, and were – as a result – at death's door. However, the fact that the signage implied that this was a permanent exhibition – permanent, for the week or so that the agricultural show lasted, that is – would imply that it was unlikely that my gruesome hypothesis could have been correct.

According to the zoo chat forums:

> "Sea snakes are not particularly hard to keep and various species have been kept long-term. This isn't a recent development but has been the case since the 1990s at least. However, only sea kraits have been seen with some regularity in aquariums in Europe and North America, probably because these coastal species are easier to source than the true sea snakes. True sea snakes have only very rarely been kept outside their native Asia and Australia. As long as they are healthy when entering captivity, they are not particularly prone to disease and readily feed on dead fish (there's also videos on YouTube: "Sea Snakes feeding at Reef HQ Aquarium" and "Sea snake feeding at Ocean Park Aquarium, Shark Bay WA"). When well-fed they evidently tend to ignore most other fish in their exhibit. For example, a wide range of small to medium sized fish (squirrelfish, wrasse, surgeonfish, angelfish, butterflyfish, moorish idol, damselfish, maskray, etc) co-inhabit the olive sea snake exhibit at Blue Planet Aquarium (Denmark); most of these have been together for a very long time without issues. Reef HQ (Australia) has successfully kept sea snakes with lionfish and stonefish for a long time. Aquarium of the Pacific (USA) and Berlin (Germany) have kept a range of small fish with their sea kraits, but I'm unaware of their "durability", i.e., if fish remain long-term or frequently switch, suggesting predation by the sea snake. However, mixing should still be done with care. Several few years ago an aquarium in Australia lost a sea snake... when attacked and eaten by a pufferfish. Since many sea snakes feed heavily on eel, especially morays, in the wild, they presumably should never be mixed. I've seen a photo from Aquarium des Lagons (New Caledonia) where a sea krait and sea turtle share a tank, but suspect this is a very risky mix."

The other sideshow that I remember was one curated by the West Australian Police, and – although, like most nine year old boys, I was a bloodthirsty little sod – my mother flatly refusing to let me go into the 'Homicide Gallery' (which considering that even then my psyche was far more fragile than I let on) was probably a good idea.

On another occasion, we visited a travelling exhibition of Australian reptiles, which had been set up in what seemed, to my memory, to be a church hall of some description. I remember that it was advertised as being an exhibition of species that were found locally, but as it included small specimens of both species of crocodile found in Australia, neither of which are found outside Queensland and the Northern Territory, this could have not have been the case.

With hindsight, it would appear that all of these animals were being exhibited in a highly unsuitable series of displays, but for the nine year old Jonathan, already obsessed with aquatic reptiles in particular, it was paradise. For the first time in my life, I had the chance to see not only crocodiles, but lots of different species of turtle ranging from the parchment shelled soft shells, still all within the family *Trionyx*, to the pleasantly grotesque *Pleurodira*, about which even now I giggle when I see them because I have always thought the long necks looked just like a penis.

There were also lizards and snakes of all shapes and sizes, including the coastal Taipan, which, allegedly, is the most venomous terrestrial snake in the world.

In the middle of the city of Perth, there is a park, whose name I have sadly forgotten. In the middle of this park, unremarkable except for its enormous size, there is a hill, which has been maintained as a wilderness nature reserve. I have told people about it over the years, and nobody has believed me, but a year or so ago, my friend and colleague, Lars Thomas, confirmed that he had been there too, and that everything that I have been saying about the place for the last half century, is completely true.

I assume that the nature reserve is far more policed than it would have otherwise seemed, especially to a nine year old who thought that it was a virgin 'bush', and that dangerous animals have – to a certain extent, at least – been removed to places where they are less likely to be a danger to visiting humans. But, the amazing thing about the place, particularly for me, was that one could see and interact with a wide variety of wild animals in their natural habitat. The three that remain most vibrant in my mind's eye are two lizards – the shingleback skink and the blue-tongued skink – and a mammal; the peculiar, egg-laying, short-beaked echidna. I had seen all three of these species in zoos earlier in our trip, but nothing could have prepared me for the intense joy that I felt seeing them wild, in their native habitats, where they were so tame that I could kneel down with my head almost at ground level, and observe them face to face.

It has been fifty years since I left Australia, and – perforce – my memories of our stay are not only those of a nine-year-old boy, but have been filtered through the intervening half century. They are as fragmented as the rest of my memories which make up the narrative of this book, but as well as the main events that I have described to you, certain other fragmented memories intermittently come to the surface, such as the cries of the little boys who sat, selling newspapers on street corners throughout Perth. They had big, checked caps on their heads and – every few minutes – would call out an incomprehensible phrase that sounded like 'ber-bee-berk', something which, for some reason, amused my little brother and me immensely. And for many years, when I had what Churchill described as 'the black dog on my shoulders', something which happened more and more as I approached puberty, Richard could always cheer me up by imitating the cry of a Perth city newspaper boy.

Although it appalled my father, I was always impressed by West Australian breakfasts. Every morning, we would sit in the small dining room of our guest house, and the waiter would stride over to us and gabble:

"Watcha-yer-want, guys? We got stike an' eggs, stike an' sausages..."

And he would rattle off half a dozen more meals, all involving large slabs of 'stike'. Once, my father asked whether there was anything on the breakfast menu that did *not* include 'stike', and the waiter looked at him in horror, as if he had asked for a vial of heroin and some nipple clamps.

I also remember an occasion, where I realised – for the first time in my life – that the concept that I had been fed for as long as I could remember (that Britain was at the hub of a great web of colonies and the Dominions, all of whom loved and respected the Motherland), was actually not true.

We were on a coach trip; where to and why, I have no idea, but the tour guide stood up at the front of the coach as we were driving along on our way to wherever it was that we were going, and said, "is there anyone here from Sydney?" and three or four people cheered. "Is there anyone here from Queensland?" and more people cheered. He continued in this vein, each time eliciting more cheers from the jolly punters, until he asked, "so, who else have we got?" and my father, showing an unusual amount of bonhomie, answered that we were from England. There was a dead silence.

The tour guide muttered something that I didn't hear at the time, but I have to assume it was derogatory, because nobody spoke to us for the rest of the trip.

During one of our last family days in the sand dunes, I wandered off, looking for wildlife. After about ten minutes, I found myself in completely unfamiliar parts of the dunes, and I began to sense that something was following me. Out of the corner of my eye, I would see something scuttling out of sight into the marram grass. I knew enough about Australian wildlife to know that the only large predators were extinct, but the memories of some of the images from the police exhibition that I had seen a few weeks earlier at the Perth show came unbidden into my mind, and I began to be truly frightened.

I was uncomfortably aware that whatever it was positioned between me and the path back to my family, and I didn't know what I was going to do.

Then, I saw what it was.

It was my father, who - partly as a prank, and partly to make sure I was alright - had followed me. I was so shocked and relieved that I burst into tears, and for the last few days which we were to spend on the island continent, I was an emotional mess, and for some reason it seemed that whatever I said was going to irritate one or both of my parents.

And it wasn't just my parents. On our last visit to the park in the centre of the city, I saw something white on the ground. I bent down to pick it up, and found it was a piece of bread. I looked around, and saw that there were other pieces of bread scattered across the grass. Over the brow of the hill came charging a bunch of angry Australian children a few years older than me. They were feeding the pigeons in the park when some 'stupid Pommie bastard' went and "fucking ruined it". My parents extricated me, but I got the impression that their sympathies were with the natives.

Later that day, we were walking past some shops, when we passed a greengrocer. I saw a long, and strange looking, root vegetable, which reminded me irresistibly of one of the pictures in my encyclopaedias at home. "Look, Mummy, it's manioc", I said in a shrill and enthusiastic voice. The shopkeeper overheard me, and snarled that it was nothing more than a parsnip, and my father cuffed me round the ear for embarrassing them.

And that is, I think, when my psyche started to fall apart.

At the time, I didn't know that I was going into my first breakdown. Indeed, I would have scoffed at the idea. I had always been raised on the concept of having a stiff upper lip, and being a true soldier of the Empire. But I was. I was a small boy, who was being subjected to the stresses and strains of things he couldn't possibly understand.

I don't want to appear as if this book is entirely me criticising my late parents. It is not. And whilst it is now self-evident to me that my father suffered from a very similar battery of mental health disorders as do I, he was never diagnosed as such, mainly because – half a century ago – mental illness, like butt plugs, nipple clamps and septic tanks, was not something that one spoke about in public. It was only forty years later when I finally received a diagnosis for myself, and I had to bully, cheat and cajole to get that. So my poor, dear father never had a chance, and so by definition, neither did I.

There is a line in one of the classic werewolf movies, featuring Lon Chaney Jr., which says something like, "until the bloodline of the wolf is severed, the ancient evil will continue". And that is basically why I have never had children of my own. I truly believe that my father's mental health conditions came from his relationship with his mother, and I suspect that it goes back, generation after generation. I have been so unhappy throughout most of my life, that I decided once I reached adulthood, that I would not pass my genes on to fuck up another generation.

As noted at the beginning of this narrative, "They fuck you up, your mum and dad. They may not mean to, but they do", said Philip Larkin, and with the benefit of hindsight, I know that he was right.

We left Australia a few days later, and I was excited to be going back to the relative stability – for me at least – of Hong Kong. It was the only home that I knew; England being an abstraction that I only knew from holidays, and although my relationship with my parents wouldn't change, the fact that I was back with my pets and a landscape and landmarks that I knew like the proverbial back of my hand, made me happy.

On our last day in Australia, my parents decided to hire a car, and so we drove out into what my parents described as 'the bush'. I kept my eyes peeled as I stared intently out of the car window. I so wanted to see a kangaroo, but I was unlucky. I never saw a wild Macropod, and I've never seen one since, although it appears that, even now, two species of large kangaroo and a whole bunch of smaller wallabies are found in the wild country inland from Perth.

We drove thirty or forty miles inland from Perth, and soon found ourselves in from some fairly wild country. Several times, we saw the bright orange/brown 'goannas' rushing across the road but, sadly, we didn't see any other wildlife of note. Peculiarly, we had seen far more native animals in the little wild hillock in the middle of Perth's biggest city park.

But, even aged nine, I could tell the difference between a strictly managed nature reserve in the middle of the large, modern city, and a place where – in the words of one of my favourite early twentieth century explorers – *nothin' would surprise.*

Except, of course, that nothin' actually did surprise. But we had nice family lunch, and all too soon, we were ready to go back to the hotel, because – I remember my mother saying – we had a particularly early start the next day.

So, we packed up, and set off for 'home'; my father driving, and my mother in the passenger seat, navigating. After an hour, it became startlingly obvious that something was wrong. On the journey out, the suburbs of Perth had slowly but surely given way to wilderness, which – equally slowly but surely – got progressively more wild. We had stopped for lunch in a cheerfully primitive stand of native trees, which cast an alien shadow down upon us, as they had for any time in the previous ten thousand years. However, on our return journey, the countryside was getting progressively wilder and more implacable, and there were no signs whatsoever of the outskirts of Perth. And there really should have been. I gingerly pointed this out to my parents, but was told, in no uncertain words, to keep my mouth shut. So, I sat back in the rear seat and gazed in interest, and not a little trepidation, at the alien landscape that was passing before my eyes. With hindsight, it is a damn good thing that - knowing my father's state of mental health at the time – I had not seen the 1971 Nick Roeg adaptation of James Marshall's 1959 novel, *Walkabout*. This is not just because it featured Jenny Agutter with her kit off, but because it opens with a mentally ill, white father having an existential crisis, shooting at his two children and everything else that moves, blowing up the family car and shooting himself in the head; leaving his young family to fare for themselves.

Again, with hindsight, I think that the events of 1967, when my father lived under the daily shadow of an imminent invasion of Hong Kong by bloodthirsty, Communist paramilitaries, as well as a whole host of other problems - not the least being a mentally ill son - had taken its inexorable toll and he was quite possibly at crisis point himself.

We carried on driving, and eventually, my father spoke up and asked my mother to check the map.

"Oh no, dear" she replied, in her most matronly manner, "I'm not using the map. I'm navigating by the sun".

All day, the tension had been rising until it was culpable, and I was scared, though resigned, for an imminent explosion.

But it was an explosion of laughter! My father, choking back uncontrollable gasps of mirth, reminded my mother that, for the first time, she was navigating in the southern hemisphere, and so King Sol was leading us further away from the city, rather than towards it.

No harm was done, and whilst it would be a much better plot twist if I told you that somehow we'd run out of petrol and been stranded amidst a host of poisonous snakes and savage tribesmen, of course nothing of the sort happened, and we made our way back to the hotel in far better spirits than we had been in days.

The next day, we made our way back to the airport and onto our Qantas flight to Hong Kong. My mother had always been given a little 'helper' from our family doctor, back in Hong Kong; a tranquiliser (probably Valium), to give to my brother and me in order that we would be calm during long air journeys. This might well be why I enjoyed long haul flights so much, and it unconsciously started my life-long habit of getting pilled-up before I fly anywhere.

Soon after we rose into the air, I was looking out of the cabin window, and could see the unmistakeable shoreline of Shark Bay, and its attendant islands, below me. It was a ground-breaking moment for me; the first time I had ever seen a geographic landmark that I recognised from an atlas in real life. I promised then that someday I would go back to Australia, preferably without my father. However, at the time of writing, fifty years on and twelve years after my father's death, I have never done so.

Pity.

I settled back in my seat for the long flight home. However, I couldn't get comfortable. The upsets in my psyche were beginning to take their toll. It was the first time that I remember, on this flight between Perth and Hong Kong, that I started to hear 'voices'. Being an imaginative child, I assumed that these voices - which never said more than a few words that were coherent, but were usually mumbling away in the background - were voices of ghosts, or aliens, or some other appropriately supernatural being from the pages of the books that I devoured so happily.

It wasn't for another thirty years before I realised that these were yet another symptom of my burgeoning mental illness. I'd always been a paranoid child, but during this flight, I was totally convinced that some disaster was awaiting us. Maybe the whole of Peak Mansions and everything in it (which, of course, included all my pets) had burned to a crisp. Maybe my beloved Ah Tim would have died, or one of her extended family (and remember that this was nearly a year before the Manson murders) had gone on a blood-fuelled killing spree. I continued to work myself up into an emotional frenzy, imagining more and more macabre and horrific scenarios happening to the people and animals that I held dear, until I was sobbing loudly and shaking violently.

All I got in return was a cuff round the ear and a lecture on how I should be a "young gentleman" like my younger brother, and stop letting my family down.

Of course, when we finally got back to Peak Mansions later that day, everyone – animal and human – was perfectly well. Nothing untoward had happened. There had been no bloodbaths or Communist invasions, and – thankfully – it was as if our six weeks away had never happened. And it was only a matter of days before I settled, more or less happily, back into my normal routine. But things were never the same again.

It is only with the benefit of hindsight that I realise how drastically those six weeks travelling around the southern hemisphere have changed me. Like most small children, I had always assumed that what my parents said was gospel, and that any time that I was reprimanded or punished, it was automatically my fault. But the chinks in that particularly armour plated truism were beginning to show, and not only did the summer of 1968 give me my first real experience of the mental illness which was to plague me for the rest of my life, but I was to realise for the first time that my parents were not always right.

But I do not want anyone, not even myself, to think that it is the memories of these horrific emotional events which are the only things that I have kept with me from that summer, half a century ago. Far from it. The things that I remember most are the animals, the land and seascapes. The gloriously solipsistic feeling of being alone on the deck of a boat with a 360 degree horizon, cleanly devoid of any land. The sight of my first (and, to date, only) platypus, and the way that I had interacted with so many gloriously antipodean creatures such as shingleback skinks, and the desolate beauty of the Nullabor Plain. It is these things which remain with me still, and which are the most important memories – for me – of that glorious summer.

But when I went back to school a week or so later, everything had changed. The teaching system was still as intractable as ever, and – without really knowing how or why I was doing it – I became more disruptive and angry, and as a result, I was punished regularly both there and at home.

Then, a few weeks later, disaster struck. Although my paranoid premonitions on the flight back to Hong Kong were nothing more than my psychotic imagination in full bloom, a much loved member of the family was to disappear suddenly, and forever.

I still remember the day vividly. There had been another outbreak of cholera in the colony. These things happened with monotonous regularity, and each time, all the Europeans (I don't know about the indigenous people, but I suspect not) were inoculated against the disease. I had a deathly fear of injections. I don't like them even now, but back then, they completely terrified me. However, my mother took my brother and I into town, to the family surgery so we could be inoculated.

The only upside for me with this was the fact that it meant that I had an afternoon off school. Richard had started at Peak School that term, but being only five years old, he only went to school in the mornings, and so this didn't affect him. But, despite the terrifying thought of having a needle stuck into my arm without a by-your-leave, I was rejoicing in the fact that I wouldn't have to return to school that day. I walked home and, finding myself with half an hour to spare, I went around (with my imaginary zoo keeper hat on) and checked on the wellbeing of all of my animals. William the mynah bird was in his wickerwork cage in the conservatory, next to my big fish tank. And, I don't think I'm being too anthropomorphic to say that he showed every sign of being pleased to see me.

Elsewhere in my menagerie, various fish and creepy crawlies did their own inimitable thing, and I noted with pleasure that the red ramshorn snails in one of my smaller fishtanks had obviously been getting on with the job that mother nature intended, because there were gelatinous masses of eggs scattered haphazardly across the glass.

I went outside into the back yard and there, in his favourite place on the outside windowsill of Richard's and my bedroom, was Augustus the cat, sunning himself with a regal air. I went up to him and scratched him behind the ears, and he made little brrping sounds of appreciation. My mother called me back into the apartment, and we left for the dolorous visit to the Doctor. And I never saw Augustus again.

When we came back, he wasn't there, but this was nothing unusual; he often disappeared for hours at a time, although it was unusual – but not unheard of - for him to be away overnight. But, by the time I got back from school the following afternoon and he was still not there, my mother and I, and even my father, who had been very fond of the animal, began to worry.

Over the next few days, we searched the countryside on the hill behind Peak Mansions, but to no avail. A few days after, Mrs Morley-John, the wife of Hong Kong's Lord Chief Justice, told me that she had seen a dead cat on the big flat roof of one of the garage blocks at the back of the art deco apartment block. I was on the way to school, and so couldn't do anything about it, but I asked her to tell my mother. When I came home, the corpse had vanished, but my mother reassured me that it had not been Augustus, but suggested that whoever the cat had been, there were two puncture marks about half an inch apart on the front leg. But, she reiterated, it was certainly was *not Augustus*.

I had more than a sneaking suspicion – though I didn't realise at the time - that, for the best possible motive, my mother was lying to me.

I think that Augustus had been carrying out his regular explorations of the hillside, and had come off worst in an encounter with a Chinese cobra.

For the next three years, until we finally left the colony in early 1971, I held out hope that – like the sagacious Siamese cat in Walt Disney's 1963 movie, *The Incredible Journey*, which had been one of my favourite films – Augustus would return home. But, not for the first time, Hollywood lied to me, and a much-loved member of our household was gone for good.

CHAPTER EIGHT
Tadpole Pond

Some time soon after we returned to Hong Kong, in the autumn of 1968, Ah Tim, Ah Tam, and their family moved out of the servant quarters at the back of our apartment. They both continued to work for my parents, but they had undergone a massive life change as, that autumn, A couple of years before, Ah Tim gave birth to a baby girl. She consulted my parents for an English name, and whilst the original suggestion of 'Rosemary' was rejected because it would be truncated to 'Rosie', which was a generally accepted *nom de guerre* used by the prostitutes of Wanchai, the alternative suggestion of 'Belinda' was accepted.

But now she was pregnant again, and in the fullness of time gave birth to a second daughter—Jennifer—and they decided that they needed somewhere larger to live than the servant's quarters at Peak Mansions,

During the latter stages of Ah Tim's pregnancy and immediately after the baby was born, her duties had been taken over by a relative of hers, called Ah Teem, of whom I can remember absolutely nothing apart from her name.

The family moved into an apartment block in one of the exclusively Chinese parts of the city, and both Ah Tim and Ah Tam commuted to work at Peak Mansions, leaving Ah Ling to look after Belinda and Jennifer as she had done for my brother, when he was a baby.

My father took over what had been the two living rooms in the servant quarters as an office, and I was given another one for my own purposes. Finally, I had a room of my own that could act as 'museum' or 'laboratory' – whichever took my fancy – and I filled the shelves that were on the walls with the various specimens that I had collected over the years, and for which there was no longer any room in my bedroom.

The pretentions to it being a 'laboratory' were fuelled not only by the various dead creatures in jam jars full of formaldehyde or bright mauve methylated spirits, but by the fact that, for Christmas 1968, I had been given the chemistry set for which I had begged for so long. If I'm honest, it was a bit of a disappointment, because once you have made crystals grow in a test tube full of copper sulphate solution, there isn't that much more you can do with the stuff. So, I proudly arranged the collection of test tubes on one of my shelves and forgot about them.

My father hadn't helped by telling me, no sooner had I unwrapped it, but he was going to be testing me on the names of different chemicals and their properties. Once again he had impinged upon what these days I would call my headspace, and made things less pleasant than they would otherwise have been.

One of the most impressive exhibits in my museum was a full-size bamboo snake, which I had found dead by the side of the road on my way to school one day. It was an undeniably impressive specimen - virulent green, and over three feet in length – and unlike so many of the items of dead wildlife that I consigned to my ever growing collection of jars of formaldehyde and methylated spirits, the snake was in remarkably good condition.

One of the characters in the Dr Dolittle books, and – interestingly – the only character apart from the titular hero who makes it through to all the different adaptations, is a parrot called Polynesia, who allegedly started life as a nestling somewhere in West Africa, although in all the movie versions, she is played by a South American macaw. Polynesia has a complicated back story which I will not go into here, but which meant that she spent most of her life in England, and whenever she is accompanying John Dolittle on his various adventures around the world, spends much of her time objecting to the local climate, as if she were born and bred somewhere in the Home County. In one of the books (and I can't remember which), she complains that in wherever it was that they were, there were only two climates; the wet season and the dry season, and went on to speak wistfully of the procession of the British seasons and the changes in the weather that they brought.

Hong Kong was much the same, although it was noticeably cooler during the winter months, but when you hit the rainy season, golly did it rain!

One of the things that I always found fascinating about the rainy season were the flying ants. One has flying ants at home in England, of course, but in the tropics they were far more prevalent, they were far bigger and there were far more of them.

When it was the appointed season for such things, and the first spatters of rain heralded the flood of biblical proportions which was to follow, the first of these ants would gingerly put its feelers out of its burrow, and fly out into the brave new world which awaited it.

They came out in their millions, which was a good thing for the future propagation of the species because the vast majority of these unfortunate insects would fall foul of the burgeoning deluge and find themselves stuck to roads or concrete pavements as their wings got waterlogged. I imagine that this would not have been such a problem for such insects emerging away from conurbations because nature abhors flat surfaces and geometric angles, but in the places where *Homo sapiens* had shaped the environment, the ground was covered with juicy, wriggling, flying ants. And with such a delectable source of portable protein, out came the predators. Domestic dogs and cats, birds large and small, frogs, toads, geckos, skinks and agamas, and even – it was said, though I never saw them myself – ferret badgers and civets. On occasion, I even saw elderly Chinese folk out with wickerwork tubs in which they placed these wriggling, juicy morsels, whether to use as food or not I never found out.

My friends and I always did our best to rescue as many of these unfortunate ants as possible; putting them into plastic ice cream boxes and taking them indoors to dry out. Although we would release many dozens of these lucky insects back from whence they came when the rain shower had finished, many hundred times as many of them perished. Many of the ones which we initially rescued had torn, frayed, or otherwise damaged wings, or wings that had become entangled with those of their fellows, and – knowing that ants do not need their wings to survive – we carefully cut them free with razor blades. I know that this sounds like the sort of thing that horrid children do to hapless insects, but our intentions were always good, and we were always on the side of the angels.

I realised a few days ago, when I was last dictating a passage of this book to my amanuensis/stepdaughter, Olivia, that I haven't actually mentioned my friends and contemporaries. Embarrassingly, this is because I have forgotten many of them. I had two particular friends, who also lived in Peak Mansions; William Topley, whose mother was an anthropologist and probably the first adult to actually take my plans for being a scientist seriously, and an Australian boy called Ricky. The three of us were inseparable for some years, but it is a sad mark of my failing memory as I get older, that I cannot remember many of our exploits.

I was also close to a boy called Michael Brown, who lived in Mount Austin Mansions, and it was he who opened one of the next chapters of my life.

Soon after returning to Hong Kong in the late summer or early autumn of 1968, I discovered the immortal 'William' books of Richmal Crompton. A relative had given me *Just William's Luck* (the only novel in the series, which otherwise consists of collections of short stories) a year or so previously, but I think I was too young for it at the time. However, when I discovered a copy of *More William* (1922) in the school library, which at that time was a medium sized room just around the corner of the main hall on the lowest level of the Plunkett's Road campus, I was immediately hooked. It was the story, 'William's Hobby', in which the eponymous hero tried to preserve a small, dead frog, by dipping it into a cup of tea, with comedy results, that completely entranced me. It reminded me of my unfortunate episode with the dead tree frog and the pickling vinegar a few years before, and – as a result – like so many other English-speaking boys in the middle of the twentieth century, I almost immediately identified with William. It wasn't until many years later that I discovered that, as well as me and many of my contemporaries, a decade and a half previously the teenaged John Lennon also based his philosophical outlook on Crompton's hero.

After this, I read as many of the William books as I could. There were thirty-eight of them by this time, with only two more to be published before Crompton's death in early 1969.

I have written earlier about how the nomenclature of various contemporary and classic children's books had influenced the names that the expatriate children had given to various landmarks on Victoria Peak. And so when, in one of the books, I read about how William and his friends visited one of their local landmarks – Tadpole Pond – I had an immediate flash of recognition.

For years, various elder children that I had met had talked vaguely about 'Tadpole Pond', but from the way that they had described it, I had got the impression that it was a very long way away from my stamping grounds. And my mother, fuelled – no doubt – by her eternal fear of poisonous snakes, had threatened me with dire and brutal punishment if I was to stray away from these proscribed areas.

This, as readers will have recognised, gave me an enormous amount of leeway, and the nine year old me was quite happy to explore the areas where he was allowed to go, and – believe or not – I very seldom broke my bounds.

One day, in the autumn of 1968, my friend Michael Brown from Mount Austin brought me a present. It was a small fishtank, containing some tadpoles and a few very small silver fish. I initially thought that these little metallic creatures were the tadpoles of a species of tree frog. It had been very recently when I'd read how certain species of tree frog laid their eggs in little 'swimming pools' they had constructed by sticking the leaves of forest trees together in order to find a receptacle where their eggs would be safe. After the eggs had hatched, the tadpoles would eventually break out of the leafy nursery and fall into a pond or stream below, where they would dart around like "little silver fish". I yearned to see such things with all of my heart, and when I saw these little creatures alongside more conventionally shaped tadpoles, I was convinced that my yearning had borne fruit. But even a proper second glance at them proved that they were undoubtedly fish. It turned out that one of the bigger boys had taken Michael to the semi-mythical Shangri-La of 'Tadpole Pond' and its location was no longer a mystery.

Michael promised to take me there at the very next opportunity, and was as good as his word.

If you travel up the Peak Tram funicular railway, right up to the highest spot at Victoria Gap, leave the terminus and venture out into the bright sunlight, you will see Mount Austin Road leading up steeply at what feels like a 45° angle before you. Even aged nine, I found the path up to Mount Austin to be a hard slog, and I very much doubt if I could walk up there now, although I hope that at some point in time that somebody will drive me up there. There is a footpath by the side of the road and as you walk up, there is seemingly impenetrable jungle to your left, in which one can see all sorts of interesting creatures on a regular basis. I even saw a bamboo snake once; (*Trimeresurus albolabris*). Also known as the white lipped pit viper, this extraordinarily beautiful, green snake, which can grow up to between two and three feet in length, is poisonous. And although the venom would not be fatal to an adult in good physical condition, children, the elderly and the infirm would die in fairly short order.

On another occasion, I saw a lantern bug, which – despite the name – are not bioluminescent. They are beautiful and very brightly coloured planthoppers, which have an extraordinary upcurving snout-like projection on their head, looking for all the world like something from the L.S.D. madness of a psychedelic album cover. The local species (*Pyroes candelaria*) feeds on plant sap, using the strange proboscis to pierce tree bark in order to extract the precious juices from the phloem.

There was always something to see in this swathe of rainforest, and ever since my earliest foray up and down Mount Austin Road with my mother and younger brother in tow, I had always dawdled, making the most of the exotic sights and sounds. But on this day, I walked as fast as I could up the steep incline, in order to meet Michael, as arranged, by the southernmost gate to the Mount Austin Mansions children's playground.

I got there on time, and Michael was there waiting for me with a huge grin on his face. "Okay, where is it?" I asked, eagerly. I was expecting there to be an arduous trek through the jungle, up the side of the mountain, into unknown territory for me. But, he continued grinning.

"It's here", he said, gesturing towards the heavy gunmetal crash barrier, which separated the path of Mount Austin Road from the rainforest that I so loved to look at.

I began to feel cross. Surely Michael hadn't brought me all the way up here to carry out some stupid practical joke. I told him that I didn't understand, and that I knew this area like the back of my hand, and that although there was a drainage ditch which, at the height of the raining season, had a small amount of water in it, and although the waterfall on the hillside fell all the way from just below Victoria Peak Gardens had a considerable amount of water that led into a subterranean drainage pipe, there was no pond, or anything like it.

He continued to grin, and told me to go with him. I was a little wary. The youth of the area was still obsessed with playing Cowboys and Indians, and it would not have overly surprised me if I had found myself tied to a tree as some sort of hostage during a complicated game of tribal warfare. But, being a trusting soul, I put these forebodings behind me, and followed him, as he led me towards the crash barrier.

Although the jungle was very thick most of the way up, there was one place just as the road turned, where if you looked over the crash barrier you could see a steepish bank, covered in fallen and desiccated palm leaves. At this point, Michael climbed over the crash barrier, gestured for me to follow, and, using some convenient tree trunks as grab rails, disappeared down the hillside. I followed him, to find that only maybe thirty feet below the level of Mount Austin Road itself, there was a large, concrete basin about half the size of the sitting room in which I am sat dictating these memoirs, and the basin was full of greeny brown water, fed from a large drainage pipe which, I assumed, once I'd had time to think about it, was the one that connected to the pipe at the southwest end of the playground, and through which the water from the great waterfall, and before that the little stream that flowed through Victoria Peak Gardens through the next step in its inexorable journey to the sea. This was a perfect secret playground for the young people of the area. I later found that, in a perfectly reasonable plan to make sure that it would remain a secret for as long as possible, and therefore out of any risk of adult intervention, that the younger children would be kept ignorant of its location until they were old enough – hopefully – not to get into trouble there. And this entirely voluntary arrangement worked well, as far as I can tell, until the time that the British left the colony.

The whole thing had obviously been a rocky nullah onto which the concrete pond had been built. It was a widely held belief amongst the children of The Peak that it had been built during the war to service military vehicles operated by the invading Japanese, but I have never been able to confirm this. There were all sorts of rocks on which one could climb, and as the little stream led from an overflow pipe out of the southernmost end of the pond, a bit like the one that comes from your bathtub, there were much smaller ponds, formed as the water filled natural crevices in the rock, each of which held a miniature ecosystem of its own.

And if you followed the stream, the twenty or thirty yards until it disappeared over the brow of the hillside, and carefully looked over the cliff, you could see that you were standing at the top of the waterfall on Harlech Road, which had intrigued me ever since my mother had first walked me past there back when I was five or six.

The revelation about Tadpole Pond was – in a minor sort of way – a life changing event for me. For the first time, I had somewhere that I could go which was *mine.* Somewhere that my parents would never go and had never been. And so, emboldened by this discovery, I began to explore further.

My friends and I had explored the three-tier ruins of the Peak Hotel on the hillside behind Peak Mansions extensively, but – for reasons I don't really know – we had not explored further up the hillside, but when we did, we discovered all sorts of other delights.

Looking at satellite photographs of the area now, it appears that much of the wooded hillside, which acted as an adventure playground for me and my friend, has now been built over, which probably makes sense bearing in mind the fact that Hong Kong is so short of space, but it is sad to almost certainly know that the places I loved so well no longer exist.

My friends and I were all interested in animals to a greater or lesser degree, and my mother suggested that we form a nature club. This we did, and it had the grandiose title of The Royal Hong Kong Society for Nature Study and Animals. My mother burst out laughing and said that she had no idea how a bunch of nine year olds could be so pompous and said that we should just call it the Peak Mansions Nature Club. With our pretentions horribly bruised, we reached a compromise and called it the Nature Improvement Club, or NIC which still managed to make my mother tut and shake her head, but she let it go. We had all sorts of grandiose plans, most of which never came to anything, but we had meetings where three or four of us would sit in my 'museum', and talk nonsense. We even had an 'anthem' which we would solemnly sing at the beginning and end of each meeting. It was to the tune of 'Oh God Our Help in Ages Past', and I am very glad that I can't remember most of the words now. It started off with us singing "The NIC, the NIC…" and I have no intention of revealing to you all the rest of the fragments that I can remember, because over half a century on, my childhood pretentions are still quite capable of embarrassment.

The hillside behind Peak Mansions, which also overlooked tiny Plunkett's Road that led up the hill, and which I walked along every day on the way to school, was covered in trees and vegetation, but they were very different to the ones that I knew back up the hill at Mount Austin.

For one thing, the trees were not rhododendrons, but a more natural mix of broad-leafed deciduous trees and shrubs, but unlike Mount Austin, there were no waterways; the nearest analogue to these would be the concrete storm drains, which crisscrossed the area. These had been put in partly at the behest of my father, after a disastrous series of typhoons during the rainy season of 1967. As a result of this, large swathes of the hillside had been washed away, and landslides made several of the major roads on the peak unusable.

But these storm drains were built on a steep incline, and were only full of water actually when it was raining, and soon dried up, so there were no little pools full of tiny wildlife.

But there were all sorts of other things.

Every child in Hong Kong knew about the fearsome *Scolopendra gigas*, the giant centipede. Bright red in colour, it was nearly as dangerous as it looked and every European child had at least one story about how "someone they knew" had died a slow and unpleasant death after being stung by one. However, to the best of my memory, nobody could actually come up with dates or times to substantiate these claims. *Scolopendra* had been relatively common on the hillside above Mount Austin Mansions, but further down on the wooded hillsides above my new home, they were replaced by another large centipede with an equally fearsome appearance. *Scutigera coleopatra* and several closely related species are less dangerous than *Scolopendra*, but the children of the colony had been so conditioned to fear any large centipede that they treated *Scutigera* with just as much respect as they did other species. The thing which I found irresistibly fascinating about *Scutigera* was the way that it moved as if it was a mechanical construct rather than a living creature. The nearest I have ever come to being able to produce an analogue of this peculiar mode of perambulation is the animated film clip which Pink Floyd used on stage to illustrate their song, *Welcome to the Machine*.

I spent much of my time on the hillside, clambering up and down and investigating little child-size dells and rills where an adult would neither have been able to venture, nor – probably, in my limited experience of the grown up mindset – would want to. The phenomenon that I noted, back at Mount Austin, that people from the incomprehensible grown up world were somewhere between unwilling and frightened to go into the forested areas which existed only a stone's throw from the places where we all lived, continued to baffle me. And it baffles me to this very day, although I am more than grateful for the fact that this inexplicable behaviour did give me and my friends (but particularly, me) places where we could retreat and be ourselves rather than whatever it was that our parents wanted for us.

About halfway up Plunkett's Road on the left-hand side was a disused garage which, in all the years I knew it, was never used for anything except for various games by children of the area. Because it was the main thoroughfare to and from Peak School, it was a place that saw the passing of a lot of children, and it became a gang hut, a cowboy stockade, or a castle, depending on what game we were playing that day. For some reason my friend, Michael Brown, and I decided that we wanted to be Martians, and played at being aliens (which usually meant that we would make beeping noises and jump out at the other children whilst wiggling our fingers on our foreheads, pretending that they were antennae) and this garage became our 'spaceship'. For several weeks we would hide in the garage after school in the afternoon, and spend a happy twenty minutes jumping out at juvenile passers-by, taking great delight in the shrieks of our female classmates when we managed to frighten them.

We didn't mean any harm by it, but in those unenlightened days, making girls squeal in fright was quite a common hobby. There was a boy called Clive, a few months older than us, who also used that garage as a base of operations, but – whatever it was that he did to the girls (and we never did find out) – it was far more serious than jumping out at them whilst wiggling one's fingers upon one's forehead. He was disciplined severely by Miss Young, our Scottish headmistress, and the garage was henceforth forbidden to the youth of the area; a ban which lasted for about six months, until everybody conveniently forgot about it.

On the right-hand side of Plunkett's Road, was a thick forest of mature bamboo, and all the local children would eagerly pull out fresh bamboo shoots on which to nibble as we walked to and from school.

On a couple of occasions during the winter of 1968/9, I attended events at the school, which necessitated me being driven home after dark, and although I never saw them in the day, every time that we drove down Plunkett's Road under cover of darkness, we would see huge, lumbering, black and white figures, the front half of which looked like huge guinea pigs. They were porcupines, and I always found it massively exciting that such exotic looking beasts could be so common just a matter of a few dozen yards from where I lived.

We would often find the traces of porcupines and other wild mammals on the hillside, but - by day at least - I don't think that we ever saw any wild mammals, living or dead, except for small rodents like the Ryuku mouse, and Sladen's roof rat.

As already described, on the south side of Hong Kong Island is a huge, natural harbour called Tai Tam Bay, and some time during the latter part of 1968, my father purchased a half share in a small cabin cruiser, called *The Ailsa*. The owners of the other half were an American family, about whom I remember very little. Because of this peculiar divvying up of ownership, we had her on alternate weekends, and so every other Saturday and Sunday we spend time down on the relatively sheltered waters of upper Tai Tam Bay, where we could all indulge our various nautical fantasies. One of the most important things, as far as I was concerned, was that it opened up a whole string of new biotopes for me to explore, and for the next couple of years, I took every opportunity to do so.

For my ninth birthday my parents gave me half shares (with my brother) in a rowing boat that we named *The Seahorse*. As I have already written, I had discovered Arthur Ransome's charming children's adventure stories, and emulating the characters in *Swallows and Amazons*, my brother and I paddled around the bay playing at pirates and explorers. My father - who not only had a history in the Merchant Navy, but had been a keen member of the Hong Kong Royal Naval Reserve - banned us from flying the Jolly Roger. At the time, I thought that he was merely being unfair, but as I now know much of the work of the Hong Kong RNR was conducting anti piracy patrols, his objection to his two young sons crewing a vessel displaying a pirate's flag is easier to understand.

My father rented a mooring, bang in the middle of quite a busy stretch of water.

Immediately to the north of us was a village of what were known then as Tanka people, the same people I had seen at Aberdeen. Since prehistoric times, these have been an important ethnic subgroup in southern China, and they traditionally lived on junk and fishing boats in coastal harbours. Historically, they were considered to be outcasts, and since they were boat people who lived on the sea, they were often referred to as 'sea gypsies' by the Chinese and the British. Both they, and the majority Han Chinese, insist that the Tanka are separate, and Tanka were not only banned from mixing with, or marrying, the land-based Cantonese and Hakka peoples, but they were also barred from Cantonese and Hakka celebrations. Some ancient Chinese sources – according to Wolfram Eberhard – claimed that water snakes were the ancestors of the Tanka and claimed that they could last for three days in the water, without breathing air.

On the whole, the Tanka aquatic village (and I am sure that there is a proper term for a conurbation of people living in boats, but I have no idea what it is), and the collection of fifty or so moorings leased by European expatriates, left each other alone. But on the rare occasions that I found myself nearer to the Tanka settlement, they seemed very different to the rest of the Chinese folk with whom we mixed on a day to day basis. And it is only now that I realise how much of a difference in mind-set being a minority ethnic group on one hand, and sea-dwelling nomads on the other, would make.

A report by the Catholic Foreign Mission Society of America in 1921 writes:

> "They are an aboriginal tribe, speaking an altogether different language from the Chinese. On the land they are like fish out of water. They are said never to intermarry with landlubbers, but somehow or other their tongue has crept into many villages in the Chiklung section. The Chinese say the Tanka speech sounds like that of the Americans. It seems to have no tones. A hardy race, the Tanka are untouched by the epidemics that visit our coast, perhaps because they live so much off land. Each family has a boat, its own little kingdom, and, there being plenty of fish, all look better fed than most of our land neighbours."

On my 11th birthday I remember seeing two enormous king crabs - refugees from an impossibly prehistoric past - swimming effortlessly into the shallow water of Tai Tam, looking for somewhere to lay their eggs. My reverie was interrupted by a young Chinese boy with a boathook. He started to try and catch them, and when he didn't succeed, was about to crush them. Appalled, I ran up and punched him on the nose. He ran away screaming and I was soundly chastised by my father.

Again, with the benefit of hindsight, this was perfectly understandable. The Cultural Revolution of 1967 had hit Hong Kong like a bombshell. As I have already described I remember seeing a troupe of Red Guards marching up the Peak Road only a few hundred yards away from where we lived. The Communist Party was, of course, banned in the colony, but the doctrine of global revolution which had politicized students in Paris, the UK, and the US, and which had already produced at least one martyr in Jan Palach and inspired many young Chinese men to follow their lead and rise up against their imperialist masters.

My father, understood the increasing fragility of race relations in the Colony, and was understandably frightened. When his oldest son became involved in an imbroglio that could have been perceived as having racist connotations, he was furious. My true defence - that I was only trying to protect two increasingly rare survivors from the Permian period from an ignominious death - cut no ice with him. Luckily, it appears that the young boy I punched could not have been the scion of a family of hardened revolutionaries because none of us heard anything about the incident again and British rule in the colony continued for another 30 years.

Sometimes, we would go on quite long voyages, but usually – presumably because my father was tired after a long week's Colonial Administration – we would only sail (and by 'sail', I mean chug leisurely along using our outboard engine) to the opposite side of Taitam Bay, some quarter of a mile away, where they was a pristine beach with a few small rock pools and a tiny patch of mangroves, whose grey-green leaves always seemed vaguely sinister to me. Unfortunately, on our first visit, my mother saw a snake in the mangroves and us children were immediately forbidden from ever exploring them. There was a steep hillside behind this silver sand beach, and although my brother and I explored the lower parts of it, one day I excitedly found a breadfruit tree and, knowing exactly what it was from my perusal of *A Swiss Family Robinson*, I bore two of the huge fruits back to my mother, who looked at them suspiciously and refused to cook them for our tea.

One Sunday, we were on *The Ailsa* and I was, for some reason best known to myself, which I cannot remember now, swimming around the boat pretending to be a dog. I was shouting "Yelp! Yelp!", and this – once again – brought me into conflict with my father. One of the things that he had impressed upon me from an early age was that one should only shout for assistance if one needed it, and – as he misheard my shouts of "Yelp!" as a shout for "Help!" – he immediately jumped to the conclusion that I was breaking this one of his most sacred commandments. Readers who have followed the history of my relationship with my father thus far will not, I suspect, be surprised to discover that I was given a more severe than usual physical punishment as a result of this.

On another occasion, my father bought a logbook for our little ship, and instructed me to write down what happened to us in my best handwriting. This was something that I did with some pride, and was – I think – understandably angry when my father wrote something unintelligible in the logbook in his diabolically untidy handwriting. My reaction was deemed to be appalling insolence, and once again I was beaten for it.

But most of my seafaring memories are good ones.

The islands that now make up Hong Kong had been inhabited, or at least *visited* by humans, for many millennia. My parents chose to visit the uninhabited islands rather than the ones that had people living there, but, on one occasion a friend of theirs - whom I discovered in a moment of alcohol-fuelled indiscretion from my father, was a high-ranking member of MI6 – who also had a boat, and on his family's excursion onto one of the outlying islands he had found a stone adze head, which someone or other had dated as being several thousand years old. This excited me massively, and for weeks following this discovery, I picked up and tried to bring home with me every peculiar looking rock I could find, convinced that it was going to be a *bona fide* prehistoric relic.

Needless to say, none of them ever were.

As I sit here, dictating this chapter to my lovely stepdaughter Olivia, I am looking at a recent picture of Tai Tam Harbour on Google Earth. Although superficially similar, it is far more built up. The Tanka settlement has vanished, and the most noticeable sign of human occupation, on the shore next to where the settlement once was, is a wakeboarding centre. A lot of the upper reaches of the bay appear to be silted up, although this could purely be that the satellite picture was taken at low tide. Following the path that goes down the north-western side of the harbour, it is hard to identify the places that I knew so well half a century ago. There are far more buildings, far more developments, and, I suspect, that much of what I once considered its charm has probably gone for good.

But the little beach, which we took so much for granted that we didn't even give it a name, still appears to be there. And sitting as a crippled man in late middle-age, desperately trying to preserve his memories of a time and place which have drifted way past the horizon of entropy, it doesn't take too much of an effort of will to remember these glorious weekends where I could study the local wildlife to my heart's content, where my father could pretend for a few short hours that he was a sailor again and my mother could read her Regency Romances, whilst my brother – still a little boy of five – gurgled happily and made mud pies by the shoreline.

Truthfully, half a century after the event, I'm not sure which of the little beaches, with their covering of white coral sand, is the one that we always thought of as our own private beach. But it doesn't matter. 1968 is a lifetime ago. And I very much doubt if I shall ever visit those beaches again.

One of the things that I had always found fascinating about Hong Kong were the crabs. There were so many of them, and they seemed to have evolved to inhabit a wide range of ecological niches. In another small clump of mangroves on the opposite side of the bay, near the slipway where we parked our car and from which a taciturn Chinese boatman would take us out to our allotted mooring, for example, lived a whole population of nutty brown crabs, even in the complex root structures of the purely terrestrial trees and bushes further away from the sea.

But if you looked harder you could see that there were dozens of small mangrove crabs; little crabs just under an inch across, which swarmed all over the arching and labyrinthine root systems and climbed quite high up the trunk and branches of these peculiarly stunted little trees. I had never considered that crabs could climb before, and I never tired of watching these earnest little arthropods as they scuttled up and down the increasingly complicated maze of branches and boughs. There was quite a wide range of colours exhibited by these little crabs, with all shades of green, brown and red being observable if you waited long enough.

There were other crabs that lived entirely in the water, and there were hermit crabs of various sizes to be found in the different rock pools that I took so much joy in exploring. However, the ones that possibly intrigued me most were the ghost crabs that lived in burrows on the sand. They would come out *en masse* and form huge swarms on the surface of the beach, where they would look for dead fish and other tasty morsels that had been left by the receding tide. However, at the first sign of any approach by a human, they would all scuttle back to the safety of their burrows in the sand, and in a few short seconds were entirely hidden. These burrows must have been quite deep, because on a number of occasions I tried to dig one of these crabs out, but I never managed it.

On one particularly memorable day on our special beach, I saw a huge (and you must remember, I was nine, so huge doesn't mean the same as it would do now), yellow crab with long legs, running from the shelter of the mangroves, across the hot sand, to the relative safety of the shoreline. I ran after it and managed to catch it. It was bright yellow with brown markings and long legs like a harvestman spider. I was unable to identify it then, and I have never been able to identify it since. This is where I wish that I still had access to my old nature diary, because I remember drawing a picture of it before letting the enormous crustacean ('enormous' being about 6-7" across the carapace) go into the warm water and noting, with interest, that its ungainly long legs were just as good for swimming as they were for running.

There are a number of fine websites and blogs which chronicle the comings and goings in the aquatic life in Hong Kong's coastal waters, and it is sad to see how degraded it is from my memories of those same waters, only half a century ago. I know that men of my age have a tendency to look at the past through rose coloured spectacles, but I have done my best to avoid this temptation throughout this narrative, and there are concrete memories that are vibrantly alive in my head, which truly seem incompatible with the depleted and degraded waters that I read about today.

I remember, for example, how, on one notable occasion when our little boat was at anchor off the family's favourite little beach, when I was swimming face down with a snorkel and I saw, to my wonder, how the sandy floor of the bay maybe a fathom and a half below me was covered in a veritable carpet of grey/brown starfish. I had seen a delicate little brittle stars on a number of occasions while exploring rock pools throughout the territory, but I had never seen proper starfish before. A brief trawl through the **HKmarinelife.blog** suggests they were of the species *Astropecten* *monacanthus*, which has been reported from a vast area of the Pacific Ocean, from South East Arabia to Japan. According to the Hong Kong Biodiversity website, which is maintained by the Hong Kong Government itself, there are three species of starfish of this genus known from Hong Kong waters, and so it may not have been this species after all, but it doesn't really matter. Because it is the sheer wonder of seeing so many of these peculiar echinoderms in one place.

Starfish Bay is a small cove in the New Territories, and in 2008, it was the location for one of the few pieces of good news for Hong Kong's marine life in recent years. Once it had been the home for enormous numbers of these attractive little creatures, but, as the *South China Morning Post* reported on Monday 12ᵗʰ May 2008:

> "Marine ecologist Paul Hodgson said all the starfish in the bay were killed many years ago partly because the water was polluted by untreated sewage from Tai Po and Sha Tin. Ms Newbery said that after a year of surveys and water testing, it was found water quality in the bay was once again suitable for starfish. So it was decided to relocate about 3,000 of them to the bay with the aim of re-establishing a viable population.
>
> In September last year, environmentalists transferred about 100 starfish from Long Harbour, which had a population of at least 300,000, to the bay as a pilot project. This month, about 60 children from Renaissance College aged from seven to 11 waded into Long Harbour over two days to collect about 2,000 starfish, which were then ferried to Starfish Bay and introduced into their new home.
>
> 'Not only did the children have a lot of fun, but they also learned a valuable lesson - from a very young age, they can make a difference to the environment,' Ms Newbery said. Yesterday's final transfer was carried out by a group of 28 Hebe Haven Brownies and Cubs aged seven to 11, who harvested about 1,000 starfish from Long Harbour and transferred them by boat to Starfish Bay.
>
> 'This is the first time that young children have ever been involved in such a marine ecosystem rehabilitation project,' Ms Newbury said. 'They have succeeded in putting the starfish back into Starfish Bay.'"

On another occasion, we sailed down the eastern side of Tai Tam Bay and anchored in the deep water of one of the little coves that pepper the coastline. My explorations in Hong Kong in recent years have been restricted to using the remarkably helpful Google Earth, and it is sad to see that many of these tiny inlets, which were once beautifully virgin and uninhabited, are now dotted with the unmistakable signs of human activity; many of them have now got buildings on them - whether they are houses or commercial buildings, I have no idea - and I would imagine that if they are indeed dwelling places, they are the weekend *pied à terre* of some unimaginably wealthy plutocrat, which is something that the anti-capitalist and anarchist Jon Downes of the 21ˢᵗ century finds indescribably abhorrent. I have never been able to identify this bay on Google Earth, which is a pity because it was an unusual bay for us: instead of the sun-baked white coral sand, which covered most of the beaches that we visited around the territory, this was a grey, silty, mudflat, with a sizeable stream running through it from a cascade, which fell down the forty five degree angled hillside, which lay invitingly in front of us. And it was the first time that I had ever had a chance to investigate the liminal interface between a freshwater environment and its marine counterpart.

The stream was surprisingly deep, and the water flow was fast enough for my mother to keep a firm grip on my little brother's wrist, because – even though he was wearing a life jacket (as we all did, during our nautical forays) – she was convinced that he would fall in, and be sucked beneath the surface by an unsuspected vortex. She was not as concerned about me. After all, I was coming up to being ten years old, which was the age that young boys in her favourite Regency Romances were liable to be taken into the army as drummer boys, or onto naval vessels as cabin boys. So, I was allowed to explore this riverlet under strict instructions that I wasn't to go in out of my depth, and that I would still wear my life jacket.

This, I rushed off to do, and found out – much to my surprise – that the water was far too cold to make exploration comfortable, so I sat on a large and comfortable rock on the bank of the deep stream, and watched with interest as a procession of large fish, which I believe were probably grey mullet, swam purposefully up and down the water course before me.

Although there are a surprisingly large number of freshwater and brackish water fish species to be found in Hong Kong, and although I have always been fascinated by aquatic ecosystems, I had not seen very many of the local fish. And these were, by far the largest that I had ever encountered.

They are an interesting species, because although they are indigenous to South China, they are also widely farmed for commercial purposes. One of the things that makes them particularly interesting, both from a biodiversity, and commercial viewpoint, is that they are one of the few species that are particularly tolerant to poor water quality, and they can even be found in the massively polluted waters of Hong Kong harbour itself. There are, in fact, six species of mullet that have been reported from Hong Kong waters, but by far the most important of these is the flathead grey mullet (*Mugil cephalus*). This species is actually found in coastal, tropical and subtropical waters worldwide. Three similar species are also found in British waters, but whilst they look very similar to the mullet that I watched that day in Hong Kong, half a century ago, and even have the same common name, I found out whilst researching this narrative, that they are an entirely different species. However, I can look back over a time which is only half as long ago as my mullet adventures in Hong Kong to another day, when I was sitting on the banks of a small creek near Looe, on the south coast of Cornwall, and watching a shoal of the British mullets behaving in a nearly identical manner to their Hong Kong equivalents. I could have sat on that rock, watching the fish all day, because as I have noticed over the years, most stretches of unpolluted water are full of little denizens who reveal themselves to anyone who is prepared to sit quietly and wait and see what happens.

And so it was here.

As well as the mullet, who were the undoubted kings of this stretch of water, there were some little vividly coloured, blue and green fish, less than an inch long, which skittered about busily. I do not know whether they were a marine species or a fresh water one, but I never saw them before or since, and I have never been able to identify them. There were also little, bright yellow shrimp, and industrious looking hermit crabs, who stalked the sandy riverbed earnestly.

But my reverie was crudely shocked out of existence by my mother calling me for a picnic lunch. This was a not unwelcome interruption, because then – as now – Jonathan Downes is largely motivated by the activity of his digestive tract.

My mother always did remarkably good picnic lunches. Big chunks of cheese, cucumber and esoteric Chinese vegetables, together with various little savoury things that I always assume that she made herself. Mealtimes, especially alfresco ones, were amongst the only times that one could always guarantee that my father would be in a good humour and might even start telling jokes. So, picnic mealtimes were things to be savoured, and – even now – I look back upon them with fondness.

This particular mealtime remains in my memory, not because of what we ate, nor because anything unpleasant happened, but because of what happened afterwards.

One of the firm rules that I remember from my childhood, and which I believed in completely until – a few years ago – I learned that it was completely fallacious, was the rule that one was not allowed in the water for an hour after eating. It was something about stomach cramps. So, although I was very much looking forward to going snorkelling and investigating the submarine coastline of the bay, like a relatively good young fellow, I trotted off to investigate the shoreline whilst keeping my feet dry. Then, as now, my favourite bit of going to the beach is looking in rock pools. But – to my disappointment – on this particular beach, there weren't any. But, what there were, were a couple of peculiar, sandy lagoons about fifteen or twenty feet across. Due to some geological peculiarity, the grey, silty sand of the beach fell away into deep, horseshoe-shaped pools of clear water. The sandy bottom to these pools meant that, although they were – maybe – ten feet deep, one had crystal clear visibility. However, to my disappointment, there was nothing in the way of fauna that was immediately apparent. But, in the second of them, whilst I was gazing into the empty waters with a jaundiced eye, I saw – to my amazement – a large, dark brown shape swimming purposefully in through the narrow isthmus bottleneck, which separated the deep lagoon from the sea. My first and immediate thought was "shark!". I was not scared of such things, anymore than I would have been scared of snakes, but my dear mother's innate paranoia - that everything in the tropics was guaranteed to be doing its best to eat her offspring - had rubbed off on me, and I felt sure that this unexpected marine visitor was – in the words of an annoyingly catchy children's song which is unaccountably popular at the time that I am writing this part of the narrative – a 'baby shark'.

But it wasn't.

It was actually something that I had already got a fairly intimate knowledge of, because I was used to eating them once or twice a month.

Once every ten days or so, an elderly Chinese hawker would come to the servants' entrance at the back of Peak Mansions with an odorous flatbed truck packed with dry ice, upon which reclined a large assortment of dead fish of various species. I was always excited when these visits took place when I was not at school, because it was the only chance that I ever got to see *bona fide* specimens of the local deepwater fish. Ah Tim or – on occasion – my mother would go out and greet the fish hawker. My mother was always more polite to him than Ah Tim was, explaining to me *sotto voce* that one should always be kind to the 'lower orders'. But there was some sort of Cantonese caste system of which I still remain in blissful ignorance, which meant that the elderly fish salesman was so far below the social level occupied by the house servants of a high ranking Colonial Service Officer that Ah Tim would forever look down upon the poor man with a haughty sneer and a curled lip.

On the days when my mother concluded her business with the 'fish man', she would always buy large steaks cut off the unprepossessing corpse of one of the groupers; a large group of a number of genera in the sub family *Epinephelinae*. They are slow swimming, impressively ugly fish, with stout bodies and large mouths, and many species grow to over a metre in length, and achieve a weight of over 100kg. They have an interesting reproductive strategy. Throughout much of their life, at least until they mature, they are all female but have the ability to change sex after having achieved sexual maturity. The largest, and oldest, male often controls harems which contain between three and fifteen females. I had read about this fascinating strategy in one of the library books that my mother regularly got me, and had received coals of opprobrium heaped upon my head after – in the middle of a formal lunch party, attended by one of my father's superiors in the internecine, not to say labyrinthine halls of power within the Colonial Secretariat – I had described the mechanism at some length, and asked (in my piercing nine year old voice) whether or not it would be possible for members of our own species to change sex. In the days before gender reassignment surgery became commonplace, the discussion of such things was something proscribed from the dinner table, and certainly from the lips of those who society still recommended should be 'seen and not heard'.

So, I knew quite a lot about groupers, but had never seen one. Not alive and in the wild, at any rate. When we drove through the little town of Repulse Bay on our way to Tai Tam and our weekend life on the ocean waves, we passed several large seafood restaurants, each of which had big fish tanks built into the outside wall so that prospective patrons would be able to see who they were going to eat. And some of these – on occasion – had contained groupers of one species or another. But, they were always lacklustre creatures who gave every impression of knowing what their sad fate was going to be. This grouper, however, despite being relatively small (only a couple of feet long), which made one suspect that she was an immature female, was obviously the mistress of all she surveyed (not that there was much to survey in this apparently empty sandy lagoon).

Groupers feed by swallowing their prey whole, rather than biting chunks off them like a shark does. And so, I supposed, that it was not impossible that there would be shoals of transparent prawns or some other marine arthropod that, though not apparent to a nine year old boy standing on the shore and gazing enthralled down into the water, were an abundant and delicious food source for this magnificent fish.

During the hour in which I stayed on the shore of the lagoon, waiting for the chance to be able to go into the water with my snorkel and assume an amphibious existence for myself, I saw her swim in and out of the sandy waterhole on half a dozen occasions. And she was still doing so when my assigned sixty minutes were up, and I ran back to my family's 'base camp', grabbed my snorkel and slipped surprisingly gracefully beneath the water's surface, to see what I could find.

About thirty feet away from the shoreline was a long, low, rocky outcrop, the utmost top of which broke the surface of the water slightly, forming a series of tiny islets, on which – as we had been arriving several hours before – I saw an immature reef egret. In recent years, two species of egret have recolonised the coastal parts of North Devon, where I now live, but – sadly – it is unlikely that the western reef egret (*Egretta gularis*) will join them, being a creature of much warmer climes. One of the things that is particularly interesting about them is that they have two distinct colour forms. Whilst many of them – like the egrets that are so common now in the Taw and Torridge estuaries – are snowy white in colour, others (my favourites) have a beautiful slatey-grey plumage, which make them almost impossible to confuse with any other member of the heron family. There is a rare, dark, morph of the little egret, and, it was a bird of this darker colour variant, which had been standing to attention on one of these tiny islands as if he was greeting us formally upon our arrival.

I swam towards this rock, taking great joy in the fact that the closer I got, the more agitated shoals of little fish were there for me to swim through. But when I got to the rocks themselves, I found myself, for the first – and I'm afraid, the only – time in my life, swimming above a tiny coral reef.

I had been so disappointed, the previous summer, when I had been thwarted in my ambition to see the world famous Great Barrier Reef, but whilst this was only a tiny conurbation of corals in comparison, it was still a coral reef, and it appeared to be a healthy one, and so I swam slowly above it, face down, occasionally taking big gulps of air in through the snorkel, and gazing in delight at the tiny world laid out below me.

I've written elsewhere about how impressed I was with the Rowland Ward Pavilion at the British Museum (Natural History), but I have also always been fascinated by model worlds. Whilst my days of playing with toy soldiers are nearly five decades in the past, until I was about thirteen and discovered rock and roll music, and the interesting fact that girls were different to boys, one of my favourite activities was to make huge, complicated layouts of toy soldiers and my model train set, each time producing a different world that unfolded kaleidoscopically in my mind's eye.

I think this is why I have always been fascinated by aquatic micro-ecosystems; each one is a little world in its own. When I was a teenager, living in the same village that I live now in rural North Devon, I used to ride my bicycle out to Ashcroft Hill, just outside the village. By the side of the road were a series of little ditches and ponds, each with a completely different mini-ecosystem. The water beetles and other tiny invertebrates, which were common in one ditch, would be replaced by a completely different selection in the next ditch over, only a few feet away. And although the ditches are long gone; the victims of land drainage and reclamation, a failing water table and increasing vehicular pollution, the memory of them remains with me still.

I have only ever seen such dramatic changes between one micro-ecosystem and the next within a marine environment a few times in my life. Usually, purely because the world's oceans are all conjoined, and – perforce – provide much larger areas for their dependent ecosystems to inhabit, the resulting habitats tend to be much larger. But on this day, over half a century ago as I write, I swam a couple of feet above the most dramatically changeable ecosystem that I have ever seen for myself, within a marine environment.

The water, surprisingly cold at this time of year, perhaps because it was being continually replenished from the little river I had explored earlier, was crystal clear: a rarity in Hong Kong, even in those days.

And I was surprised to see how – even within the space of a foot or so – the corals would change form and colour dramatically. There were little brain coral of pink and pastel yellow, then there were the similar, richly textured *Platygyra*, which looked bizarrely like the interlocking weaving roads and lanes of an ancient English country village, seen from the air; a beautifully intricate series of patterns of pinks, yellows and browns, sometimes erupting into organic turrets and parapets that looked for all the world like some of the more bizarre imaginings of whoever it was that designed the covers for cheap editions of classic science fiction novels during the 1970s. Less common were bright orange puffballs that I have never been able to identify properly, and complex pink anemones, amongst whose labyrinthine tentacles various species of clownfish took refuge. Tiny, jewelled, clownfish were also seen patrolling the pink antlers of a series of magnificent branched corals, which looked like intricately tended topiary. At intervals, all the way along this ever varied and always magnificent undersea garden, were giant clams, considerably smaller than the one that had caused the death of one of my favourite characters in a novel by Willard Price that I had read a few months previously, but still, if I had been foolhardy enough to allow my naked feet to penetrate their chitinous mantrap, would have caused me significant damage.

The huge, glossy, black sea cucumbers with whom I had become familiar a few years earlier during my aquatic explorations of the little beach owned by Stanley Prison, on the opposite side of Tai Tam Bay, were ever present but they were joined by various multi-coloured and more ornate relatives. Little fish of every colour and every morphology flitted busily throughout a coral garden, and occasionally I saw what I now know to be mantis shrimps, probably *Psuedosquilla ciliata*, strange little creatures that looked like elongated woodlice that had been plonked into the middle of one of the more disturbing pieces of 1970s science fiction art by the late Patrick Woodroffe. A gunmetal grey, these little crustaceans were oddly secretive, which added to their slightly sinister demeanour - to my eyes, at least.

Slowly, I swam around the entire circumference of the little reef, arriving back where I'd started after about an hour. I had tried to count the number of different fish species that I had seen, but I gave up after about fifty. I had always heard about what a rich diversity of creatures were to be found in such a habitat, but – believe me – until you have seen it for yourself, the reality simply doesn't begin to sink in. And the fact that habitats like this across the world are being destroyed as a result of climate change, pollution, and crass commercial interests, becomes even more of a tragedy.

I was slightly disappointed that there were no cephalopods to be seen, nor were there any seahorses. These were two animals that I dearly wanted to see, and I was disappointed by their absence. I never was to see a living seahorse in Hong Kong, in the wild, at least, and I have never seen one to this day, outside tropical fish shops or public aquaria. But, a year or so later, I did find a dead one floating amongst a tiny floating bed of garbage and I salvaged it to be enshrined in a jam jar of methylated spirits, back in my 'museum'.

It was also round about then that I had my first, and only, encounter with a wild cephalopod. Back in the shallow, sandy waters of our favourite bathing beach, I was exploring one day and found a half beer bottle from the San Miguel brewery on Lamma Island. I was, and always have been, impressed by the way that the sea will take pieces of broken bottles and batter them into submission, forming beautiful, opaque, glass pebbles. I dove down to the sea bed three or four feet below me, to retrieve this bottle, which would – I hoped – have been the largest 'glass jewel' that I had found yet. Sadly, the action of the sea had not yet worked its magick upon the bottle, but – to my great excitement – inside the bottle was a small, and rather bad tempered, octopus.

Reverently, I placed it into a bucket and took it home, where I planned that the 'beer bottle octopus' would take pride of place in my burgeoning zoological gardens on my windowsill. But, I hadn't learned the lessons of my ill-fated marine aquarium back in

Guernsey, a year or two before, and the poor octopus was dead before I got it back to Peak Mansions.

But, although I would have spent a veritable lifetime lost in the wonder of this fantastic landscape, over which I had swum, gazing in awe at the ever-changing vista of life below me, only too soon was it time to swim back to the boat, hoist the anchor, and make our way back to harbour. Although all this happened fifty plus years ago, I cannot ever remember going back and visiting this strange, dark grey beach, with its cold river and Lilliputian coral reef, again. I can only imagine that, whilst it was full of things that fascinated me, it was not a pleasant place for my parents, my little brother, or any of the other people who occasionally came along with us on our marine excursions.

My vote would have been counted as insignificant, if a vote had ever been called; something which would have been anathema to my autocratic father. But this was only one adventure in a series of excursions that took place most weekends, for something in the region of two years, and whilst it does indeed stick in my mind for all sorts of reasons, it is not the only one that does so by any means.

On the western side of Tai Tam Harbour was a concrete slipway, which we used for all sorts of things, and we had many picnics on the shallow, shingly beach adjoining it. On the other side from the beach was a small patch of mangroves. I am not even going to attempt to identify them as a species, because – according to those jolly nice fellows at Wikipedia - about one hundred and ten species of plant can be considered 'mangroves', as the term is used for any shrub or small tree that grows in coastal saline or brackish water.

Whilst my father did whatever it was that he did, and my mother tended to my younger sibling, who had an unfortunate habit of trying to eat everything that he came across, including the slower moving wildlife of this liminal zone, I spent as much time as I could investigating the peculiar world of this tiny mangrove swamp. Mangroves can be found all over the world, and they sometimes cover great areas of land, but these of which I write, only covered a few square yards; an area about half the size of my sitting room. I think that every television show that has ever depicted mangrove swamps shows film of mudskippers and fiddler crabs. Mudskippers are peculiarly amphibious little fish which have become adapted for a semi-terrestrial lifestyle. Fiddler crabs, equally brightly coloured, are asymmetrical crustacea, the males of which have one in enormous claw that they use for fighting, signalling and generally impressing their womenfolk. Animals of both these types *are* found in Hong Kong, but sadly, they didn't seem to exist in my little mangrove swamp, or at least I never saw any. This didn't stop me looking, and I spent many industrious hours trying to find them.

On the upper branches of these strangely stunted little trees, one could usually see kingfishers of a number of different species perched and surveying the ground beneath them with a slightly sinister gleam in their eyes. I've always liked kingfishers, and it is one of the things that I have always found slightly disappointing about British wildlife that we only have one species. But it is an undeniably gorgeous one, which is found in Hong Kong as well. But my favourite were the black-capped kingfisher (*Halcyon pileata*), a more heavyset and muscular looking creature than the tiny common kingfisher. Both in flight and at rest, these birds reminded me of the interceptor aircraft flown by Earth pilots in the Gerry and Sylvia Anderson series, UFO. Their bright red, boat-shaped bills looked too big for their bodies, and indeed did seem to effect their flight patterns. They have a black head, white neck and breast, and glossy blue back and tail, and once seen were never forgotten.

Another favourite was the much rarer crested kingfisher (*Megaceryle lugubris*), which, despite being black, brown and white (with small splashes of orange on the breast of the male in the breeding season), had these drab colours in such a beautiful and intricate mosaic that – to this day – they are one of my favourite birds of all time. At low tide, a small area of mudflat was revealed, again maybe half the size of my sitting room, and whilst I was still unsuccessful in my ongoing search for mudskippers or fiddler crabs, I did find that even a surprisingly cursory amount of digging would reveal some pleasantly prehistoric appearing bristly polychaete worms, and some small, conical gastropods, which resembled larger versions of the Malayan trumpet snails that infest so many home aquaria.

Most winters, my wife and I went down to see the mudflats at Appledore and Fremington to happily watch the North Devon wading birds, which – for some reason – are far more numerous during the winter months. We saw redshanks, greenshanks, curlews, whimbrels and a dozen others, and it is mildly disappointing – with hindsight – that I have no memories of any wading birds on my favourite stretch of mudflats in Hong Kong.

There were a few large (and by large, I mean between four and six feet in length) rocks lying embedded in the mud, and – to my delight – I found that, on the leeside of each of them, was a small pool that would have been called a rock pool if it had not been made by a combination of freshwater run-off and mud. Mostly, these pools were disappointingly empty, but sometimes they would be full of tiny fish, including baby pufferfish. I never did find out why the pools could be empty one day and a teeming metropolis of little fishes and crustacea the next, nor did I ever identify the pufferfish as a species. There are, apparently quite a few species of pufferfish in Hong Kong waters, but apart from these miniscule examples in the muddy pool on the leeside of these two half-buried rocks that looked like beached whales, covered in knobbly barnacles and chitins the only other pufferfish that I encountered were two or three porcupine fish, which I found, fully inflated though dead and desiccated, on a broad, sandy beach on the south side of Beaufort Island, an uninhabited member of the Po Toi group, a few miles south of Hong Kong island. This is, again, where I am frightened that my memory might be playing tricks with me, because through the magic of Google Earth I can "fly" only a few hundred feet above the coast of the island, and – try as I will – I cannot find any sandy beaches there. However, I suppose that the satellite pictures may have been taken at high tide, and if I have sadly misremembered the exact location where I found some dead fish over half a century ago, it isn't really the end of the world. After a bit more digging, I found an aerial photograph, which I think shows *my* beach, but as it is on a website highlighting plastic pollution in the South China Sea, in many ways I am saddened by my discovery and wish that I hadn't bothered.

The island was, and as far as I can ascertain, always has been uninhabited, probably because there is no natural fresh water apart from what collects in natural basins in the granite bedrock when it rains. Lying through my teeth, I told my mother that snakes couldn't swim, and so she was far more lenient about letting me explore this little island than she would have been if we had merely landed on one of the hundreds of little coves either on Hong Kong island or the mainland. For some reason, she never asked me how snakes had found their way to Hong Kong Island, or to Stonecutters Island, which was known locally as the 'Snake Island' because there were so many there. Incidentally, the Japanese, during their occupation of the then-British colony, used the unique isolation and the fauna of the little island to house a snake farm. Venomous snakes were bred there and milked of their venom to provide antidotes to Japanese soldiers bitten while on active duty in the Pacific Theatre.

I don't know why this little beach on Beaufort Island was such a favourite destination for my family, but it suited me down to the ground. There was not only a beach with both sand and rocks, but an entire island to explore. Despite my mother's fondly held reassurances, one of the first things I ever found on the island was a large and very dead MacClelland's Coral Snake, which – had it been alive – would have had no difficulty in subduing (and probably killing) the nine-year-old me with one bite. This specimen, however, was both dead and desiccated and my avaricious nature was just too much for me to ignore, and I slipped it into a plastic sandwich bag and put it in the bottom of my rucksack, deciding to "find" it somewhere less contentious, on Hong Kong island. I can't remember the details of how I did this, but it took pride of place in my home museum for many years, until I had to get rid of it when it was time to go back to England for good.

Ironically, I never saw another specimen, on Beaufort Island or anywhere else for that matter. Nor did I see any other reptile on the little island. However, on one of our visits, I discovered something much more disturbing.

I always thought that Beaufort Island, in shape at least, looked like a chocolate blancmange. Ah Tim made wonderful chocolate blancmanges to a recipe that some previous 'Missee' had taught her. They tasted delicious, but – although she made them in the prescribed manner by keeping them in the pudding bowl until they set, and then turning out the pudding bowl onto a plate that was there waiting for it – they never did set 100% correctly, and there were always little jagged bits missing near the top; just like on Beaufort Island. So, I always thought of the main hill of the island (and, therefore, by definition the island itself) as 'Chocolate Pudding Mountain', and

– on the various times that we went there – it was another of my little kingdoms, where I could roam untrammelled.

On one occasion, however, we went there and the island looked very different. Usually, the 'chocolate pudding' was covered by an uneven carpet of green scrub, but today it was completely changed. About a third of the scrubland had disappeared and was replaced by black, charcoal skeletons. A hill fire had wreaked tremendous damage on *my* hillside, and although just under half of the island appeared to be undamaged, the effect on the island as a whole was horrific. As soon as we had landed, I scrambled up the hillside to see whether I could ascertain the cause of the massively destructive conflagration, and to my satisfaction, I think that I probably did. There was a small, flat and mostly clear area, about three quarters of the way up the main hill. Although the Downes family had always preferred – for reasons I don't know and don't really care, and which certainly don't matter, half a century later – to have their picnic meals on the beach, I had noticed on previous occasions that we were not the only visitors to this remote islet, and that other visitors preferred to have their meals at this open air natural picnic ground. And so it had appeared to be, on this occasion. Not only did the picnic area appear to have been the epicentre of the fire, but there was what was unmistakably a broken Coca Cola bottle that had been half melted by the blaze. And it took no great leap of imagination to theorise that it had been this glass which, magnifying rays of the searing hot summer sun, out into which – of course – only mad dogs and Englishmen would venture, that had been the immediate cause of the blaze.

Something had put the fire out before it had done too much damage, and again I hypothesised that it was one of those weird flash rainstorms which blow up, seemingly out of nowhere, across the tropics. My hypothesis was strengthened by the fact that the twigs that had been reduced to charcoal no longer had the fluttering debris of charred vegetation left dangling upon them, and – to my nine-year-old mind, at least – this was mostly likely to have been caused by the action of sudden wind and rain.

One side effect of all this was that there were a couple of new locations for me to explore; places that, on previous visits, had been covered with dense scrub and thorns, which created such an impenetrable barrier that even an adventurous nine-year-old *gwei-lo* was unable to fight through it. But now, it was all gone, and I made my way intrepidly into the depths of the island, cheerfully swinging a stick from side to side, knocking off the charcoal twigs and clearing quite a serviceable path. I truly was not expecting to find what I did. Because, there, where it had been hidden by vegetation for the previous two decades and where – looking at Google Earth pictures of it now - it appears to be hidden by vegetation again, was unmistakeably a Japanese army 'foxhole'.

Whereas, as you will find elsewhere in this narrative, there were once – and still might have been at the time – a subspecies of the Eurasian red fox (*Vulpes vulpes hoole*) found in the territory, and the story of their existence is actually quite an interesting one; the British colonists deciding that it was their God-given right to hunt foxes wherever they damn well pleased, and in doing so causing just as much havoc in Hong Kong as their descendants still do today – illegally – across many parts of Britain. But, the use of the word 'foxhole' in this context is to describe a type of earthwork constructed in a military context, and although some such constructions can be quite complex, and large enough to hold a whole team of soldiers, this one could not have held more than one. It had been built out of naturally occurring boulders, augmented by sandbags, which – after a quarter of a century or so – were rapidly falling apart. Martin Booth describes how, during his enchanted childhood in Hong Kong, he found a similar foxhole; although his foxhole, as described in Gweilo [2004] contained the mortal remains of a hitherto missing Japanese soldier.

There was nothing so exciting in mine, although – believe me – I searched very hard. There weren't even any cartridge cases or any other typical evidence that could give a historical context to what I had found. I didn't even know for sure whether the army that had constructed it was the Imperial Japanese one, but any other explanation seemed to me then (and seems to me now) to be unlikely.

Whilst there were guerrilla fighters – both Chinese and European – active in the wilder parts of the New Territories during parts of the Second World War, the invading Japanese would have carried out a thorough door-to-door, and island-to-island, search for British renegades, following which summary justice would be carried out (usually execution, but sometimes with some unpleasant oriental torture added). And, it seemed highly unlikely that a European or Chinese renegade could have hidden out on Beaufort Island for any length of time, especially as there was a complete absence of natural freshwater.

I scrambled back down the hillside to my family, only to have it pointed out that after scrabbling through carbonised scrubland, I was as black as soot. My mother was angry that I had got my clothes so dirty, and my father made a racist comment that would probably have resulted in him being taken to court in the days in which I write. But, I managed to convince my father that this was something he really should see, and, slightly diffidently, I led him back up the hillside to my little piece of military history.

He was far more interested than I thought he would be, although it has taken fifty years for me to come up with a workable hypothesis as to why.

As I have said elsewhere in this narrative, my father was a fairly senior officer in the Colonial Service, and had been involved with various plans to combat the communist menace from over the border. He had also been – until the organisation was shut down as a result of various budget cuts by Harold Wilson's Labour government back in London – an avid member of the Hong Kong Royal Naval Reserve [RNR]. And, from what I have discovered in the intervening half century, the Hong Kong RNR's compliment of ships; two minesweepers called *HMS Cunningham* and *HMS Etchingham* were not just involved in anti-piracy patrols and thwarting illegal immigrants, but may well have been also involved in more proactive anti-Communist activity.

What I do know is that this was the last day that we ever went to Beaufort Island, and I've often wondered whether my interpretation of what I had found was wrong. Was it a lonely outpost inhabited by a solitary Japanese soldier, keeping watch for incoming ships from the South China sea or taking pot shots at American dive bombers who most certainly *were* active from 1943 onwards? We know this because Herklots himself, who was by then a prisoner of war in what had been, and was to be again, Stanley Prison, noted how the deeper sea fish had been killed as a result of this dive bombing and how enterprising POWs had snuck beneath the parameter fence to salvage such tasty and nutritious treats from the beach where they had washed up. Or could it have been something else entirely?

Over the last half century, I have often wondered whether there was a network of outposts on a lot of the outlying islands, where British soldiers, or volunteers, with machine guns and binoculars, sat out night after long, lonely night, looking out for the Communist invasion that never happened. It also makes me wonder whether there was something else hidden in the blackened charcoal scrubland that my father already knew about, but which a nine year old boy should never see.

On occasion, my father would do something far more adventurous with our little boat. I remember one day when, instead of just sailing to one of the little deserted beaches in Tai Tam Bay, he took a course due south and headed right out to sea, right past the Po Toi island group before heading east and out into the open sea.

We were well into international waters when we stopped and my father revealed the reason for this mighty incursion into the High Seas. He consulted his chart and dropped anchor, and I was terribly impressed to know that his calculations as to the amount of the anchor chain which would be needed were spot on. He then got out a lump of grey coloured metal which he told me was lead that he had melted from the tops of bottles of fizzy wine that he had collected over the previous year. It had a rough eyehole at the top, through which was threaded the end of five fathoms of nylon, and at the other end was a depression into which he had melted a considerable amount of candlewax.

He looked very proud of himself as he told me it was a home made sounding lead, and that he and I were just about to test it. Using an arm windmill motion made famous by Pete Townshend, (someone of whom I am sure he had never heard) he whirled the lead around and threw it into the water feeding the rope out until he could feel that visit was resting on the ocean floor. It was only then that I noticed that he had marked off the rope every 6 feet so we could tell how many fathoms of water there were below us.

He checked the chart, having triangulated our position with a compass and his old brass sextant, and showed me exactly where we were. The chart was exactly right.

The sounding lead was exactly 3 1/2 fathoms beneath us. I never did find out why he took us into international waters to carry out the experiment, but I imagine that the frisson of being somewhere that the Hong Kong Coast Guard and marine police had no jurisdiction was considerable.

Then he had me pull the rope back in, coiling it over my left-arm as I did so. And the sounding lead had one more surprise for me. The big blob of candle wax had grains of sand embedded in it which confirmed the statement from the Admiralty chart, that the seabed directly beneath us was sandy.

Something which I shall always remember about that day was that come swimming earnestly past the boat I saw a tiny blue and yellow lobster. It swam quite easily into my net, and I observed it for about 10 minutes before releasing it back into the sea. I have never seen anything quite like it before, and never since, but I've always wondered whether it was a naturally tiny species, or the young adult of a much larger one.

That day, I was feeling closer to my father than usual, and so, as he was in a benevolent mood, I was happy to have one of his lessons in seamanship. He pointed at the flag folded neatly in the corner of the cabin. "That is a Union Flag. It is not a Union Jack. It is only called a Union Jack when it flies on the Jack Mast of a ship. Most People get it completely wrong, but from now on you are not one of those people. I never want to hear you refer to it as a Union Jack again".

He said this sternly, but with love – both of me, his country, and the naval tradition – in his voice. So I vowed to him, and to myself, that I would never misname the Union Flag again.

Some weeks later in the history lesson about James I, I was told that the term 'Union Jack' came from the French for James, i.e. Jacques. And together with the rest of my class I was instructed to write this into my exercise book. But I wrote that "The Union Jack is called because it flies on the jack mast of the ship". For some reason, this was taken as another example of Jonathan refusing to conform. And I was eventually chastised by my father, after having been reported for insolence.

"Jonathan will not conform?" Who the fuck was I supposed to be conforming to? It was another one of Roger's 'bricks in the wall'.

Just behind Tai Tam bay was a series of reservoirs. The largest of these - Tai Tam Tuk - had been created in the early 20th century when a river was dammed and a steep wooded valley was flooded. At the bottom of the reservoir are the remains of at least one (and according some sources two) small villages that had been an unfortunate victim of the burgeoning Crown Colony's need for more and more fresh water. Some of my fondest childhood memories are of walking through the winding paths that lead through the thick woodland, as the whole family went for another of our regular Sunday walks. During my researches for this chapter I was trying to find some photographs of the PG Farm when I discovered this account of an encounter with some particularly frightening mystery animals in the heavily wooded hillsides surrounding the reservoir:

> "We got to our chosen area and set up camp for the weekend under a concrete bridge that had once been part of a more permanent track around the reservoir. Through the night we heard an animal howling, it was a very strange sort of howl, quite indescribable really. As dawn broke we could see some trees about fifty yards along the bank swaying as something moved through them. The first animal appeared on the bank no more than forty yards form us followed by another half dozen or so, they looked like a cross between an orangutan and a chimpanzee. They stopped dead when they saw us and then very slowly started to walk towards us, one of the lads with us got very nervous and after shouting something quite incoherent, threw a rock at them. This caused the apes to start jumping about, they started to make their weird howling noise and having previously seen my friends reaction to aggressive animals I quickly picked up all my bits and was the first one to leg it up the track, the others no more than a second behind me.

> "There had been an Irish kid with us called Pat and none of us had noticed that he was asleep when the apes arrived, he had woken up to find himself being watched at close quarters by the apes and his friends all gone. Apparently the apes had spent a couple of hours playing around on the bank and then just wandered off into the trees. When he hold us about this I wished I had stayed but was then glad I hadn't as I hadn't been wearing brown trousers. Pat returned to the reservoir on his own several times and the apes always came to see him but as winter approached they stopped coming."

The above quote is taken from the fishing memoirs of a man named Nick Buss, who lived in Hong Kong during the early 1960s. Despite spending many happy hours in those woods at roughly the same time I never saw any monkeys there. Indeed, if you discount the semi-tame rhesus macaques that I mentioned earlier when describing the Botanical Gardens, I only ever saw two wild monkeys in Hong Kong. This sighting occurred one afternoon in 1970 when I was on my way home from school. I had to take the Peak tram from Island School in Bowen Road to the terminus at the top of the Peak that was only a few hundred yards from where my family lived at Peak Mansions. On this particular afternoon, the little green tram car had to halt its journey for about five minutes to allow a female monkey with at least one small child gripping precariously on to the hair on its back, to make a leisurely crossing (using the masts and cables that propelled the trolley cars up and down the Peak) to traverse the tram line.

The first connection that would be made in the minds of most people between monkeys and Hong Kong is the widespread belief in the Chinese custom of eating raw monkey brains, often out of the trepanned skull of a living monkey. It is interesting to note that whereas some television documentaries shown on British TV during the late 1980`s repeated this story with glee, others denied that this was more than a historical curiosity that certainly doesn't happen any more. I am certain that whatever perversity can be dreamed up by the human psyche is catered for somewhere on the globe, and as most human perversities are catered for somewhere in Hong Kong, monkey brains are probably still scooped out and eaten somewhere in the less well traversed areas of the territory.

The living monkey population of Hong Kong is no less mysterious. Although there is no doubt that monkeys have existed in Hong Kong since at least 1918, and probably have always existed here, their status is far less certain. In 1870 Robert Swinhoe - a man who can justifiably be described as the Father of Hong Kong natural history - described a small monkey species which he named *Macacus Sancti-johannis*. He wrote that: "This rock monkey is found in most of the small islands about Hong Kong and is like a Rhesus with a very short tail."

He continued: "Dried bodies of this animal split in two are often exhibited from the ceiling in druggists shops in Canton and Hong Kong; and its bones are used for medicinal purposes."

Writing in 1951 Herklots reported: "There are still monkeys wild on the Lema Islands south of the Colony. On the island of Hong Kong a monkey family was watched early one morning near Tai Tam reservoir in 1947, and I have had occasional accounts of monkeys having been seen on The Peak and in the Deep Water Bay valley. It is possible, but not certain that these are descendants of the original wild stock."

Herklots identified the original wild monkeys as Rhesus Monkeys, that (at least when he was writing), had a range stretching from "India to the whole of China south of the Yangtze." However, when Swinhoe had originally described *M. Sancti-johannis* he specifically said that the Hong Kong monkeys were like a rhesus but with a short tail. The rhesus monkey has a long tail, and was first described by Zimmerman in 1780. It is an animal with which Swinhoe was bound to have been familiar, and therefore if he drew a distinction between the "Hong Kong Rock Monkey" and the rhesus then we can safely assume that they were two different animals.

Herklots noted that monkeys were released into the woodland near the Kowloon reservoir during the First World War. During the Japanese occupation of the Colony in the Second World War, and after the trees had been cut down, the surviving animals scattered. Since the war they have been reported from several districts in the New Territories including their own haunts. Patricia Marshall then added a few more pieces to an ever more complicated jigsaw by announcing in 1967 that a second species - the long tailed macaque - had either been released or escaped from captivity during or shortly after the 1939-1945 hostilities. But we still need to consider Swinhoe's original record.

Macacus Sancti-johannis is said to have a very short tail. As we have seen, both of the species that were found in Hong Kong before 1981 have quite noticeable tails. By the end of the 20th Century there were at least four macaque species (and various hybrids) living in the colony. It was claimed that all of these were introduced, and that the indigenous population had died out. But none of these species has anything approaching a "pig tail."

According to my late friend, the noted zoologist C.H.Keeling, *Macacus Sancti-johannis* is generally considered as a synonym of the Rhesus Monkey. A female specimen, was presented to London Zoo on the 14th January 1867 by R. Swinhoe. It had been caught on North Lema Island, just south of Hong Kong territorial waters. It is said to have been found on St. John's Island in the South China Sea and both the monkey and the island were named after Commander St. John R.N.

Despite spending many happy hours in those woods at roughly the same time as Nick Buss I never saw any monkeys there. Indeed, if you discount the semi-tame rhesus macaques that I mentioned earlier when describing the Botanical Gardens, I only ever saw two wild monkeys in Hong Kong. This sighting occurred one afternoon in 1970 when I was on my way home from school. I had to take the Peak Tram from Island School in Bowen Road to the terminus at the top of the Peak that was only a few hundred yards from where my family lived at Peak Mansions. On this particular afternoon, the little green tram car had to halt its journey for about five minutes to allow a female monkey with at least one small child gripping precariously on to the hair on its back, to make a leisurely crossing (using the masts and cables that propelled the trolley cars up and down the Peak) to traverse the tram line.

Even if we ignore the mystery of where the Hong Kong island animals disappeared to between 1947 and 1970, and even if we ignore the fact that some of the later records do not mention monkeys on the island itself, there seems no doubt that Rhesus monkeys are, and have been, resident on Hong Kong island.

Whether or not we are to accept that *Macacus Sancti-johannis* is distinct merely at sub-specific level (and the interbreeding between three of the four species described as being naturalised residents of the Colony in 1992 suggests that there is more to be learned about the genetics of the Macaque family), then the animals were certainly distinct enough morphologically with a pig-tail, (suggesting a curly tail), that they were for a while considered to be a distinct species.

And the animals that frightened the group of young fishermen in 1964? The fact that they were described as apes rather than monkeys suggests that within the past sixty years there were, indeed, pig-tailed monkeys living wild in the more remote forests on the south side of Hong Kong island. The fact that they were reported in the very location where Herklots noted them in 1947, suggests that they were a well-established population, and I fervently hope that they are still there!

Even if they are not, it seems likely that the genes which produce this pig-tail are hidden somewhere within the gene pool of the Rhesus monkeys on Hong Kong Island itself. It also seems most probable that these genetic differences may yet assert themselves once more; and even if they no longer exist there at the moment, Hong Kong Island will eventually once again be the home to a distinctive pig tailed monkey!

I would love to say that I knew all about these peculiar tailless monkeys, back during my school days, and that I had even compared them with the stories of orang pendek from elsewhere in the book, but in all honesty I cannot pretend anything of the sort. However, it is interesting that there are reports of unknown species of small ape from all across the Far East, and although some people like to hypothesise that they are all members of the same species of distinctive primitive hominin, I think that it is more likely that, as seems to be the case with pig-tailed monkeys of southern Hong Kong island, they are elusive members of unusual morphs, or in some cases genetic throwbacks of primitive members of known species of monkey. And because monkeys and other primates are, by nature, secretive and more intelligent than most animals, it seems likely, to my mind at least, that they will be more elusive.

And as I have noted again and again in this narrative, back in the sixties, at least, the native Chinese were known to shy away from the forest as much as possible, as did most of the European expats. It was only a certain brand of mad dog and Englishman who not only "went out in the noonday sun" but ventured into the deepest part of the forest, and so I am not at all surprised that our only record of these stubby tailed, black, primates comes from an intrepid group of boy scouts!

Anyone who has known me in later life, will probably be surprised to learn that when I was in primary school I was a keen amateur boxer. I have a sneaking suspicion that in these politically correct days at the beginning of the 21st century, young boys of seven and eight are probably not encouraged to beat the living crap out of each other in the name of sportsmanship. As my career as a pugilist only lasted for a couple of years in the mid-1960s, I cannot really comment as to whether it did me any harm or not. I don't think so. However, for a couple of years, I was taught the 'Royal and Ancient Sport of Kings' by a man called Billy Tingle who ran a sports club for boys in the Colony. He taught me to swim and box and he singularly failed to teach me to play cricket. His wife was the proprietor of the nursery school at which I started my education, and the couple were - as far as I remember - leading lights within the expatriate community on the island. Once again, whilst preparing this chapter, I took recourse to the Internet in a vain attempt to try and find out some biographical information about this man who was such a pivotal influence on generations of young people in Hong Kong. I found one reference - the biography of a local boxing champion - that made a veiled jibe at the "institutional racism" of Tingle's establishment. As my mother is now dead, and it was she who arranged my attendance at the various establishments run by Mr. and Mrs. Tingle, there is nobody left for me to ask.

It was Billy Tingle, however, who first told me about one of the greatest mystery animal stories of Hong Kong. During my short career as a pugilist, I attended boxing lessons in the hall of my *alma mater.* One evening I overheard my instructor talking to one of the teachers about tigers. Once again, I had been aware that tigers occasionally visited Hong Kong. One of my earliest memories of Hong Kong natural history was a warning broadcast on the local Rediffusion radio station warning hill-walkers not to venture into the wilds of the Sai Kung Peninsular on that particular weekend because a female tiger - with cubs - had been spotted there. So, when I heard my boxing instructor and his friend mention the great striped cat - the villain of the *Jungle Book* - my ears pricked up, and ignoring the strictures that children were to be seen and not heard, I asked him for some more information.

He told me that during the Second World War, when civilian internees had been incarcerated in what was now the maximum-security prison at Stanley, Japanese soldiers had shot a tiger. I rushed home, and grabbed my figurative bible. As has probably become almost painfully obvious, it is Herklots's book, *The Hong Kong Countryside*, that became the most important book ever written on the natural history of the territory. I believe that large portions of Herklots' book were written whilst he was interned by the Japanese in Stanley Internment Camp. I also believe that he was lucky enough to take his complete set of *The Hong Kong Naturalist* into captivity with him. It was during the war, while all Britons and their allies living in the colony were interned in prison-camps, that the next, and possibly the most intriguing chapter in the story of the tigers of Hong Kong took place. Herklots seemed unsure of what had actually happened:

> "During our internment at Stanley a remarkable story filtered into the camp that there was a tiger at large on Hong-Kong Island. Later it was reported to be on Stanley Peninsula. The guards got excited and it was risky walking about in the evening for an excited guard might fire at a prisoner mistaking him for a tiger! Soon pug-marks were seen at the camp: I examined some myself but was by no means convinced. Then the story was spread that the tiger had been shot and finally there came into camp a Chinese or Japanese paper containing a photograph of the dead tiger. This photograph I saw. People said that it was a menagerie animal that had got loose; a likely story! It is strange how loath people are to believe that tigers do visit the Colony and occasionally swim the harbour and visit the island."

Even at the age of eight I felt that there was something rather peculiar about this statement. It was almost as if Herklots didn't believe the story himself. It was almost certain that *something* had happened. But what? At the time I had just discovered Lewis Carroll and I misquoted "Alice" that "someone" had certainly killed "something" and that the "something" was a large Tiger.

Again, my enquiring mind young was tempered by the prevailing "children are to be seen and not heard" attitudes which were prevalent in Colonial Society fifty years ago. So, once again, I had to work by stealth. Over the following years and months I gingerly asked various grown-ups if they had heard of the event, and much to my surprise quite a few of them had.

The Second World War was the defining event of my generation - even though hostilities had ceased fourteen years before I was born. I don't know what it was like in the UK for a young child growing up during the 1960s, but for me growing up in

Hong Kong - a British Colony which had suffered four years of intense brutality under Japanese occupation the reminders were everywhere.

My friends and I played soldiers in the disued gun emplacements that still stood along parts of Lugard Rd., and amongst my parents' friends and acquaintances were several who had been prisoners of war during the years of occupation. There was no shortage of source material for me to draw on. Over the years and months I pieced together the facts of the case from snippets of information that I could glean from those who had been there. About ten years after my quest began - when I was approaching adulthood and living in England I discovered the following passage in a book of reminiscences about the history of Hong Kong written by someone with the pen name of *Thagorus:*

> "During the war, a tiger was shot by a party of Japanese Militiamen near Stanley in May 1942. A Mr. E.W.Bradbury, who was once a butcher with the Dairy Farm Company, was brought from the Stanley Internment camp to skin the animal, the meat from which subsequently provided a feast for members of the Hong Kong race club. The animal was three feet high, six feet long, weighed 240lbs and had a nineteen-inch tail. The skin of the tiger was stuffed and mounted in the hall of Government House, from which it was subsequently transferred to Japan in 1944. One theory about its presence on the island was that it had escaped from a menagerie during the Japanese invasion; another and more likely theory was that it had swum over from the mainland."

Unlike my quest for the elusive red fox, I found that my elders and betters were happy to talk about their exploits during the war, and on this occasion evidence was relatively easy to get hold of. However, making sense of it all was far more complicated. My primary school had a small library, and for some reason - best known to the Gods of cryptoinvestigative theory - it contained several back issues of *The Hong Kong News*, an English language newspaper published by the occupying Japanese. Leafing idly through these one day I hit paydirt. I found a contemporary account of the incident: 'Fierce Tiger shot in Stanley Woods! Successful Hong Kong police hunt in early morning.'

> "Although for some years past, rumours had circulated that there were tigers roaming the Hong Kong hills, it was only yesterday morning that such was shown to be fact, and the feat of shooting the first tiger on the island was accomplished by Nipponese gendarmes and Indian and Chinese police at the back of Stanley village. Early yesterday morning the lowing of wild beasts was heard by many residents in Stanley village and gendarmes and police and military set off fully armed to search the hills. The search party, consisting of Nipponese gendarmes and Indian and Chinese policemen, was headed by Lt. Colonel Hirabayashi. The party was divided into smaller groups and a net was spread around the woods. After going over the ground for some considerable time, one group of searchers came across the tigers lair. They immediately opened fire but despite all efforts and the use of big wire netting the beast succeeded in evading the hunters. Not discouraged by the failure of the first attempt, the Nipponese police continued their search and a bigger cordon was thrown around the whole area.
>
> Apparently alarmed by the noise the tiger rushed about the forest for some time when it was again encountered by the police party. The police opened fire, and shots from an

Indian policeman this time found their mark, causing the tiger to halt. The Indian fired three shots, hitting the tiger in the head, left shoulder and lungs.

Despite its wounds the tiger continued to struggle against the efforts of the policemen to tie it up. In the struggle, one of the Indian police was injured. However, the work of the Nipponese and Indian Police was fully rewarded as the tiger was finally subdued. The dead Tiger was then taken to the vacant ground outside the gendarme office at Stanley."

Eventually, in the mid 1990s, due to the good offices of Richard Muirhead, I obtained a number of books and photocopies which confirmed the story. The day that they arrived in the post I was laid low with the flu, but I eagerly sat up in bed, tore open the packaging and read the documents which finally confirmed the details of the incident which had obsessed me for nearly thirty years. A book about the Japanese occupation included a photograph of the dead beast, credited to Lady May Ride, which is captioned: "The famous Stanley Tiger which was shot by the guards in 1942. This appears to be the only unofficial photograph taken by an inmate at Stanley."

If this is the photograph from the Japanese newspaper, referred to by Herklots, why was it taken by an internee, whoever he or she was? Collaborating with the enemy to the extent of becoming an unofficial press photographer for a newspaper full of propaganda, which was published by the occupying power would have been considered almost treasonable.

However, the photocopy of the original newspaper cutting that I had first read back in the little whitewashed library at Peak School showed that the Lady May Ride photograph was not the one used by the occupying Japanese. This is a far less impressive piece of photography than the Lady May Ride photograph that, despite the claims that it is an unofficial photograph, is obviously posed and well composed. The stringency of Japanese security arrangements, especially earlier on in the War is legendary. Violence, torture and even executions were relatively commonplace for what the Japanese considered to be infringements of security. If, indeed, it was taken by an internee and not by a Japanese Press Photographer, then the evidence suggests that it was done so with the connivance, tacit, or overt knowledge of the Japanese Military. The head of the creature is being supported by a man who appears to be an Indian, and presumably the policeman that shot it. If the man in the picture is a guard or policeman, as seems probable, he was certainly aware that he was being photographed. He is even smiling for the camera! It seems almost impossible that the Japanese Security Forces could not have been aware of the photograph.

When one compares it with the crude picture which accompanied the item in *The Hong Kong News* then the whole affair becomes even more unlikely. There may have been three thousand internees but it seems almost impossible that Herklots, who was after all Hong Kong's leading naturalist and the editor of the *Hong Kong Naturalist* magazine, and a minor celebrity in his own right, would not have known about the tiger incident from more than hearsay and rumours. Dr. Herklots was important enough to be put in charge of revitalising the post-war fishing industry for the region, in a successful attempt to restore food stocks as quickly as possible. Another history of the Japanese occupation gives more details of this affair and implies that Herklots, whom he describes as a "Biologist just released from Stanley Internment Camp," was a person of considerable importance. Even if Herklots had not been taken to view the carcass in person, it seems certain that the photographer, who obviously did see the carcass, would have spoken to Herklots about it!

We have examined enough evidence from Herklots already in this book, to suggest that he is a reliable and indeed an expert witness. His mind may have been vague about minor details, but surely an event as important to the sum total knowledge of the zoo-fauna of Hong Kong as this would have remained fresh in his mind. As a Fortean, I have often been accused of paranoid conspiracy theorising, but in this case, something doesn't add up!

The mounted skin was taken to a place of honour in the newly restored Government House and eventually ended up in the Tin Hau Temple in Stanley village.

Back in the late 1960s I remember talking about the affair to my beloved amah - Ah Tim. She told me that according to Chinese belief, the tiger was the King of Beasts and the arrival of a tiger unexpectedly in a neighbourhood was often seen as an omen that a new Emperor or King was about to take the throne. It is certain that some people at the time saw the death of the unfortunate tiger in Stanley Internment Camp as being a signal that the reign of the King-Emperor George VI was nearing an end, and the reign of the God-Emperor Hirohito was about to begin!

It also seems likely that the invading Japanese would have been determined to extract the maximum of publicity from the event by exploiting local folk beliefs. Near the end of the war when it was obvious that they would lose, they were still fermenting Chinese Nationalist feelings, often through the use of cultural motifs, and sometimes by recruiting collaborators, in an attempt to ensure that at least the British would no longer be in power in Hong Kong. They failed, as history has proven, but the different stories I managed to unearth over a period of some thirty years suggested that someone, either wittingly or unwittingly, was not telling the whole truth.

The whole affair is a real mystery, and excitingly it is a mystery that I hope that eventually I shall be able to solve. Although there is no doubt that South China tigers did visit Hong Kong on many occasions, it is very tempting to speculate that the unfortunate creature that was shot in 1941 was, indeed, a captive animal which had been released in the area by the occupying Japanese forces as a crude - but remarkably successful - piece of psychological warfare.

The affair has become somewhat of an obsession with me since I first heard about it from Billy Tingle back in the mid 1960. One of these days I have every intention of going back to Hong Kong, and somehow obtaining a DNA sample from the pelt. It should then be a reasonably simple job to ascertain whether this was the last verified Tiger to visit Hong Kong Island or whether it was just one of the sadder casualties of the most terrible conflict of the 20th century.

Now, thanks to a passage in an excellent book called *Prisoner of the Turnip Heads* by George Wright-Nooth, which tells the often harrowing story of his time spent as a P.O.W in Stanley Internment Camp on Hong Kong Island during WW2, the mystery is a little closer to being solved.

30 May, 1942.
Last night Langston and Dalziel who were sleeping outside at the back of the bungalow were woken up at about 5.00 am by snarls and growls. Langston, at Dalziel's instigation, got up to have a look. He went to the edge of the garden and looked down the slope to the wire fence. There Dalziel saw him leap in the air and fly back into the boiler room shouting 'There's a tiger down there' .... Next morning, on being told the story we were inclined to laugh.

31 May, 1942.
Slept very badly owing to stomach trouble. During the night we were woken by three rapid shots and much shouting.

1 June, 1942.
Early this morning there was much activity on the hill behind the camp which was being searched by parties of Chinese and Indian police under Japs .... One of the Chinese supervisors told me that an Indian policeman had been mauled by a tiger at about 2.00 am."

Two tiger guards were instituted, one armed with a gong, the other with a gardening fork. The bungalows had no doors or windows so for several nights there was considerable apprehension at night.

4 June, 1942.
As usual we all slept outside. At about 3 am I heard Colin say, 'Geoffrey! Don't move there's a TIGER eating a bone behind your bed!' Then he said, 'Stephen, nobody move. The tiger is at the foot of Stephen's bed.' My bed was around the corner so I loosened my mosquito net and very gradually slipped out of bed ready to take some action, but what I, or anyone else, could do was doubtful. Then Colin said, 'Where is Farrar? My God! He's eating him.' This was too much for Searle who came along to see what was happening. Colin then shouted, 'Don't move, you fool Searle!' Just then Farrar woke up and it was discovered that what Colin had seen was a black coat lying across Farrar's body with one end lying on his white pillow. The pillow he thought was the bone and the coat the animal."

A tiger was indeed on the loose, probably from a circus that had been located at Causeway Bay. It was subsequently shot and the carcass, which weighed some 240 lbs, was given to an internee called Bradbury to be skinned. He had worked as a butcher at the main dairy farm and was probably the most unpopular man in the camp a real life Uriah Heap as I will explain later. As the reader is aware this skin is still on display today in the Stanley Tin Hau temple.

Bradbury's photograph subsequently appeared with the dead animal in a Japanese newspaper, although I did not see it in the *Hong Kong News.*"

So, it looks like it was a circus animal after all, rather than a *bona fide* South Chinese tiger. But one day I should like to put this mystery to bed once and for all.

CHAPTER NINE

There must be Trouble Ahead

"We`re not in Wonderland anymore, Alice."~

Charles Manson

Bizarrely – because, by the time we returned to England a few years later, my parents always gave every indication that they disliked Christmas as much as I do as an adult - back in Hong Kong in the late 1960s, they made a very big deal about it. There were always lots of people at a sumptuous Christmas lunch, including a pair of middle-aged Roman Catholic priests, whom my parents had befriended, and who they dropped like the proverbial hot coals once they left the priesthood to get married. One of them also committed the additional sin of getting married to a Chinese girl, and 'going native'. In my parents' eyes, and those of Mother Church, for having committed the appalling sin of having rejected a life of devotion for a life of inter-racial rumpo, they were forever damned. There was also 'Aunty Chad', who had some connection with the cartoonist responsible for the popular World War II era British cartoon character, 'Mr Chad'. And my parents always contacted the Captain of whichever American or Canadian, or indeed British, warship was currently moored in Hong Kong Harbour, asking that a couple of sailors - who would otherwise spend Christmas aboard ship - join the Downes family for their celebrations.

The Christmas of 1968 was particularly poignant, because it has gone down in history as the week when Apollo 8 first carried out ten successful orbits of the moon by human astronauts, a few months after the Soviet Union had done something similar with tortoises, mealworms, and various flies.

After dinner, my father, as he always did, proposed toasts to 'The Queen' and 'Absent

Friends', before asking one of the aforementioned Roman Catholic priests to say a prayer for the Apollo 8 astronauts.

Although I had been aware of the American (and to a lesser extent, the Soviet) space missions before, they had not really impacted upon my consciousness.

But, in common with the vast majority of my peers, I almost immediately became 'space mad'.

The children of Peak Mansions started to play at being astronauts *en masse* and one of the most enduring of our games was to fashion what we fondly believed to be our own miniature space capsule out of a one gallon plastic ice-cream box, with two cricket stumps tied to it in a cross pattern, which we believed looked more than somewhat like radio antennae.

We would then defy our parents instructions not to go up onto the flat roof of the apartment block in which we all lived, and throw our makeshift 'spacecraft', to which we had attached a parachute made of a pocket handkerchief (boys still carried such things back in those days) and string. And we would marvel as our gallant craft drifted to earth, some six storeys below.

So impressive was this game that we played it solidly, for months, just as the people at NASA sent two more missions into space, before the big one in July that year, which was to land the first men on the moon.

My relationship with my schoolteachers and my parents continued to deteriorate. Some years ago, I watched a documentary presented and narrated by British actor and comedian, Stephen Fry, in which he revealed that he had been a 'manic depressive' all his life, and that this condition – more properly called Bipolar Disorder – had affected his life massively, both for good and for ill. As a schoolboy, he had spent three months in what is now HM Prison Ashfield in Gloucestershire, after an incident when he absconded with a credit card of a family friend. He was also expelled from at least two private schools, and was the last person that anyone would ever have expected to turn into a 'National Treasure' a quarter of a century or so later.

Well, I am not a national treasure, nor have I been to prison, but the spring of 1969 saw my psyche finally implode in upon itself. Throughout my life, from 1969 to somewhere in the early years of the 21st Century, when my condition was finally brought – sort of – under control, I underwent numerous episodes when I did something stupid, and often criminal, without being able to explain – even to myself – why I had done it. I became quite good at coming up with excuses for why I had done these things, which gained me a reputation as both a bad child and a liar. But it wasn't until the massive amounts of therapy that I went through between 1996 and 2005 that I realised that many, if not all, of these obfuscations were the result of me trying to explain to myself why I had just done something so bloody stupid.

No doubt, there were episodes before, but in the late spring of 1969, I was caught shoplifting at the Dairy Farm mini-supermarket just up the road from where we lived. Although I remember the fallout from this, and the horror of my parents' reaction and subsequent punishments, in common with most of the other, similar, psychotic episodes that I have had over the years, I can't actually remember what happened, or what it was I stole. I do remember that, somehow, I implicated one of the boys who had bullied me over the years, although – as far as I remember – he was innocent of that crime at least.

For the first time in my life, I began to hallucinate, and I spent most of my time – whenever I could, at least – hiding up on the hillside in one of the little dens I had made. As I have written in an earlier chapter, I had three particularly close friends; an Australian boy called Ricky, whom my father disliked intensely for reasons known only to himself, and the two English boys; Michael Brown and William Topley. Despite the coals of opprobrium that had been heaped upon my head by a vengeful society, these three boys stuck with me and were ever-loyal, to the extent of even trying to bolster up the alibi which my psychotic psyche had created out of nowhere.

I would like to think that, these days, a child who was as obviously mentally ill as me, would receive some sort of psychiatric help. I was, indeed, sent to a psychologist by my parents, but he couldn't have done that good a job, because not only did he not notice that I was suffering from a serious psychotic illness, but a few months after he pronounced me to be cured, and I went out and did exactly the same thing again.

There were only two things that I remember happening as a result of my psychologist's advice. The first of these was that, instead of having a 'nursery tea' with my little brother, at about half past five each evening, my father would make a real effort to get home from the office early enough for us all to sit down and eat as a family. This made me feel incredibly grown up, and – I suppose – that was exactly what was supposed to happen.

The other thing that the psychologist recommended was that I joined the Cub Scouts.

And so, for reasons best known to themselves, my parents enrolled me in a Troop of this venerable organisation, based at St. John's Cathedral in the part of Victoria City known as 'Central', for obvious reasons. There were thriving outposts of the Cubs, Brownies, Scouts and Girl Guides at my *Alma Mater* on Plunkett's Road, but for the rest of my time in Hong Kong, every Thursday evening I went down to the little community centre attached to the great, stone Cathedral, to learn about life through the Baden-Powell lens.

And I adored it.

It was the first time in my life that I had something of my own; something which I belonged to, and that my parents and little brother didn't. I looked forward to

Thursday evenings with a passion, and learned all the oaths and obligations of the Scouting movement rigidly. But, even then, my poor, dear father managed to fuck it up. Every time I got a bad school report, or did something wrong, he would make me stand to attention in front of him, and recite the part of the Scouting Oath about "doing ones best", which left me both humiliated and even more angry than I had been before.

But, I did get something else that spring, and it is something that has stayed with me ever since. Presumably because she, too, was trying to improve my lot, my form teacher, who I believe was called Miss Stuart, put me in charge of the class Nature Table, a position that I immediately equated as 'Curator'. And for the next four months, I truly did do my "best".

One of the things that truly helped me in my new endeavour was the fact that there was a little stream that flowed down the far perimeter of the playing field that was situated just above Peak School. In fact, to refer to it as a stream is probably hyperbole, because it was a tiny, slow moving water course no more than a foot across at its widest point. It had probably been originally constructed as a drainage ditch, intended to stop the playing field from getting waterlogged during the rainy season, and – much to my sorrow – when I tried to look it up both on Google Earth and on the Peak School website, it appears that what was once a slightly shabby, grass playing field has now been covered with AstroTurf, and although it looks all very swish and shiny, I strongly suspect that my little "stream" has gone the way of all flesh. But, during the spring and summer of 1969, the water course still flowed, slowly but surely, and although at its narrowest point it was only a few inches wide, the constriction of the water flow produced a series of little lagoons, none more than a few inches deep, but all containing a rich and varied selection of wildlife.

As freshwater zoology has always been, and remains to this day, the thing that interests me most, I set up a series of three or four inside ponds on my nature table. It so happened that my mother's twin tub washing machine had recently exploded; she always insisted that it was Ah Tim who was unable to get her head around the functioning of this huge, noisy and unwieldy item of domestic equipment, but I have always had a sneaking suspicion that it was actually my mother, a lady who had the mechanical acumen of a small newt, who continually managed to break the washing machine, necessitating a regular stream of expensive repairs. Finally, the poor bloody machine gave up the ghost for good in the spring of 1969 and – my father being in a surprisingly good mood that day, despite the imminent necessity of having to purchase another washing machine – gave me two shallow trays of enamelled metal, about three foot square and three inches deep, which had once been an integral part of the *quondam* washing machine. I took them to school, and they comprised the centre piece of my exciting new nature table.

As my main 'go-to book' for general natural history information was *The Children of Cherry Tree Farm* by Enid Blyton, I had got into my head that there were two types

246

of batrachian – frogs and toads – and it never really occurred to me until I took over the Class Five nature table that, in a place like Hong Kong where there were dozens of different types of tailless amphibian, that this would necessitate there being a whole range of different types of tadpole. In the little stream alone, there were four.

The most common were, of course, those of the Asian common toad, then known as *Bufo melanostictus*, which has since been moved into the genus *Duttaphrynus*. This was (and apparently still is) the most widespread of Hong Kong's amphibians. There was also a small, very dark, and remarkably aggressive type of tadpole, which Herklots said was probably the larval form of one of the Spadefoot Toads. Unfortunately, however, I have done a little research and found that there are no Spadefoot Toads known from Hong Kong. In fact, they are only found in Europe, northwest Africa and western Asia. I would love to extrapolate from this that Herklots had identified a creature that is now well and truly within the realms of cryptozoology, but I think that it is far more likely that he just totally misidentified one of the more commonly accepted local species. I have found, however, that *Megophrys brachykolos*, which is usually referred to as the 'short-legged toad', has been referred to as the 'Peak Spadefoot Toad', although it is no such thing. The species was first properly described by John Romer in 1952, although the species had first been collected as far back as 1917, but it had been misidentified. The citation by Romer and Robert Inger, from 1961, gives no indication why this creature, which is a fairly standard looking *Megophrys*, or Asian horned frog, should be given a name associated with an entirely different genus. As everybody knows, whilst Wikipedia is a useful reference tool, it is fatally flawed, and although I have found various southeast Asian frogs being described as 'Spadefoot Toads' when they're nothing of the sort, I have not been able to ascertain why. I don't suppose it matters particularly, but this is the sort of minor zoological mystery upon which I thrive, and it is the sort of thing that's going to bug me until I finally find out the answer.

I have the problem that I have always had when trying to rear any of the Lissamphibians, in that whilst rearing them from eggs or larvae is relatively easy, persuading the resulting young frog or toad to graduate successfully to adulthood (especially in the days before I discovered fruit flies and micro-crickets) was a practically impossible task and, as a result, I usually released the tiny frogs back into the wild where they could fend for themselves. So, of the four types of tadpole, I was only able to identify two of them, and only then because I had seen the adults – the aforementioned Asian common toad and the giant spiny frog (*Quasipaa spinosa).*

I set up one of my smart, new enamelled metal 'ponds' to illustrate the wide range of different creatures (at the age of nine, I had never come across the word 'biodiversity' but this is what I meant). It contained all four different types of tadpole, until I realised that the aggressive ones - which I am beginning to be convinced are *Megophrys* of some description - were no respecters of my carefully laid out aquatic diorama and promptly decided to eat all of their fellow exhibits, until I segregated them off with nothing more vulnerable than water weed and pretty stones as companions.

There were also various aquatic insect larvae, and although I found various grotesquely attractive dragonfly larvae, even then I realised that these veritable 'tigers' of my little stream would also eat anything that they were placed with and I was forced to – once again – exhibit them in a mini-aquarium of their own.

Much to my disappointment, the tiny stream didn't have any fish in it; it was far too small, but, after a week or so of diligent netting every break time, I had amassed quite an extraordinary diversity of different creatures, many of whom lived – apparently – quite happily together.

It was about three weeks into my explorations of this tiny stream, when I found a new species of animal, which presented me with a mystery that I was not to solve for many years. In one, and only one, of the tiny lagoons, I caught a number of what appeared to be transparent tadpoles. I caught them, and transported them proudly to my aquarium, where they bumbled around in the way that tadpoles are wont to do, for several days before they disappeared. I assumed, quite reasonably, that they had been eaten by something else. So, using one of a selection of empty plastic ice-cream boxes that my mother had given me, I set up a small 'mini-pond' for them alone, and went out to capture another exhibit's worth of these peculiar little creatures. This time, it took longer to find them, but eventually find them I did, and I took them back to the classroom, where they lived happily for a week or so before they – too – disappeared. Gutted, because I had – to my mind – done all that I could do provide them with palatial accommodation, even capturing some tiny midge larvae to augment the Tetra Min fish flake, which I have sworn by ever since I started keeping aquatic creatures, and still swear by today, I went through the contents of this ice-cream box with a figurative fine tooth comb, and I found a couple of small lumps of cloudy 'jelly', which I could not explain, and which I assumed were the mortal remains of my prized translucent tadpoles.

As has been so often the case in my life, it was Gerald Durrell who came to the rescue, although he didn't come to the rescue in this particular case for another thirty-three years! I wrote earlier in this book of how I came to read Douglas Botting's biography of Gerald Durrell after I had the worst breakdown of my life in September 2002. I was practically catatonic and this was the most severe attack of any condition associated with my bipolar disorder that I have ever had, and I truly hope that nothing like this happens to me again.

In one of the chapters dealing with Durrell's childhood on the Greek island of Corfu, it describes how the young Gerald found some peculiar translucent tadpoles, and how his – too – had disappeared mysteriously. It turned out that Gerry's 'tadpoles' had been nothing of the sort. They had been larvae of the biggest, and nastiest, of the local mosquitoes. Until then, I had no idea that a mosquito larva - rather than looking like peculiar, robotic, comma-shaped creatures like something off a progressive rock album cover from forty years ago – could actually appear to be tadpoles. And so, over three decades after the event, I had finally discovered an explanation for the disappearance of my 'translucent' tadpoles that I could live with.

But, there was one creature that I dearly wanted to exhibit in my newly won exhibition space. Over the years, as I have written, I had become mildly obsessed with the existence – or otherwise – of the bright red freshwater crabs that people told me about, of which I had seen the occasional mortal relic in the shape of discarded claws or fragments of bright red shell, but which I had never seen for myself. In a very real sense, they were – to my eyes at least – 'cryptids' in that they were creatures that were 'ethno-known' (were seen reasonably regularly by people who lived on The Peak) but which were unknown to the mainstream scientists of the area (me). There was even a perfectly valid alternative theory to explain "why they should not exist". I did not know it at the time, but these interesting little crustacea presented me with a classic cryptozoological paradigm, similar to those with which I would be confronted – on and off – for the rest of my professional life.

I had been looking diligently in all the ponds and streams that I frequented (this sounds grand, but in actuality, these were all fed by the same main watercourse: the one that started at Victoria Peak Gardens, gathered pace, fed the waterfall that tumbled down the face of Mount Austin, and ended up at Tadpole Pond). But, sadly, I never found any.

It is strange how literal minded children are, or at least I was. I had been visiting Victoria Peak Gardens, both with and without my parents, for the previous four years, but I had never even *thought* of following the little stream beyond the decorative bridge, which marked the eastern border of the park. Similarly, I had explored the tiny plateau that lay at the top of the waterfall on many occasions, but it had never occurred to me to see what happened above it. I knew, intellectually, that the two watercourses were interlinked and it seems ludicrous to me now that I never thought about exploring this further, but like Syd Barrett, I have always had a very 'irregular head' and, over the years, many expensive therapists have done their best to unravel its workings, and if they couldn't manage it, how the hell can I?

I don't know what it was that finally 'persuaded' me (if that is the correct word, which I don't think it is) to explore the stream in the 'unknown' stretch between the bridge and the waterfall, but one fine day in the early summer of 1969, I finally did so, and I found something that – to me at least – seemed completely miraculous.

Here, let me digress for a minute, although I promise you it is a digression that will – eventually – make sense.

As I have written elsewhere in this narrative, large parts of my childhood were defined by the books that I read, and in the year when The Beatles broke up, the media decided that the hippy dream was defined by the Woodstock Festival and decided that it all ended at Altamont, and Charlie Manson and his family were running amok in California, I was obsessively reading Hugh Lofting's *Doctor Dolittle* books. For those of you who have either never heard of them, or whose only introduction to them were the 1998 film and its sequels, I shall resist the temptation to rant on about the way that the film industry rides roughshod over much loved pieces of literature, and explain that the books that I loved so well were set in Gloucestershire during the early part of Queen Victoria's reign, and featured a tubby, white, country doctor, who learned to converse with animals and became a notable vet.

One of my favourites of these books was *Doctor Dolittle's Post Office*; a subplot of which featured a storyline about an island off the coast of West Africa, where no human (apart from the doctor) had ever stood. John Dolittle MD changed the name of this island from 'No Man's Land' (which I strongly suspect was a grimly funny joke on the part of the author, who was in the trenches of the First World War when he wrote these stories, to send home episodically in letters to his children) to 'The Animal's Paradise', because it was such a rich and happy home for a wide variety of creatures. Well, despite the fact that my newly discovered stretch of stream - which was no more than two hundred yards long, and probably less - didn't contain surviving dinosaurs and an enormous range of other birds and mammals, hitherto unsuspected in that part of the world, it did contain a whole string of little rock pools, several of which contained my elusive freshwater crabs. As there were all sorts of other tiny, aquatic creatures there, very few of which I had ever seen before, I took a leaf out of *Dr Dolittle's Post Office* and – to myself, at least – I named this tiny rocky nullah and its attendant rock pools 'The Animal's Paradise', and have used that name ever since, whenever I think of it.

To me, a nine year old boy obsessed with the tiny creatures that can be found in ponds and streams, this was a veritable paradise, and I spent many happy days perched on one of the big, smooth, boulders, observing the complex and interrelated lives of the creatures who lived there.

Here, I am afraid I need to put in a slightly disappointing interjection. In 1980, many years after my family had left Hong Kong, I inherited some money from a deceased relative, and the first thing I did was to pay for a return visit to the land that I loved so well. It was not altogether a success, and – at the tender age of twenty-one – I discovered for the first time that things get smaller as one grows older. What, in 1969, had seemed like a glorious vista of ponds and animals had, by the time I was twenty one, been reduced to a small, dried up and grubby little watercourse that – even then – was clogged with rubbish that had been washed downstream in the previous rainy season from the picnic grounds high on Victoria Peak. But, let's return to the summer of 1969, when the world was freshly minted for my delight.

I was delighted to find that the simple expediency of turning over some of the largest stones that lay on the stream bed revealed freshwater crabs of various colours and sizes. They were all basically red, or purple, in colour and it never occurred to me that there would be more than one species of crab living in these little ponds. It was only whilst putting this book together that I read about a newly discovered species of freshwater crab in the tiny Chinese territory of Macau; a former Portuguese colony only a few miles west of Hong Kong, on the other side of the Pearl River estuary. I looked at this dark purple creature, *Nanhaipotamon macau*, and thought to myself that this little decapod, which is thought to be endemic to Macau, looked awfully familiar. Perhaps it is, or at least was, more widely distributed than the present authorities expect, but most of the crabs were the species that is now known as *Nanhaipotamon hongkongense*, a bright red creature that is a true freshwater crab, because – unlike so many of its relatives – it does not need to go back to the sea in order to breed. I knew this, not because I had read it somewhere (my only written resource on the subject of freshwater crabs in Hong Kong described a 'green' creature in passing by Herklots when he was talking about something else) but by observation. I knew that freshwater crabs elsewhere in the world (having read about the hermit crabs of Florida) had to go down to the sea to breed and that the larval form of these creatures lived for many months in a planktonic state, which could not be replicated in freshwater. However, even on my first day in 'The Animal's Paradise', I found a dozen or so tiny – but fully formed – crabs, but no sign of any larval crabs in any approaching a planktonic state. The nine-year-old me deduced that this meant that this particular population of crabs must breed in a different way.

And the nine-year-old me was right.

This was confirmed upon a later visit to the ponds, when I discovered a female crab with a whole clutch of juicy eggs tucked untidily underneath the triangular flap of the abdomen. When I held her up to the light, I could see the shapes of the larval crabs wriggling about inside the eggs. *This* was where the elusive planktonic stage of this species took place.

I couldn't wait to exhibit these fantastic creatures in my washing machine 'show tank' at the school nature table, and – a few days later – I did just that! Sadly, nobody was as impressed as I was with these fantastic little crustaceans, and - not for the first time and certainly not for the last – I realised that the things that excited me didn't necessarily excite anybody else!

Then summer arrived, and you must remember that I was only nine years old. And at the age of nine, at the beginning of the summer holidays (and you must remember that in order to facilitate the families of school children who were all, or very nearly all, either colonial service officers, army officers, or ex-pats of some degree or other, the summer vacation was eight weeks long), the next two months stretched endlessly before me like the golden road to Samarkand and the weeks and months ahead were full of exciting and wonderful opportunity.

For the fourth year running, my father had chosen to take his annual leave in a six week block. Many years later, during the short months before he died, when we were actually close friends, he confided in me that all three of my surviving grandparents had used all sorts of egregious social 'blackmail' in order to make sure that the Downes family came back to England on holiday this time, instead of another jaunt round foreign parts like the one we had enjoyed the previous year.

Whilst we had been at the Royal Perth Agricultural Show in Australia, the previous summer, my father had seen a herd of the eponymous cattle from North Devon with which he had worked whilst working as a farm manager between Bideford and Barnstaple, twenty years earlier, when he and my mother first married. And these 'ruby red' (actually a purplish brown) bovids had evoked such pangs of homesickness, that - although my mother wanted to go to South Africa on holiday for the summer of 1969 – my father was quite happy to give in to the family pressures and spend six weeks in Devonshire.

My father was actually born in Tavistock, a small market town some miles north of Plymouth, right on the edge of Dartmoor, and for the first few years of his life – before his family underwent one of the periodic episodes of financial unrest that both sides of my family (and indeed, myself) have suffered over the years – lived in a large country house, which was almost a mansion, just inside the parameter of Dartmoor National Park itself.

So, my parents decided to base our family holiday at a guesthouse just outside the village of Widecombe-in-the-Moor. It was called Dunstan House, and was a large and well-appointed farm house with a huge paddock behind it, and various dogs and cats with which my brother and I could play.

Of the four six-week vacations that the family took, this is probably the one that I look back with most pleasure. This is partially, of course, because I was older and able to experience and enjoy my surroundings more than I had when I was younger. But I think that the real reason that I enjoyed it so much was that my father – being so close to his original home, and back in the Devonshire that he had truly never wanted to leave – was happier and more content than I had ever seen him. As a knock on effect from this, I didn't seem to piss him off as often as I usually did and – for most of the time, at least – we enjoyed a happy *detente*, which was both welcome and unfamiliar to us both.

The establishment was run by a lady called Mrs Cruikshank, who lived with her teenage daughter, Diana, whom I shyly adored from afar, but who – being sixteen – was very nearly grown up in my eyes, and so quite out of reach. A few years ago, when Mrs Cruikshank's son, whom I had never met, telephoned here to tell me that his mother had died, he got the John Downes and me – Jon Downes – completely mixed up, and when I told him during our affable conversation that I'd had an enormous crush on his sister back in 1969, there was a shocked silence until I explained that I had been the shy nine-year-old, rather than his autocratic father. Once we had sorted that out, and each commiserated with the other upon the death of their parents, the phone call ended on a friendly note. I've never heard from him since, nor is there any reason why I should, but every time I am on Dartmoor I always drive out to Dunstan House and gaze longingly at it from the safety of my car (or whosoever's car I happen to be in), as if intently involved in a surrealchemical ritual to revisit one of the happiest summers of my life. You never know, perhaps that's exactly what I am always doing.

One of the things that I always found a delight about being in the Mother Country, was the fact that there are so many things that one can safely eat in the hedgerows and byways of the English countryside. Back in Hong Kong, my mother had strictly forbidden us to eat any of the berries and nuts that grew in profusion in the various plants that I saw everyday in the lush forest. She was convinced that they were all deadly poison, and it is probably a good thing that she never knew how my friends and I would chew happily on fresh bamboo shoots, suck the honey out of the pretty black and yellow daisy shaped flowers that grew on the verge of Peak Road as it climbed the great mountain, and even ate the wild bananas when we found them. Although tasting reasonably familiar to those of us who were used to the taste of cultivated bananas, the stumpy bluish purple fruits, full of large seeds which had to be spat out with relish, were very different indeed.

However, in the lanes of Devonshire, which I was exploring for the first time, it seemed that there was an enormous range of different things that one could eat. There were blackberries, wild raspberries and strawberries, the delicious milky-green unripe hazelnuts, and – just down the lane from Dunstan House – the hedge was full of wild gooseberries. This totally and utterly amazed me, and started an interest in hedgerow cookery that I have vaguely had ever since, to the chagrin of various of my loved ones over the years, who have had to put up with my various experiments from the pages of Rosamond Richardson's *Hedgerow Cookery.* As I have got older, less mobile, and as the once fecund hedgerows have become ever more polluted by the emissions from motorcars, this activity has waned away to nothing. But it is still something that fascinates me, and when my friend Amy, who is a self-avowed forager, starts to talk about wild food sources, I sit back and bask in her words like a slow-worm on a dry stone wall on a summer's day.

I compare myself to a slow-worm here, because this was the first time I had ever encountered these peculiar legless lizards. I had read about them, of course, in books like my beloved *The Children of Cherry Tree Farm*, but this was the first time I saw one for myself. Despite my mother's strictures to leave well alone, I had followed Herklots' warning that all the poisonous snakes in Hong Kong have stripes, to a greater or lesser degree, and had handled and examined several different species of stripeless serpent over the years. This included a snake called the Red Necked Keelback, which, it turned out many years later, was actually highly venomous despite having no stripes. I was only ever bitten once by a snake; I was climbing the steep path which led from Peak Mountain up to the ruins of the hotel behind it. As usual, I was wearing open-toed sandals and grey socks. Joyfully scampering through the long grass, I felt a sharp pain in the big toe on my right foot. Looking down, I saw two little puncture marks bleeding slightly, but hard as I looked, I couldn't find the perpetrator. I am still alive, half a century later, so I assume that it could not have been one of the poisonous snakes of the territory. I never told my mother, indeed I never told anyone until now, because I knew that if I did, this would inflame her hatred of serpentiformes to a greater degree than it already was. And, considering that she seemed to be in a permanent state of Defcon One on the matter, the repercussions of telling her about my incident would have been unthinkable.

Slow worms, however were a totally different kettle of squamata. When I first found one of these charming little legless lizards basking in the late-July sun, on a dry stone wall, round the side of Dunstan House, I picked it up and ran to show my parents, secure in the knowledge that when my mother started her normal anti-serpent protests, I could explain that it was not a snake at all, but a lizard, and point out that it had both external ears and eyelids. Surprisingly, this worked, and despite the fact that it looked like one of the serpents that terrified her so, the fact that it was in possession of ears and eyelids placated my mother so much, that I was eventually able to keep these animals as pets, handling them every day.

Dartmoor is a strange and often bleak place, however it has been inhabited for at least four thousand years, and there are many prehistoric remains scattered about the National Park, including dolmens, standing stones, and stone circles, as well as an estimated five thousand hut circles, which are circular or oval depressions in the ground with evidence of where a stone wall once stood. Although Hong Kong has been inhabited for at least two thousand years longer than Dartmoor, and – if you know where to look – one can still find evidence of these first settlers, the summer of 1969 was the first time that the nine year old me had ever been confronted with physical evidence of prehistory.

And it was a heady experience.

It wasn't as if one even had to go searching for these prehistoric monuments. I had been excited enough to see Stonehenge for the first time, back in the days when one could visit the place untrammelled by authority and walk right up to, and even climb upon, the stones. But to the nine-year-old me, the fact that it was right by the side of the A303, one of the great arterial trunk roads of the British Highway system diminished somehow my feeling of communing with the past. On Dartmoor, I had no such problem.

Because, in those days, as it was everywhere in the country, there were far less cars on the road than there are now. And, if – as my parents liked to do – we frequented, like Wordsworth's Lucy, the "untrodden ways", when we came across a Neolithic stone circle nestled in the furze by the side of the road, it was if it was a special gift to the Downes family from benevolent Gods.

Again, with the same poem by Wordsworth:

"A violet by a mossy stone
Half hidden from the eye!
—Fair as a star, when only one
Is shining in the sky."

I explored the ever-changing landscape with delight. So unimaginably big, though so perfect in miniature, it was a whole world of things that I had never seen, or even imagined before.

A significant chunk of the northern part of Dartmoor, particularly the part accessible through a little road that goes up a steep hill in the middle of Oakhampton town centre, has been used a British Army firing range for over two hundred years. Like all small boys, I was fascinated with things ascertaining to the military, and eagerly collected spent cartridge cases that I found, although I was upset to be told by my father that – because of the draconian legislation that had been brought in in the wake of the 1967 Communist uprising – I would be unable to take them back to Hong Kong with me. On one occasion, I discovered proof - as if any proof were needed - of the history of military activity on the moor, when I found a spherical object which was unquestionably a piece of grapeshot, probably dating back to Napoleonic times.

Whilst I had, of course, been aware of the bare bones of history, this was the first time that I was confronted with it as a living, breathing thing. And I greedily soaked up as much of it as I could.

On the far side of Hay Tor is a quarry, which was built in 1820 in order to provide fine granite to the newly expanding cities of England. A peculiar stone tramway was constructed to carry the granite a journey of ten miles to a canal which led from southern Dartmoor to Newton Abbot from whence it would go down the river Dart by barge, to the sea. I found the derelict tramway and the little groups of ruined huts adjacent to it, which, although they had been built and destroyed in the middle of the 19th century, truly didn't look much different from the remains I had found elsewhere on the moor that dated from several thousand years before that, totally fascinating. Not only did I cajole my family into spending as much time as I could there, but I have gone back at intervals ever since, and it is one of my greatest sorrows that now I am disabled and mostly confined to a wheelchair, I shall most likely never go back again.

The quarry had been full of water for about a century, and the resulting ponds were a fascinating little ecosystem of their own.

Because they have never been fed by anything except for rain, there are none of the animals that one would normally expect to find in a body of still freshwater on Dartmoor. There are no fish. But, actually, that isn't quite true!

255

Somebody, at some time in the past, had introduced goldfish and they had made themselves at home. Behaving like wild animals rather than the fat, sleek, and lazy denizens of every garden pond, one would occasionally see a brilliant flash of orange as one of these delightfully feral *Cypriniformes* skittered from the clear water in the middle of one of the three or four interconnected pools to one of the myriad of intricate granite hidey holes.

The other vertebrate animal that lived there was a large colony of palmate newts. It was the first time I had ever seen a tailed amphibian in the wild. There is an indigenous newt in Hong Kong, called – unsurprisingly – the Hong Kong newt, but whilst they are not uncommon – apparently, in some of the mountain streams – I had never seen one. The closest I had ever come was the fire bellied and paddletailed newts, which were occasionally sold as pets at P.G. Farm. As a direct result of my fascination with the palmate newts of this quaint little quarry behind Hay Tor, I cajoled my parents into letting me buy one of these delightful pet amphibians. I had it for some months in an enormous goldfish bowl (which I think had originally been a punch bowl) but, sadly, it escaped (newts can climb up the sides of perpendicular glass walls with relative ease and are great escape artists) and its mummified corpse was sadly found underneath the corner of my bedroom carpet some months later.

Back on Dartmoor, these beautiful little caudates were a continual source of a fascination to me. They moved through the water with surprising grace, like tiny dinosaurs doing some sort of strange sub-aquatic ballet dance, and I never tired of looking at them. Also living in the cool, still waters, was a whole pantheon of different invertebrates, some of them similar to those that were already familiar to me from the hill streams of Mount Austin, and others – like water scorpions – that seemed to me to be wildly exotic. As always, my fascination with life in ponds and streams was unsatiated, and I took every opportunity to indulge it.

There was an intricate system of little lanes, which criss-crossed the hinterland of Widecombe-in-the-Moor, and there was a pleasant walk of a mile or so, which started at our lodgings, went down the hill, over a stream, past a tiny hamlet consisting of an old farmhouse and a few attendant cottages, and a small patch of oak woodland, before emerging into an area of moorland and a surprisingly steep hill that led down to the village. I was particularly keen on this walk, because there was a tiny stream that went alongside the base of the perimeter wall of the farmhouse, and which contained a mysterious inhabitant. Every time we walked past, we saw a fishy flash out of the corner of our eyes, as the little animal – whatever it was – darted out of sight. It was dark brown, and about the size of the top joint of my thumb, and – although I never could catch it – I suspect it was one of those peculiar little fish called miller's thumb, or bullhead. It got its common English name because of a fanciful similarity between this tiny fish, the only British freshwater sculpin, and the largest digit of the right hand of someone whose lifestyle choice was to be someone who milled corn. Apparently, such people have a depressed and flattened thumb because of all the time spent pressing down upon the millstone. Anyway, that's the way that I read it, back aged nine, and I have never looked into the matter in any depth to verify it one way or another. This is something that I suppose I really should do at some stage, but like so many other things in my life, it has to be put on the metaphorical back burner, because there just isn't enough time in the day to do all the things that interest me.

Many years later, I found out that this little hamlet, which had been remarkable to me only for its mysterious fishy inhabitant, was actually somewhere of cryptozoological importance. In May 1988, a farmer, quite possibly the man who lived in the aforementioned walled farmhouse, which reminded me so much of the place where Amyas lived in Rosemary Suttcliffe's *Simon*, which was my favourite book that summer, shot an animal that was attacking his poultry. It turned out to be an Asian leopard cat (*Prionailurus bengalensis*). It turned out that it was one of two that had been illegally kept by a local drug dealer. When he had been busted, his animals escaped and history does not relate what happened to the other one.

The summer of 1969 was the summer of firsts for me. As well as seeing and interacting with physical evidence of prehistoric men, I also discovered pop culture for the first time. Not, I hasten to add, pop culture of the musical kind, although it was the summer that produced some absolutely remarkable music, at the time – at least – it passed me by. My father's strictures on "long haired twits" were still too near the front of my increasingly dysfunctional cerebral cortex. But, for the first time, I found myself in a time and place where I could buy comics on a weekly basis. Whilst educational publications, like *Look & Learn* and – for the younger readers – *Treasure,* did percolate out to the furthest flung outpost of the empire, the more frivolous and indeed anarchic ones didn't. I had seen occasional issues of *The Beano*, but had no idea that this was only one of maybe a dozen weekly publications aimed at kids. And I was thrilled to discover them all.

When one lived in a tiny British colony on the southern coast of China, where even those periodicals which *did* arrive in the colony took something like three months to do so, it was hardwired into one's brain that all the parts of these publications that were aimed at interacting with their readership could basically be glossed over. By the time that anybody wrote to enter a competition, for example, and the resulting letter had sped all the way from the Orient to the offices of the Scottish company who published *The Beano*, *The Dandy*, and various other similar magazines, it would be too late.

Likewise, the adverts for collectable postage stamps, and the various bits of childish tat that – back then, at least – were dotted throughout these publications, were also not applicable to those of us living an expatriate existence. So, I decided that I should take advantage of this, and pledged to myself that on our next visit to Ashburton (the local Metropolis) I would send off a load of letters inspired by my newly found cultural discovery.

At the time, my favourite joke (which – ironically, when one considers what happens next - had been told to me by my father) was something to do with 'shark infested custard' being 'yellow and dangerous'. So I decided that I would send this *bon mot* to the letters page of *The Beano*, which on every issue promised to reward children who sent in the funniest jokes.

For some reason, that I still don't understand, my father reacted extremely badly to this news and told me not to send the joke in. Being still somewhat of a dutiful child, I acquiesced, but said in passing that there were all sorts of other letters that I wanted to send. I meant to the vendors of the aforementioned esoteric tat that could be found advertised in the back pages of all of these magazines, but for some reason, my father interpreted my reply as me being insolent, and I was physically reprimanded. I very much doubt whether it was, but this is the only occasion during the long, hot summer of 1969 that I remember my father beating me. On the whole, my relations with my parents were quite good, for a few weeks at least, and my memories of this time are amongst the happiest of my childhood.

Although, as already mentioned, I had been brought up on various stories from South Chinese mythology and folklore, and was only too aware that the shadow realm was far more tangible (if you can say such a thing about something that is, by its very nature, intangible) than had been portrayed on American TV cartoons, it was – once again – something that happened during the summer of 1969 which brought this home to me with a bump.

About a mile northwest from Hound Tor is a small burial mound. It is allegedly the last resting place of a girl called Kitty Jay, who allegedly killed herself some time in the late eighteenth century. In 1901, P. F. S. Amery wrote:

> "..Jay's Grave, which is by the side of the Ashburton and Chagford road, where the Heytree and Hedge Barton Estates meet. A workman of mine, aged 74, informs us that about forty years ago [...] he was in the employ of Mr. James Bryant, of Hedge Barton, Manaton, when he remembers Jay's Grave being opened, in which a young unmarried woman who had hung herself in Cannon Farm outbuildings, which is situated between Forder and Torhill, was said to have been buried, but no one then living at Manaton could remember the occurrence.
>
> The grave was opened by order of Mr. James Bryant in the presence of his son-in-law, Mr. J. W. Sparrow, M.R.C.S. Bones were found, examined, and declared to be those of a female. The skull was taken to Hedge Barton, but was afterwards placed with the bones in a box and re-interred in the old grave, a small mound raised with head and foot stones erected at either end. Such is the present appearance of the grave."

The thing that is most notable about this grave is that there are always fresh flowers put upon it. When this was first noted, in the 1950s, it was suspected that a local author, Beatrice Chase, was responsible, but she died in 1955 and the custom continues. Indeed, in recent years, all sorts of other things have been put there, presumably as some sort of votive offerings; things like coins, candles, crucifixes and shells, and in 1997, my friend and colleague Richard Freeman and I even found the dismembered tail of a cat.

Back when people were less cynical than they are today, some folk (including my father) believed, or at least *liked* to believe, that the flowers were placed there by pixies, and it was this story that entered the consciousness of the nine-year-old Jonathan. Over the years, many people, including some that I know personally, have driven past the grave late at night and reported seeing shadowy, hooded figures bent over it. Such things sent a *frisson* of excitement down my spine, and, to a certain extent, still do.

Although the iconography of 'pixies' was everywhere in the various tourist shops that proliferated in Widdecombe, but could be found dotted all over the area, I soon found that my father was not the only person who believed that the 'little people' had some kind of objective reality of their own.

Many years later, a friend of mine told me about how she had been visiting the Dartmoor base of the Field Studies Council, and how, in a layby just down the road, she had stopped for a picnic lunch. There was a loose pile of unworked granite to the side of the layby, and as she looked at it idly while munching her sandwich, she saw something moving.

Thinking that it was probably a weasel, she moved closer to have a look, and was astonished to see "a little man in a brown suit" only a few inches high, clambering between the spaces in the rocks. She made no attempt to interact with him, but let him be, "feeling privileged" that she had been granted a brief insight into a world that would normally have been closed to the members of our species.

And she is not the only one. One day I will have to get around to telling the story of another friend of mine, who at the time was what was known as a 'New Age Traveller', whose converted school bus was parked up near Stibb Cross, in North Devon. There, she and her then-boyfriend had a series of encounters with the 'little people' that markedly shaped her life from then on.

> "My boyfriend at the time had a series of encounters with what he described as a little grey alien, very similar to those depicted on the front cover of Whitley Streiber's book Communion.
>
> One night he was driving along the road together with my daughter Jenny who was about eight years old at the time. She remembers seeing a ball of white and yellow light about the size of a football suspended in the road in front of them. With no time to stop they drove straight through the light which appeared to enter the car and go to straight through it. She remembers how the light felt strangely warm although she can remember suffering no ill effects from her experience. My recollections of Mark's account at the time, however, are somewhat different. I remember him telling me how, terrified, he

reversed away from the light and drove away as fast as he could, and that another car on the same road did exactly the same thing and both cars reversed down the road as fast as they could.

My boyfriend started to suffer from unusual tiredness and used to go to bed extremely early. Each morning when he awoke he had strange triangular red burns on his arms, and I think once, on his neck. Although they appeared to be burns these regular isosceles triangles did not blister and seemed not to cause him any pain. He was convinced that these marks were somehow linked to the alien entity that he nicknamed George. He even claimed that George had sat in the car with him one night and attempted to communicate with him. A Druid friend of mine, known to the cognoscenti as Badger was driving my car one night when she had a momentary sighting of what appeared to be a very similar entity in the rear view mirror. This activity seemed to be inextricably linked to the location where we were camped because when we left Stibb Cross we seemed to leave George behind us.

Jenny also saw what she described as little figures running off into the undergrowth on a number of occasions, although now, she has half convinced herself that they were rabbits or birds going about their natural business. Other weird things happened at the same time. On a number of occasions we saw strange flickering lights in the night outside our bus. On one night a car which was parked outside rolled downhill into a convenient bush but although the ground was wet there were no tyre marks. A few days later a similar incident happened but this time the events were even more inexplicable as the car seemed to roll uphill into a muddy ditch from whence it had to be pulled out by a tractor!

Another day we found a burnt out car in the middle of the moor. The strangest thing about it was that there were no scorch marks on the ground around the vehicle and it seemed as if it had somehow been transported to the place where we found it.

My boyfriend became obsessed with the imagery of the archetypal Grey after his encounters with George, and for months afterwards he made tiny alien heads out of modelling clay. Long after we left Stibb Cross, the psychic reverberations of that sinister spot haunted our whole family, and even now the memories leave us all with a chill down the back of our necks.

I would rather not venture an opinion as to the nature of the things that I have seen. Whether or not they are beings from another part of the Galaxy, from another dimension, from another reality I don`t know. I have a sneaking suspicion that they are just part of the way that things are, and that they can be experienced by anyone who turns their back upon the city for a simpler existence beneath the stars".

Although I'd always been interested in mythology and folklore, it was this summer that made me realise that such traditions were a living, breathing, thing and that there was a world of infinite possibility that existed outside the universe, unconstrained by our personal reality tunnels.

Another thing that I found totally fascinating was the range of ice creams and ice lollies that were for sale. The concept of such things wasn't new to me, of course: there was a wide range of ice creams in tubs, and ice lollies on sticks, which were available to the youth of Hong Kong. But they were all manufactured by a company called *The Dairy Farm*, which was one of the longest established Hong Kong retail businesses, having been started back in 1886 by a bloke called Sir Patrick Manson.

His initial aim was to:

> "...to improve the health of Hong Kong people by providing them with non-contaminated cows' milk and to import a herd of dairy cattle so as to decrease the price of milk by more than half."

It is now a major pan-Asian retailer, involved in processing and wholesaling food and personal hygiene products across the Pacific region and China. By the late 1960s, it had already established a monopoly in certain areas, and the ice creams and ice lollies that my friends and I devoured so eagerly were one of these areas. However, when I got to England, I found that the twin frozen confectionary behemoths of *Lyons Maid* and *Walls* were competing against each other for this lucrative market, and did so by providing ever more exotic confections. But, luscious as they were, it was the wrappers of these various frozen treats that fascinated me the most. Like the back pages of the comics, these were full of special offers whereby you could get hold of some massively desirable artefact just by saving up a certain number of these wrappers and sending them off, together with a postal order for two and six. It is a pity that I was not interested in pop music at that time, because one of the aforementioned prizes was an extremely limited-edition EP from Apple Records, The Beatles' record company. This four-track record, containing music by Mary Hopkin, Jackie Lomax, James Taylor, and The Iveys (soon to become Badfinger), now commands prices in excess of a hundred quid, and I have never even seen one.

What I was most obsessed with were the lollies produced to tie in with the then-popular *Thunderbirds* TV show, and I played with the toys that I got a results of these offers for several years.

In lots of ways, this six-week sojourn in the heart of Dartmoor was a real game changer for me. Things that I had always taken for granted, and had not even really thought about, such as history, folklore, and the paranormal, which had always been completely overshadowed by my obsessive interest in natural history, had begun to assert themselves in my sphere of interests, and have stayed with me to the present day.

My father had been happier than I had ever seen him; and as a result, I think I realised – subconsciously at least – that if he couldn't be in his beloved Africa, somehow the rolling hills and ancient landscape of Devonshire were an acceptable substitute. It is probably the only period of time from my childhood of which I have any concerted stretch of memories when I don't remember either of my parents being angry with me, with the almost inevitable physical punishment that this entailed.

On the day that The Beatles came together for the last time to take a series of photographs at John Lennon's then-home of Tittenhurst Park, near Ascot in Berkshire; pictures which were used – amongst other things – for the cover of the *Hey Jude* compilation LP, I celebrated my tenth birthday. Together with Gran (my father's mother was always known as 'Grandmother'), my brother, parents and I went out to tea and ate coconut cake at one of the little cafes that still can be found opposite the church in the village of Widecombe-in-the-Moor. Richard and I then had our photographs taken, holding a squirrel monkey wearing a little red velvet jacket, which was touted around the village by a rather unsavoury looking fellow, brandishing a camera. These days, I am completely appalled at the idea of a sentient higher primate being forced into servitude for the amusement of a succession of small children. The poor thing was quite probably terrified, and might even have been drugged to keep it docile enough to be held, but at the time, Richard and I were completely entranced, although it did – I'm afraid – pale into slight insignificance compared to the equally unethical photograph taken in Australia of us holding a koala, the year before.

God alone knows where the photograph is. I haven't seen it in many years.

After tea, the whole family walked back along the old Devon lane that led out of the village and back to our lodgings at Dunstan House, and as we strode along – on one of the happiest evenings of my childhood – we sang the song for which the village is still best known:
> "Tom Pearce, Tom Pearce, lend me your grey mare.
> All along, down along, out along lea.
> For I want for to go to Widecombe Fair,
> With Bill Brewer, Jan Stewer, Peter Gurney,
> Peter Davy, Dan'l Whiddon, Harry Hawke,
> Old Uncle Tom Cobley and all,
> Old Uncle Tom Cobley and all."

Many years later, my friend the Rev. Lionel Fanthorpe told me that the song had first been collected in 1890 by the legendary Sabine Baring-Gould, a fellow clergyman and collector of cultural and Fortean esoterica, although the song itself was much, much older. It had a far less salubrious than one might have hoped from the – now popular – family favourite folksong, telling the story of a romantic tryst that got severely out of hand. Apparently, the historical 'Uncle Tom Cobley' was an amorous bachelor, who, when he had been young, was possessed with a head of a bright red hair. As he continued his carnal journey around the young ladies of the area, there were many claims that he had fathered illegitimate babies. However, when the baby in question did not have red hair, he refused to acknowledge his paternity, and thus his responsibility for financially supporting his child.

Although the historical 'Tom Cobley' was allegedly around in the late 18. Century, the final verse in which Tom Pearce's grey mare - with or without the seven men who rode her to death – still haunts the Devonshire lanes, gives an intriguing insight into the possible origins of the song. The last verse reads:

> "And all the long night be heard skirling and groans,
> All along, down along, out along lee,
> From Tom Pearce's old mare in her rattling bones
> And from Bill Brewer, Jan Stewer, Peter Gurney, Peter Davy, Dan'l Whiddon,
> Harry Hawk, old uncle Tom Cobley and all, old Uncle Tom Cobley and all."

Noted Fortean Paul Devereux, unearthed a paper by the legendary folklorist, Theo Brown, in which she suggested that the ghostly horse was identical to German legends from the Harz mountains of *Der Schimmelreiter*, who was a psychopomp that would lead the souls of the departed from the world of the living to the venerated realms of the dead. She argued, as described by Tim Sandals, that:

> "Therefore in the contexts of Tom Pearce's grey mare, the reason he, "sat down on a stone, and he cried" was because he realised that the grey horse's death meant all future spirits were condemned to oblivion as they would have no spirit guide to take them to the Otherworld. The whole concept of the belief was that the grey mare represented an entity which hovered between life and death and acted as a, "boundary figure" without out which no human soul can be led into the life-after. It is this very concept that is a much later and darkly humorous invention that used the theory of the grey horse spirit guide as its motif."

But I didn't know any of that at the time, and probably wouldn't have cared. For once, I was happy.

This idyll was not to last long. A week or so later, we left Dartmoor, drove to Hampshire to return Gran to Grandad (who had spent a few weeks of respite care at the local cottage hospital) and – after only a few days in Hampshire – returned to London and thence to Hong Kong.

Before we left Devon, however, we went on a sort of family 'pilgrimage' to a part of North Devon that I never thought I would see for myself. As I alluded to earlier, at school, we had been learning about the English Civil War, and – as part of this – I'd been reading a charming book by North Devon author, Rosemary Sutcliff. The book was called *Simon*, and was largely set in and around Torrington, and as we drove up what is now the A386 and the A3124 between Dartmoor and North Devon, I supressed little squeals of excitement as I saw places for myself that I had previously only seen in my mind's eye.

Rosemary Sutcliff was a remarkable woman, but she had been stricken with Juvenile Idiopathic Arthritis when she was very young, and spent most of her life in a wheelchair in near constant pain. Many years later, I found out that she spent much of her professional life sitting in a pub called *The Black Horse* in Torrington Square, where she sat at the table in the window, writing her remarkable series of historical novels for children. *The Black Horse* was better known to North Devon malcontents of my generation for being the subject of a song by the notorious punk rockers, The Cult Maniax.

> "If you ever go to Torrington
> The old pub in the square
> Don't you ever go in the door
> 'cos they don't want you there.
> The Black Horse is a very fine pub
> The building's what I mean
> The landlord is a bastard though

He won't let us be seen...
In The Black Horse..."

But it was the last verse that caused all the problems, and prompted a high court order to have all the remaining copies of the record destroyed:

"The landlord is a Nazi
His wife's a fucking Jew
Don't you ever go in the door
'cos they'll be banning you..."

But all of this was over ten years in my future, and on this final jaunt of our memorable Devonshire holiday, I gazed in awe as the ancient sunken lanes revealed places and scenes from the book I had read and loved so many thousands of miles away.

We had afternoon tea with some acquaintances of my parents, who lived in Northam, and about whom I can remember absolutely nothing apart from the fact that they ran a small hotel, and then we went on to a little village called Clovelly, about eight miles down the A39, which featured a steep, cobbled main street, up and down which donkeys and tourists made their way with more than a little difficulty.

My father explained to me that his grandparents, my grandmother's Mum and Dad, had moved to Clovelly in the 1870s, and my great-grandfather had been the head coastguard of this picturesque but tiny fishing port, which was then, and remained for some years, a place where significant amounts of smuggled goods made their way into the United Kingdom. He told me another story, which produced a *frisson* of ghoulish delight down my spine, about how – at some point during the 17. century – a family of notorious cannibals had lived in one of the caves that could still be seen in the middle distance along the beach at Clovelly. He told how, after their depredations upon the local populace became too much for the authorities to ignore, dragoons from the local barracks at Hartland raided the bestial encampment, and a pitched battle took place, following which the few survivors of the cannibal family were burned at the stake.

This wasn't actually true, but my father wasn't to know this. The mythos of the Cannibals of Clovelly was a very similar story to that of a Scottish legend featuring a certain Sawney Bean and his cannibal family, who allegedly preyed on hapless travellers in a part of the West coast of Scotland, at roughly the same time. It has been suggested, with a great deal of corroborative evidence, that both stories were concocted by local smugglers, who wished to dissuade superstitious locals from investigating a local cave system too hard. The caves at Clovelly bay, which are still named the Devil's Kitchen, were allegedly linked to the Iron Age hill fort, at Clovelly Dykes by a subterranean passage, and unidentified smugglers preferred that timorous local souls think that shadowy figures and flickering lights seen around the dykes on moonless nights were supernatural in origin.

Whilst we were in Devonshire, I read an article in *Look and Learn*, about the making of the highly acclaimed *Battle of Britain* movie, and – for some reason – this triggered off another one of my obsessions.

So, on my return to Hong Kong, I started to collect everything that I could find on the subject, and spent all my meagre pocket money on small, plastic Spitfires. Like all my obsessions, then and now, this rapidly got out of hand and – for the first, but certainly not the last, time – I started making grandiose plans for a film of my own on the subject. The fact that I didn't have a movie camera, that video cameras had hardly been invented, and that, with every day passing, my parents were getting more and more annoyed with my ceaseless rantings on the matter, didn't actually dissuade me. And so, I made complex plans for how I would suspend my model aeroplane collection on pieces of cotton and film complicated dog fight scenes, and these totally unrealistic plans took up much of my headspace for the next year.

The autumn term began, and I looked forward to restarting my curated nature table. At the end of the previous term, I had let all the animals go back into the streams from whence they came, and I looked forward to starting it all over again. But it was not to be. My form teacher of the previous year had gone on to pastures new, and the new teacher wasn't interested in my aquacultural plans, and even decided that I wasn't allowed to study pond life in my nature study lessons, and had to do a 'project' on something completely dull involving mould, and so the brief spark of joy that education and learning can bring was once again snuffed out peremptorily, at the altar of bourgeois conformity.

In October each year, the annual Michaelmas Fair was held in the grounds of St John's Cathedral, and this year – for once – I'd had the foresight to save up some of the money that I had been given by doting relatives for my birthday a few months before, and thus had the princely sum of twenty or thirty dollars (about four quid) to spend.

Although, when I had been younger, I would have spent all of my money on sideshows such as a coconut shy, and mountains of pink candyfloss - the thought of which, now, with fifty years' hindsight, makes my poor beleaguered pancreas feel like shrivelling up and making a run for the hills, there was one thing that I particularly wanted, and that was a proper butterfly net. Most of the sideshows at the fair were run by various worthy causes, including a Leper Home, which was on one of the outlying islands of the colony. In order to help finance their lives, and pay for small luxuries, the lepers would sell handicrafts at events like Michaelmas fair, and – for some reason – one of the things that they always made were butterfly nets. And they were bloody good ones, too.

When I tell my younger friends and relatives that leprosy was rife in certain parts of Hong Kong when I was young, and that at a young age I was used to seeing these poor wretches, hideously disfigured by this disgusting disease, some of them just don't believe me. In fact, only a few years later, when I returned to England, even my new friends in North Devon found it hard to believe, and it's not something I talk about very much. These days, the disease has been eradicated in much of the world and I doubt whether there is a *lazaretto* left outside certain parts of the tropics.

I went to the stall run by the religious order that maintained the Hong Kong lazar house, paid over my three dollars for a swish new butterfly net, and went to see what other exciting things I could find. In recent years, I have told various TV and radio interviewers that there were three major epiphanies in my life; my discoveries of cryptozoology, rock and roll, and girls. But, in fact, there was a fourth. And this fourth epiphany, which took place at the St John's Cathedral Michaelmas fair of October 1969, was just as tumultuous as the other three, and may even have affected my subsequent life even more profoundly.

I discovered a second-hand bookstall.

I had always loved books, but because my access to bookshops was relatively limited, the books in my collection were largely limited to those things that were chosen for me by parents, friends and relatives. And, although as I have said already in these pages. my father – in one of his most liberal moves – had never forbidden any of the books on his or my mother's shelves to me, they were – obviously – reflective of his and my mother's tastes. I had read, or attempted to read, them all, and my mind was opened to all sorts of exciting new possibilities.

But this was the first time that I had ever been presented with a whole range of books for sale, at remarkably low prices, when I was lucky to have significant largesse in my pocket.

I bought about a dozen books that day, for a total price of under ten dollars. These included the complete and unexpurgated *Robinson Crusoe* and *Gulliver's Travels* (the latter, complete with the dirty bits), several books by Captain W. E. Johns, whom it turned out had been a friend of my paternal grandfather when my dad was a boy, and when I took them home, my father was very excited to see copies of titles that he had not read since he had been my age, and he diffidently asked me if he could borrow them. Remembering how generous he had been in letting me read his library of highly unsuitable books on the subject of medieval Indian sexuality, Chinese communism, and various things that had scared me shitless about the Devil riding out, I was magnanimous and said that of course he could. These books about Captain James Bigglesworth were in the original editions rather than the ones deemed suitable for children of my age in the 1960s, which have been expurgated more and more over the intervening years, so that now they contain nothing that the virtue signalling brigade could find even slightly dubious. In the books I was now reading, Britannia ruled the waves, Biggles and his pals flew sorties against First World War Germans, with a prize of a case of whiskey for whosoever achieved the highest number of kills, and all sorts of things in the various adventures around the world that some people now would deem to be casually racist, although I doubt whether that had been their intention. And finally, I bought two hardback books by Anthony Buckeridge, one of which was to set me off on another of the great adventures which has defined my life.

Buckeridge's most famous, and certainly the most successful, series of books concerned the trials and tribulations of an eleven year old school boy called Jennings, who attended a preparatory school somewhere in Sussex. Buckeridge himself was a teacher at boarding schools in Suffolk and Northamptonshire, which – together with memories of his own school days – provided plenty of material for these books. The stories are cleverly, intelligently and deftly written, and his use of the English language has been compared favourably with his contemporary wordsmiths, like P. G. Wodehouse. I already owned several of the books in this series (at the time there were seventeen of them) and had enjoyed them all immensely (I still do). One of these new books concerned Jennings and his friend Darbishire's attempts to start a museum (something else that I have done on several occasions over the intervening years), but the fourth book in the series – *Jennings and Darbishire* (1952) – concerned the adventures they had when they started their own newspaper, called the *Form Three Times*. I thought that this was an absolutely fantastic idea, and so, together with my friend Michael Brown, I decided to do likewise. And so, the *Form Six and Upper Six Weekly* was born. It was my first taste of being a magazine editor.

Following in the footsteps of Jennings and Darbishire, and – although I didn't know it at the time – *The Fifth Form at St. Dominics*, written a lifetime before by Talbot Baines Reed, my new 'magazine' was published in an edition of one, which I pinned up proudly on the class notice board, and stood back smugly, waiting for people to read it. And, slightly to my surprise, they did.

It was partly handwritten, and partly typed out by my mother (that was – I am afraid – until my father put his foot down and said that I was making her work too hard and forbade me from asking her to do it ever again). Once again, my plans had been thwarted, but I continued to 'publish it' for the next four or five months until it fizzled out with the advent of summer and some very disturbing personal news.

It contained articles about various sporting events and other things, which my classmates had done, and items of news such as the fact that a classmate called Clive (yes the same one who had been convicting of doing something he shouldn't to his female classmates in the garage halfway up Plunkett's Road) had been caught setting off a stinkbomb in the local convenience store.

Talking of the Dairy Farm, once again during the early summer of 1970, I was caught shoplifting there, together with another boy, called Keith. Once again, I have no memory of how, what and why, but I do remember that – at the time – I didn't know how or why I had done it either and – with hindsight – it was just another incident in the slow but inexorable decline of my mental health. No matter how many visits I made to the child psychologist, nobody came to the conclusion that I was seriously mentally ill, and in desperate need of help. Indeed, no-one ever did this, until I was in my late thirties when – in the wake of a horrific divorce – I was diagnosed as being Bipolar.

But all that was in the future. Each week, I proudly pinned up the latest copy of the magazine for my friends and peers to peruse at their leisure, and each week those set in authority over me by a benevolent Colonial Administration, totally ignored it.

One thing that I do remember in the wake of the disaster of my second shoplifting incident is that my father did try to reach out to me, and on a couple of occasions he and I went down to Tai Tam Bay on a Saturday evening and spent the night aboard *The Ailsa.* I particularly remember the first time, because – in the middle of the night – my father woke me from my slumbers and called me on deck. I was mildly grumpy about this, because then – as now – I don't like my sleep being disturbed, but the grumpiness vanished when I saw what he had to show me. It was like the water was on fire. Each wave, as the new tide flooded in from the South China Sea, glowed with bioluminescence. I know now that what my father called 'phosphorescence' (although even now, I don't know which type of photoluminescence it was, and it really doesn't matter) is caused by tiny algae suspended in the water, and that the glowing lights which turned the familiar bay into something out of Fairyland was a direct result of these tiny plants being buffeted by the incoming tide. We sat and watched this marine firework display in wonder. Occasionally, a foot or so below the surface, we could see the liquid movements of large fish, presumably chasing smaller fish that – again – had been driven into the bay by the incoming tide. Here, I would love to say that we saw sharks or porpoises, but we didn't, and I only ever felt disappointed by this many years later, when – in one of Gerald Durrell's books – I read an account of a similar experience from his boyhood in Greece. But he had seen dolphins. Once again, the young Gerry outdid me.

On another visit to the boat, but I cannot remember whether this was one of Daddy's and my excursions or a family day out, I was lying stretched out on the deck at the bow of the ship (I'm sure there is a technical term for this, but I don't know what it is). What I remember vividly is that my parents noticed that my legs were not stretched out as straight as they should be. My paranoia was so acute that I took this as a personal slight, but my parents took it far more seriously and referred me first to the family doctor and then to a specialist at Queen Elizabeth Hospital. My father told me, as honestly as he could, that one of four things would be necessary. They might ignore it, I might have to go to physiotherapy, I might have to wear a leg brace, or I might need surgery. Praying as hard as I could that it would not turn out to be either of the second two options, I went along to the appointment, and after having been examined, poked and prodded thoroughly, my parents were told that a diagnosis, together with details of the recommended treatment, would be posted to them in the next couple of weeks.

It was a Friday afternoon, and – with the innocence of youth – even the fact that I had a Sword of Damocles hanging over me, the fact that it would not fall for several more weeks was good enough for me. The birdsong in the air had never seemed so cheerful, and the multicolours of butterflies flitting about the blooms on the lantana bushes had never seemed to bright. The next day, we went back to *The Ailsa*, and spent a lovely weekend on board. For the first time, I encountered sea-squirts. Better known as Tunicates, the adults look like unprepossessing leathery lumps of masticated chewing gum stuck onto the side of rocks. They are known as 'sea-squirts' because, when prodded, they squirted out a languid stream of water, which was no-where near as impressive as the water-pistol-like qualities of the huge, black Bêche-de-mer with which I had been familiar for years. No, the thing that really fascinated me about these peculiar little animals, was that, despite looking like retarded sea anemones, they were actually primitive Chordates, meaning that – like fish, reptiles, amphibians, birds, mammals and me – they have a spinal cord. Yes, you have read it right. They were far more closely related to humanity than anyone would have guessed.

We visited one of my favourite picnic spots; a small rocky beach that no-one else ever seemed to visit. On each side of the tiny cove were impressively fierce, though surprisingly easily scalable rocks, and there was one particular place where the rocks were dotted with tiny indentations an inch or so deep. I know now that they were probably caused by one of a number of small invertebrates, such as *Polydora* that, despite their soft bodies, commonly make their mark upon much harder bits of their environment. But, at the time, I was convinced that they had been made by meteorites.

Ever since I first read *Comet in Moominland* by Tove Jansson, I had become mildly obsessed with comets and meteors. Ironically, one day during the spring of 1970, I actually saw something that the adult me would have turned cartwheels if he had seen. One lunchtime, high above the playground of Peak School, I saw a round, bronze coloured object, hovering high above me. I pointed it out to my companions, and they saw it too. I have no idea what it was, but nowadays I would have no problem in categorising it as a 'UFO', although then I was convinced that it was a comet. After all, it was an object, it appeared to be flying, and neither now or then have I been able to identify it. I have seen UFOs since, on a number of occasions, but until the summer of 1997 when – together with several other people – my wife and I had a very close sighting of a huge flying triangle above my garden here in North Devon, I was not to see any UFO quite as clearly again.

Whereas once upon a time the whole of the island of Hong Kong had been lush jungle, it had been deforested at various times during the past few centuries and although the jungle was growing back, there were areas where the main vegetation was either bamboo or tall lush elephant grass similar to the pampas grass which you can buy in any garden centre, but far less refined with a wiry feral quality. It was here that I had played as a child, creeping through the tall stems which towered five or six foot over the ground and living out my boyhood fantasies of Red Indians, Robinson

Crusoe and Swallows and Amazons. During our weekend, when we visited some of the smaller islands, which were too small to have ever been able to support a forest environment, I again explored these weird grassland areas and marvelled at the rich eco-system of small animals which lived there. There were beetles, lizards, snakes (although I never told my mother, who was always terrified that I would get bitten) and on several occasions I even found the places where one of the most spectacular of Hong Kong mammals, the Himalayan Porcupine (*Hystrix hodgsoni*) had been. The only times I ever saw live porcupines were (as I wrote earlier) occasionally at night when my father was driving us home after dark. Once or twice I remember seeing the distinctive black and white shapes lumbering at the side of the road. However, I saw them dead as road-kill several times, and once during an expedition, which was so secret I have never told anyone to this day, I found one of their skulls.

I had been visiting some family friends at a place called Mount Kellett. Like the apartment block in which I had lived, it had been built to house senior Government officials, but unlike my domicile at Peak Mansions, the countryside immediately around Mount Kellett was much more exciting to the naturalist. Peak Mansions was an exciting enough place to be – within a 100 yards of our front door was the top of a long winding footpath which led through a couple of miles of deep forest down to the reservoirs at Pokfulam, and a little further on the Lugard Road – which circled Victoria Peak and from whence one could see snakes and lizards aplenty and a variety of the local birdlife. But Mount Kellett boasted a far lusher stretch of jungle, and one could regularly see Barking Deer, Civet Cats and - so it was rumoured – the remnants of the once plentiful population of Dhole or Red Dogs. It also boasted one of the best resources for children that I have ever seen. Successive generations of colonial sprogs had built a massive tree-house complex in two or three interlocking banyan trees which grew, gnarled like old men with arthritis, only a few yards from the politely manicured lawns of the apartment block. I loved to visit Mount Kellett - I had several friends there, I always enjoyed playing in the tree-house and at the age of ten – although my days of actively pursuing the fairer sex were well over half a decade in the future – I was beginning to evince some curiosity about the female of my species and, for some reason, the free and easy atmosphere which seemed to prevail amongst the youthful population of Mount Kellett was conducive to my being able to satisfy my curiosity.

One afternoon, while my mother was drinking tea and chatting to her friend, I and the daughter of the house, went to explore. We climbed over the small perimeter wall which bordered the Mount Kellett car park and found ourselves within only a few minutes deep in unexplored jungle. Whatever thoughts I had had of a game of "Doctors and Nurses" disappeared, as whatever genetic predisposition I have of being an intrepid explorer took hold, and for the first, but certainly not the last time in my life, I put exploration and pursuit of knowledge before my interest in the opposite sex. Stealthily the two of us explored and found, much to our surprise, that there were a couple of small, dilapidated, but obviously still inhabited huts deep in the jungle only a couple of yards away from the block of flats which we knew so well. This was amazing! At the time I spun a complex story to explain them. Even then I was interested in cryptozoology and had also read a number of pieces of classic juvenilia in which heroes like Biggles discovered lost tribes. OK, with hindsight, I think even at the age of ten I should have realised that a lost tribe of primordial Chinese would not be found only a couple of yards away from a block of flats in which resided dozens of senior civil servants, but at the time I thought I had made a momentous discovery. The huts were – also we found out a few days later – where the elderly Chinese couple who maintained the gardens of Mount Kellett resided. They had been built only twenty years or so by the Urban Services Department and there was no mystery whatsoever. However, we didn't know this as we poked and prodded our way around and found that just downhill from the huts was a small but flourishing kitchen garden. At the side of this garden were two wire traps, one containing bones and quills and the other containing the very putrefied corpse of a dead porcupine.

I carefully opened the trap, removing the skull and some of the quills. I still have them somewhere as a *memento mori* of the first time in my life where I eschewed women in favour of adventure.

I have written elsewhere about the intermittent occurrence of the Chinese water monitor in Hong Kong, but the largest species of lizard which was regularly found there when I was a child was *Calotes versicolor*, a member of the agama family, which boasted a number of different names. It was known as the changeable lizard, the Cantonese garden lizard, and even the bloodsucker, because the male developed a brightly coloured head and neck during the breeding season.

I was always fascinated by these lizards, and dearly wanted to keep them in my collection and try to breed them. Sometime during 1969, workmen from the Urban Services Department replaced the bath in one of our bathrooms, and I cadged the old one, putting it in my museum as the centrepiece display. I made quite an impressive little diorama there, with rocks, small plants and tree branches. But, sadly, the only time I ever mentioned to catch one of these impressive little reptiles, it died within hours of me putting it into its new home, and – disheartened – I never tried again, the dead lizard joining some of its fellow fauna in one of my ever growing collections of jars of methylated spirits.

Some of my favourite childhood memories are from weekends spent on *The Ailsa*; my father had always been a sea-farer – he only left the merchant navy in order to marry my mother – and, with hindsight, I can see that each weekend spent exploring the myriad of tiny islands in the estuary of the Pearl River were something which gave him a certain degree of solace from a job he despised in a land that he hated.

We spent most weekends on board her, and every Sunday, when it was time to go home, our sadness was partly assuaged by the fact that in only six more days' time, we would be able to do it all again.

So, on the Monday morning, rather than complete despair at a whole week of schooling in front of me, I was always remarkably happy, because I was daydreaming about our adventures and the animals I had seen over the weekend before.

And then, in early July 1970, I had one of the worst, and certainly the most pivotal, days of my life. After an uneventful morning, I went back home for lunch, to be told by my mother that *The Ailsa* had drifted her moorings and been wrecked irreparably on the sharp rocks at the side of the bay. And just as I was reeling from that news, she opened a letter from the hospital. I had a serious case of *Genu Valgum* or knock knees. This is a normal part of many children's growth, and most people grow out of it. However, a small percentage don't, and needed a series of painful operations (notice I put this is in the past tense, because medical technology has improved immeasurably in the last half century) in order to stop them becoming cripples in early adulthood and wheelchair bound by middle age.

Guess which percentage I fell into?

As I have mentioned earlier, my friend William's mother was the only person to take my ambitions of being a scientist seriously, and when – at the beginning of 1970 – William followed the more traditional educational pathway of boys of his age and went back to England to boarding school, his mother spent more and more time with me. Looking back, I can see that she was lonely and missed her firstborn, but at the time—selfish little beast that I was—I only saw the positive benefits for me of having an adult who actually took me seriously.

On several occasions, she took me to various temples, both in Kowloon and on the island. I found this insight into a completely different culture compelling, and quite probably made a nuisance of myself, asking her and her friends amongst the Chinese clergy endless questions.

One should remember that, at the time, Chinese communism was far more severe and austere than it is now, and both religious freedom and capitalism were frowned upon. Therefore, the temples in Hong Kong were the only places for hundreds of miles where one was not only free to worship whatever Gods one chose, but were also free to buy and sell a bewildering amount of quasi-religious tat.

As somebody who'd been brought up in a Christian household, I was perfectly aware that other customs and creeds existed, but I found the vast pantheon of Chinese Gods almost overwhelming. I was also both amused and fascinated by the idea that one could ease the path of your loved ones into and through the underworld by burning large handfuls of 'Hell Bank Notes', which could be purchased for a matter of pennies at each of the myriad stalls, which seemed to exist by each of the temples. Indeed, unlike a Western church, the temples – the larger ones, at least – seemed to be the hub of a whole variety of buildings, which included the dwellings of various Chinese priests, past and present, and stalls selling food, knickknacks, and things to be burnt as offerings.

There were also large numbers of beautiful young women. My father later told me that these were temple prostitutes, but although I have managed to find well attested sources for the tradition of temple prostitution in the Indian subcontinent, whilst the history of prostitution in China is undoubtedly a rich and fascinating one, I am forced to draw the conclusion that my father was being more than usually racist. He didn't like the Chinese, never wanted to live in Hong Kong, and I think was probably quite capable of having mixed up the traditions of China and India to the detriment of the Chinese.

In early 1970, there was a spate of sightings of large sharks in the colony. Whether or not anyone had actually been attacked by these sharks, I don't know, but my friends and I became ever so slightly obsessed with the subject. My parents were regular readers of the *South China Morning Post*, which was the best known and most reputable of Hong Kong's English language newspapers. These hallowed pages only tangentially mentioned the elasmobranch invasion, but there were several more downmarket English language newspapers in the colony, and they soon sported a series of dramatic (and probably not very factual) articles insinuating that there was going to be a whole spate of shark attacks in the colony over the next few weeks and months.

I diligently bought these less salubrious periodicals, and cut out the relevant articles, pinning them up on a noticeboard in the corner of my museum.

I also made sure that, from then on until I forgot about it, whenever we went out to sea at weekends, I took my bow and arrow with me, often augmented by some homemade spears that I had constructed from the bamboos which grew on the hillside immediately behind Peak Mansions.

This was also my last summer at Peak School, and I remember very little about it. In the spring, various girls in my class came to school in tears because The Beatles had split up. I paid no attention, not only because I wasn't interested in The Beatles (remember, my father had beaten it into me that they were nothing but lower class long-haired twits) but because six months before, the same girls had come to school weeping the same tears because Paul McCartney was allegedly dead. Rumours to this fact had spread across the civilised world, and were only proved to be untrue when an interview with McCartney, liberally sprinkled with pictures showing him and his young family alive and well in Scotland, was published in *Life* in November 1969. In so much that I cared at all, the ten year old Jonathan was fairly convinced that the rumours of the band splitting up would turn out to be equally fallacious.

They weren't.

But I didn't care. I was far more worried about the ordeal that I was to face this coming summer.

In the meantime, my collection of the local freshwater wildlife was increasing exponentially, and now took up a ramshackle table the whole width of my bedroom windowsill – some eight feet or so.

My father was friends with the Chief Commissioner of the Hong Kong Prison Service, and for my birthday he had commissioned the prison workshop to make me a large aviary, which stood outside the French window in our backyard. In it went William the crested mynah bird, together with three budgies, which I had acquired along the line, and a pair of red vented bulbuls that had been given to me by Ah Tam.

This was not the first such commission they had received from my father. Way back when we had been living in Buxey Lodge, I had a pair of white mice. Apparently, my father had mentioned these mice to the Commissioner of Prisons, and between them they had cooked up the jolly idea of getting the inmates in the prison workshop to build me a plywood mouse 'prison' in which my pets could live happily. What they didn't take into consideration was the fact that mice can chew their way through wood, and also that somebody had been stupid enough to give a four-year-old boy a boy mouse and a girl mouse. So, within a pressingly short period of time, there were hundred of mice in the mouse prison, and they had not only escaped into the flat itself but were causing enormous amounts of damage.

The saga of the mouse prison ended soon afterwards.

But even as my menagerie expanded, I wanted, above anything, to have a seawater aquarium.

My parents were also friends with the Chief Justice of Hong Kong, who lived with his wife and a huge boxer dog in one of the other ground floor flats at Peak Mountains. Most impressively, it was the only one of the apartments in the huge building to actually have a bona fide garden, even though it was triangular in shape, and only about the size of my sitting room here in North Devon. But it was, undoubtedly, a garden.

Mr Justice Morley-John was a keen stamp collector, and encouraged me in my intermittent forays into the hobby. I could never be described as having been in thrall to the hobby, but I was reasonably enthusiastic, and it was kind of the eminent judge to look after me, and encourage me as much as he did. His wife had a marine aquarium, the first in private hands that I had ever seen, and I longed to emulate her.

She had stocked it herself, and it contained all sorts of little fish, hermit crabs, prawns and other tiny animals, and I longed to be able to do the same. I spent many long and happy hours sitting cross legged in front of the 36" fish tank, and discussing the behaviour of its inhabitants with their owner. And, probably because they wanted to do something nice for me, knowing that I was just about to undergo a series of unpleasant operations, my parents finally agreed to let me have a marine fish tank of my own. A few days before my birthday, the tank, filters, and pump arrived, and the day before my birthday, we went down to Tai Tam Harbour with some five gallon jerry cans to collect some sea water, and on my birthday itself, we went back there to catch some fish for my new aquarium.

It was one of those golden days of childhood, which seemed to go past in slow motion as if my psyche was determined to preserve every detail for posterity. And, forty nine years later, an elderly cripple in North Devon, sitting in my favourite armchair dictating this narrative to my stepdaughter, as I fuss the badly behaved Jack Russell Terrier that is sitting on my knee, I still remember every moment.

A few months earlier, I had carried out what I considered to be an animal collecting expedition on behalf of Mrs Morley-John. I caught various small and interesting crustacea, having – reluctantly – had to release an enormous spider crab that was far too large even to fit in Mrs Morley-John's aquarium. Whether or not it was the same species as the Japanese giant spider crab which is popularly believed to be the largest crab in the world, I don't know. But at the time, I certainly believed it was. I also found some sea anemones, but they perished on the way back to Peak Mansion, and Mrs Morley-John told me how they would have had to be fed individually with tweezers, and that they would not make good additions to her menagerie. So, I knew vaguely what I was doing, and I spent my eleventh birthday happily catching small fish, including two pufferfish, and some small invertebrates – shrimps, hermit crabs and two small sea urchins.

I knew from bitter experience the perils of overstocking an aquarium, and even at the age of eleven, I exercised restraint and common sense.

At the end of this magical day, there was ice cream and cake, and we went back home to introduce my new exhibits to their tank. We had placed the tank next to my bed, and that night I drifted to sleep watching these little creatures bustling about their increasingly complex daily lives.

Despite it being my birthday, I had to go to bed early, because the next day was to be a very important one, and we had an early start. Why? Because I was to go to hospital.

I was terrified. But, I had obediently swallowed the doctrine that an English gentleman always keeps a stiff upper lip and doesn't show emotion, especially in front of foreigners, drummed into me and so – despite all my inclinations on the subject – I marched into the hospital with my parents as bravely and with as much insouciance as an eleven-year-old boy with severe mental health problems could muster. This hospital was to be my home for the next month. I don't remember any more details of the hospital itself, but I remember my father taking my hand and my mother kissing me goodbye as they left, leaving me alone in the single occupant whitewashed room in Queen Elizabeth Hospital.

A Chinese orderly came in and, in a very formal manner, told me to get changed into my pyjamas and lie on the bed. Being an obedient child, I did as I was bid, and lay down to await my fate. However, nobody had actually warned me about what was going to happen next, and I was completely unprepared for, what seemed to me like, a series of exquisite tortures and humiliations.

First, the Chinese orderly came in again, and without actually giving me any warning, pulled my pyjama bottoms down and got out a huge cutthroat razor. Being a child possessed of quite a macabre imagination, I naturally thought that he was going to geld me, and I started to cry. The orderly just looked confused, continued to sharpen the razor on a old-fashioned leather strop, lathered up a handful of creamy suds from some old fashioned shaving soap, and covered first my left leg then my right leg in slippery foam all the way from my groin down to my calves. He then began to shave me.

Having been told that adults were always right, it didn't occur to me at this stage to ask what was going on and why he was doing all this. Indeed, it wasn't until he had finished shaving both legs and sprayed them with what I believe was chlorhexidine and pulled my pyjama bottoms back up, that I realised that I was not going to be turned into a eunuch. He shuffled out with his paraphernalia and it was only then that I realised that this whole embarrassing and humiliating interchange had taken place without a word having been spoken on either side. My next visitor was a very old, Portuguese nun, presumably from one of the convents in the Portuguese territory of Macao, just across the Pearl River estuary. The Portuguese first arrived in Macao in the 1550s, and therefore had been colonial masters of the territory for three hundred years by the time the British arrived in Hong Kong in the mid 19th Century. Macao had also not been formerly occupied by the Japanese during the Second World War, and it could well be said that Macao was far more Portuguese than Hong Kong had ever been British. Portugal being a Roman Catholic country, there were more convents and monasteries in their territory than had been in ours, which resulted in the fact that if you were to meet a nun in Hong Kong, she was quite likely to have been of Iberian origin.

This particular nun seemed absolutely ancient to me. She was, I thought at the time, probably the oldest person I had ever seen; bent, shrivelled, and with almost translucent skin through which a network of interlocking blood vessels could be easily seen. And, it appeared that she spoke very little English.

But my father had always taught me that, despite cultural differences, all religions basically worship the same God, and I took comfort from the fact that this tiny, shrivelled old lady, who looked remarkably like one of the semi-transparent prawns back in my marine aquarium at Peak Mansions, wanted to pray for me and with me. Despite the fact that the Second Vatican Council had been a decade or so before, she prayed in Latin, or at least I think she did. It might have been in Portuguese, but it doesn't matter. We prayed together, she made the sign of the cross on my forehead, and disappeared as swiftly and silently as she had arrived.

During the next month that I was to spend in the hospital, she would arrive to see me most days, always unexpectedly, and always when there was no-one else there and at the most peculiar and erratic times of the day or night. It was as if she was only there to see me, and that her only objective reality coincided with one of the more arcane parts of my reality tunnel. Practically half a century later, I am not convinced that this wasn't, indeed, the case.

These days, I would like to think that things would have been organised differently. But in Hong Kong at the end of the 1960s, boys of my age were meant to exhibit the stiffest of upper lips, and to remember that the First World War had been won on the "playing fields of Eton" or something like that.

So, I was left alone in the empty room until – half an hour or so later (and to me, it seemed like an eternity) – the orderly came back in, unceremoniously turned me onto my stomach, and pulled my pyjama trousers down, before parting my buttocks and thrusting a suppository deep inside me. Or at least *now* I know what he was doing, but at the time I was terrified. I was an eleven year old boy, and during my informal upbringing (the one which I had received from my peers at school and in the Cub Scouts, rather than the formal one that I had received from my parents and my teachers) I had been told all sorts of things about "bumming" and whilst I hadn't believed most of them, I was convinced was this was the unlovely fate for which I was destined.

However, apparently not. The orderly bustled out again, leaving me in an undignified and vulnerable position, lying face down on the unmade bed. Soon, I wanted to use the lavatory very badly indeed. But I was a reasonably obedient child, and nobody had given me permission to leave my room, or – indeed – to change position, so I lay there, terrified.

Soon, I was in tears, and in imminent danger of losing control of my bowels. I was praying aloud that someone, anyone, would come back in and rescue me, and eventually my prayers were answered. It was the elderly Portuguese nun, who must have been a nursing sister, because she produced – as if by magic – a bed pan, manoeuvred me onto it, and left me to carry out my long-overdue call of nature. Using a mixture of pigeon English and sign language, she told me to stay where I was, and disappeared out of the door, returning a few minutes later with a Chinese doctor who, it turned out, could speak English.

The doctor and the nun removed the bed pan, cleaned me up and made me comfortable, and then the doctor explained to me in faultless English what my ordeal had been all about, whilst castigating the absent orderly for his insensitivity and boorishness.

The elderly nun sat in the chair by my bed, tutting with concern, muttering in Latin, and occasionally genuflecting as she gazed up to the Heavens with a despairing look on her face. But the doctor, having somehow extracted from the terrified eleven-year old-boy lying on the bed before him, that I was interested in the natural sciences, treated me as an equal and explained exactly why my bowels had needed to be emptied and all the hair on a vast proportion of my lower limbs had been shaved away. Once I realised that the motive for my ordeal had been purely scientific, and that nobody was going to be "bumming" anybody, I sat up and took an animated, and surprisingly dispassionate interest in the subject.

The nun and the doctor stayed with me until I fell asleep, and the next thing I knew, I was being woken by my mother, who promised that she would go with me as far as she could before I was to enter the operating theatre, and would be with me once I awoke after the surgery.

In came the orderly, who appeared somewhat chastened, and I like to think that he had been soundly reprimanded for his behaviour towards me the previous evening. In fact, I like to think that the Portuguese nun had followed in the grand traditions of her country's empire and ordered him to have been chastised with the *bastinado*, but it was 1970 in a territory under British administration, and things like that just simply didn't happen.

It was just like one of those tear-jerking scenes in a hospital drama on television. The orderly picked me up and put me onto a wheeled gurney, and slowly pushed me down the long, winding corridors of the hospital. For some reason, hospitals of a certain era always seem to have corridors painted the same shade of bilious watery green, and I could see what seemed like miles and miles of these interlinking pale green corridors stretching out before me. Occasionally, a small gaggle of doctors or nurses bustled past earnestly, but mostly the three of us were alone: me on the gurney, the orderly pushing me, and my mother walking steadily by my side, holding my hand as we trundled on towards the operating theatre. It took quite a few minutes to get there, but – all too soon – we were facing two swing doors, each sporting a round porthole of the sort of corrugated glass containing square wire mesh, that is often seen of the windows of old bathrooms. My mother kissed me goodbye, and promised that she would be there when I woke up, and the orderly pushed me into the room, relinquishing me to a colleague of his, wearing a long, white, lab coat, a tunic and a surgical mask. Much to my surprise, the orderly patted me on the shoulder and muttered, "zoi gin", which is one of several ways to say goodbye in Cantonese. I realised then that he was probably as shy as I was, and feeling just as awful.

The surgical team were kind, but business-like, and they told me in a sensible amount of detail what they were about to do. One of them swabbed down the inside of my arm with some quick drying alcohol, which smelled a little like acetone, but I don't know what it was. And then gave me an injection, telling me to count backwards from ten. I can't remember how far I got, but it wasn't very far, and soon I was deep beneath the waters of Lethe... and then I woke up. It was apparently three hours later. I was in the recovery room, again painted in the watery bilious green that looked for all the world like the colour of an unhealthy *Pierid* caterpillar. As she had promised, my mother was sitting in a chair by the side of my bed. Yes, somehow while I was asleep, I'd been transferred back into a standard hospital bed. My mother had, apparently, been waiting for quite a while for me to wake up. Although it never occurred to me to ask how long 'quite a while' was, half a century later it really doesn't matter. But she looked pale and drawn, and it is only now that I have a family of my own that I realise quite what an ordeal the poor woman must have been through.

I couldn't move the bottom half of my body, but there was a dull ache in my knees, which was getting progressively worse. Again, I like to think that in these more enlightened times, a child would not have been left in as much pain as I was for any length of time, but – once again – the concept of English Gentleman of any age having to display a "stiff upper lip" came to the fore, and despite the fact I was soon in so much pain that I was gripping my mother's hand far tighter than I had ever done before, I was determined that – in front of my mother, at least – I would behave like an English Gentleman, and that Lord Nelson must have been in far worse pain when he lost his arm. After about half an hour of this, along came the orderly once again, and I was wheeled through the labyrinthine corridors back to my room.

An hour or so after my mother and I had been left by ourselves in my solitary side room, and the orderly had left us with a cup of tea and a glass of orange squash (for Mummy and me, respectively), I had two more visitors. My father and the cheerful and kind Chinese doctor turned up almost simultaneously. The doctor asked me if I was in pain, and I could see my father glaring at me disapprovingly as I admitted that I most certainly was. The doctor gave me a little capsule to put under my tongue, and within minutes I could feel the pain receding and a warm glow of wellbeing creep over my body as if I was being comfortably swaddled in pink cotton wool. For the first, but by no means the last, time in my life, I was discovering that I really rather liked Morphine Tartrate. Like so many other of my lifetime's habits, I started early.

The recovery process was supposed to take something in the region of a month, but – somehow (and I suspect that my father pulled a few strings, and used his position as a senior member of the Colonial Administration to facilitate this) – I was allowed home at weekends. Every Friday evening, my wheeled hospital bed was pushed into an ambulance, and I was driven up Victoria Peak to the service area behind Peak Mansions, whereupon a bevy of burly orderlies would carry me off the ambulance, and Ah Tam would wheel me through the servant's quarters into the part of the flat with which I was more familiar, and thence to my bedroom. I was still in pain, and still bedridden, but I could watch the complex lives of my little fish in my bedside aquarium, and have bedtime stories from my mother. After a week in hospital, this was absolute paradise.

In the daytime, I was often wheeled out through the hallway and the huge living room to the conservatory, and Ah Tam would open the French windows and let me gaze out upon the heavily forested hillside, which tumbled down for miles to the town (now city) of Pokfulam. This forest was the haunt of leopard cats, pangolins, civets, and porcupines, and within living history had been home to tigers and possibly even leopards. It was a magnificent place, and I spent much of my childhood exploring it, and much of my adulthood dreaming about it, and after a week of surgery and physiotherapy, just to lie in my bed looking through the open French windows at the jungle below was bliss.

Outside the windows, a shallow sloping stretch of lawn led down to the road, and my mother was wont to recline on a sun lounger there and sunbathe. Occasionally she would be joined by her friends, and on this particular occasion a lady called Sheila Muirhead, with an irritating young son aged four, had come to visit. I was annoyed. Now my mother would not be willing to tell me stories, or make too much of a fuss of me, and what was worse, her son was too young for me to be able to talk to on any meaningful level, and as both my legs were in plaster, and I was wracked with agony every time I moved, I couldn't do anything more boisterous in terms of play.

Then I had an idea.

For my birthday, the day before I went into hospital I had received a copy of *Hong Kong Butterflies* by Major J.C.S Marsh, and I was desperate to put my newfound book to use. I was at the age when I had just begun to realise that some creatures were more closely related than others, and I wanted to identify the myriad animals that surrounded me. Fluttering along a few inches above the closely mown grass were dozens of small, blue butterflies. Major Marsh listed several dozen members of this family, quite a few of which looked very similar.

So I called to the toddler who was earnestly chuffing up and down the sloping lawn pretending to be a goods train. "Hello" I said. "I'm Jonathan. What's your name?"

"Richard". He said. "What are you doing in bed?"

So I told him, and despite the seven year gap in our ages, he not only seemed to sympathise with me, but – after I explained my predicament re. Major Marsh and the blue butterflies - he expressed - as well as a four-year-old can express anything – a willingness to help me in my investigations. So I told him where my bedroom was, and where I kept my butterfly net, and where my precious copy of *Hong Kong Butterflies* was, and he trotted off inside. About ten minutes later, after a few false starts, I was sitting up in bed with Major Marsh's *magnum opus* on my knee, and a Robinson's marmalade jar in one hand, as my young assistant – still making enthusiastic train noises – rushed up and down in search of butterflies.

When, eventually, he captured one, my quest was at an end. It was a fine male specimen of *Lampides boeticus* otherwise known as the long-tailed blue. Having identified the poor little thing, Richard and I liberated it, and I thought nothing much more about the matter for about twenty-four years.

Nearly a quarter of a century later, whilst the nascent Centre for Fortean Zoology was in its infancy, I received a letter from a young man called Richard Muirhead, who was very interested in the stranger aspects of the natural world. It took months for me to make the connection, but eventually the penny dropped.

This time around, the seven-year age gap was of no importance whatsoever, and we soon became firm friends. A further quarter of a century later we still are.

Lampides boeticus is an interesting little insect; it is one of the most widespread and common butterflies in the world. The wingspan is between 24-32mm for males, with the females sometimes being a little larger. Like many of the lycaenids, it is markedly sexually dimorphic, with the female only having a small amount of blue colour in the centre of the wings, whilst the rest is brown. The males, however, are like gorgeous, tiny, flying jewels, and are a bright violet blue in colour. Both sexes, however, have a thin, long tail at the apex of the hind wing, from which it gets the English name, 'long tailed blue'. Now, it is found across much of Europe, Africa, southern and south east Asia, and even Australia. In parts of the United States, it is classified as an invasive species, and known as the 'bean butterfly' and it considered as a major pest of legumes in agriculture. But whilst they are common over much of the world, and despised in some of it, in England they are a very rare and very welcome visitor.

Because – even after the effects of global warming – the United Kingdom, even the southern half, has comparatively cold winters, all the resident British butterflies either spend the winter as eggs or pupae, or hibernate (either as adults, or caterpillars). *Lampides boeticus*, however, is what they call 'continuously brooded', which means that they can produce three or four generations a year, always on the leaves of plants of the pea family. However, each generation begets the next generation like something out of *Genesis*, and neither caterpillars or adults are able to hibernate. They are also very sensitive to temperature fluctuations, and so, even though most years a few intrepid members of this species reach the shores of southern Britain and sometimes even breed, they will never become British residents, at least not until Britain's climate changes beyond all recognition. Although they regularly turn up in the United Kingdom, first having been recorded from Brighton and Christchurch in August 1859, they are not natural migrants and so – unlike painted ladies (*Vanessa cardui*), for example – they will not migrate south again once the autumn chills make southern Britain impossible for them to live in.

Between 1859 and 1939, a mere thirty-six sightings had ever been recorded, and by 1988 only another eighty-five sightings were noted, thirty eight of these taking place in 1945. However, in 2013, enormous numbers turned up in southern Britain, with them breeding successfully into October. Much of my research over the past fifteen years has been into the fluctuating nature of biodiversity in areas where once it had been thought that species lists remain static. Events like the *Lampides boeticus* 'invasion' of 2013 are, therefore, a particular interest to me, but even now whenever I read about these delightful little insects, I involuntarily picture Richard Muirhead as a little boy, pretending to be a train, and earnestly catching these little insects for my perusal.

But despite the solace of weekends with my family, every Sunday night, the ambulance would come and take me back to the hospital for another week of horrors. The beginning of the second week was the worst: for reasons that I cannot remember, and which don't really matter nearly fifty years later, I had to have a second operation on my knees because part of the first operation had not gone according to plan. The only thing I remember about this second operation was that the kindly anaesthetist asked whether I wanted an injection or gas? As I believe I have mentioned elsewhere, I've always been terrified of injections and chose the latter option. I always remember this as one of the worst decisions of my young life, because breathing in whatever noxious chemical was then used to send hapless patients across the Waters of Lethe was a frightening and totally disorientating experience. It probably only took a few seconds, but I found myself terrified, struggling against the heavy rubber mask held over my face as everything changed shape, colour and form with a psychedelic intensity. This is what always comes to mind whenever I read about gas chambers, either during the Third Reich, or more recently as a means of judicial execution.

I have spent a lot of the last twenty-five years travelling, both internationally and within the United Kingdom. And something that I have noticed increasingly is that the actual process of travelling, when you are in somebody else's hands entirely and in a process of transit between the part of the real world, where you live normally, and the part of the real world to which you are going, puts me (at least) into a state of limbo. It is as if one's normal emotional and sensory faculties are suspended for the duration of the journey, and one behaves as if one were a piece of luggage on a conveyor belt; passive to the extreme, and almost apathetic as regards the things that are going on around you.

So it was, for me, aged eleven, during my first major bout of hospitalisation.

During my increasingly welcome weekends at home, despite the fact that I was bedridden, and had to use a bedpan, and pee in a bottle, I was still surrounded by the things that I knew, and able to interact with them pretty much as normal. But, back in the hospital, I just did what I was told, and waited ungrumblingly for the next stage of my rehabilitation. After the day or so following each of my operations, I cannot actually remember being in pain. This was either because I wasn't, or – more than likely – because I was under quite severe medication. More recently in my life, I have found myself in a similar state, either because I have been prescribed various psychoactive medications from the doctor, or because I have self medicated. I have never made any secret about the fact that over the years I have taken fairly large amounts of various drugs, both recreationally and therapeutically (although the demarcation line between these two categories is often blurred), and it took me many years to discover how to function reasonably normally whilst ripped to the tits. This was originally a workaround, but as I get older and my health declines, I am on more and more daily medications, and this coping mechanism that I taught myself, back during my misspent early middle age, has become more and more useful to me.

But back in the late summer of 1970, the bedridden eleven-year-old boy that I was then had no such knowledge, and – without the sensory and intellectual stimuli provided by my family and homelife – I drifted along with the flow in a state of acquiescence. My mother came to visit me every afternoon, bringing comics, and books, and staying to read me stories. It was the first time since our return to Hong Kong back in 1964, when – waiting for our apartment at Mount Austin Mansions to be ready – we stayed for some weeks at the Repulse Bay Hotel, that I had a concerted programme of stories read to me by my mother, and – sadly – it was to be the last.

My mother read me books from her own collection that she thought I would like. Back in 1964, it had been the collected works of Gerald Durrell, but I'd read them all many times myself by 1970, and so we progressed onto the mystery stories of Dorothy L. Sayers, and the more entertaining Regency Romances of Georgette Heyer. Neither of these were the sort of books that a 'normal' eleven-year-old boy would enjoy, but I was far from being a 'normal' eleven-year-old boy. Both of these authoresses have remained dear to me, on and off, ever since.

After my second weekend visit home, I was allowed to get out of bed and was allocated a wheelchair, in which I could propel myself around my room and up and down the corridor. I thought this the most enormous fun, and when there was nobody else around to complicate things, my wheelchair became a Spitfire or Hurricane, and I became either Biggles or – with a slight nod to my current disabled state – the legendary legless airman, Douglas Bader, and I 'flew' up and down the long, green corridor that smelled of antiseptic and efficiency, engaged in complicated manoeuvres and dogfights with the cream of the Luftwaffe, always victorious despite overwhelming odds.

It was towards the end of that third week that I had to go through the process of learning to walk again. It was a long, drawn-out and torturous procedure, but I threw myself into it with total enthusiasm because I knew that as soon as I was upright, even if I had to walk using crutches, I would be able to use the lavatory under my own steam and the humiliating process of bedpans and bottles would finally be in the past. The third weekend that I went home, I was on crutches - although I still had the mobile hospital bed to transport me to and from Queen Elizabeth's Hospital - but in the fourth week, I graduated to using first two walking sticks, and then one, and by the end of the fourth week, I was discharged.

I would like to think that in these more enlightened days, a child who had been through such a searing ordeal would have been given some emotional time to recuperate. However, we lived in less enlightened times, and the week after I was discharged from hospital, I was thrown into the tumultuous process of starting at a new school. As those of you who have followed this narrative so far will – no doubt – be aware, the relationship between me and school was not, and never had been, a particularly positive one. And so, I faced this uncertain future with trepidation.

One thing that I don't remember worrying me was the fact that in twelve months' time, I would have to go back to hospital for another operation, this time to remove the two or three metal staples that had been hammered into my kneecap. But when you are eleven, a year is such an unimaginably long time that one cannot even imagine what is going to happen twelve whole months in the future.

But the new school was something else entirely.

CHAPTER TEN
Changes

For most of the time that the British had custodial supervision over the territory of Hong Kong, the only secondary school for the children of British expatriates was King George V School in Kowloon. Better known as KG5, it had originally been founded back in 1894 as Kowloon College, but after a chequered history during the war years (during which the school was used as a hospital for prisoners of war, and it has even been rumoured that the pavilion was used as a torture chamber by the occupying Japanese authorities), it was redesignated as King George V School, as King George V had been the monarch on the throne of the British Empire when the foundation stone of the school had first been laid.

Peculiarly, during the final months of preparation of the current volume, my late wife was in the hospital in Barnstaple. And the name of her ward? KGV. King George the Fifth had been a busy man.

However, for reasons that remain obscure, in 1967, a new secondary school was founded on Hong Kong Island. Named, unimaginatively, 'Island School', it was originally housed in the buildings of the former British Military Hospital on Bowen Road, although five years later it also moved to the mainland. Again, it had been built in the early years of the 20th Century, and had been used as an internment facility by the occupying Japanese between 1941 and 1945.

For some reason, it never – at least, during the time I was there – shook off its long term *genius loci* as a military hospital. Although I had disliked the structure of my previous primary school, the regimented structure of Island School was very different, and unlike the schools in England that I was to attend later on in my adolescence, I actually enjoyed and appreciated the place. Something that I found very hard to come to terms with was the adoption of a strange format for the timetable. Instead of having one's week mapped out in front of you from Monday to Friday, the schedule actually was mapped out into seven 'days'. So, for example, if day one was on a Monday, day five would be on the Friday, and days six and seven would be on the following Monday and Tuesday, and so on, *ad infinitum*. This is, apparently, something that is far more common in American seats of learning, and in military establishments, but it was something that took quite a lot of getting used to, as far as I was concerned.

The most exciting thing about the new school, for me, at least, was the fact that it had its own zoo. Called 'The Zoo Club' and run by a lady called Mrs Maylett, it contained an impressive range of animals, ranging from what I have always thought of as 'Pet Shop Species', like budgerigars, white rats, red-eared terrapins, and bunny rabbits, to some undeniable exciting animals, like a huge Asian water monitor (*Varanus salvator*), who was housed in a room about the size of my present sitting room, which had made no attempt to disguise its military and medical history. It had small, high, windows of the sort of frosted glass that one sees most usually used as bathroom windows, but with a criss-cross lattice work of wire embedded deep inside the glazing to give it extra tensile strength. No attempt had been made to provide decor for the huge lizard, but I was also so overawed with seeing a reptile, considerably longer than I was, that I paid no attention to the rest of the layout of its captive habitat.

The Asian water monitor is found across a lot of southern Asia, from India and Sri Lanka, east to southern China, and down to the Sunda islands of Sumatra, Java, Bali and Borneo. There is no doubt that it was originally found in Hong Kong, and it is still found there today, although the people who monitor the biodiversity of the territory tend to think that it was hunted to extirpation by the 1970s or 80s, and that the specimens which are seen and even captured now, well into the 21· Century, are specimens that have been released from captivity in recent years. The species is very popular as a pet, but the fact that it grows up to a length of 10.5 feet (3.21 metres) precludes it from being kept as a pet by an urbanised population who mostly live in relatively cramped apartment blocks. When the young monitors get too big for captivity, they are often released, along with specimens bought at local food markets by well-meaning Buddhists, who believe that they are 'acquiring merit' by releasing a captive animal and saving it from a certain death in the cooking pot. The most recent information that I have read about this species in Hong Kong claims that these released animals probably breed there, but admits wryly that there is no *prima facie* evidence for this having taken place.

This seems particularly likely to me. After all, another lizard known from mainland China, but not known from Hong Kong until the beginning of the 21· Century, is the Chinese water dragon (*Physignathus cocincinus*). No-one knows exactly when they appeared within the Hong Kong fauna, but at the time of writing in 2019, they are quite widely distributed in Hong Kong, and are the second species of agamid to be found there after *Calotes versicolor*.

The zoo was also home to various birds, including two or three species of parakeet, at least one gibbon, several monkeys (both, as far as I remember, long tailed macacques (*Macaca fascicularis*), one of the two species of monkey that you will remember are to be found wild, if introduced, in Hong Kong.

Starting a new school was more traumatic than I liked to admit, and was the second or third (depending on which way you decide to count them) of the big traumas which happened to me during the summer and autumn of 1970, and which would shape the rest of my life. Looking back with undeniably rose-tinted spectacles, I actually quite enjoyed my brief sojourn at Island School. Certainly, compared to the horrors I was to face once I returned to the Motherland, my first taste of secondary education was quite a pleasant experience. But, the abrupt culture shock from scholastic childhood to scholastic adolescence was as traumatic for me as it was for most other children. What made it worse was that for the first time I was totally embarrassed by my appearance. I could still only walk with a stick, and on bad days, crutches, and unlike me fellow male pupils who all wore the enviable long trousers of adulthood, I still had to wear shorts, because my knees were still enveloped with plaster and bandages. Even after the plaster was removed, a couple of weeks into my secondary education, if I did anything strenuous my left knee would ooze blood and lymphatic fluid, staining the ever-present bandages with the tell-tale stigmata of surgery. This meant that, right from the beginning, I was a pariah amongst the other boys in my class who all – it seemed, to me, at least – were obsessed with sport and athletic prowess, whereas I had to sit on the sidelines with a book.

Most of the teachers had, I think, been briefed to be kind to me because of my various ailments and disabilities, but at least one teacher was spectacularly nasty to me when I continually arrived late for lessons because I could only hobble along, rather than walk at the stiff pace of my classmates. I have always been quite forgetful, and although these days I can blame it on my imminent dotage, the eleven-year-old me had no such social get out clause. And so, when I forgot my textbooks, leaving them at home or on the other side of the campus, I was – quite understandably – reprimanded. During my five years at Peak School, I had gone from being the youngest boy in the school to one of the oldest, and it was a culture shock to find myself back in the lowest form, surrounded by older children who were well on their enviable path to adulthood.

For the first time in my scholastic existence, I actually showed some interest in my work, and – in the subjects that interested me, at least – did rather well. However, it wasn't long before I got into trouble and was given my first detention. It was for some heinous crime involving spilled water in the art room, but I can't remember the details. Whereas, with the benefit of hindsight, detentions for stuff like this are a normal part of school life, my parents treated it as if I had done something absolutely appalling, and my father beat me for the crime of having "besmirched the family honour". Apparently, the husband of the art teacher was one of his colleagues at work in the Colonial Secretariat, and my father felt that he would never live the shameful experience down.

Stuff like this did nothing but push me further into my own private world, which, when I was still living in Hong Kong, existed up on the hillsides behind and below Peak Mansions. As I got older, I explored further afield, and found tiny woodland glades, miniscule waterfalls and streams, and dense bamboo thickets into which I ventured and made little dens, which were my own private sanctum. My two best friends, William and Ricky, were no longer around; William had been sent back to England to a boarding school in Suffolk, and Ricky went back to Australia with his mother, following (according to my father 40 years later, although I knew nothing about it at the time) his parents' acrimonious divorce. In Hong Kong, in 1970 at least, divorce was a rude word that one never spoke about, and my parents were scandalised enough to do their best to stop me associating with somebody that, even on his deathbed, my father referred to as a "vulgar little oik". I missed them both, and although I became friendly enough with my new school companions, nobody came along to fill those gaps of friendship.

I spent more and more time alone, either out in the countryside or with my nose in a book. And, with the power of hindsight, I can see that I was becoming more and more isolated. My little brother was a remarkably well adjusted and happy child, and indeed has stayed so throughout his life, whereas I lurched from one crisis to another until I settled down, to a greater or lesser extent, around about the turn of the millennium, as a result of effective therapy, medication and my second marriage.

I remember in the September of 1970, lying on my back on one of the grassy hillocks which overlooked the ruins of the Peak Hotel, high above the apartment block where we lived. I lay for hours, watching the swallows and other migratory birds wheeling around in the sky above me. It is actually quite surprising how similar much of the fauna of Hong Kong is to the fauna of the United Kingdom. The bird that we know as simply the swallow (*Hirundo rustica*) is also found in Hong Kong, though it is known as the barn swallow, and it too migrates south for the winter, although its journey is nowhere near as long or arduous as it is in Europe, merely having to go into Indochina rather than having to navigate all the way from the United Kingdom to sub-Saharan Africa. Together with a bird called the red-rumped swallow (*Cecropis daurica*), which is also found in Europe but which is a very rare vagrant in the UK, it congregated in relatively large numbers, preparatory to flying south. This biannual migration was something which I always enjoyed watching, partly because of its undeniably spectacular nature and partly because the migration of swallows and their relatives was such an iconic trope in some of my favourite books, such as *The Wind in the Willows* and *Doctor Dolittle's Post Office*. As remarked upon earlier in this narrative, the classier end of children's literature provided one of my most important set of cultural landmarks during my childhood and adolescence, and – to a much greater extent than one would imagine – still does so today.
Each autumn, I looked forward to climbing the hill and watching the thousands of little birds return again in the spring, and so it was in the autumn of 1970. What I

didn't know, and couldn't possibly know, was that this would be the last time I would ever watch this migration. Because the final bombshell that was to rock my world during this peculiar cataclysmic year was just about to drop.

My father was a strange man; alternately outgoing and affectionate or cold and withdrawn, with flashes of bitter anger. Many years after the events described here, I was diagnosed with bipolar disorder and a mild schizoaffective disorder, and ever since, I have wondered whether my father suffered from one or both of these. If so, it would explain a lot. There is a history of mental illness in his family, and if he had suffered from one of the family maladies, but had never been given a diagnosis, it would explain why I always found him so difficult to deal with.

I was not given a firm diagnosis until after my first marriage imploded. For years, my strange behaviour and mood swings were thought of as just "Jon being Jon" and they certainly contributed towards a lot of the difficulties which I had been through in the first forty years of my life. It is notable, I think, that I have been considerably more successful in both my professional and my emotional lives since the disease that has blighted the lives of so many of my family over the years was diagnosed.

But by the autumn of 1970, even the neurotic and self-absorbed eleven-year-old me, dealing with the painful aftermath of two orthopaedic operations and negotiating the social minefield of secondary school for the first time, could see there was something wrong. My father suddenly became far less active than he had been, and continually complained of a bad back. I only knew a fraction of what went on at the time, but apparently it had become so bad that he had to have a couch installed in his office so that he could work lying down. But still, his symptoms got worse, and at some point during the autumn of Hong Kong, he was diagnosed with chronic osteoarthritis, the debilitating effect of which meant that he was no longer able to do his job.

So, with the large family Christmas already visible on the horizon, my brother and I were told that in a few short months, in the February of 1971, we would be leaving the only world I had ever known as home and returning to the Motherland.

Even now, I truly cannot explain to anybody reading this narrative the complete enormity of what this meant to me. England was a nice place to visit; both my grandmothers and my surviving grandfather lived there, but it was cold and weird, and everybody behaved completely differently to us Colonial Ex-pats. And what was going to happen about my animals? On hearing the news, and beginning to digest the various implications of it, I burst into tears, was cuffed around the ear, and sent to bed without any supper for being selfish.

I cried myself to sleep that night.

My brother, who by this time had reached the ripe old age of seven, had recently matured enough for him to join in with my games, and share in my dreams, hopes and fears.

The children of Peak Mansions had recently discovered that if one took a hacksaw, it was possible to cut a path through the thick bamboo forest on the slope above the ranks of garages behind our apartment block. And that the severed bamboo canes were perfect to use as spears or to make bows and arrows, and even to be used in the construction of makeshift huts. I think that a book by Anthony Buckeridge, called *Jennings's Little Hut* had quite a lot to do with this.

So all of us children made a series of complex, labyrinthine tunnels, pathways and makeshift dwellings all the way through the tiny bamboo forest, taking care that our parents, guardians and the Chinese servants set in power over us didn't know what we were doing, because of the ever present fear of poisonous bamboo snakes, now known as the white-lipped pit viper (*Trimeresurus albolabris*).

My brother joined in these activities with gusto, and soon became part of the various games (usually cowboys and Indians, pirates, or soldiers) that we played, and was a perfectly satisfactory 'Redskin brave', junior soldier or 'cabin boy'. And, for the first time I realised how much fun it was to have a junior collaborator with whom I could share my various activities. I even told him about my burgeoning interest in cryptozoology, and he joined in with some of my early hunts for surviving Hong Kong red foxes, or other animals thought – at the time – to be extirpated in the territory.

To digress a moment, it is interesting to note that several of the creatures which, at the time, were considered not to exist in Hong Kong anymore have since either returned or have been found to have been living there all the time.

Wild pigs (*Sus scrofa*) were almost extinct in Hong Kong by the end of the 1960s, but have since recovered their numbers and have now reached pest proportions, even being found on the island, probably having got there either through one of the cross-harbour tunnels which have been constructed since my time or by swimming. Billy Higginbotham of Texas A & M University is quoted in *National Geographic* on the 6. June 2015 as saying that "pigs are excellent swimmers, crossing water to seek food sources, escape danger or find better habitat". There are other changes in the list of currently resident Hong Kong mammals; the crab eating mongoose (*Herpestes urva*) had not been seen since the early 1950s and was considered to have been extirpated from the area. However, 30 years or so later, it turned up again, without a by-your-leave, and those few of us who are interested in such things still argue whether it was a reintroduction, a recolonisation, or whether they have been there all the time. I, by the way, mostly believe the last of the three. Then, soon afterwards a second species of mongoose, the small Asian, or Javan, mongoose (*H. javanicus*) was discovered in the new territories in the late 1980s and has apparently become quite successful. Two smaller mustelids, the yellow throated marten (*Martes flavigula*) and the yellow bellied weasel (*Mustela kathiah*) have now both been recorded from the colony, the

Eurasian otter (*Lutra lutra*) has made a comeback, and as mentioned earlier perhaps weirdest of all, it turns out that the Chinese, or Reeve's, muntjac (*Muntiacus reevesi*), which was relatively common, if elusive, in Hong Kong when I was a boy, has actually turned out to be something completely different; the Indian muntjac (*M. muntjak*). It is unclear whether *M. reevesi* does actually, or indeed, ever has, existed in the former British colony. The list of rodents, shrews, whales and bats have also changed quite dramatically over the years, and three species, the dhole (*Cuon alpinus*), the red fox (*V. vulpis*) and the large Indian civet (*Viverra zibetha*) are now considered to be extinct. On top of that, two subspecies of squirrel were introduced to Hong Kong in the 1970s.

And I was leaving all this behind! I was inconsolable, but Richard was so much more excited to be seeing his grandparents again and my parents, quite understandably, I suppose, were more worried about my father's condition and what they were going to do once they only had my father's pensions to live on, and so a mentally ill eleven year old snivelling for his soon-to-be lost paradise was of very little concern to them.

At school I did my best to keep a stiff upper lip and started to bequeath as many of my animals as they would take to the Island School Zoo Club, who were good enough to say they would have my various birds and fish, although the serried ranks of jam jars containing various invertebrates (mostly aquatic) were of very interest to them, so I realised that my precious freshwater crabs, water snails, diving beetles, ladybirds, caterpillars and cicadas would have to be released from whence they came.

The cicadas had been a relatively new addition to my menagerie. I had read about this charming little insects in various books by Gerald Durrell, and had deduced from his description that the sweet chirping sound which sounded almost like a small bird (which is what I thought it was at first) rather than one of the grasshoppers or crickets with which I was familiar, was made by a cicada. So, in one of the stands of elephant grass which stood on the left hand side of Plunkett's Road as one was going downhill towards Peak Mansions, and after several hours very hard work, during which I saw my only living specimen of a many-banded krait (*Bungarus multinctus*) which would have been quite capable of killing me (and no, I didn't tell my parents, who would have dispatched the servants to go, burn down the stand of elephant grass and kill any serpents that they found therein) I finally found myself the owner of four beautiful, pale green cicadas, each about the size of the upper joint of my thumb now I am a morbidly obese sixty-year-old.

Interestingly, they were not living on, or feeding off, the elephant grass which provided protection for them. They were actually upon small, succulent, light green plants which, as my pretensions to being a botanist are even more tenuous than my pretensions to being a zoologist, I have never been able to identify but which I was very familiar with as a child. And so, as I brought my new pets home in triumph to live in a twelve-inch fish tank with a muslin lid on my bedroom windowsill, I dug up several of these food plants and arranged them in what I felt was a pleasingly artistic manner before introducing my cicadas to feed upon them.

The whole episode was one of my most successful, because the cicadas seemed to be very happy in their new home, and even started to sing first thing in the morning, when the rays of sunlight penetrated the usually dank back yard outside my window.

Someone had given me a very sturdy wooden box without a lid, and I had a stroke of what I believed then was genius. I put it on my windowsill with the open top plumb against the glass, so I could go out into the backyard and look at the things that I had placed inside. I fantasised that this was the latest enclosure in my personal zoo, and as such would need something particularly impressive to live inside. I had become very interested in the various members of the ladybird family, which could be found living on the hillside above Mount Austin Mansions and my home at Peak Mansions. I noted that they would always arrive in numbers soon after there had been a swarm of tiny green aphids, and concluded – correctly – that they fed upon them. So, I collected ladybirds of various species, and some large, dark, metallic blue scarab beetles that I have never been able to identify and kept them in my new 'enclosure'. I kept the ladybirds happy on a diet of as many aphids as I could find, and when – as they inevitably did – the aphids escaped and started to infest various parts of our apartment, I stringently denied that they had anything to do with me. Why would I want to keep aphids? I lied, thanking the gods of natural history that my parents didn't know and didn't care that they were food for my ladybirds. Sadly, I could never find what the blue scarab beetles liked to eat, as they refused all the different plants that I put in there for them, and so after they were obviously becoming more sluggish, I took them up to the ruins of the hotel, high on the hillside, and let them go where I had found them.

Soon after, I was given another wooden box, and so my second 'special enclosure' came into being. I used this to keep a small colony of what I called 'shell slugs'. Over the years, I had kept various Hong Kong snails, including the invasive and very successful giant African land snail (*Achatina fulica*), which had arrived in the colony on imported vegetables in the 1920s. But I had never really paid attention to slugs. But these beautiful little creatures, with dappled light grey and pink bodies, and an incongruously small shell as translucent and shimmering as the finest mother-of-pearl, totally transfixed me, and to my great pride, I even managed to breed them. I don't know, with the benefit of hindsight and the increased zoological knowledge I have gained over the last half century, whether they were actually slugs, or a highly specialised species of snail. But I was very proud of them, and quite disappointed that Mrs. Maylett at the Island School Zoo Club was not interested in taking possession of them.

When you are eleven years old, five months is an absolute lifetime. And so, it was that, although I knew at the back of my mind that my life in Hong Kong had a fixed time limit, it was September, and we wouldn't be leaving the colony until February, and so I put the entire matter aside to be dealt with when it finally became necessary.

I was much more interested in my ongoing obsession with the Battle of Britain, and when the movie finally arrived in the orient, I bulled my parents into taking me twice. My father was typically scathing about the whole thing, but he had always been scathing about my various interests even when they were relatively harmless, and this was something which carried on up until the last few months of his life. So, I ignored him, and carried on my daydreams of making a film on the subject which would put the Guy Hamilton movie of 1969 completely in the shade. I had ambitious plans for filming most of it in our backyard, using my collection of Airfix model aeroplanes suspended on lines of cotton purloined from my mother's work basket. These fantasies kept me happily employed for months - when I should have been busily concentrating on my education - and would rear their head again on and off for the next two years.

As anybody who has followed my subsequent career (if you can call it that) will know, I have been involved in film making quite a lot over the past two and a half decades, both in front of and behind the camera. And it was, I believe, my grand cinematic plans for a World War II *tour de force*, hampered only by the fact that I had no funding, no cine camera, and that my plans were – on the whole – unworkable, that set me off on one of my current career trajectories. I would spend hours trying to work out in my head how one could fabricate a scene featuring plastic toy aeroplanes on string and make it look half believable. At the upper terminus of the Peak Tram, which was, you may remember, only a few hundred yards away from my home, there was a tourist kiosk which sold – amongst many other things – 35mm transparencies of many of the more touristy parts of the colony. I bought copies of all the ones which purely showed jungle or sea without any trappings of humanity, and carefully (or as carefully as a cack-handed eleven year old could be) drew pictures of fighter 'planes from various angles, and tried to persuade myself that I had achieved a stunning technical breakthrough.

I hadn't.

As well as this, my other main non-natural history obsession of the time was the forthcoming third man mission to the moon. Actually, it was the fourth, but as we all know, the astronauts on Apollo 13 told Houston that they had a problem and the whole thing went tits up, although not as tits up as it could have done.

Apollo 14 was scheduled to take place in January 1971, considerably over a year after the previous successful excursion in November 1969. Despite the fact that my entire family were scheduled to be leaving Hong Kong a couple of weeks after Alan Shepherd, Edgar Mitchell and Stuart Roosa were scheduled to return to Earth, my obsession was at a fever pitch. I was convinced that it was my bounden duty as a young man who still wanted to be a scientist, to chronicle every inch of the mission, from the preparations to their triumphant return. I religiously watched every television programme on the subject that I could, and whenever I could get away with it, I was to be seen wandering around with my tiny transistor radio held intently against my ear, and with an earnest look on my face. Many teenagers, and what are now known as pre-teens, of that period were seen doing likewise, but I was listening to the minutiae of the exploration of the 'final frontier', rather than the latest from the ex-Beatles or the Rolling Stones.

That long autumn, however, did see the first of my capitulations in the face of pop culture's inexorable assault upon my senses.

Whenever my parents were at home, they would always watch the RTV evening news at 6 o'clock. They encouraged me, as a young man on the cusp of teenagerhood, to do likewise, and – because, believe or not, I didn't like to annoy my parents, and I couldn't think of any reason why I shouldn't watch the news – it became part of my daily routine to sit down just before six o'clock to see what horrors had been happening in the world about me.

Back in the autumn of 1970, the Rediffusion TV people always put on something that they believed was of cultural significance just before the news. Usually, it was something like a pair of ballet dancers doing their thing to the accompaniment of some pre-recorded Tchaikovsky. Sometimes it was a string quartet, sometimes a sad looking man playing *Greensleeves* on a lute. Once, it was Simon and Garfunkel. I remember nothing about their performance apart from the fact that I sniggered all the way through it, thinking that 'Garfunkel' sounded like it was a rude word. But I usually paid very little attention, except on one glorious occasion, when the guest star was Basil Brush.

But then, one night in November 1970, the announcer said that the cultural significant offering which we were just about to enjoy was something called 'Deep Purple'. What a stupid name, I thought to myself. How can a performer also be a colour? Five hirsute young men stood in the middle of the stage. My parents had always told me that people like this were 'long haired twits', and so I paid very little attention.

They took their places behind their various instruments. And it started:

Dum dum de-dum dum-de, dum dum de dum-dum-dum DA-DUM DA-DUM

It was the first time that rock music had ever drilled its way into my consciousness. It was like a mainlined shot of every endorphin in the world squirting deep into my vena cava. I was immediately hooked. The song was *Black Night* and it was absofuckinglutely marvellous. Even now, half a century later, I still get that visceral rush of excitement when I hear that riff.

My life was never going to be the same again.

A month or so before receiving the news that he was about to be invalided out of Her

Majesty's Overseas Civil Service, for reasons which I never did understand because both of my parents were 'cat people' rather than 'dog people' and unlike many young boys, neither my brother or I had ever begged for a dog, my father came back from work one day brandishing a small Dachshund puppy whom he named 'Frankie'. She was very small, very neurotic, and so highly strung that the phrase truly seemed to lose its meaning. Whilst my parents had been stationed in Nigeria they had owned several Dachshunds, because this was a breed of dog that was particularly good at divesting whatever compound they were living in at the time of its resident members of the serpent tribe. Whilst, as already described elsewhere in this narrative, there were species of poisonous snake in Hong Kong, many of them potentially deadly and Augustus had, on one occasion, proudly brought in a young cobra, except in my mother's paranoia we could not truly be described as having a snake problem, but I guess that my parents both truly liked Dachshunds. And I imagine, a couple of years after the sad disappearance of Augustus, they thought that it was time that we had a house pet again.

Even on the cusp of the 1970s, purebred dogs were liable to be far more neurotic and needy than their crossbred analogues, and she was an excessively needy creature. Unlike a cat, she had to be taken for long walks twice a day and for some reason it fell to me, as the eldest son, to take her out each morning before I went to school. I didn't actually object to this, and, indeed, I quite enjoyed seeing the places which were so familiar to me from my day to day existence over the previous few years in a completely different aspect. The people who frequented this otherwise familiar places were completely different in those hours before the 'foreign devils' ventured out to go to work or school. In those days there were still a few Victorian-era gas lamps in parts of Harlech Road, and I was always fascinated to see the Municipal Lamplighter going about his business. Though I had seen him, on occasion, lighting the lamps of an evening, the process of snuffing the flame out using a long pole with a peculiar brass implement on the end of it for some reason fascinated me, and I never tired of watching it. The lamplighter himself was a peculiarly wizened little man, with a chestnut brown face carunculated like a walnut and several fingers missing off his left hand. With the innocence of childhood, it never occurred to me to wonder about the mishap which must have caused his disability, but now I recognise, with half a century's hindsight, the markings on his face to be scar tissue and his missing fingers to be corroborative evidence that, at some time during his life, he must have been the victim of some violent incident, and as it was only three decades after the brutal occupation of the British Colony by the invading Imperial Japanese army, it is a fair guess that my friend the lamplighter had been a victim of these horrific times.

I call him my friend, because, although he appeared not to speak a word of English and my Cantonese was rudimentary, although far less rudimentary than it is now, he would always acknowledge Frankie's and my appearance on the scene with a cheery wave and a muttered "cho san" [good morning] and I always made sure that I had a bar of chocolate in my pocket which I could share with him. My parents had always impressed upon me that I should not 'talk to strangers' but, like so many other things which they impressed upon me, I ignored them with impunity and no great harm ever came to me.

I slowly began to adjust to secondary school life, but – for me, at least – it took a lot of adjusting. It seemed to me that everything that happened in our history or English or even geography lessons tended to have – as a subplot, at least – a nuance of animal cruelty, and this disturbed me very much. It was to be worse when I got back to England and did my first year again, twelve months later, because – as I have written elsewhere – I had a seriously peculiar Latin master with apparent mental health difficulties, who insisted on telling us all about the nastier aspects of the Roman Colosseum. But, it was bad enough during the final months of 1970 in Hong Kong. The lessons seemed to be all about blood sports and cruelty, and death and decay.

With hindsight, I have no idea if this was just a reflection of the way my brain was functioning at the time; after all, I was just about to leave the only world I had ever known for an uncertain future in a Motherland which I had only explored through the pages of English literature, and for which I was completely unprepared.

The whole ethos of death and decay, especially in the animal kingdom, was made worse for me by the fact that the building – which at that time held the Island School campus – was still in the process of being renovated, and that the Chinese workmen who were involved with the renovation process occasionally made their presence known when I would find dog-faced fruit bats (*Cynopterus sphinx*) dead and nailed to the trunks of trees. Whether they had been dead when put there, I don't know, but I hope so. It was my second indication of how little the local people liked bats. There are two species of fruit bat known from the colony, as well as least twenty-one species of micro-bat. A year or so earlier, one of the children who lived in the same apartment block as me at Peak Mansions came running into to tell me that, the previous night, when her baby amah was putting her to bed, a small bat had flown into the room and that when she ultimately caught the little creature, she wrapped it in toilet paper and threw it into the bin. As soon as her baby amah had beat a dignified retreat, my friend (whose name, I am embarrassed to say, I have forgotten, but it has been fifty years) leapt out of bed and ran to the bin in the corner to rescue the tiny bat. But, it appeared to be injured and didn't fly away when she gave it a chance. So, as soon as she could the next morning, she brought it to me.

I had a look at it, and it appeared that at least one of the 'fingers' which make up the skeletal structure of a bat's wings was broken, and the wing membrane was torn.

Having, at the time, a touching belief that grownups could fix anything, I insisted to my friend's mother that we telephone the HKSPCA and take the injured chiropterid into them. The phone call was, of course, to prepare them and their crack team of surgeons for the complicated surgical procedure that would have to happen next.

Looking somewhat bemused, my friend's mother let me use her telephone (and remember, fifty years ago, children were very rarely allowed to use telephones and the idea of the telephone culture which would evolve amongst children and young people over the next few decades would have been completely incomprehensible to us) and I called the HKSPCA. A bored sounding Chinese woman answered the call and didn't seem to understand anything that I was trying to say to her, and seemed convinced that I was talking about a dog. Nevertheless, I did my best, and my friend's mother drove us hell for leather down to the HKSPCA headquarters in Central District, where, in a fever pitch of self-importance, I strode in and presented the woman behind the reception desk with my little parcel.

"You must get it to surgery immediately", I said, with as much authority as I could muster. But she took one look at it, and ended our adventure with three words.

"It is dead", she said, and threw the dead bat and the toilet paper into her waste paper basket.

My friend and I were distraught at this sad end to our mercy dash, but her mother took pity on us, and took us both to see *Chitty Chitty Bang Bang* at the cinema, and so the day was not a complete write off.

However, the whole affair gave me the beginnings of a lifelong suspicion of the animal rescue services, at least where wild animals are concerned.

On another occasion, things worked out better. I was walking our dog down Pokfulam Road one afternoon after school, when I heard the howling of a dog in distress. Frankie was, as I have written earlier, a highly neurotic and unpredictable beast, with all the worst bits of what happen to pedigree dogs when they get too inbred. So, I tied her to the trunk of one of the trees, and climbed up the steep incline to investigate.

I found a small dog, complete with collar, that had managed to get its foot stuck in one appeared to be a porcupine trap. Ever since discovering the porcupine traps of Mount Killitt the year before, I kept an eye open for them, and found – to my dismay – that they were more common than one would have liked to have thought. I never found another one with a porcupine in it, but whenever I found these traps I would always destroy them. The problem here was that the dog was both frightened and angry, and I had enough sense not to go too near it.

One of the things which was always drummed into any child brought up in the tropics was that dogs not only could bite but the results of that bite would mean that the unlucky recipient would have to undergo the excessively painful and unpleasant treatment for suspected rabies, even if it was not clear whether the animal had that bitten them was affected or not. This has remained with me all my life, and thirty years after the events which I am recounting, I was out one night with my friend and colleague, Graham Inglis, in one of the more formal parts of Mexico City. There was a small group of friendly looking stray dogs stretched out against the side of one of the ornate marble fountains near the Plaza del Revolucion. Graham – who is quite a fan of dogs – made his way over to make friends with them, until I shouted incoherently something about rabies, whereupon the two of us beat a hasty retreat.

Back in 1970, I took Frankie back up the hill to Peak Mansions and telephoned the HKSPCA. This time, they were faced with something with which they knew how to deal, and the animal control officer turned up within about forty-five minutes, and the two of us went and rescued the little dog. He gave it a sedative, we found the address of the owner on an engraved disc on the creature's collar, and the dog was restored to the bosom of its family. The owner gave both of us a crisp ten dollar note, which was quite significant largesse for me at the time, being something in the region of a couple of quid.

For someone like me who has always been more interested in what Herklots and my mother both referred to as 'creepy crawlies' than the larger and more spectacular beasts of the field, my last winter in Hong Kong was notable because of a remarkable number of huge silk moths. In *The Hong Kong Countryside,* Herklots wrote that he suspected that these magnificent insects, which despite it all were only the third largest of the saturniids to be found in the region, were the 'cynthia moth', now known as *Samia cynthia.*

It has been nearly fifty years since I last saw them in the wild, but I have bred them here in my home in North Devon on a number of occasions, and I tend to agree with Herklots's identification. There are, apparently, several subspecies and I would not like to hazard a guess which of these I found so delightful back in the winter of 1970. There must have been something in the air which was favourable to the saturniids, because that winter, I also saw a couple of Chinese moon moths (*Actias sinensis*). Perhaps the most lovely moths that I have ever seen, the moon moth complex are spread across much of Asia and parts of north and central America. They are beautifully patterned with light brown markings on a pale green background, and they sport long, delicate tails at the bottom of each wing which flutter in the breeze like the bridal veil of a fairy princess. Despite the fact that there are quite a few different species scattered around the world, I have only seen three of them alive and in the wild; the Chinese species, the Mexican species and the North American one, although I have seen various specimens of the Indian moon moth (*A. selene*) in various butterfly farms around the world.

Nobody else in my family was even slightly interested. My brother was at his wits end because having reached his turn to take his class hamster home for the weekend, the little rodent – which for some reason was called 'Honey Fred' – did what members of the hamster family are so good at and escaped, living a feral existence underneath the floorboards of what had once been the servant's quarters and now was my father's office. Some weeks later, Ah-Tam, who still came to work for the family on occasion, managed to capture the errant rodent and present it back to my brother, who, greatly relieved, took it back to school whereupon it escaped again, but this time it was not the responsibility of any member of the Downes family.

My parents were even more distant and preoccupied than they had been before. At the age of eleven I didn't realise that, because my father was being invalided out of Her Majesty's Overseas Civil Service, that there were going to be all sorts of problems with his pension and that although my father, at least, longed to back in England after two decades in foreign climes, for a while it looked like he would have no money when he did take his family back to the Motherland.

My parents had to go to an interminable round of farewell dinners – the sort of black tie, formal events that my father hated, and my mother tolerated – all the time with my father arguing with the Colonial Secretariat in Hong Kong and the Secretary of State for the Colonies back in Whitehall. But he was still the Assistant Colonial Secretary and had a gruelling workload which he still continued with up until the very day that he retired. Bear in mind here that his crippling osteoarthritis was getting worse by the day. He could no longer sit at his desk, and – for a while – he stood at a lectern that had been borrowed from one of his friends in the Royal Hong Kong Police.

My father had a long and complex relationship with the Hong Kong Police force. During the 1960s, there were a number of serious corruption scandals, and – from what I can gather – my father had been the senior civil servant in charge of not only organising some of the enquiries but also restructuring the new and improved Police service which would go forward into the 1970s and beyond. As a result of that, he was presented with a ceremonial police truncheon; what our transatlantic chums call a 'nightstick'. When my father finally died in February 2006, his coffin was draped in the Union Flag and the black, ebony truncheon was placed atop it for the duration of the ceremony.

Because of my father's special relationship with the new hierarchy of the Royal Hong Kong Police, the family – which in practice meant my father and me – were invited to various police service parades, and I remember being very impressed by a magnificent billy goat that was marching as the police service mascot. A week or so later, I was upset though interested to hear from my father that the goat had been attacked and killed by a civet cat. This must have been one of the last records of the large Indian civet (*Viverra zibetha*) in the colony, because by the time I started studying the wildlife of Hong Kong again in the late 1980s, this impressive carnivore, which can reach a head and body length of up to thirty seven inches with another two foot of tail attached behind, was finally declared to have been extirpated from the colony. There are three species of civet cat that have been found in Hong Kong and the large Indian civet, with its total nose to tail tip length of five feet, is by far the largest. Any animal capable of taking down a hefty adult goat needs to be treated with a damn sight more respect than many people would accord to one of the south Chinese civet cats.

Many decades later, having – in the interim – studied the predation methods of both civet cats and mongooses, I put the arcane knowledge which I had gathered to good use when I spent two sojourns on the island of Puerto Rico in the lesser Antilles in 1998 and 2004, when I was studying the alleged activities of a creature called the chupacabras which many people suspected was responsible for a string of quasi-vampiric attacks on livestock across the island. Another experience of mine during those last months before we left Hong Kong for good, and also – coincidentally, although we all know there is no such thing – involved the Royal Hong Kong Police. A senior police officer who may actually had been the Chief of Police but I can't remember, sent out an armed guard when he was convinced that communist insurgents were responsible for having attacked his prize banana tree. This might not have been quite as ridiculous as it sounded. There were communist activists and wannabe revolutionaries aplenty in Hong Kong at the time, and one of the important facets of Chinese character is that many place a great deal of importance on not 'losing face'; something which onlookers like those of us in the west would do well to remember when trying to understand things happening on the world stage, like the violent protests against the regional government which are going on at the moment (December 2019) as I dictate the final chapters of this book.

So, when the police commissioner (if it was him), angry at the destruction of one of his prize-winning banana trees, set an armed guard on the other, he wasn't over-reacting as badly as one might have thought. In the middle of the night, a few nights later, the marauders struck again and this time a shot rang out, and the blood of the bandit soaked into the virgin Hong Kong earth.

The bandit was a porcupine. Attacks by porcupines upon banana trees were not, and are not, an uncommon occurrence. Indeed, Herklots himself relates a very similar story which happened somewhere near Pokfulam in the years before the Second World War. But I saw the mangled remains of the once proud banana tree, and this was instrumental in my formulating a hypothesis to explain the existence of the chupacabras of Puerto Rico over three decades later.

It's strange how, after a gap of nearly half a century, certain things stick in your mind. I don't remember my last day at school, for example, and I don't actually remember much about my last month in Hong Kong. But I do remember our last Christmas in the colony.

For reasons which are lost to the mist of time, my father's secretary and her family, who had recently returned to the colony, came and spent Christmas with us. My brother and I had always been quite friendly with her children, and so having another family join ours for Christmas Day was by no means an imposition.

What I do remember, however, is that, unlike my family who were stolidly Anglican, Mrs Everett and her family were Roman Catholics. This made no difference to me, because my father had a pleasingly ecumenical attitude towards his faith, and indeed towards people of other faiths. Racial and religious prejudice were something completely alien to me. However, as I have noted elsewhere in this narrative, over the closing years of the 1960s I became more and more aware of events on the world stage that didn't directly impact upon my own life, and during 1969 and 1970 I had become aware of the 'troubles' in Northern Ireland. But I was horrified to discover that, while my friends' father – a high ranking army officer - had been on a short posting to Belfast and his family had gone with him, whilst attending a local catholic school my friends had been severely bullied. Why? Because, having attended a school for army officers' children in Hong Kong, the exercise books they took with them to their new seat of learning were emblazoned with the Union Flag and a Royal crown. Although I only heard about this second-hand, it was my first real experience of racial prejudice, and it upset me greatly.

Another incident which remains fresh in my mind for some reason, although it was of no more than tangential importance then or now, was what happened when Ah Tam one day presented me and my brother with a cage of white mice. As you will have gathered by now, much of my menagerie over the years had come as a gift from Ah Tam, and I was thrilled with the white mice until I realised, which a start, that we were leaving Hong Kong in just over a month, and that there was no way I would be able to take this kindly meant but ill-judged gift with me. I immediately burst into tears, but through my sobs I counselled my mother that she should not tell my brother about the inconvenient rodents because he would also be equally upset. My mother, showing one of the earliest examples of the syndrome which they were to exhibit for the rest of their lives; that my brother was far more sensible than me, foolishly ignored my advice and Richard immediately burst into tears as well. What happened to the mice, I do not recall.

The last few weeks in Hong Kong went by in a blur, and it is only now that I realise quite how unhappy I was at leaving the place that I had spent all of my sentient life. What I now know to be my usual mental defence mechanisms kicked in, and I strutted around the place – both at home and at school – like a cock of the walk, boasting about all the exciting things I was going to do back in England. For some reason that I still don't really understand, although it embarrasses me whenever I think back about it, I started borrowing money from everyone who would lend it to me. What I wanted it for and indeed what I spent it on, I have no real memory, although I do know that this was the time when I first started comfort eating. I was desperately unhappy about leaving Hong Kong, but I was determined not to show it.

Getting rid of my collection of odds and sods which I proudly called my "museum" was particularly difficult. Some things, like my collections of sea shells, skulls and bones, and the huge death's head hawk moth that I had found one morning a few years earlier on one of the stone pillars that supported the covered walkway outside Peak School, I could take with me. But the vast majority of my collection I couldn't.

As described earlier, I gave most of my animals to the care of Mrs Maylett at the

Island School Zoo Club, and I had already returned my various creepy crawlies to the wild. Frankie the dachshund was given to the family who lived next door, and thus – for the first time in as long as I could remember – I had no animals at all to share my life.

I gave all the various exhibits from my "museum" to the science department at Island School. Whether or not they were as pleased with the collection of dead lizards and snakes in methylated spirits, the mortal remains of the beer bottle octopus, two dried porcupine fish that I had found on a beach during one of our voyages of exploration, my dead and desiccated coral snake and two enormous dried breadfruit that I had found in the scrubland that fringed one of the beaches in Tai Tam Bay, I do not recall. But I assume that they were gracious about it, because my embarrassingly selective memory often remembers the nastier things better than the nicer ones.

There was one of my exhibits that caused my father and me more than a little difficulty in its disposal. One of the other children who lived at Peak Mansions was a girl called Deborah, and her father was a *bona fide* scientist working in a criminal forensic department of the Hong Kong police. I don't remember her family being particularly close to mine, but I do remember that he invited me to spend a day with him in his laboratory; an offer which I was very excited to accept. It was a very interesting experience for me and was remarkably prescient of parts of my future life, because most of what Deborah's father did was to analyse suspicious substances to find out whether they were illegal drugs or not. At this stage in my life I had no real conception of drugs or drug culture. Someone, probably my mother, had described them as things people took to make themselves feel good but which always ended up killing them instead, and the whole subject was of very little interest to me. As an aside, I also remember hearing the word 'rape' for the first time, and asking my mother what it meant. She told me that it was when somebody "married" a woman when she didn't want to be, which gave me a totally unrealistic definition of the term which stayed with me for several years.

However, I digress.

Back at the police forensic laboratory, in early 1970, I "helped" Deborah's father analyse several batches of suspicious pills, and before we went out to lunch at a local restaurant he told me that after lunch he would show me some human organs, which had been salvaged from an autopsy. This was immensely appealing to a rather macabre ten-year-old boy, but I was also far more sensitive than I pretended and the idea of this put me off my usually hearty appetite. In the end, it was a bit of an anti-climax. And although I have a vague memory of seeing various bottles with lumps of meat floating in them, I cannot remember being either impressed or disgusted by the sight. What I was impressed by, however, was an enormous house plant, growing in the corner of the laboratory. It looked a bit like one of the tomato plants that my grandmother was so proud of, back at her home in Hampshire, but with much larger leaves. I assumed that this was some kind of giant tomato and asked Deborah's father why the Royal Hong Kong Police were so interested in cultivating it. He burst out laughing, and explained that this was a plant of the species *Cannabis sativa*.

Even I knew what cannabis was, although I had no interest in taking it at that time. But I very badly wanted a leaf of the dreaded heaven and hell plant for my museum. For some reason, Deborah's father seemed to find this exceedingly funny, and so he picked a single, large and impressive leaf, and showed me how to put it through the office laminator. He even got his secretary to type out a little white sticky label describing what this plant was, and at the end of my day in the forensic laboratory, I bore my exciting trophy home in triumph, telling my mother and anyone else who would listen, that I had decided that I was going to be a forensic scientist when I grew up.

A year and a half later, however, we were left with the conundrum of how we would get rid of this particular trophy of mine. I was old enough to realise that taking controlled drugs through international customs lines and then importing them into England, even if I had only the interests of science and a career as a forensic scientist in my sights, was a complete no-no. The fact that I did exactly this on several occasions when I was in my early thirties and travelling back to the Motherland from rock and roll shows in Amsterdam and the Republic of Ireland, is irrelevant here.

My father suggested that we should burn the specimen, but, again in total contrast to the way that I would be only a few short years later, I pointed out that we couldn't possibly do this in case we accidentally inhaled some of the fragrant smoke. I suggested we give it along with my other specimens to the science department of Island School but, for some reason, my father was unimpressed by the idea of the son of the Assistant Colonial Secretary making a gift of narcotics to a place where young people went to learn various golden rules and moral precepts. In the end, I believe, we buried it somewhere, but the full details are lost in time.

CHAPTER ELEVEN
Homeward Bound

"If you're going to do something, do it well. And leave something witchy."

Charles Manson

I don't remember my last day at school, or my family's last day at Peak Mansions. As for our last few days in the colony, we decamped to the world-famous Peninsula Hotel. I remember dribs and drabs of our stay there, but they are disjointed and not at all cohesive.

I remember my mother apologising to my brother and me because we didn't have a television set in the room. This didn't bother either of us at all, because then, as now, 'the one-eyed goggle box' is something which I can take or leave, and usually leave. I remember reading a copy of *Reader's Digest*, describing student protests in America, complete with descriptions of mass nudity and debauchery at various rock festivals which I found exciting and oddly compelling. The article was peppered with references to "coeds" which I now realise meant co-educational, or female students in a hitherto male-only seat of learning. However, at the time, I thought that it was a piece of thrilling adult code referring to women of ill-repute and dubious morals, and the thought that there were such girls on the planet gave me great hope for the future.

I remember that there was a bar or restaurant with the theme of Noël Coward's immortal *Mad Dogs and Englishmen*. Although my interest in world affairs was mostly to do with moon landings and my retrospective obsession with the second world war, I was vaguely aware that the British Empire which I had always been brought up to believe was inviolate and solid as a rock, was actually crumbling away faster than I had realised and that there were surprising amounts of anti-British sentiment across the world. I then filled myself with righteous indignation at the fact that somebody could equate Englishmen with 'mad dogs' and assumed that this was a particularly egregious example of anti-British sentiment. I got angry and upset until my mother – rather brusquely – explained it to me.

...and that's about it! The next thing I remember was being on an Air India jet, taking us towards Bombay.

Our great exit from Hong Kong began to go awry within a few hours. We were flying over the jungles of Indochina, the first (and last) time that I had done so in daylight, and there was no cloud cover whatsoever. I was in a window seat, and stared down at the verdant green forests below me, occasionally punctuated by slow, muddy blue rivers, and let my imagination run riot. I was imagining tigers, elephants and crocodiles, lurking amongst the huge trees, and – presciently – wondered whether there were any lost populations of the Javan rhinoceros left there. It wasn't until the late 1980s that a population of this, probably the rarest large mammal in the world, was found in Vietnam, to the excitement of all, especially the dealers in traditional Chinese medicine, at whose door the blame can be laid for the fact that this population – the last mainland group, as far as we know – was wiped out in the early 21st Ccentury.

I also wondered whether, as we flew over Vietnam and Laos, there were pitched battles going on beneath me, and I peered intently at the forest below until I fell asleep. I have always found it particularly easy to go to sleep whilst on aeroplane flights, and I must have slept for some time because when I awoke it was because my mother was shaking me and telling me to fasten my seatbelt, because we were making an unscheduled stop in Bangkok. Apparently, something was wrong with the aeroplane.

Five decades later I cannot tell you what was wrong, if I ever knew, but, to my great excitement, we were told that we would be spending a night or two in the beautiful capital city of Thailand.

For some reason, I have always thought that cities such as Bangkok had remained, inviolate for centuries, but – actually – Bangkok traces its roots only as far back as a small trading post during the 15th Century, but the parts that we saw, at least, were undeniably beautiful; strange, flat buildings with golden turrets and spires, and huge temples made of a pinkish red stone. There were many slow-moving rivers, canals and creeks in which I imagined there to be all sorts of exciting creatures, although we didn't see anything apart from a few goldfish. The vivid blue sky was full of multi-coloured kites with long flowing tails, and it turned out that our visit had coincided with the national kite-flying competition, which was apparently a very big deal. I was particularly impressed to see several kites in the shape of enormous flying dragons and – even more incongruously – immense flying paper goldfish; anatomically correct to the smallest detail.

Richard and I spent the whole taxi journey from the airport to the hotel with our faces glued to the window, drinking in the details of this wholly unexpected but utterly delightful anabasis.

When we got to the hotel, there was a further delight in store for us in the shape of a baby elephant and its lavishly costumed keeper standing as a ceremonial guard outside the sumptuously decorated doorway. These days, I would have been appalled; the poor creature had probably been orphaned deliberately by the authorities in order to provide a four-legged and betrunked tourist attraction. It was probably not cared for properly, and almost certainly had a short and unhappy life ahead of it. But to two little boys, one eleven and one seven years old, it was yet another delightful facet of this completely unexpected delay in our exodus from Hong Kong.

We settled into our hotel rooms, and I was already making all sorts of highly impractical plans, which would have certainly disappointed me by not coming to fruition. These mostly consisted of an investigative trip deep into the jungles of Thailand's interior, where I would discover all sorts of new species of animal and maybe even encounter one of the fabled mystery hominids which have been reported from swathes of jungle all across south east Asia. The fact that these jungles would have been far too far away from Bangkok to have made a visit even to the outskirts of them even slightly practical was not an issue to my feverish eleven-year-old mind. But in any case, it was not to be. No sooner had we settled in, but my mother came down to Richard's and my room (which, for some reason, was on a different floor to the one occupied by my parents) to tell us that plans had changed and that we were going straight back to the airport. Apparently Air India had managed to lay on a substitute aircraft, and we were to resume our interrupted journey right away.

So, we packed our cases again, went down to the foyer, bid goodbye to the baby elephant, and got back into the taxi. I was disappointed that my plans for elaborate expeditions into the interior had been thwarted, but nevertheless I was excited at the fact that we would soon be in India, which was, after all, the home of my beloved Kipling.

I have no memory whatsoever of the flight across the sub-continent, but I do remember that within about half an hour of landing, we were all nearly arrested.

You will recall, I'm sure, that the reason for our long journey back to England was that my father had been invalided out of Her Majesty's Overseas Civil Service because of serious osteoarthritis. One of the treatments that was being tried for this debilitatingly painful condition was a rigid surgical corset, which was – of course – the last thing that the members of India's security services were expecting to show up on their X-Ray machine. The scanner picked up some strange and anomalous pieces of metal, and when the soldiers frisked him it was confirmed that he had what felt like a weapon shoved underneath his clothing, on his back. The soldier in question shouted for back-up, and we were immediately surrounded by grimacing Indian military men, pointing submachine guns in our direction. My mother, brother and me were all frisked, and our luggage searched for any sign of military hardware. Of course, they didn't find anything, and when my father's surgical corset was revealed, the forces of law-and-order let us go. It was the first, but by no means the last, time in my life that I was to fall potentially foul of a country's immigration security services.

My first morning in the city which was still called 'Bombay' back in 1971, is something that will remain with me for the rest of my life. I have vague memories of the drive from the airport to the hotel after our brief brush with the forces of Law-and-Order, but apart from the election posters for Indira Ghandi, reading "A vote for Indira is a vote for India" and other similar slogans, I can't remember much else. But that first morning, waking up to the sight of a white coral beach, palm trees, and various sleek and well-fed monkeys playing on the shore, will remain with me forever. Of course, I had seen palm trees, coral sand, and monkeys before, but the concatenation of these three items of exotica combined with the azure blue Indian Ocean which stretched out towards the horizon and the Persian Gulf many hundreds of miles away, was too much to resist. I was in the land of Kipling, I was Kim sitting on *Zam Zammah* outside the Wonder House, and I was totally enthralled.

My other memories of these few days in a subcontinental paradise involve my father breaking one of the local by-laws. I was sat in a deckchair at the edge of the swimming pool, whose tiles of lapis lazuli blue somehow paled into insignificance in comparison to the vista of the Indian Ocean, at which I couldn't help but cast furtive glances every few minutes. I was reading one of Enid Blyton's Famous Five books (the one that featured the titular children up on the Yorkshire moors with an entomologist schoolteacher and tunnels full of "spook trains"). My father was in the pool, diligently swimming length after length. One of the chiropractors or osteopaths that he had consulted had, I remember, told him that swimming would be good for his osteoarthritis, and so he swam as often as he could. Like his eldest son, he never did anything by halves, and if he was told to swim, he would swim obsessively, cutting most other things out of his mind.

Up came an exotically clad Indian bellboy, or something like that. Emphatically, but with due deference, he called to my father to get out of the pool. Apparently, some of the lady guests were offended by the fact that my father's swimming trunks were far skimpier than was the current mode on the west coast of India. In fact, they were so brief, that my father was in danger of infringing the local legislation on the matter. Then, as now, I found the whole affair rather amusing, but knowing what an irrational 'old chap' (he was actually fifteen years younger than I am now) he was, and also what a devotee of not "sparing the rod" in order to not "spoil the child", I thought that it was wiser to keep my own counsel on the subject. This is something that I have done for forty-nine years.

But, our main objective in Bombay (or, I suppose, I should call it 'Mumbai', but as it wasn't 'Mumbai' back then, I don't feel inclined to) was neither swimming, Enid Blyton, nor monkeys. It had to do with the Sea Cadet Corps.

My father was always, at heart, a sailor, which was why – at his funeral – I read Robert Louis Stevenson's *Requiem* about the "sailor home from the sea". He had always wanted to be a sailor and he spent the second world war as a radio officer in the Merchant Navy all the way through the Battle of the Atlantic. He was torpedoed, swept overboard in a hurricane, and had all sorts of other horrific adventures. When the war was over, he continued in the Merchant Navy for a couple more years and only came ashore in order to marry my mother. But saltwater was always in his veins, and even when he was working on a North Devon farm in the years before he and my mother emigrated to Africa, he felt the pull of the great oceans, and so was pivotally involved with setting up the North Devon Sea Cadets.

Years later, in 1968, he was also pivotally involved with setting up the Hong Kong Sea Cadets, and although I was never a member I was one of the poster boys for the organisation, as I appeared on a widely distributed publicity photograph alongside a Chinese boy in full Sea Cadet uniform. I was stripped to the waist and posed in what these days would probably be seen as a somewhat homoerotic stance. This was purely because – not actually being a member – I didn't have a uniform, but my father (whose idea it had been) wanted to show that European boys and Chinese boys could stand together without prejudice in this brave new organisation. I was just embarrassed that all and sundry would see my nipples. I had no particular problem with family and friends seeing me in a state of undress, but the idea of everybody who read the *South China Morning Post* being able to see my semi-nakedness was more than my natural eleven year old modesty could stand.

Interestingly, whilst writing this chapter of my memoirs, and prompted by my amanuensis and stepdaughter, Olivia, I ended up looking up the beginnings of the Hong Kong Sea Cadet Corps. According to those jolly nice chaps at Wikipedia, it was started in 1968 by former members of the Hong Kong Royal Naval Reserve. As I have written elsewhere, my father was a keen member of this organisation, in which he was – I believe – a Lieutenant Commander. I still remember, vividly, how incandescently angry he was when, as a result of Harold Wilson's defence cutbacks in the 1968 budget, the Hong Kong RNR was one of the colonial organisations which was disbanded. He ranted about socialism for days, and was even more of a martinet towards me than usual. I can only imagine that being instrumental in forming the Hong Kong Sea Cadet Corps was his defence mechanism to make sure he managed to keep the saltwater in his veins.

A couple of years later, and along came the International Sea Cadets Association, which – again – he was one of the people involved in setting up, and with which he was involved until his death in 2006. Somehow, he had become friends with the person who set up the Sea Cadet Corps of India, or at least the part of it that was based in Bombay. I have a vague recollection that the two men had served together in some capacity either in Hong Kong or during the war, but I cannot be sure, in the same way as I have no memory of the man's name nor of anything else much about him. However, my father was scheduled to pay a semi-official visit to this man and his 'ship' in Bombay, either on behalf of the Hong Kong Sea Cadet Corps or for its international big brother.

I put the word 'ship' in quotation marks because it was actually an enormous concrete edifice, like the 'ship' on the shore of Portmeirion as made famous by *The Prisoner*. I remember it being a full-size battleship, made of concrete and stuck on the shoreline of some docks. However, I was eleven years old, and many gallons of alcohol and not a few ounces of various narcotics have gone through my veins in the intervening years, so forgive me if I don't remember.

Olivia and I had a quick shufti on the internet and she soon found a photograph of something called the *T.S. Jawahar* (T.S. standing for Training Ship) which is, indeed, a massive concrete battleship looking far more impressive than I remember it, named after and having been consecrated by Pandit Jawaharlal Nehru, the first Prime Minister of India and the bloke who allegedly was shagging Lady Mountbatten, the wife of the last Viceroy.

We were shown, reverently, around this monolithic structure and although I remember my father being ecstatically impressed and my mother being graciously polite, my little brother and I were both slightly bored and I spent most of my time daydreaming about all the exotic wildlife that I was certain that I would have been able to find had I not been stuck on an ugly, vast, concrete boat for one of my only precious afternoons on the Indian subcontinent.

That evening, we went to dinner with my father's colleague and ate a meal that I'm sure now I would have found delicious, but which was a little too exotic for my eleven year old palette. I was more interested in the fact that there were two huge tokay geckos which scampered up and down the wall and along the ceiling of the sitting room of our hosts, brazenly feeding off the myriad insects which were attracted to the ceiling light fitting.

The next day was my last in Asia for nine long years. In fact, apart from a brief trip back to Hong Kong financed by a legacy from my dead great-aunt in December 1980, it was my last time in Asia to the present day. This was not intentional, it is just that my explorations have taken me to Central America instead, over the past forty years, although I fully intend to return one day. However, as I am now in my seventh decade, and in fairly dire health, I am only too aware that my options are fast running out, and that if I am going to return to the place that I dream of nearly every night, I am going to have to get a move on. Dictating this narrative to Olivia, who doubles as my stepdaughter and my secretary, has filled me with a yearning to return to Hong Kong, and to take my family with me so they can see for themselves what all the fuss is about. But I have to say that I am terrified at the prospect; the places I have described in this narrative were beginning to disappear fifty years ago, and I have to admit that the totalitarian Special Administrative Region of the People's Republic of China – which, at the time of writing, is displaying a distinct whiff of tear gas to the world outside – does not seem to be the inviting homeland that I remember so fondly.

But I digress.

At the dock, we boarded a huge (or it seemed huge to me, but it was nothing like the leviathan cruise ships that are so depressingly familiar these days) ocean liner, whose name I am embarrassed to say I have forgotten. It was owned by an Italian company, had something like a hundred passengers, and was to carry us home to Europe with stops off at various African locations along the way.

We had to queue in a rather grubby building at the edge of the waterside, and – not for the first time in my life, or indeed, this narrative – my imagination ran away with itself. Underneath the ubiquitous election poster for Indira Ghandi ("Indira's people are India's people") was a sign warning that:

"Taking Indian currency out of India is a serious offense punishable by incarceration".

I had a few rupee coins in my trouser pocket. I doubt whether in total they came to more than twenty or thirty pence in value, but I dearly coveted them for my coin collection, and didn't say anything about them, even though I was afraid that I was risking "incarceration" at the pleasure of the Indian Government. After all, Indira's people were India's people, and a little white boy who was not sure whether he belonged in Hong Kong or in England was highly unlikely to be treated leniently by the powers that be.

So I was terrified as we went through the disembarkation procedure and was literally sweating from every pore. When we got on the ship, I realised that my mother had become seriously worried about me and took my temperature, fearing that I had succumbed to my father's old nemesis of Tropical Malaria. Shamefacedly, I admitted that I had put the whole family's liberty in jeopardy just in order to further my nascent career as a numismatologist.

For some reason, my mother found that immensely funny and kindly explained to me that there had been some recent high-profile fraud cases where high-ranking Indian government officials had smuggled large sums of money out of the country in order to trade it at profit on the international market. She was sure, she explained, that I was unlikely to have committed any crime that the authorities, either in India or England, would have the slightest interest in.

We found our way on board and an impressive looking fellow from the Purser's office showed us to our cabin. He was positively dripping in gold braid, his white uniform was spotless and his shoes were – literally – so high polished that, as he walked, they not only reflected back what was around him but caused fast moving reflective shapes to be projected on the walls and ceilings of the corridors through which we were being ushered. The corridors were all painted in refreshing blues and greens, all the signs were in Italian and English, and the projected reflections from his uniform footwear skittered like ethereal fish along the walls and ceilings. Although my parents had originally tried to get a stateroom, for some reason none were available, and we had to make do with two fairly small adjacent cabins; one for Richard and me and the other for my parents. This was exciting enough as far as my brother and I were concerned, but we didn't understand the complicated social structure of life on the ocean waves, and my parents both sulked massively for the rest of the voyage.

Having left our luggage in the cabin, my mother took us on deck, leaving my father fulminating like a bad-tempered water buffalo on their bed. My parents had a double bed in their cabin, whereas Richard and I had highly nautical bunks. We immediately fell in with the nautical mindset, and replied "aye aye sir" and saluted whenever anybody asked us anything, which must have been mildly embarrassing - not to say irritating - for my mother, whom I remember being astonishingly forbearing to us.

Navigating our way through the labyrinthine passages and out on deck into the tropical sunshine was far more difficult now we didn't have the Italian naval officer as guide. But we got there in the end, and, as always, were immediately enthralled by the sights, sounds and smells of a tropical harbour.

But this tropical harbour had something which I had never seen before, and have never seen since: a resident population of dolphins in a busy harbour. I had been excited enough three years earlier to see one dolphin. This was overkill.

These were delightful creatures, although I have no idea what species. One of the signature animals of Hong Kong is their resident population of pink dolphins. It seems, these days, as if you only have to type 'Hong Kong wild animals' into a search engine and you will find a hundred different accounts of dolphin watching expeditions. However, in all my family's explorations of the Hong Kong archipelago, we never saw a single one. The Hong Kong pink dolphins are, by the way, a race of the Indo-Pacific humpback dolphins (*Sousa chinensis*).

They are roughly the same size as the more well-known bottle-nosed dolphins, but are born black, gradually changing their colour to grey and then white when they get older. But sometimes, the adults appear a bright shade of pink – as pink as bubblegum – due to the blood vessels located very close to the skin, which act as a cooling mechanism. Like all dolphins, they have a layer of blubber, but when in warm, tropical waters, they need to lose heat by passing blood through the surface blood vessels. So when they get hot, this cooling mechanism kicks in, and they – literally – blush.

The freshwater dolphins of the river Amazon can also be pink in colour, but this is mostly because the males lose the outer layer of skin due to fighting and other rough and tough delphinic activity.

The dolphins which I watched, enraptured, for the next hour or two were mostly grey, although I remember their pectoral fins were pinkish in colour, presumably also as a heat regulatory mechanism. They spent most of their time feeding from the enormous shoals of little fish, which darted through the water like quicksilver or the reflections from the boots of the Purser's Mate. These, I hypothesised, had been attracted into the harbour by the lure of all the edible garbage that was cavalierly chucked in by people working on the boats or the wharfs alongside. You could even see vast shoals of little silver fish swimming bravely in from the ocean, towards their doom, and I would probably have felt sorry for them if it had not been for the fact that the dolphins were so immeasurably groovy.

Yes, you did read me right. Although I was still of the mindset that had been drilled into me by my parents, that people with long hair were 'twits' and beneath my contempt, the youngsters of Hong Kong had adopted some of the vocabulary of the hippie and beatnik movements, and 'groovy' was a word that I adopted aged ten, and have used intermittently ever since, much to the embarrassment of my nearest and dearest.

When the dolphins weren't actively hunting their supper, they appeared to be just playing. I know that it is anthropomorphic in many people's eyes to say such a thing, but these fantastic marine mammals gave every impression of conducting their complex nautical acrobatics for the sheer hell of it. Much to my great delight, these dolphins (or, at least, very similar ones) were to accompany us all the way across the Indian ocean on the next stage of our journey.

My only other memory of this day is a far less pleasant one.

I know that I am referring to events which are now half a century in the past, but a lot has changed over that half century. And changed for the better.

My father decided that it was his duty as paterfamilias to join his family on deck, and so – despite his ever present pain in his back and legs – he rose from his rest, locked the cabin, and made his way to join the rest of us. Along the way, he encountered a small English boy whose name I completely forget, and in some manner that I also completely forget, the boy was cheeky to him. Cheek from the younger generation was one of the things that was anathema to my old man, and he immediately retaliated by picking the boy up and giving him a sound spanking on his bare bottom. These days, quite rightly, this would have ended up with my father being arrested and charged with assault, or even worse. And it shows how far we have progressed as a society, that when the little boy ran to his parents in tears to complain, his parents came and apologised to my father rather than reporting him to the police.

Although in most ways, I miss the world in which I was brought up, in some ways we have definitely progressed in the past fifty years.

And so, we set off on an intrepid voyage across the Indian Ocean, towards the Red Sea. Unlike our voyage to Australia three years before, this journey was far less interesting both from a natural history point of view, and – indeed – from any other. For one thing, the boat was much larger, which meant that the complement of passengers was also larger and that the experience of the voyage was far more conventional.

There were quite a few children on board, and both Richard and I did the things that children on cruise ships always have done, like energetic games on deck, and other such activities laid on for our benefit by the authorities. Richard, by this time nearly eight years old, fitted into this society much more readily than did I. I, as I have done at various other times throughout my life, retreated into the ship's library, and descended into the cerebral world of books.

It was on this journey that I first discovered the stories of Edith Nesbitt. As I have written elsewhere, I had discovered the fantasy tales of C. S. Lewis nearly five years before, but even the eleven-year-old me could realise that, with Nesbitt, here was the motherlode. Despite the fact that I loved the Narnia books (and still do), it was so obvious that Nesbitt's books had been a massive influence on Lewis, and it was quite an eye-opener for me to discover that authors did not exist in a vacuum; that they – like the rest of us – had things that inspired them and influenced them in the same way as their books have inspired and influenced me.

As has always been the case throughout my life, I have taken inspiration where I can find it, and it was one of the books by Nesbitt that inspired my next project. In one of them, the child protagonists had done something to annoy or antagonise one of the family servants...

[As an aside here, I know that other people of my age living in England had found the idea of a family with servants a difficult one with which to grapple. But remember, I wasn't an ordinary English lad. Until only a few weeks before, I had lived with my family servants, and the idea of such things was not at all difficult for me to understand.]

... and as an apology to her, they had taken photographs of themselves, "floated the image off the card backing", and made a picture for her, drawing an intricate and decorative border to each photograph.

"I could do that", I thought to myself. I had a small but functional Box Brownie camera with which I could take photographs of which I was very proud (despite the fact that they were in black and white and I could only get seven pictures to each roll of film). So, I decided that I would enlist the other children on the boat to be bit part players in my new project; a mixture of drawings and photographs in book form, called 'Fun Aboard Ship'. I'm afraid that I remember very little about this, mostly because it was half a century ago as I write, but I do know that I took my precious rolls of film back to England and then – for whatever reason – never did anything with them. That is probably an encapsulation of the story of my life, but I remember vague bits of my complex scenario, including one segment whereupon a gaggle of my 'cast' leaned over the rail, pointing out to sea, as if they had seen a sea-serpent. But that's about all that I do remember.

I don't have any nasty memories of that particular voyage, mainly because I don't really have any memories at all, it was just there; another experience in a lifetime that seems to me to have been crammed with them.

A week or so after we had left the docks at Bombay, we arrived in the eastern African maritime city of Mombasa. This was the first part of the voyage which really interested me, because, for the first time in my life, I was about to go on safari.

All the way through my life, the concept of the dark continent of Africa, full of exotic animals and even more exotic people, had been what I believe is currently known as a trope. My early readings in cryptozoology, mixed with the adventures of Allan Quartermain and various other things that I had read over the years, had led me to expect wonderful things. Even as the vast majority of the passengers on the ship made their way towards the small flotilla of open-topped trucks which were to take us to the world famous Tsavo National Park, I was convinced that this journey would see me being the first English scientist to prove the existence of the 'missing link' and capture (or at least photograph) a hulking manbeast, finally ensuring myself – at the age of eleven – a place within zoological history. As we drove along the red dirt road which led from the busy port to the jewel of the Kenyan conservation services, I was convinced that, if I looked hard enough at the mountains silhouetted in the distance, I would see a pterosaur like the one that may or may not have been encountered by Ivan T. Sanderson many years ago in a different part of Africa. Truly the imagination of an eleven year old boy is a pretty remarkable thing, and I like to think that, whilst I have developed a healthy dose of cynicism over the years, that the wide-eyed eleven year old boy drinking in the first sights and sounds of the dark continent is still in there somewhere, and still comes out on occasion to irritate his elders and betters.

I don't know how long it took us to get to Tsavo, and it doesn't really matter, but get there we eventually did. And I still vividly remember the first two things that happened.

A few months before, my family had been watching a nature documentary on television about what it called 'Small Game'. The premise of the show was that everybody went to Africa and filmed elephants, lions, and rhinos, but that there were just as many interesting creatures to be found hiding underneath rocks, or the loose bark on trees. So, the first thing that I did once we got out of the truck in order to stretch our legs, was to look under the loose bark of a dead tree, twenty or thirty feet away from where our rusty vehicle had been parked. And yet, for one of the first times in my life, television had not lied to me. There, shivering in the light, was a brace of extraordinary looking geckos. They had thick scales that looked like the armour worn by a medieval percheron, and were blotched in dark brown and virulent green; so much more exciting than the three or four species of gecko I knew so well from back in Hong Kong.

I ran back to my parents, babbling in excitement, and my father had a soft and tender look in his eyes as he came over to admire the lizards with me.

He then pointed out two insanely colourful lizards, which I recognised as a type of agama because they were so remarkably similar, morphologically, to the big garden lizards I knew back in Hong Kong, on a large rock nearby. But these were brightly coloured, and I could see why they had acquired the English name of 'rainbow lizard'. We watched them for ten minutes, fascinated by the way that the dominant male lizard would display colourfully to attract one or more of the adoring females of his species that skittered up and down the lower reaches of the rock, and how – on occasion – his colours would get even more impressive, as he entered into territorial skirmishes with other males.

I was still fascinated by the social behaviour of these resplendent agamas, but then my father took me by the hand and told me that he wanted to show me something I'd never seen before.

Ten or twenty yards away was a small hillock, maybe thirty feet tall, certainly no great shakes in the mountain department. But it was steep enough to climb in the vivid heat of an east African noonday sun, which was far hotter than anything I had ever experienced on the shores of the South China Sea. But we made it to the top, and my father and I looked out over the vast east African plain. I could see what looked a little bit like a group of grey boulders, but which my father said was a small family group of elephants. More obvious, and less self-effacing, were various antelopes of different shapes and sizes, which were scattered willy-nilly across the landscape; some solitary and others in small herds. And there, in the distance, was a unmistakable giraffe.

My father took my hand. "You've never seen this before, or not since you were a baby. But you know what it is you are looking at?"

I shook my head, aware that this was a peculiarly pivotal moment in my relationship with my father.

"It's miles of fucking Africa! And once you get that red dust in your veins, it never leaves, and it will be with you forever", he said, softly. And I could see that he was crying.

Seeing the wide-open plains of East Africa for the first, and – indeed – only, time in my life was an absolutely awe-inspiring experience. Having been brought up with both factual and fictional television programmes set amongst the huge herds of what was still known as 'big game', and having avidly read the mammoth pile of *National Geographic* magazines that one of my father's work colleagues had given me, I thought that I was prepared for Tsavo National Park, but I was sadly mistaken. Nothing could have prepared me for the sheer, primal rush of seeing the birthplace of humanity for the first time.

I had read all about Doctor Louis Leakey and his discoveries of our distant ancestors, just over the border in Tanzania, and so I knew only too well that the red laterite dust, which was everywhere before me, had flowed in the veins of the human race since long before we existed. I understood what my father had said about Africa being an addictive drug, but for me it was quite understandable. I was standing on the same ground that the very earliest humans stood upon, and therefore, it was not at all surprising that I was experiencing such an existential rush of emotion.

I could probably have stood on that little hillock, holding my father's hand, and staring out over the trackless waste before me – all day. But, we didn't have all day. The jolly looking African driver was tapping his watch impatiently, and so my father and I left the intimacy of our bonding reverie, and climbed back onto the peculiar looking charabanc, which had been painted in the obligatory zebra stripes that identified it all and sundry across the world as a safari vehicle.

And so, our own little safari began.

I had, of course, seen elephants in zoos and as I note elsewhere in this narrative, I had made friends with, and - in the mildly annoying current vernacular – got 'up close and personal' with a baby Asiatic elephant a couple of weeks or so before, outside our hotel in Bangkok, but nothing was to prepare me for quite how majestic a small herd of African elephants - the women and children being chaperoned along by a huge, fully tusked, male - was actually going to be. In fact, that's not quite true.

I have written elsewhere about how my grandfather had taken me to the British Museum of Natural History for the first time, back in 1964. One of my favourite exhibits there was something which has been locked up in the voluminous vault of this magnificent building, as it is no longer seen as appropriate for the sensibilities of our current age. James Rowland Ward (1848-1912) was one of the most famous British taxidermists, and amongst other exhibits, he constructed a magnificent series of dioramas at the museum in South Kensington. I was completely flabbergasted by the Rowland Ward Pavilion, as it was called, and it remained one of my favourite places to visit whenever I went to the metropolis for the next thirty or forty years. But one of the reasons that I am so disappointed that the Rowland Ward Pavilion was dismantled in 2004 is that it did manage to convey a little of the incredible feeling of awe that one experiences when first seeing these mighty animals in their own habitat.

We met several small family groups of elephants throughout the day, and on one occasion the alpha male of one particular herd even charged our vehicle in a half-hearted sort of way, but it was a fearsome enough experience that our jolly driver hastily got into reverse gear and drove backwards up the track as fast as he could, until the bull elephant, obviously thinking that honour had been satisfied, glared at us one last time before turning on his tail and marching back to join his family, who stood staring at him admiringly.

We also saw rhinos, mostly black but also – we were told – the much rarer white rhino, although, whilst putting this narrative together, and checking with those jolly nice people at Wikipedia, they imply that the northern white rhinoceros was never found in Kenya. Here, I suppose, I should point out to those who do not know, that the specific common names 'black' and 'white' don't actually refer to the colour of the creature, as both species are a uniform greyish colour. 'White' actually is a corruption of the Afrikaans word 'wijd', meaning 'wide', referring to the width of the rhinoceros's mouth.

It is sad to note that the northern white rhinoceros is now functionally extinct, with only two specimens – both female – still alive. There is hope, although I am not a geneticist or anything like it, and so I cannot truly comment upon the subject with any great authority, that frozen sperm from the testes of deceased males of the species could be used to fertilise the females, but – at the time of writing in March 2020 – all these attempts have failed, possibly because the two females are now too old to easily become pregnant.

Bizarrely, the only giraffes that we saw all day were the ones that my father and I had spotted from our earlier vantage point, but we saw all sort of other ungulates; big and small, mostly antelope of varying sizes, shapes and colours. Something that I hadn't realised until seeing them in the flesh, is that each of these various species of antelope behaved in a completely different manner. Each filled a different ecological niche, and it was only then that I understood what my spiritual mentor Gerald Durrell had said, when he wrote of what a tragedy it is when humankind lets a species go extinct, because it completely upsets the balance of nature.

Driving along a steep escarpment, we looked down and saw a slow-moving shallow river, and on the banks what seemed to be long planks of wood lying languorously in the tropical sun. But they weren't planks of wood, they were huge Nile crocodiles. It was the last time I was to see a wild crocodilian until 2003, when my mate Nick Redfern and I were driving along a long, straight, road through the swamps on the Texas/Louisiana border. We pulled into a layby to answer a call of nature, and as I gazed vaguely over the shallow swampy pond by the side of the road, I saw a small American alligator slipping off the bank into the water.

I was disappointed that we didn't see any of the big cats, but as we were leaving the national park on our way back to Mombasa, we saw a lean and hungry looking lioness, slinking furtively through the undergrowth only a few hundred yards away from our vehicle. I fantasised that she had been one of the descendants of the famous 'man-eaters of Tsavo', a pair of peculiarly maneless male lions which were responsible for the deaths of up to 135 people in the district, back in 1898.

I had read J. H. Patterson's 1926 book, *The Man-Eating Lions of Tsavo*, back in Hong Kong, and had become morbidly fascinated by the whole affair. At the end of the crisis, the British Prime Minister, Lord Salisbury explained why work on the East African railway had been so badly delayed:

> "The whole of the works were put to a stop because a pair of man-eating lions appeared in the locality and conceived a most unfortunate taste for our workmen. At last the labourers entirely declined to carry on unless they were guarded by iron entrenchments. Of course it is difficult to work a railway under these conditions and until we found an enthusiastic sportsman to get rid of these lions our enterprise was seriously hindered."

We saw baboons, monkeys, ostriches and vultures, but all too soon it was time to return to Mombasa, re-join our ship, and get on with the next stage of our voyage.

And so, the Downes family, together with perhaps another hundred or so passengers, continued our voyage; and we sailed down the east coast of Africa towards our next ports of call. And do you know what? I can hardly remember a thing about it.

My diaries of the time have long since vanished, and so I have nothing really to act as an *aide memoire.*

My only memories of this part of the voyage are disjointed and mostly unhelpful. I, of course, remember the big kerfuffle when the ship passed through the equator going south, and Lord Neptune (again, in reality, one of the crew) presided over the ceremony of Crossing the Line. All the young people on board enjoyed this immensely, but I was a seasoned traveller and this was my third time travelling in between hemispheres, and the whole thing left me rather jaded.

I remember one of the other young people on the passenger list telling me proudly how he tormented frogs while living at his home in India. And I remember another swarthy young man, a year or two older than me, who, followed at a discreet distance by what seemed to be all the young women under the age of twenty-five on board, swaggered up and down the deck as if he owned it. As it turned out, as he was some sort of Arabian princeling, he probably did. Me? I mostly kept myself to myself, sitting alone on deck reading my beloved Edith Nesbit, or gazing out to sea, hoping to spy a sea-serpent.

Somewhere along the line, my parents decided that I was putting on weight, and so they unilaterally said that I was not to eat midday meals from then on. It was about thirty years before I was to discover that fasting is actually one of the worst ways of trying to lose excess adipose tissue, and so my sufferings were completely useless. All they did was to upset and alienate me, and to sow the seeds of the eating disorder which I have had pretty much ever since.

Luckily, although I was – unsurprisingly – lonely, and isolated from the rest of the people of my own age upon the vessel, I could, and did, gain endless satisfaction from watching the flying fish skitter out the way of our approaching craft, the dolphins playing in the bow wave, and the albatrosses which became more and more common the further south we went.

The next port of call was Durban, the European settlement of which had been founded a hundred and fifty years before, when *HMS Salisbury* – a fifty-eight-gun 'fourth rate Ship of the Line' – was travelling from the Portuguese colony of Mozambique to the British at the Cape of Good Hope. They got caught in a terrific storm and pulled in to a convenient shelter in the Bay of Natal.

They started a small trading colony in order to engage in commerce with King Shaka kaSenzangakhona, also known as Shaka Zulu, who was a minor character in several of the books of Henry Rider Haggard, an author of whom I was (and am) very fond. We stayed in Durban for a day and a half, and – although I know full well that we explored parts of the city – I cannot remember anything about it. Together with a few members of the ship's passenger list, and a motley group of locals and trippers, we took a coach trip to a 'wildlife park', where - it was alleged – that we would see more of the giants of the African veldt. But, after the magnificence of Tsavo, this was very small beer indeed. I remember a few zebra and a few bored-looking antelopes, and a solitary, bad-tempered-looking rhinoceros. This was no valuable slice of unspoiled Africa, and there was certainly nothing here for my father to share a bonding moment with. To be honest, it felt both civilised and genteel; more like a semi-cultivated piece of parkland in rural England, than a virgin portion of the dark continent. My father was obviously as unimpressed as I, as my only real memory of this sojourn, apart from the disgruntled rhino, was my father adopting an outrageous South African accent and singing a song about a South African boy who wanted to visit the big city of Durban, in order to buy 'Eskimo Pie', which was apparently some sort of ice cream. The South African members of our company looked annoyed by this, but kept their own counsel, as we returned to the ship and made ready for our departure.

Having been totally underwhelmed by Durban, I was actually very much looking forward to the next item on our itinerary, which was to brave the stormy seas off the Cape of Good Hope, which had first been rounded in 1488 by Portuguese explorer Bartolomeu Dias. Herodotus, writing in the fourth or fifth century BC, implies that unnamed Phoenician mariners had done the same thing five hundred years before the birth of Christ, but even in 1971, to sale 'round the Cape' was a nautical excursion worthy of Nancy Blackett.

Much to my surprise, my father and I were two of the only passengers on deck to brave the salt spray and to see the southernmost tip of Africa (actually, it's not, but that is besides the point) looming out of the mist, many miles to Port. I prattled incessantly, and probably – with fifty years hindsight – annoyed my father immensely, but – for once – he kept the annoyance to himself.

A couple of days later, we sailed into Cape Town.

I remember a little bit more about Cape Town than I do about Durban. Our coach trip this time was to the Constantia Valley, which was (and probably still is) a major grape-growing and wine-making district, which, as my first dabblings with the 'Demon Drink' were six or seven years in the future, and there was no wildlife to be seen whatsoever, left me completely uninterested.

What was more exciting, as far as I was concerned, was the steam railway locomotive that puffed away in a corner of the docks, pulling wagonloads of cargo from one place to another, with eternal industriousness. It was the only time, as far as I'm aware, in my life, that I ever saw a steam locomotive which wasn't just preserved for its own sake, and was actually doing the job for which it had been originally built.

Another thing which sticks in my mind was the fact that park benches, public lavatories, and drinking fountains were sometimes dedicated as 'Whites Only'. This both intrigued and upset me: back in Hong Kong, where the white minority were also the rulers, no such thing had been enforced! I had played alongside some Chinese children in school, sat with Chinese children at various sporting and cultural events, gone swimming with them in the vast South China sea, and I had even appeared, bare chested, alongside a Chinese boy in an advert for my father's Sea Cadet Corps. And this new (to me) manifestation of racial disunity was quite upsetting.

My mother whispered in my ear that she also found this racial segregation to be both disturbing and nauseating, and I remember this when – a decade or so in the future – the young hippie activist Jonathan, by then in his early twenties, had a flaming row with his parents about their regular holidays in P. W. Botha's South Africa.

As we sailed out of Cape Town to continue our long journey north towards Europe, we passed a whaling station, where, apparently, enormous piles of whale skeletons were visible. Another passenger, an adult who knew about my passion for natural history, pointed it out to me, but I had been looking at something else and totally missed it.

The 'something else' that had, and was to, occupy my mind fully during our time in South African waters, was the legendary *Flying Dutchman*, a ghost ship which is said to never make port, and which is doomed to sail the oceans forever.

George Barrington wrote this in 1795, in chapter six of *A Voyage to Botany Bay:*

> "I had often heard of the superstition of sailors respecting apparitions and doom, but had never given much credit to the report; it seems that some years since a Dutch man-of-war was lost off the Cape of Good Hope, and every soul on board perished; her consort weathered the gale, and arrived soon after at the Cape. Having refitted, and returning to Europe, they were assailed by a violent tempest nearly in the same latitude. In the night watch some of the people saw, or imagined they saw, a vessel standing for them under a press of sail, as though

she would run them down: one in particular affirmed it was the ship that had foundered in the former gale, and that it must certainly be her, or the apparition of her; but on its clearing up, the object, a dark thick cloud, disappeared. Nothing could do away the idea of this phenomenon on the minds of the sailors; and, on their relating the circumstances when they arrived in port, the story spread like wild-fire, and the supposed phantom was called the Flying Dutchman. From the Dutch the English seamen got the infatuation, and there are very few Indiamen, but what has some one on board, who pretends to have seen the apparition."

Even the future King George V saw the phantom vessel, in 1880, and wrote:

"July 11th. At 4 a.m. the *Flying Dutchman* crossed our bows. A strange red light as of a phantom ship all aglow, in the midst of which light the masts, spars and sails of a brig 200 yards distant stood out in strong relief as she came up on the port bow, where also the officer of the watch from the bridge clearly saw her, as did the quarterdeck midshipman, who was sent forward at once to the forecastle; but on arriving there was no vestige nor any sign whatever of any material ship was to be seen either near or right away to the horizon, the night being clear and the sea calm. Thirteen persons altogether saw her ... At 10.45 a.m. the ordinary seaman who had this morning reported the *Flying Dutchman* fell from the foretopmast crosstrees on to the topgallant forecastle and was smashed to atoms."

Although I had no wish to be "smashed to atoms", I dearly wanted to become one of the exclusive club of mariners who had encountered this spectral vessel. But, sadly, it was not to be.

About the only other thing that I can remember about our time in South Africa was that at one of the brace of ports we visited, the family of the swarthy boy about my age, with whom I had exchanged the sort of pleasantries that eleven year old boys do, and whom I mentioned in passing above, came on deck with his family, all of them in the highly ornate formal dress of Arab royalty. The whole family marched down the gangplank with an undeniably regal air, their robes and burnouses flowing behind them in the breeze. Their decorative keffiyeh held in place with an agal circlet, which sparkled with golden threads and precious stones. I have never seen anything like it before or since, and for about half an hour, as the boy's entire family disembarked slowly and were greeted by equally ornately dressed Arab men and women on the quay, we felt that we were witnessing something out of *Lawrence of Arabia*; a social interaction to which people like us were usually never privy.

That was probably the most memorable part of our visit to what was still then a state viciously divided upon racial lines. Even at the age of eleven, I found this institutionalised segregation deeply disturbing, and it upset me for many years that my parents seemed to feel so at home there that they visited regularly and made so many friends among the minority white community.

Soon, we were back at sea, heading northwards and leaving the land of apartheid behind us for good. I would love to tell you that I had adventures on that leg of the trip, but – truthfully (and I have always endeavoured to be truthful in this narrative) – I can't remember anything about it. Some days, or maybe a week, I don't know, later, we arrived in the Canary Islands. My only knowledge of the place was from one of Hugh Lofting's Dr Dolittle books, in which he said that the islands were distinguished by the huge flocks of bright yellow birds, which could be seen flying everywhere. And I was massively disappointed when I found that this was not the case.

The Atlantic canary (*Serinus canaria*), known worldwide simply as the wild canary and also called the island canary, canary, or common canary, is a small passerine bird belonging to the genus Serinus in the finch family, Fringillidae. It is native to the Canary Islands, the Azores, and Madeira. Wild birds are mostly yellow-green, with brownish streaking on the back. The species is common in captivity and a number of colour varieties have been bred.

The name Islas Canarias is most probably derived from the Latin "Canariae Insulae", meaning "Islands of the Dogs". According to Pliny the Elder, the Mauretanian King Juba II named the island Canaria because it contained "vast multitudes of dogs of very large size".

The Canary Islands are particularly interesting because, like many other of the Atlantic archipelagos, they are politically part of Europe, thought geographically part of the continent of Africa. They are also very interesting from a cryptozoological point of view. In the late 1990s, or the early years of this century, a species of large lizard which had only been known from fossil records was found to be living quite happily on the islands. But there are other less well-known cryptozoological aspects to the Canary Islands.

An old friend of mine, who has family on La Gomera, tells of a local belief that there are small, brown, rodents looking very much like guinea pigs, that were to be found in the wilder parts of the island when he was a boy. As he is roughly the same age as me, these animals would have been seen at about the same time that I visited Tenerife, back in 1971. The island, which is about fourteen miles in diameter, is of volcanic origin and is very mountainous. It has been described as being rather in the shape of an orange that has been cut in half and then split into segments, leaving deep ravines called barrancos. The upper most slopes of these barrancos are covered by a laurel rainforest which has up to fifty inches of rain a year. The upper reaches of these densely wooded regions are almost permanently shrouded in clouds and mist, and for complicated meteorological reasons, there are a whole string of fascinating microclimates, and so, the idea of there being unknown species of small mammal living there is a perfectly cogent one.

But what could these creatures be?

I have always had a theory that they might be exactly what they seem to be – guinea pigs. The cavy family is composed of rodents native to South America, and six species – although they have never been found in Guinea, and are certainly not porcine - are known as guinea pigs; the best known species being of a domestic guinea pig (*Cavia porcellus*) which is an important meat animal in South America and a common household pet in the rest of the world. I wonder, although I have never investigated it properly, whether cavies were commonly taken from South America on board Spanish trading ships as a food source, and could possibly have escaped and become naturalised in parts of La Gomera.

In my book, *The Island of Paradise* (2007), I use a similar theory to explain some of the sightings of what has become known as the chupacabras, positing that the trade ships from Africa carrying slaves or other tradable goods, may have taken West African porcupine species to the new world as food, and that they, in turn, may have escaped into the porcupine-friendly habitat of Puerto Rico.

But, I knew nothing about this then. And, quite apart from my disappointment at not seeing huge flocks of bright yellow canaries, the day and a half that we spent on Tenerife was massively underwhelming. It was raining continually, and most of the island was shrouded in mist. We went in a minibus up to one of the higher peaks of the island, where it was raining too hard for us to get out, but I noted the strange black sands and rocks which were everywhere in this peculiar volcanic island. But, I am afraid, after our extraordinary time in Kenya, most of the other ports of call on our voyage 'home' were a disappointment.

My first and only sighting of the Rock of Gibraltar was also surprisingly underwhelming. It was one of those big icons of the British Empire that I had been having instilled into me from my earliest childhood. But unlike the Gateway of India, in what was still Bombay, constructed between 1911 and 1924, and to which we had paid homage during our stay in India some weeks before, the Rock of Gibraltar – to me, at least – was just a rock; a bloody big rock, but a rock for all of that. And, as we were not close enough to see the monkeys, I was sadly uninterested.

But in the seaway approaching the straits of Gibraltar, where I was inwardly disappointed to find that the twin monsters Scylla and Charybdis no longer dwelt, I did have a zoological encounter which I have sadly never repeated.

Whilst, as you have read, at various times during our voyage from Hong Kong back to Europe, we saw various species of dolphin and porpoise, it had (and still is) been one of my dearest wishes to see one of the great whales. And in the seaway approaching the Rock of Gibraltar, I had my wish.

Well, sort of, anyway.

I was on deck with one of the senior crewmen. I have no memory of how, why, or who he was, but he grabbed my shoulder and pointed towards the murky, foggy horizon, which was far closer than it would have been on a clear day. For a few precious seconds, I saw a large, dark hump breaking the surface of the water, and the remains of a plume of spray, which the sailor told me was diagnostic of the exhalation belonging to a humpback whale. To date, and I am now sixty-one, it has been my only encounter with one of the Mysticeti.

It wasn't until many years later that I realised that I should not have been disappointed at the absence of Scylla and Charybdis. And not just because - as monstrous creatures - they never existed. I had taken my perusal of as many books on cryptozoology as I was able to get hold of very seriously, and – even at the age of eleven – believed firmly that there was probably a germ of truth behind any zoomythological creatures. And I had built up the possibility somewhere in my subconscious that Scylla and Charybdis were actually 'real' but immensely rare sea creatures, which, of course, would surface just as our gallant ship sailed through their hiding places.

I still remember the teacher who told us about Greek myths back in Hong Kong, four or five years earlier, saying that Scylla and Charybdis lived by the 'Pillars of Hercules' which most scholars agreed were the straits of Gibraltar.

But that is just not true.

Most authorities actually believe that the twin monsters were alleged to inhabit the Strait of Messina, which separates Sicily and the mainland of Italy, most significantly in the area of a natural, but treacherous whirlpool.

A day or so later, we pulled into the port of Barcelona, and I am afraid that – once again – there is very little that I remember about it. We were only there for a day, and all I can remember is my father repeatedly saying how good it was to see that, even though there had been no Spanish king on the throne since 1939, when General Franco and his coalition won the Spanish Civil War, the crown of the kingdom of Spain was everywhere, and it was well known that the young King Juan Carlos de Bourbon was poised to take leadership of the republic whenever Franco finally died.

After sixteen years without monarchy or kingdom, in 1947, Spain was made a Kingdom again by General Franco, who claimed to rule Spain as Head of state of the Kingdom of Spain through the Law of Succession. However, without a king on the throne, he ruled through a coalition of allied organizations from the Spanish Civil War including, but not limited to, the Falange political party, the supporters of the Bourbon royal family, and the Carlists, until his death in 1975.

My parents were unquestioning monarchists, and would pardon General Franco anything, because – according to things they read whilst in the country – he was 'grooming' the young Prince for Kingship. At the time of writing, King Juan Carlos has abdicated in favour of his son King Felipe, and appears to be being investigated for Fraud.

And then, from Barcelona, we travelled east across the Mediterranean towards our final destination of Brindisi. Having been an avid reader of the Roman Empire fiction of Rudyard Kipling and Rosemary Sutcliffe, I was prepared to be far more impressed by Italy than I had been Spain. After all, the only way that Spain had insinuated itself into my cultural world view was through the relevant chapters of *The Voyages of Dr Dolittle* which waxed lyrical about the evils of bullfighting. But Italy had produced Romans, and the Centurion Pertinax, and it was to be another year or so before I had my mind polluted with stories of the horrors of the Roman arena.

We sailed up the eastern coast of Sicily, and I saw my first live volcano. Mount Etna grumbled away implacably with a small but steady wisp of smoke coming out of her summit. But she was unquestionably a volcano, and she was the last active volcano I was to see until driving past Popocatépetl nearly thirty years later, whilst on an expedition to Mexico in search of the grotesque, vampiric chupacabras. We pulled in to the quay at Brindisi and disembarked, leaving our home of the previous five or six weeks. We said our goodbyes to our erstwhile companions, but even at the age of eleven, I knew that the promises to stay in touch with our friends were empty ones, and that we would never see each other – or even think of each other, much – again. We had three hours or so to kill before catching a train north to Milan, and there was somewhere that I particularly wanted to see. And much to my surprise, both of my parents agreed.

The Appian Way is one of the earliest and strategically most important Roman roads, and was the first long road specifically built to transport troops outside the smaller region of Greater Rome. Thus, it was the first of the complex network of roads which crisscrossed the empire, and which made the Roman Empire the political and military success that it was. At the end of the Appian Way is a monument; an impressive stone tower which for over two thousand years has stood as a monument to the majesty of Imperial Rome. I wanted to see it, and it didn't cost anything, so my parents happily acquiesced, and I spent a happy half hour gazing at it in awe.

It is strange how the passage of time can leave one with enormous blanks in one's memory. When I wrote my autobiography, *Monster Hunter*, back in 2004, I found that when I got to writing about events from only three years earlier, I couldn't remember anything that I'd done. This was mostly because of the bad behaviour which characterised much of my early middle-age, but I cannot use that excuse here. I was eleven, and eleven-year-olds – or this one, at least – didn't indulge in substance abuse in 1971.

Somehow we got from Brindisi in Southern Italy to Milan in the north of the country, and as I have vague memories of being on a train at Milan Railway Station, I assume that we got there by train. But I am afraid that I have absolutely no concrete memories of Italy whatsoever. It was Easter weekend, and the next thing that I remember is waking up in a hotel in the beautiful Swiss city of Lausanne. My father was unwell; I think the journey had finally been too much for him, and he was spending the morning of – what I think was – Easter Saturday in bed, while my mother took Richard and me out into the city to let off steam. She was as tired as my dad, but she sat down on a park bench, looking at Lake Geneva, while Richard and I wandered about, exploring, vaguely responding to her exultations not to go too far away.

This was the biggest lake I had ever seen, and as it is the second or third largest lake in western Europe (depending on your definition of a lake), because the two largest are actually inlets of the sea, which have been closed off by The Netherlands, this is not really surprising. There were no lakes in Hong Kong, and I don't think I had ever seen a body of freshwater much larger than Tai Tam Tuk reservoir. So, with my head full of cryptozoology, I was sure that such an impressive body of water had to have had a mysterious denizen or two, so I set out to look for lake monsters.

And it wasn't long before I saw one.

If I remember correctly – and, unlike my memories of Italy, my memory of that morning in Lausanne are crystal clear – my young brother was pretending to be a racing car and speeding up and down an imaginary track, whilst I furrowed my brow and, using my right hand as a sunshade, surveyed the surface of the water intently. Suddenly, hardly believing the evidence of my own eyes, I saw a black hump break the surface of the water, and a few minutes later, it was followed by a matte black flipper. I don't think I had ever been so excited in my young life. I didn't know whether Lake Geneva had been reputed to be the haunt of a monster, or not, but I was just about to go down in history for having discovered it.

The most famous monster from Lake Geneva is, of course, none other than Frankenstein's very own monster, because Mary Shelley famously wrote the book whilst on holiday with her husband, Lord Byron, and various other members of their collective household. There are various stories of a more traditional lake monster in Lake Geneva, but the stories are vague and difficult to substantiate. But I, eleven-year -old Jonathan Downes, knew that they were all completely true. And I would go down in cryptozoological history as a result. I started to plan what I would tell the world's press when I told everyone about my discovery, and I think that I was being presented with a gold medal by The Queen when the scuba diver I had been watching surfaced, and I mentally kicked myself for not having realised what it actually was that I had been gawping at for the last few minutes.

I went back to my mother, feeling rather chastened, and I don't think I ever told anyone about this non-experience for many years. At least not until I had learned not to take myself quite so seriously.

The people at the hotel were very kind to Richard and me, and, because it was Easter, they made a big thing about having these two small English children from Hong Kong come into the hotel kitchen to decorate eggs for our breakfast the next day.

Then, on Sunday afternoon, we went as a family on an excursion up one of the Swiss mountains. Again, my cryptozoological Spidey Sense was triggered, as I was convinced that I was going to find a tatzelwurm.

For those of you who are unaware of this peculiar central European cryptid, in Alpine folklore, the tatzelwurm or tollenwurm, a lizard-like creature, often described as having the face of a cat, with a serpent-like body which may be slender or stubby, with four short legs or two forelegs.

The alleged creature is sometimes said to be venomous, or to attack with poisonous breath, and to make a high-pitched or hissing sound.

Anecdotes describing encounters with the creature or briefly described lore about them can be found in several areas of Europe, including the Austrian, Bavarian, Italian and Swiss Alps. It has several other regional names, including bergstutz, springwurm, praatzelwurm, and in French, arassas.

Those of you who have followed me through this long and rambling narrative will remember that, some years before I had annoyed my teachers by saying that the reason that I wanted to go to Switzerland was to see one of their magnificent green lizards. So, I had high hopes in our expedition to the edge of the snowline. Not only was it one of the few times in my life I'd actually seen snow, but if I wasn't going to capture a tatzelwurm, I was certainly going to see a whole bevvy of bright green lizards. Well, I actually did a find a lizard. It was about an inch long, very dead, and very smelly, and my parents refused to let me take it to England with me as the first item in my nascent cryptozoological museum. At the time, I thought they were just being unkind, and even worse, unscientific, but now – a decade and a half older than my father was at the time – I understand their motivation and sympathise with them wholeheartedly.

My only other memory of Switzerland was seeing a pen containing a family of wild boar, with their spotted babies looking for all the world like giant bumblebees, and making similar guttural grunting buzzy noises as they bumbled along.

Then it was time for another train, and we made our way towards France, travelling through a huge tunnel which I assume was the Mont Blanc Tunnel, linking Switzerland and France.

For years, after having read *The Lure of the Falcon* by Gerald Summers, I tried to fool myself that an episode in the book when he – at the same age as I was, travelling by train through the vast forests of central Europe – saw a lone wolf by the side of the track actually happened to me. Although I can remember it vividly, I am sure that I made it up.

By the time we arrived in Paris, I was heartily sick of our journey. It had been quite sedate and civilised whilst we had been on board ship, but trains and taxis were beginning to grate upon me, and I annoyed both my parents by not being wildly excited or impressed by our visit to the most beautiful city in western Europe. The statues of scantily clad young women, which would have been alluring had I been by myself, were nearly embarrassing while I was holding my mother's hand, and I was disappointed to find that The Louvre was shut on the day we were there, and so I couldn't see the Mona Lisa, or, indeed, the Tomb of Napoleon for some reason or other. And these are the only reasons that I actually wanted to go to Paris in the first place. And then, while walking as a family alongside the Great River Seine, I was excited to find market stall vendors selling magnificent specimens of various species of crested newt. But my parents were adamant that we were not going to arrive back in the Motherland for their retirement, clutching bags full of lissamphibians, whether or not it would have been legal for us to do so.

So, our visit to Paris was a disappointment on practically every level. At the hotel that night, my mother did what she always did under these circumstances, and went out "foraging" and came back with a medley of various things to eat, of which I can only remember *pain au chocolat*, which didn't impress me very much. However, I was tired, grumpy and cross, and I don't think anything would have impressed me very much at that stage.

And so, early the next morning, we took the train to Calais and caught the ferry across the channel. Despite the fact that I had been on our little boat *The Ailsa* during the beginnings of a typhoon, and been round the Cape of Good Hope, and the edges of the Bay of Biscay, all with no ill-effects, the ferry across the English Channel made me feel very queasy indeed. I said as much to my parents, but my father told me I was being an idiot, and that I would be letting down the honour of the family if I were to be sick, and so I manfully resisted.

Peculiarly, although I have been in other rough waters since with no problem, the only other times I have been out across the channel I have also felt more than slightly unwell, although on those occasions it was neither the threat of chastisement, or the existential danger of letting down the good name of the Downes family that stopped me voiding the contents of my stomach overboard, but somehow I still managed to avoid the ignominy.

As we approached the White Cliffs of Dover for the first time, I was disappointed not to hear Vera Lynn singing something in my inner ear. All my fantasies of the Battle of Britain, and everything that I had been taught about the Motherland, came to mind as the ugly ferry pulled into the quay.

Then, as I have written elsewhere, a few moments after we stood on English soil for the first time and whilst we were still in the queue leading towards the Customs Shed, a large and malevolent seagull swooped down, and shat copiously in my little brother Richard's eye. We had arrived home to England, but that is – as they say – another story.

The End.

Postscript

And there is not much left to say, although there are a whole lot more stories that I *could tell, and may do at some point, but this current volume is already the longest book that I have ever written and I want to get it out in time for Christmas.*

When my Auntie Pip died in 1990, I inherited £1000 from her estate, and spent the vast majority of it on going back to Hong Kong for a week. I went back to most of my old haunts and was mildly disappointed that – for example – Tadpole Pond looked incredibly small compared to the way that it had done in my memories. Ah Tim's daughter Belinda was now an incredibly sexy 16-year-old, and it was hard to stay appropriate.

Luckily for my head, the place hadn't changed that much, and that week gave me a whole lot more pleasant memories for my memory bank. And I've never been back since. Adult concerns, two marriages, a divorce, widowerhood (if that is the correct term), stepfather and grandfatherhood, mortgages and the necessity for earning a living got in the way. And nowadays, although I could probably afford to go home, neither myself or the political situation in Hong Kong mean that it would be a particularly good idea. And not only am I ill, at the time of writing, Corinna, my darling wife of the last 15 years, died of cancer during the final stages of preparing this manuscript, and if I can't take her with me, there seems very little point in going.

Reading back through this manuscript there are several things that I want to make clear. First of all, I loved both my parents very much. My mother died in 2002, and my father four years later. I never really got along with either of them until right at the end of my father's life when - totally unexpectedly - we became friends just in time for us to be able to heal all the old hurts on both sides, and when he died I was holding his hand.

However, they were both complex and difficult people. The way I was treated as a child was ridiculously old-fashioned even by the standards of the fag end of imperialism, and I am more angry with the educational authorities, who were perfectly aware of what was happening in the Downes household, than I actually am with my parents.

My parents felt that by treating me like they did, they were carrying on a proud Victorian tradition of *Mens Sano in Corpore whatsit, and by not sparing the rod, they were not spoiling the child. Actually they were completely fucking up the Child beyond recognition, and preparing him for a life of manic depression, psychosis and substance abuse. But they didn't know that, and they thought they were doing the right thing. The authorities in my schools both in England and in Hong Kong had no such excuse and were not only complicit in what happened to me, but – to my mind – were mostly responsible.*

But my parents also were completely responsible for teaching me how to do all the things which have can of use to me throughout my life. They gave me my love of books, my love of knowledge, my knowledge of how to use the English language, the ability to speak and perform in public, and even taught me how to play the guitar. At the age of 61 I look back as a life spent as a journalist, an author, a citizen scientist, and a rock musician, and I realise that I have much for which I should thank them. I have many fond memories of them and I have tried to include them here alongside the horrific ones.

Totally by happenstance, whilst I was making the final adjustments to this manuscript, Richard Muirhead gave me a copy of Martin Booth's book *Gweilo, for my 61st birthday. It had been some years since I read it for the first time, and as my birthday fell less than a week after the death of my darling wife, I needed the literary equivalent of comfort food, and the story of Booth's childhood in Hong Kong ticked all the right boxes.*

And just as in the first time I read it, I realise there were so many parallels between his life and mine. We both lived in Mount Austin Mansions, I arrived in the colony on the boat that took the Booth family back to England, and a whole wallage of others (if you'll excuse my lapse into Devonshire dialect). But there were some enormous differences, most notably regarding his father and my father.

Martin Booth hated his father. I never did. I was terrified of my father, and spent most of my life in a fruitless attempt to gain his approval. But I loved him and we occasionally had precious times together, whilst Mr Booth, at least as his son described him, was a complete bastard, my father was just an undiagnosed manic-depressive with PTSD and a drink problem. The only difference between him and me apart from my haircut is that my bipolar was diagnosed eventually. And, as I have said elsewhere, we became friends in the final eight months of his life, and when he died I was holding his hand.

But this directly leads on to one of the controversial things that have come up from those who have read this book before publication. My old friend Ve Macrinnon, who himself has more than his share of skeletons in his own particular closet, has commented about my use of quotes from a convicted mass murderer at the beginning of each chapter. Whilst I am not prepared to accept everything that has been written about this particular case, I am quite prepared to admit that the person in question was guilty of some fairly horrific crimes. But he was also a philosopher of some renown, and I have quoted him at the beginning of each chapter, because underlying what could be read as the story of a relatively idyllic childhood in the tropics by a privileged white child, is a theme of horror.

There is not only the horror of watching, in slow motion, as a child's mental health is irreparably warped, but there is the horror of history. The horror of my father's war time experiences, the horror of what happened during the Japanese occupation of Hong Kong, the horror of my parents' ingrained, but selective, racism; they were friends with people of all sorts of religions and races, but always believed in the tenets of Apartheid, and up until the end of his life, my father would quote something that he claimed was first told him by the Imam of the Emir of Sokoto in northern Nigeria: "above the white man, there is only God".

This was one of the things which always reduced me to either unbelievable anger or tears throughout my whole relationship with him. But it was part of the man in the same way that it is not a part of me.

And above all, I have always tried to be honest, because although I have written this book for lots of different people - particularly my stepdaughters, nieces and nephews (both real and acquired) - above all I wrote it for myself. Because it was a time which has stayed with me for the rest of my life. When my nephew Greg went to Hong Kong a few years ago, I remembered exactly how he should take the clandestine path down to Tadpole Pond, something that very few adults would know, and cried with joy when I saw his photographs. I still dream in Cantonese, and I still have a mostly unrealistic hope that, when I take my last breath, it will be looking up at the white ceiling of the Peak School hall.

But remember one last quote from Charlie Manson: "No sense makes sense," which is, I think, a reasonably good place to say goodbye.

Jon Downes,
Woolsery,
North Devon,
Summer 2020.

STILL ON THE TRACK OF UNKNOWN ANIMALS

The Centre for Fortean Zoology, or CFZ, is a non profit-making organisation founded in 1992 with the aim of being a clearing house for information, and coordinating research into mystery animals around the world.

We also study out of place animals, rare and aberrant animal behaviour, and Zooform Phenomena; little-understood "things" that appear to be animals, but which are in fact nothing of the sort, and not even alive (at least in the way we understand the term).

Not only are we the biggest organisation of our type in the world, but - or so we like to think - we are the best. We are certainly the only truly global cryptozoological research organisation, and we carry out our investigations using a strictly scientific set of guidelines. We are expanding all the time and looking to recruit new members to help us in our research into mysterious animals and strange creatures across the globe.

Why should you join us? Because, if you are genuinely interested in trying to solve the last great mysteries of Mother Nature, there is nobody better than us with whom to do it.

We publish a journal *Animals & Men*. Each issue contains nearly 100 pages packed with news, articles, letters, research papers, field reports, and even a gossip column! The magazine is Royal Octavo in format with a full colour cover. You also have access to one of the world's largest collections of resource material dealing with cryptozoology and allied disciplines, and people from the CFZ membership regularly take part in fieldwork and expeditions around the world.

The CFZ is managed by a board of trustees, with a non-profit making trust registered with HM Government Stamp Office. The board of trustees is supported by a Permanent Directorate of full and part-time staff, and advised by a Consultancy Board of specialists - many of whom are world-renowned experts in their particular field. We have regional representatives across the UK, the USA, and many other parts of the world, and are affiliated with other organisations whose aims and protocols mirror our own.

You'll find that the people at the CFZ are friendly and approachable. We have a thriving forum on the website which is the hub of an ever-growing electronic community. You will soon find your feet. Many members of the CFZ Permanent Directorate started off as ordinary members, and now work full-time chasing monsters around the world.

Write to us, e-mail us, or telephone us. The list of future projects on the website is not exhaustive. If you have a good idea for an investigation, please tell us. We may well be able to help.

We are always looking for volunteers to join us. If you see a project that interests you, do not hesitate to get in touch with us. Under certain circumstances we can help provide funding for your trip. If you look on the future projects section of the website, you can see some of the projects that we have pencilled in for the next few years.

In 2003 and 2004 we sent three-man expeditions to Sumatra looking for Orang-Pendek - a semi-legendary bipedal ape. The same three went to Mongolia in 2005. All three members started off merely subscribers to the CFZ magazine. Next time it could be you!

We have no magic sources of income. All our funds come from donations, membership fees, and sales of our publications and merchandise. We are always looking for corporate sponsorship, and other sources of revenue. If you have any ideas for fund-raising please let us know. However, unlike other cryptozoological organisations in the past, we do not live in an intellectual ivory tower. We are not afraid to get our hands dirty, and furthermore we are not one of those organisations where the membership have to raise money so that a privileged few can go on expensive foreign trips. Our research teams, both in the UK and abroad, consist of a mixture of experienced and inexperienced personnel. We are truly a community, and work on the premise that the benefits of CFZ membership are open to all.

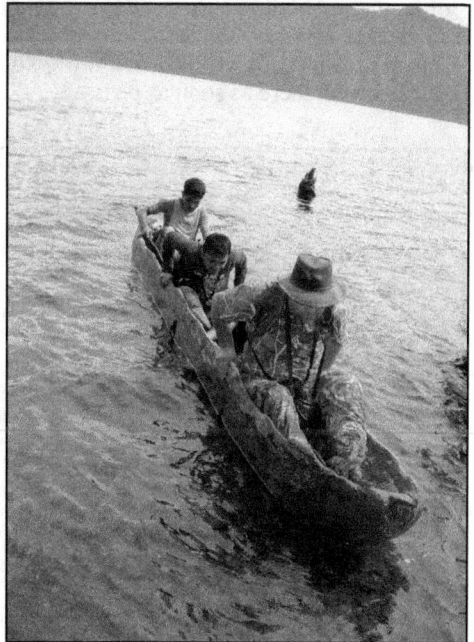

Reports of our investigations are published on our website as soon they are available. Preliminary reports are posted within days of the project finishing.

Each year we publish a 200 page yearbook containing research papers and expedition reports too long to be printed in the journal. We freely circulate our information to anybody who asks for it.

We have a thriving YouTube channel, CFZtv, which has well over two hundred self-made documentaries, lecture appearances, and episodes of our monthly webTV show. We have a daily online magazine, which has over a million hits each year.

From 2000—2016 we held our annual convention - the Weird Weekend. It went on hiatus because of the illness of several of the major personnel and the eventual death of one of them. But we plan to bring it back soon. It is three days of lectures, workshops, and excursions. But most importantly it is a chance for members of the CFZ to meet each other, and to talk with the members of the permanent directorate in a relaxed and informal setting and preferably with a pint of beer in one hand. Since 2006 - the Weird Weekend has been bigger and better and held in the idyllic rural location of Woolsery in North Devon.

Since relocating to North Devon in 2005 we have become ever more closely involved with other community organisations, and we hope that this trend will continue. We have also worked closely with Police Forces across the UK as consultants for animal mutilation cases, and we intend to forge closer links with the coastguard and other community services. We want to work closely with those who regularly travel into the Bristol Channel, so that if the recent trend of exotic animal visitors to our coastal waters continues, we can be out there as soon as possible.

Apart from having been the only Fortean Zoological organisation in the world to have consistently published material on all aspects of the subject for over a decade, we have achieved the following concrete results:

- Disproved the myth relating to the headless so-called sea-serpent carcass of Durgan beach in Cornwall 1975
- Disproved the story of the 1988 puma skull of Lustleigh Cleave

- Carried out the only in-depth research ever into the mythos of the Cornish Owlman.
- Made the first records of a tropical species of lamprey
- Made the first records of a luminous cave gnat larva in Thailand
- Discovered a possible new species of British mammal - the beech marten
- In 1994-6 carried out the first archival fortean zoological survey of Hong Kong
- In the year 2000, CFZ theories were confirmed when a new species of lizard was added to the British List
- Identified the monster of Martin Mere in Lancashire as a giant wels catfish
- Expanded the known range of Armitage's skink in the Gambia by 80%
- Obtained photographic evidence of the remains of Europe's largest known pike
- Carried out the first ever in-depth study of the ninki-nanka
- Carried out the first attempt to breed Puerto Rican cave snails in captivity
- Were the first European explorers to visit the `lost valley` in Sumatra
- Published the first ever evidence for a new tribe of pygmies in Guyana
- Published the first evidence for a new species of caiman in Guyana
- Filmed unknown creatures on a monster-haunted lake in Ireland for the first time

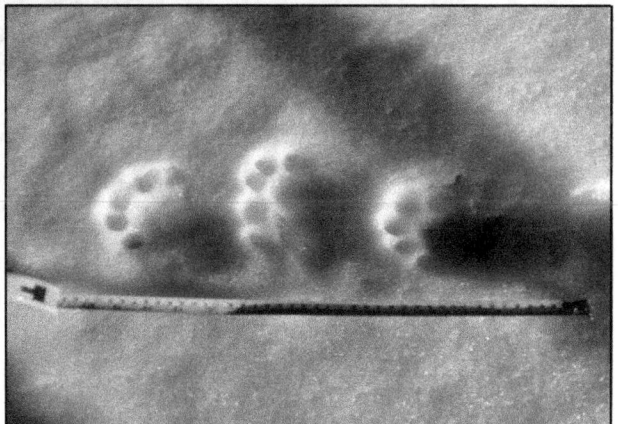

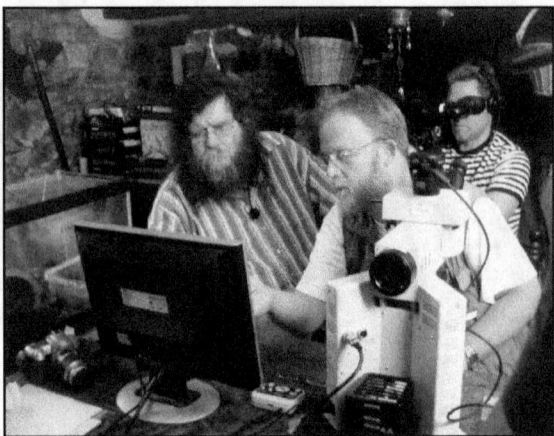

- Had a sighting of orang pendek in Sumatra in 2009
- Found leopard hair, subsequently identified by DNA analysis, from rural North Devon in 2010
- Brought back hairs which appear to be from an unknown primate in Sumatra
- Published some of the best evidence ever for the almasty in southern Russia

CFZ Expeditions and Investigations include:

- 1998 Puerto Rico, Florida, Mexico (Chupacabras)
- 1999 Nevada (Bigfoot)
- 2000 Thailand (Naga)
- 2002 Martin Mere (Giant catfish)
- 2002 Cleveland (Wallaby mutilation)
- 2003 Bolam Lake (BHM Reports)

- 2003 Sumatra (Orang Pendek)
- 2003 Texas (Bigfoot; giant snapping turtles)
- 2004 Sumatra (Orang Pendek; cigau, a sabre-toothed cat)
- 2004 Illinois (Black panthers; cicada swarm)
- 2004 Texas (Mystery blue dog)
- Loch Morar (Monster)
- 2004 Puerto Rico (Chupacabras; carnivorous cave snails)
- 2005 Belize (Affiliate expedition for hairy dwarfs)
- 2005 Loch Ness (Monster)
- 2005 Mongolia (Allghoi Khorkhoi aka Mongolian death worm)

- 2006 Gambia (Gambo - Gambian sea monster , Ninki Nanka and Armitage's skink
- 2006 Llangorse Lake (Giant pike, giant eels)
- 2006 Windermere (Giant eels)
- 2007 Coniston Water (Giant eels)
- 2007 Guyana (Giant anaconda, didi, water tiger)
- 2008 Russia (Almasty)
- 2009 Sumatra (Orang pendek)
- 2009 Republic of Ireland (Lake Monster)
- 2010 Texas (Blue Dogs)
- 2010 India (Mande Burung)
- 2011 Sumatra (Orang-pendek)
- 2012 Sumatra (Orang Pendek)
- 2014 Tasmania (Thylacine)
- 2015 Tasmania (Thylacine)
- 2016 Tasmania (Thylacine)
- 2017 Tasmania (Thylacine)
- 2018 Tajikistan (Gul)
- 2020 Forest of Dean (Lynx)

For details of current membership fees, current expeditions and investigations, and voluntary posts within the CFZ that need your help, please do not hesitate to contact us.

The Centre for Fortean Zoology,
Myrtle Cottage,
Woolfardisworthy,
Bideford, North Devon
EX39 5QR

Telephone 01237 431413
Fax+44 (0)7006-074-925
eMail info@cfz.org.uk

Websites:

www.cfz.org.uk
www.weirdweekend.org

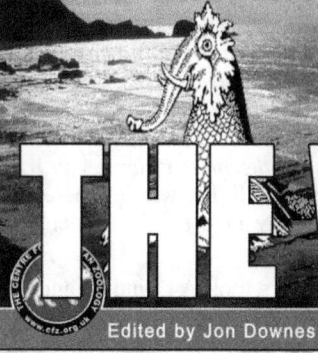

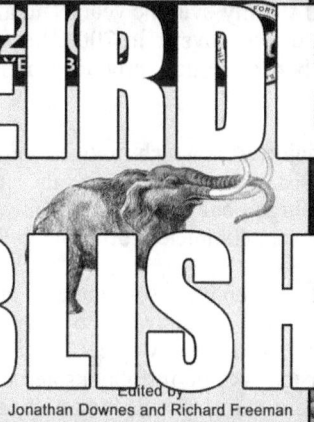

THE WORLD'S WEIRDEST PUBLISHING COMPANY

HOW TO START A PUBLISHING EMPIRE

Unlike most mainstream publishers, we have a non-commercial remit, and our mission statement claims that "we publish books because they deserve to be published, not because we think that we can make money out of them". Our motto is the Latin Tag *Pro bona causa facimus* (we do it for good reason), a slogan taken from a children's book *The Case of the Silver Egg* by the late Desmond Skirrow.

WIKIPEDIA: "The first book published was in 1988. *Take this Brother may it Serve you Well* was a guide to Beatles bootlegs by Jonathan Downes. It sold quite well, but was hampered by very poor production values, being photocopied, and held together by a plastic clip binder.

In 1988 A5 clip binders were hard to get hold of, so the publishers took A4 binders and cut them in half with a hacksaw. It now reaches surprisingly high prices second hand.

The production quality improved slightly over the years, and after 1999 all the books produced were ringbound with laminated colour covers. In 2004, however, they signed an agreement with Lightning Source, and all books are now produced perfect bound, with full colour covers."

Until 2010 all our books, the majority of which are/were on the subject of mystery animals and allied disciplines, were published by `CFZ Press`, the publishing arm of the Centre for Fortean Zoology (CFZ), and we urged our readers and followers to draw a discreet veil over the books that we published that were completely off topic to the CFZ.

However, in 2010 we decided that enough was enough and launched a second imprint, `Fortean Words` which aims to cover a wide range of non animal-related esoteric subjects. Other imprints will be launched as and when we feel like it, however the basic ethos of the company remains the same: Our job is to publish books and magazines that we feel are worth publishing, whether or not they are going to sell. Money is, after all - as my dear old Mama once told me - a rather vulgar subject, and she would be rolling in her grave if she thought that her eldest son was somehow in `trade`.

Luckily, so far our tastes have turned out not to be that rarified after all, and we have sold far more books than anyone ever thought that we would, so there is a moral in there somewhere…

Jon Downes,
Woolsery, North Devon
July 2010

CFZ PRESS

CFZ Press is our flagship imprint, featuring a wide range of intelligently written and lavishly illustrated books on cryptozoology and the quirkier aspects of Natural History.

CFZ Classics is a new venture for us. There are many seminal works that are either unavailable today, or not available with the production values which we would like to see. So, following the old adage that if you want to get something done do it yourself, this is exactly what we have done.

Desiderius Erasmus Roterodamus (b. October 18th 1466, d. July 2nd 1536) said: "When I have a little money, I buy books; and if I have any left, I buy food and clothes," and we are much the same. Only, we are in the lucky position of being able to share our books with the wider world. CFZ Classics is a conduit through which we cannot just re-issue titles which we feel still have much to offer the cryptozoological and Fortean research communities of the 21st Century, but we are adding footnotes, supplementary essays, and other material where we deem it appropriate.

http://www.cfzpublishing.co.uk/

Fortean Words is a new venture for us. The F in CFZ stands for "Fortean", after the pioneering researcher into anomalous phenomena, Charles Fort. Our Fortean Words imprint covers a whole spectrum of arcane subjects from UFOs and the paranormal to folklore and urban legends. Our authors include such Fortean luminaries as Nick Redfern, Andy Roberts, and Paul Screeton. . New authors tackling new subjects will always be encouraged, and we hope that our books will continue to be as ground-breaking and popular as ever.

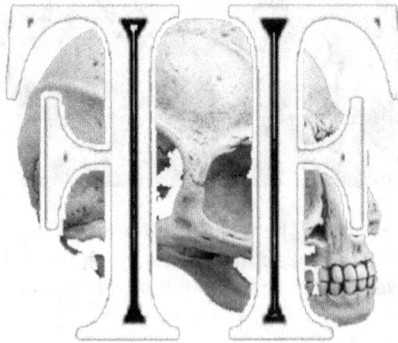

Just before Christmas 2011, we launched our third imprint, this time dedicated to - let's see if you guessed it from the title - fictional books with a Fortean or cryptozoological theme. We have published a few fictional books in the past, but now think that because of our rising reputation as publishers of quality Forteana, that a dedicated fiction imprint was the order of the day.

http://www.cfzpublishing.co.uk/

www.ingramcontent.com/pod-product-compliance
Lightning Source LLC
LaVergne TN
LVHW022111080426
835511LV00007B/749